John Rawls

John Rawls

Debating the Major Questions

Edited by

JON MANDLE AND SARAH ROBERTS-CADY

OXFORD
UNIVERSITY PRESS

OXFORD
UNIVERSITY PRESS

Oxford University Press is a department of the University of Oxford. It furthers the University's objective of excellence in research, scholarship, and education by publishing worldwide. Oxford is a registered trade mark of Oxford University Press in the UK and certain other countries.

Published in the United States of America by Oxford University Press
198 Madison Avenue, New York, NY 10016, United States of America.

Library of Congress Cataloging-in-Publication Data
Names: Mandle, Jon, 1966– editor. | Roberts-Cady, Sarah, editor.
Title: John Rawls : debating the major questions / edited by Jon Mandle and Sarah Roberts-Cady.
Description: New York, NY : Oxford University Press, [2020] | Includes bibliographical references and index.
Identifiers: LCCN 2019054113 (print) | LCCN 2019054114 (ebook) | ISBN 9780190859213 (hardback) | ISBN 9780190859206 (paperback) | ISBN 9780190859244 (epub) | ISBN 9780190859220 (online)
Subjects: LCSH: Rawls, John, 1921–2002. | Political science—Philosophy. | Social contract. | Justice. | Equality. | Philosophers—United States—Biography.
Classification: LCC JC251.R32 A25 2020 (print) | LCC JC251.R32 (ebook) | DDC 320.01—dc23
LC record available at https://lccn.loc.gov/2019054113
LC ebook record available at https://lccn.loc.gov/2019054114

1 3 5 7 9 8 6 4 2

Paperback printed by Marquis, Canada
Hardback printed by Bridgeport National Bindery, Inc., United States of America

Contents

Acknowledgments   ix
Contributors   xi

An Introduction to Rawls on Justice   1
Jon Mandle and Sarah Roberts-Cady

PART I: PUBLIC REASON

Introduction   15

1. Public Political Reason: Still Not Wide Enough   21
   David A. Reidy

2. Just Wide Enough: Reidy on Public Reason   35
   James Boettcher

PART II: IDEAL AND NONIDEAL THEORY

Introduction   53

3. The "Focusing Illusion" of Rawlsian Ideal Theory   61
   Colin Farrelly

4. The Value of Ideal Theory   73
   Matthew Adams

PART III: LIBERTY AND ECONOMIC JUSTICE

Introduction   89

5. Rawls's Underestimation of the Importance of Economic Agency
   and Economic Rights   95
   Jeppe von Platz

6. Rawls on Economic Liberty and the Choice of Systems of Social
   Cooperation   109
   Alan Thomas

PART IV: LUCK EGALITARIANISM

Introduction   125

7. Rawls and Luck Egalitarianism   133
   Kasper Lippert-Rasmussen

8. The Point of Justice: On the Paradigmatic Incompatibility between
   Rawlsian "Justice as Fairness" and Luck Egalitarianism   148
   Rainer Forst

PART V: THE CAPABILITY CRITIQUE

Introduction   163

9. Sen's Capability Critique   170
   Christopher Lowry

10. Specters of Democracy: Detouring the Limitations of Rawls
    and the Capabilities Approach   183
    Tony Fitzpatrick

PART VI: THE DEPENDENCY CRITIQUE

Introduction   203

11. The Dependency Critique of Rawlsian Equality   206
    Eva Feder Kittay

12. A Feminist Liberal Response to the Dependency Critique   219
    Amy R. Baehr

PART VII: RAWLS AND FEMINISM

Introduction   233

13. The Indeterminacy of Rawls's Principles for Gender Justice   237
    M. Victoria Costa

14. A Feminist Defense of Political Liberalism   249
    Christie Hartley and Lori Watson

PART VIII: RAWLS AND NONHUMAN ANIMALS

Introduction 265

15. Extending Rawlsian Justice to Nonhuman Animals 273
    Sarah Roberts-Cady

16. Rawls and Animals: A Defense 285
    Patrick Taylor Smith

PART IX: INTERNATIONAL ECONOMIC JUSTICE

Introduction 303

17. Rawls on Global Economic Justice: A Critical Examination 313
    Rekha Nath

18. Rawls's Reasoning about International Economic Justice:
    A Defense 329
    Gillian Brock

PART X: INTERNATIONAL JUSTICE AND TOLERATION

Introduction 345

19. Right-Wing Populism and Noncoercive Injustice: On the Limits
    of the Law of Peoples 354
    Michael Blake

20. Tolerating Decent Societies: A Defense of the Law of Peoples 371
    Jon Mandle

Index 383

Acknowledgments

Sarah Roberts-Cady is grateful to her colleagues in the Department of Philosophy at Fort Lewis College, Justin McBrayer and Dugald Owen, for their guidance, feedback, and encouragement throughout this project. It was Justin's great suggestion to structure this book as a dialogue between philosophers with different views. Both Justin and Dugald read multiple drafts of the book proposal and the chapter on animals, offering thoughtful and challenging feedback that improved the work. Sarah is also thankful to her husband, Tony, and her children, Elsie, Adelaide, Irie, and Brooklyn, for their support and patience all those weekends when she missed family bike rides and didn't fold the laundry because she was working on this book.

Jon Mandle thanks his colleagues in the Department of Philosophy at the University at Albany, and especially Kristen Hessler, for creating such a positive and supportive philosophical home. He also thanks David Reidy for sharing years of conversation and reflection about Rawls's work. And he is grateful for the loving care of his family, Karen Schupack and Anna Schupack, who contributed the cover portrait of Rawls.

Contributors

Matthew Adams is a Postdoctoral Fellow at the McCoy Family Center for Ethics in Society at Stanford University. He specializes in political philosophy with a focus on non-ideal theory and topics at the intersection of justice and applied ethics. His work has been published in journals such as the *Australasian Journal of Philosophy* and *The Monist*. He is the editor of *Methods in Bioethics: The Way We Reason Now* (Oxford, 2017).

Amy R. Baehr is Professor of Philosophy at Hofstra University, where she teaches political philosophy, philosophy of law, and women's studies. Her work on feminism and liberalism has appeared in journals including *Law and Philosophy, Ethics, Feminist Philosophy Quarterly*, and *Hypatia*; and in anthologies including *The Philosophy of Rawls: A Collection of Essays* (Garland, 1999), *Feminist Interpretations of John Rawls* (Penn State, 2013) and *The Original Position* (Cambridge, 2016). She is editor of *Varieties of Feminist Liberalism* (Rowman and Littlefield, 2004) and author of the *Stanford Encyclopedia of Philosophy*'s entry on liberal feminism. She is currently working on an edited volume, *Caring for Liberalism: Dependency and Political Theory*, with Asha Bhandary (Routledge).

Michael Blake is a Professor of Philosophy, Public Policy, and Governance at the University of Washington, where he is jointly appointed to the Department of Philosophy and to the Daniel J. Evans School of Public Affairs. He is the author of three books: *Justice and Foreign Policy* (Oxford, 2013); *Debating Brain Drain: May Governments Prevent Emigration?* with Gillian Brock (Oxford, 2015); and *Justice, Migration, and Mercy* (Oxford, 2020). His current research focuses on the ethics of migration policy, and the liberal rights of the dead.

James Boettcher is a Professor of Philosophy at Saint Joseph's University in Philadelphia. His research is focused on public reason. His work has been published in *Journal of Political Philosophy, Journal of Social Philosophy, Ethical Theory and Moral Practice*, and *Public Affairs Quarterly.*

Gillian Brock is a Professor of Philosophy at the University of Auckland, New Zealand. She has published widely on political and social philosophy, including more than two hundred peer-reviewed publications. Her books include *Justice for People on the Move* (Cambridge, 2020), *Global Justice: A Cosmopolitan Account* (Oxford, 2009), *Cosmopolitanism versus Non-cosmopolitanism* (Oxford, 2013), *Debating Brain Drain*, with Michael Blake (Oxford, 2015), and *Global Health and Global Health Ethics*, with Solomon Benatar (Cambridge, 2011).

M. Victoria Costa is an Associate Professor of Philosophy at William and Mary. She has numerous peer-reviewed publications on social and political philosophy, particularly on

John Rawls's liberalism and Philip Pettit's neorepublicanism. Her papers have appeared in *Politics, Philosophy, and Economics, Hypatia*, the *Journal of Social Philosophy, and Critical Review of Social and Political Philosophy*, among others. She is the author of *Rawls, Citizenship and Education* (Routledge, 2011).

Colin Farrelly is Professor and Queen's National Scholar in the Department of Political Studies at Queen's University in Ontario, Canada. His books include *Justice, Democracy and Reasonable Agreement* (Palgrave Macmillan, 2007), *Virtue Jurisprudence*, coedited with Lawrence Solum (Palgrave Macmillan, 2008), *Biologically Modified Justice* (Cambridge, 2016), and *Genetic Ethics: An Introduction* (Polity, 2018).

Tony Fitzpatrick is a Reader in the School of Sociology and Social Policy at the University of Nottingham. His recent books include *International Handbook on Social Policy and the Environment* (Edward Elgar, 2014), *Climate Change and Poverty* (Policy Press, 2014), *A Green History of the Welfare State* (Routledge, 2017), and *How to Live Well: Epicurus as a Guide to Contemporary Social Reform* (Edward Elgar, 2018).

Rainer Forst is Professor of Political Theory and Philosophy at Goethe-University in Frankfurt. He specializes in the foundations of morality and the basic concepts of normative political theory. In 2012, he was awarded the Leibniz Prize by the German Research Foundation. His books include *Contexts of Justice* (University of California Press, 2002), *Toleration in Conflict* (Cambridge, 2013), *The Right to Justification* (Columbia, 2012), *Justification and Critique* (Polity, 2014), and *Normativity and Power* (Oxford, 2017).

Christie Hartley is an Associate Professor of Philosophy at Georgia State University. She has published articles on political philosophy and feminist theory in *Social Theory and Practice, Law and Philosophy, Philosophy Compass, Journal of Ethics and Social Philosophy*, the *Journal of Social Philosophy*, and *Philosophical Studies*. With Lori Watson, she is the author of *Equal Citizenship and Public Reason: A Feminist Political Liberalism* (Oxford, 2018).

Eva Feder Kittay is a Distinguished Professor of Philosophy at Stony Brook University. She has published widely in feminist philosophy, political theory, and disability studies. Her books include *Learning From My Daughter: The Value and Care of Disabled Minds* (Oxford 2019), *Love's Labor: Essays on Women, Equality and Dependency* (Routledge, 2009, Revised 2nd Edition 2019), *Cognitive Disability and the Challenge to Moral Philosophy* (Wiley-Blackwell, 2010), *The Blackwell Guide to Feminist Philosophy* (Blackwell, 2007), and *Theoretical Perspectives on Dependency and Women* (Rowman and Littlefield, 2003).

Kasper Lippert-Rasmussen is a Professor in the Department of Political Science at Aarhus University in Denmark and a Professor II in the Department of Philosophy at UiT—The Arctic University of Norway. He has published extensively on issues of ethics and justice. Recent books include *Luck Egalitarianism* (Bloomsbury Academic, 2015), *Relational Egalitarianism* (Cambridge, 2018), and *Making Sense of Affirmative Action* (Oxford, 2018). Presently, he is working on a book manuscript on being in a position to blame.

Christopher Lowry is an Associate Professor in the Department of Philosophy at the University of Waterloo. His research interests include political philosophical methodology, justice and disability, and the intersection of egalitarianism and bioethics. His work has been featured in the *Journal of Social Philosophy* and in the collection *From Disability Theory to Practice*, edited by Christopher A. Riddle (Lexington Books, 2018).

Jon Mandle is Professor of Philosophy at SUNY Albany. His scholarly work focuses on political philosophy and ethics, with a special emphasis on John Rawls. He is the coeditor of *The Cambridge Rawls Lexicon*, with David Reidy (Cambridge, 2015), and *A Companion to Rawls*, with David Reidy (Blackwell, 2014). He is also the author of three monographs: *Rawls's "A Theory of Justice": An Introduction* (Cambridge, 2009), *Global Justice* (Polity Press, 2006), and *What's Left of Liberalism? An Interpretation and Defense of Justice as Fairness* (Lexington Books, 2000).

Rekha Nath is an Associate Professor of Philosophy at the University of Alabama. Her research in ethics and political philosophy has been published in journals such as *Bioethics, Journal of Ethics and Social Philosophy, The Monist,* and *Social Theory and Practice*. She is currently working on a book on the injustice of weight stigma.

Jeppe von Platz is an Assistant Professor of Philosophy at University of Richmond. He is the winner of the American Philosophical Association Fred Berger Memorial Prize 2008, which he shares with David Reidy. His research on political philosophy can be found in the book *Theories of Distributive Justice: Who Gets What and Why?* (Routledge, 2020) and in articles published by *Ethics, Politics, Philosophy & Economics,* the *Journal of Value Inquiry, Public Affairs Quarterly,* and the *Journal of Social Philosophy.*

David A. Reidy is a Professor of Philosophy at the University of Tennessee–Knoxville. He works in political and legal philosophy with a special focus on John Rawls. In addition to publishing many articles, he coedited *A Companion to Rawls,* with Jon Mandle (Blackwell, 2014), *The Cambridge Rawls Lexicon,* with Jon Mandle (Cambridge, 2015), *Rawls* (Ashgate, 2008), and *Rawls's Law of Peoples: A Realistic Utopia?* with Rex Martin (Wiley-Blackwell, 2006).

Sarah Roberts-Cady is a Professor of Philosophy at Fort Lewis College. Her work on ethics and political philosophy has been published in journals such as the *Journal of Social Philosophy; Ethics, Policy & Environment; International Journal of Applied Philosophy;* and *Politics and the Life Sciences.*

Patrick Taylor Smith is an Assistant Professor of Philosophy at the University of Twente, where he focuses on global and intergenerational justice as they relate to technology and the environment. His work has been published in *The Monist, Journal of Applied Philosophy, Ethics, Policy, and the Environment, Philosophy and Public Issues, Critical Review of International and Social Philosophy,* and *Transnational Legal Theory.*

Alan Thomas is a Professor of Philosophy at the University of York in the UK. He has published extensively in ethics, political philosophy, and the philosophy of mind. His books include *Value and Context* (Oxford, 2006), *Thomas Nagel* (Acumen Press and McGill/Queen's University Press, 2009/2015), *Bernard Williams* (as editor and contributor) (Cambridge, 2007), and *Republic of Equals: Pre-distribution and Property-Owning Democracy* (Oxford, 2017). He is currently completing a book titled *Ethics in the First Person.*

Lori Watson is Professor and Chair of Philosophy at the University of San Diego, and affiliate faculty in the School of Law. She has recently published two books with Oxford University Press, *Equal Citizenship and Public Reason: A Feminist Political Liberalism,* with Christie Hartley (2018), and *Debating Pornography,* with Andrew Altman (2019). Her third book, *Debating Sex Work,* with Jessica Flannigan, is forthcoming. She has also published numerous articles on topics in political philosophy and feminism.

An Introduction to Rawls on Justice

Jon Mandle and Sarah Roberts-Cady

For almost fifty years, the work of John Rawls (1921–2002) has played a central and guiding role in the development of Anglo-American political philosophy. This is certainly not to say that his views have been uncritically accepted. On the contrary, an enormous literature has been generated criticizing and explaining where Rawls goes wrong. But each of Rawls's three major books, *A Theory of Justice*, first published in 1971 (revised edition 1999), *Political Liberalism*, first published in 1993 (expanded edition 2005), and *The Law of Peoples*, first published in 1999, set the agenda for many other philosophers' major research projects.[1] In this introduction, we provide only the barest overview of the key ideas of his first two majors volumes, with discussions of *The Law of Peoples* found in the introductions to Parts IX and X.

Rawls's aim in his first major book, *A Theory of Justice,* is to identify principles of justice for guiding the basic terms of cooperation within a society. In particular, he wants to offer an alternative to utilitarianism, which he argues cannot "provide a satisfactory account of the basic rights and liberties of free and equal persons."[2] Rawls was immensely successful in establishing "justice as fairness" as at least a credible alternative to utilitarianism. In addition to defending nonutilitarian principles for evaluating social justice, he also developed a distinctive method of justifying them, an account of moral psychology and development, and much else. But there were important limitations and simplifying assumptions that Rawls explicitly noted. For example, he was narrow in his focus on principles of justice for evaluating the "basic structure of society"—the system formed by a society's basic social institutions—rather than other possible objects of evaluation, such as the justice of particular laws and policies. And he put aside (until *The Law of Peoples*) questions about the justice of relations among different

---

[1] His other books, which we will here treat largely as supplemental, are *Collected Papers*, ed. Samuel Freeman (Harvard University Press, 1999); *Lectures on the History of Moral Philosophy*, ed. Samuel Freeman (Harvard University Press, 2007); *Lectures on the History of Political Philosophy*, ed. Samuel Freeman (Harvard University Press, 2007); his undergraduate thesis, *A Brief Inquiry into the Meaning of Sin and Faith*, ed. Thomas Nagel (Harvard University Press, 2009); and *Justice as Fairness: A Restatement*, ed. Erin Kelly (Harvard University Press, 2001).

[2] John Rawls, *A Theory of Justice*, rev. ed. (Harvard University Press 1999), xii.

Jon Mandle and Sarah Roberts-Cady, *An Introduction to Rawls on Justice* In: *John Rawls*. Edited by: Jon Mandle and Sarah Roberts-Cady, Oxford University Press (2020). © Oxford University Press.
DOI: 10.1093/oso/9780190859213.003.0001.

societies. He also said little about the transition from an existing society with its injustices of various kinds and degrees to a more just arrangement. He believed that the distinctive contribution that philosophers could make was to develop and defend principles to be used in evaluation, but that the application of these principles to actual societies and the consideration of the implications of various alternative arrangements depend on the kinds of expertise that political scientists, economists, sociologists, historians, and others could provide. Social critique is an interdisciplinary endeavor, with philosophers having an important but limited role.

Rawls's approach to justifying principles of justice is antifoundational. He rejects the attempt to reduce moral principles (including principles of justice) to a nonmoral foundation. "A conception of justice cannot be deduced from self-evident premises or conditions on principles; instead, its justification is a matter of the mutual support of many considerations, of everything fitting together into one coherent view."[3] Fortunately, there is no special urgency to provide nonmoral foundations since we do not come to the project of justification in complete moral ignorance. On the contrary, there are certain "considered convictions" about which we are quite confident. Indeed, he writes, "Some judgments we view as fixed points: ones we never expect to withdraw, as when Lincoln says: 'If slavery is not wrong, nothing is wrong.'"[4] In A Theory of Justice, he gives the examples of the injustice of "religious intolerance and racial discrimination."[5] However, at the same time, there are many questions of justice where we are unsure or disagree with one another. Rawls mentions "the correct distribution of wealth and authority" and notes that in such cases, "we may be looking for a way to remove our doubts."[6] The idea, then, is to develop a theory that provides a unified perspective on the questions where we are relatively confident as well as the areas where we are unsure, thus helping to illuminate the latter. Presumably, there will be tensions and conflicts among our considered convictions and proposed principles. The ideal in which we achieve coherence at all levels, as well as the process of working toward this ideal, is called "reflective equilibrium."

Rawls does not simply tell us to go off and try to reach reflective equilibrium. He develops a tool to help us do so. Putting himself in the tradition of Locke, Rousseau, and Kant, he has us consider the principles of justice as the product of a social contract that would be made in an imaginary but fair initial choice situation. Rawls calls his choice situation "the original position," and its most striking feature is that the parties there are to agree to principles of justice from behind a

---

3 Rawls, A Theory of Justice, 19.
4 Rawls, Justice as Fairness, 29.
5 Rawls, A Theory of Justice, 17.
6 Rawls, A Theory of Justice, 18.

"veil of ignorance." That is, they are to agree to the principles to be used in evaluating the basic structure without knowing any specific features of themselves or their situation. The veil prevents them from knowing, among other things, their gender, race, ethnicity, level of wealth, social position, religion, or particular conception of the good (what specific ends and activities they find valuable and worth pursuing). Therefore, it forces them to consider the principles from *everyone's* point of view because they must make a choice knowing that when the veil is lifted, so to speak, they might turn out to be anyone.

There is an apparent problem, however, with this brief overview of the original position as so far described. If the parties making the social contract do not know anything about themselves or their specific system of values (their conception of the good), on what basis do they make any choice at all? Rawls's answer is that they *do* know, among other things, that they would prefer a larger to a smaller share of "social primary goods." These can be understood as broadly based resources that are not tied to or dependent on any particular conception of the good. When Rawls initially introduces them, he includes "rights, liberties, and opportunities, and income and wealth."[7] He later adds "the social basis of self-respect," which he identifies as "perhaps the most important."[8] (A somewhat more specific list and changes to their justification is given in *Political Liberalism*, 181. See our introduction to Part V.)

Having specified the motivation of the parties in the original position as well as the constraints of the situation that they find themselves in, Rawls can consider which principles it would be rational for them to choose. He argues that the nature of the choice would force the parties to compare alternative sets of principles with special attention to the least advantaged social position that each set of principles might generate. In *A Theory of Justice*, the details of this argument are somewhat obscure and are spread over many sections, but it is presented in a much more straightforward way in *Justice as Fairness: A Restatement*, part III. Although we will not reproduce this argument here, the conclusion of the argument from the original position is that the parties would choose the following two principles:

First principle: Each person is to have an equal right to the most extensive total system of equal basic liberties compatible with a similar system of liberties for all.

Second principle: Social and economic inequalities are to be arranged so that they are both:

---

[7] Rawls, *A Theory of Justice*, 54.
[8] Rawls, *A Theory of Justice*, 348.

    (a) to the greatest benefit of the least advantaged . . . and
    (b) attached to offices and positions open to all under conditions of fair equality of opportunity.[9]

The first principle is sometimes called the "liberty principle," and it takes priority over the second principle in the sense that no violation of the first principle can be justified by better satisfying the second principle. The liberty principle holds that there is a basic and extensive set of political and civil liberties to which all citizens have an equal right. The second principle concerns the distribution of economic and social (primary) goods. It has two parts called (a) the "difference principle" and (b) "fair equality of opportunity." The difference principle holds that inequalities among social positions in social and economic goods are acceptable only if the inequalities work to the greatest benefit of the least advantaged position. That is, in order for a structural inequality to be just, that inequality must result in the least advantaged position doing better than it would without that inequality, that is, in a condition of equal distribution. In short, those who are better off cannot justify their advantaged position if it comes at the expense of others. The principle of fair equality of opportunity requires that society must be arranged so that all have an equal opportunity to develop their talents and abilities, such that all can compete fairly for the various social positions, and in particular, for those positions associated with greater wealth or power.

Rawls holds that "the social system is not an unchangeable order beyond human control but a pattern of human action."[10] Therefore, the achievement of a just basic structure and the stability of such a structure once achieved depend on the development of a sense of justice among citizens. This sense of justice must be adequate to overcome conflicting sources of motivation, for example, those grounded in one's particular conception of the good. The issue of stability is infrequently addressed by political philosophers, but Rawls extensively discusses the issue in the final third of *A Theory of Justice*. As he conceives it, the problem of stability has two parts. The first is to describe the acquisition of a normally effective sense of justice as a child matures into a citizen. The second is what Rawls calls "congruence," and it concerns the consistency or "fit" between a citizen's sense of justice and her conception of the good.

In comparison to the massive secondary literature on the other elements of the theory, the material in this third part has been relatively neglected, despite Rawls's comment in 1993, "The part of the book I always liked best was the third, on moral psychology."[11] Yet, in the years following the publication of

[9] Rawls, *A Theory of Justice*, 266.
[10] Rawls, *A Theory of Justice*, 88.
[11] Quoted in Samuel Freeman, *Rawls* (Routledge, 2007), 6.

A Theory of Justice, Rawls himself came to doubt the success of the congruence argument. In the introduction to *Political Liberalism*, Rawls refers to "a serious problem internal to justice as fairness, namely . . . that the account of stability in Part III of *Theory* is not consistent with the view as a whole." He continues: "I believe all differences [between *A Theory of Justice* and *Political Liberalism*] are consequences of removing that inconsistency. Otherwise these lectures take the structure and content of *Theory* to remain substantially the same."[12] As conceived in *A Theory of Justice*, principles of justice aimed to ensure that the shared institutions of the basic structure were fair to individuals who, while they shared a sense of justice, differed from one another in their conception of the good. Fair treatment required: (1) an equal scheme of liberties entitling each to a formal right to form and to pursue her (permissible) ends; (2) a fair share of resources with which to pursue her ends.

But Rawls came to believe that the pluralism that will inevitably characterize a free and just society is not limited to the different ends that individuals will pursue (their conceptions of the good).[13] Rather, the pluralism is deep, in that each individual will typically have a (fully or partially) comprehensive religious, philosophical, or moral doctrine within which she will embed and seek to justify her conception of the good *and* her sense of justice. This pluralism is (or may be) reasonable, since it is not (necessarily) the result of failures of reasoning. On the contrary, we should see this reasonable pluralism "as the inevitable long-run result of the powers of human reason at work within the background of enduring free institutions."[14] Since there is not a shared comprehensive doctrine, there cannot be a single argument based on such a doctrine that would establish congruence for all citizens between the principles of justice and their other comprehensive values. Indeed, there cannot be a single comprehensive argument to establish the *content* of the principles of justice. Fortunately, the argument from the original position does not need to be understood as a comprehensive argument, based on some particular comprehensive doctrine. Instead, as Rawls came to recognize, it could be presented as establishing a *political* conception of justice.

Political Liberalism aims to develop the ideas and arguments necessary to understand justice as fairness, and a family of other liberal conceptions of justice, as forms of a political conception of justice. "While such a [political] conception is, of course, a moral conception, it is a moral conception worked out for a specific kind of subject, namely, for political, social, and economic institutions."[15]

---

[12] John Rawls, *Political Liberalism*, expanded ed. (Columbia University Press, 2005), xvi.
[13] For a thorough accounting of the difficulties Rawls found in the congruence argument and how *Political Liberalism* responded to them, see Paul Weithman, *Why Political Liberalism?* (Oxford University Press, 2010).
[14] Rawls, *Political Liberalism*, 4.
[15] Rawls, *Political Liberalism*, 11.

A political conception of justice aims to be compatible with a wide range of reasonable comprehensive theories. As such, it does not depend on any particular comprehensive doctrine. Instead, "Its content is expressed in terms of certain fundamental ideas seen as implicit in the public political culture of a constitutional regime."[16] These public, political ideas are assumed to be shared by the diverse, reasonable, comprehensive doctrines in the society.

While a political conception is presented as not being dependent on any comprehensive doctrine, each reasonable comprehensive doctrine, from its own point of view, can go beyond the political conception and embed it within its own values and worldview. Thus, "The political conception is a module, an essential constituent part, that fits into and can be supported by various reasonable comprehensive doctrines that endure in the society regulated by it."[17] When different reasonable comprehensive doctrines each affirm the same political conception of justice, each for its own comprehensive reasons, a society has achieved an "overlapping consensus of reasonable doctrines." This idea fills the conceptual gap left by the unrealistic aspirations of the congruence argument from *A Theory of Justice*. A society characterized by an overlapping consensus will be "stable for the right reasons."[18] Rawls notes that "the idea of an overlapping consensus is easily misunderstood given the idea of consensus used in everyday political."[19] It might be thought, for example, that the idea is to "look to the comprehensive doctrines that in fact exist and then draw up a political conception that strikes some kind of balance of forces between them." But: "This is not how justice as fairness proceeds; to do so would make it political in the wrong way."[20] A political conception of justice is developed as a free-standing "normative and moral idea."[21] It is crucial to note that the overlapping consensus is among *reasonable* comprehensive doctrines. Any actual society will undoubtedly have some unreasonable persons and doctrines. There is no principled reason (although of course there may be practical reasons) to compromise in order to accommodate them. Indeed, Rawls notes, "In their case the problem is to contain them so that they do not undermine the unity and justice of society."[22]

A just society, for Rawls, is a democratic society in a particularly deep sense, with its own ideal of democratic citizenship. The political relationship among members of such a society is one of "free and equal citizens who exercise ultimate political power as a collective body."[23] This raises the question of how

---

[16] Rawls, *Political Liberalism*, 13.
[17] Rawls, *Political Liberalism*, 12.
[18] Rawls, *Political Liberalism*, xxxvii.
[19] Rawls, *Political Liberalism*, 39.
[20] Rawls, *Political Liberalism*, 39–40.
[21] Rawls, *Political Liberalism*, xxxvi.
[22] Rawls, *Political Liberalism*, xvii.
[23] Rawls, *Political Liberalism*, xliii.

they can make a *collective* decision—at least regarding what Rawls calls "constitutional essentials and matters of basic questions of justice"[24]—when they do not share a comprehensive doctrine. Part of the answer, of course, is that they must rely on what they *do* share—a political conception of justice. But principles do not apply themselves, so a broader framework of collective reasoning regarding such matters is required. Rawls calls this framework "public reason," and he writes: "Since the exercise of political power must be legitimate, the ideal of citizenship imposes a moral, not a legal, duty—the duty of civility—to be able to explain to one another on those fundamental questions how the principles and policies they advocate and vote for can be supported by the political values of public reason."[25] Like a political conception of justice, public reason is, of course, a moral and normative ideal. It is an exercise of reason, not simply the de facto points of agreement among actual individuals. Yet it is exclusionary in that it rejects some considerations that might have normative force in other contexts or frameworks. Specifically, it "excludes comprehensive religious and philosophical doctrines (the whole truth, as it were) from being specified as public reasons."[26] It does not say that these reasons are false, only that they fail to provide appropriate political justification for democratic citizens who affirm a diversity of reasonable comprehensive doctrines. The exact contours of public reason and how the duty of civility is to be realized more concretely continue to be subject to dispute and will be explored in Part I. But this is yet another element of an extremely rich legacy that Rawls has left us to develop and make our own.

The Structure of This Collection

This book takes the work of John Rawls as a launching point for exploring major issues in contemporary political philosophy. It is divided into ten parts, with each part covering a significant area of philosophical debate inspired by Rawls's work. For each part, there is an introductory essay, providing an overview of the relevant arguments from Rawls's work and some of the contours of the debate that ensued. Each introductory essay is followed by two essays written by scholars who take opposing positions on the debate, moving the discussion forward in a fruitful way.

Part I of this volume explores the strengths and weaknesses of Rawls's idea of public reason. As described previously, public reason is an ideal of democratic discourse in which citizens must justify the principles guiding shared society

---

[24] Rawls, *Political Liberalism*, 10.
[25] Rawls, *Political Liberalism*, 217.
[26] Rawls, *Justice as Fairness*, 90.

in terms that all citizens will find reasonable, despite their differences in comprehensive doctrines and theories of the good. Rawls's ideal of public reason raises a number of challenging questions: Do the restrictions of public reasoning unfairly exclude certain arguments from the dialogue, such as those based on deeply held religious convictions that are not generally shared? Will there be a sufficient overlapping consensus among reasonable views such that public reasons will be adequate for resolving issues of justice? In this volume, David Reidy argues that there are good reasons to doubt that public reason can resolve all important questions concerning justice. In particular, he focuses on questions about the boundaries of citizenship, such as the definition of death. In response, James Boettcher explores a way that public reason can be understood to address this problem.

Part II explores Rawls's choice to approach philosophical questions of justice through ideal theory. Rawls argued that an important role of political philosophy is to identify the ideal standards of justice at which we should aim. Other philosophers challenge this approach, arguing that Rawls's ideal principles are useless as a guide for action in the real, nonideal world or, worse, that they are an impediment to addressing injustices in the world where racism, sexism, ableism, and other forms of discrimination intersect to create complex forms of domination and subordination. They argue that political philosophy ought to be focused on theorizing about how to identify and eliminate real injustices in the world. In this volume, Colin Farrelly argues against ideal theory, claiming that Rawls's idealizing assumptions have a distorting impact on values and our recognition of injustice. In contrast, Matthew Adams defends Rawls on ideal theory, arguing that nonideal theory depends on ideal theory in important ways.

Part III explores the place of economic liberty in Rawls's work. Libertarians, especially, raise many important questions about the relation between liberty and justice: What, if any, economic liberties are basic liberties that ought to be protected under Rawls's first principle of justice? How ought economic liberties be weighed against the importance of other social goods, such as equality of opportunity? In this volume, Jeppe Von Platz examines three different libertarian criticisms of Rawls's theory. Although he argues that ultimately the libertarian arguments he examines do not succeed, he also believes that libertarians are correct to hold that economic liberties are more important than Rawls recognizes. In the companion essay, Alan Thomas argues that libertarians are insufficiently concerned about protecting citizens from domination by each other. Since one important way we dominate each other is through the control of capital, he argues citizens will be best protected from domination by protecting a right to fair and universal access to capital. Further, he argues this right is best protected by property-owning democracy, an economic structure that Rawls describes as an alternative to both socialism and welfare-state capitalism.

Part IV explores controversies about Rawls's egalitarianism. Rawls describes his theory as "egalitarian," but there is a vigorous philosophical debate about how this is to be understood and what kind of equality is fundamental. Luck egalitarians take justice to aim at eliminating inequalities that are the result of luck, while relational egalitarians aim to establish and maintain relations of equality among citizens. Both have found resources for their ideas in Rawls's work. In this section, Kasper Lippert-Rasmussen defends a luck egalitarian view, carefully examining the limited role that luck egalitarian assumptions play in Rawls's theory, as well as defending luck egalitarianism against critics. Rainer Forst argues against luck egalitarianism and in favor of a Rawlsian relational egalitarianism.

Part V explores the question of what it is that should be fairly distributed in a just society. Rawls's principles of distributive justice—including the difference principle—focus on the distribution of social primary goods rather than the distribution of welfare, utility, capabilities, or some other equalisandum. But people differ in their abilities to make use of primary goods in pursuit of their ends. Accordingly, equality of primary goods may not result in equality of welfare. For this reason, Amartya Sen famously argues that one must use some other measure—equality of capability—to determine when a society is just. In this volume, Christopher Lowry explores Amartya Sen's capabilities critique, identifying what is important about it and developing a way of modifying Rawls's theory to respond to it. In the companion essay, Tony Fitzpatrick argues that both the primary goods approach and the capabilities approach face an "elasticity problem." He proposes a way forward that is "multiperspectivist," allowing some flexibility in using primary goods and capabilities as measures, depending on practical policy demands.

Part VI explores the adequacy of Rawls's theory of justice for respecting citizens who are deeply dependent on others, such as children and people with significant disabilities. In *A Theory of Justice*, Rawls describes his project as attempting to find fair principles of cooperation between free and equal people who are capable of full participation in the social order. Often inspired by developments in feminist philosophy, some philosophers have expressed concern about Rawls's overemphasis on human independence, autonomy, and equality to the neglect of the asymmetries created by human dependence and interdependence. Does Rawls's neglect of human relations of dependence result in a political theory that will create or ignore injustice for those who are dependent or who care for dependents? In this volume, Eva Kittay argues Rawls's liberal conception of equality falls short in addressing the needs of humans who are dependent and those who care for them. In response, Amy Baehr proposes a way of developing Rawls's theory to address justice for dependents by adding Rawlsian principles of justice in caregiving.

Part VII explores whether Rawls's theory provide adequate resources for critiquing gender inequality. In this volume, Victoria Costa argues that Rawls's two principles of justice are indeterminate on some key feminist issues. For example, she argues they do not provide determinate answers on questions of sexual and reproductive rights. Christie Hartley and Lori Watson respond by arguing that *Political Liberalism*, and in particular the criterion of reciprocity, contains the resources for a robust feminist critique of the social conditions that create and sustain domination and subordination.

Part VIII explores the question of justice for nonhuman animals. Does Rawls's theory of justice have the resources to address issues of justice as they impact nonhuman animals? In her contribution, Sarah Roberts-Cady argues that Rawls's theory can and should be extended to include nonhuman animals. In contrast, Patrick Taylor Smith argues that Rawls was right to restrict direct duties of justice to humans, but that Rawls's theory leaves open the possibility of indirect duties of justice to nonhuman animals.

Part IX explores debates about international economic justice. In *The Law of Peoples*, Rawls developed his long-awaited arguments on issues of international justice. Many scholars were surprised that Rawls did not advocate a direct extension of his egalitarian principles of domestic distributive justice to the international order. In fact, Rawls argued that a much less demanding principle—the "duty of assistance"—should guide economic aid in the global order. Cosmopolitan critics argue this was a mistake. What are fair principles guiding economic relations between states or peoples? Rekha Nath explores some possible defenses of Rawls's limited duty of assistance, arguing that each ultimately fails to provide adequate reasons for Rawls's rejection of global egalitarianism. In contrast, Gillian Brock defends Rawls's position on international economic justice against criticisms, arguing that Rawls offers important insights on international development aid.

Part X explores the question of the extent that liberal peoples ought to tolerate nonliberal peoples. Critics of *The Law of Peoples* argue that Rawls's attempt to establish principles founded on the common ground between liberal and decent nonliberal peoples is an unprincipled compromise that results in an inadequate set of human rights and a foreign policy that is too tolerant of nonliberal states. Is Rawls too tolerant and is his conception of human rights too meager? In this volume, Michael Blake argues that the emergence of right-wing populism and the international interference in democratic systems through troll farms illustrate some significant weaknesses in Rawls's position on international toleration. In contrast, Jon Mandle defends Rawls's position on international toleration, arguing there are good, principled reasons for setting the limits of toleration where Rawls does.

For Further Reading

Brooks, Thom, and Martha Nussbaum, eds. *Rawls's "Political Liberalism"* (Columbia University Press, 2015). This collection includes a valuable overview of *Political Liberalism* by Nussbaum and chapters discussing many aspects of the book.

Freeman, Samuel, ed. *The Cambridge Companion to Rawls* (Cambridge University Press, 2003). This important collection includes interpretations by many leading contemporary political philosophers.

Freeman, Samuel. *Rawls* (Routledge, 2007). Written by one of the leading interpreters of Rawls, this work aims to provide a comprehensive overview of his intellectual life and work.

Laden, Anthony. "The House That Jack Built: Thirty Years of Reading Rawls." *Ethics* 113 (2003), 367–390. This article offers a compelling but somewhat unorthodox interpretation of the core motivation and importance of Rawls's project.

Mandle, Jon. *An Introduction to Rawls's "A Theory of Justice"* (Cambridge University Press, 2009). This work offers an introductory guide to *A Theory of Justice*, including chapters on each of the three parts of the work, as well as chapters on the relationship to *Political Liberalism* and on some of the more important criticisms.

Mandle, Jon, and David Reidy, eds. *The Cambridge Rawls Lexicon* (Cambridge University Press, 2015). With over two hundred entries, this reference volume covers most aspects of Rawls's thought.

Martin, Rex, and David Reidy, eds. *Rawls's Law of Peoples: A Realistic Utopia* (Wiley-Blackwell, 2006). This influential collection includes both critics and defenders of Rawls's project in *The Law of Peoples*.

Weithman, Paul. *Why Political Liberalism? On John Rawls's Political Turn* (Oxford University Press, 2011). This work is the most insightful and comprehensive account of the motivation and changes that occurred in Rawls's thought between *A Theory of Justice* and *Political Liberalism*.

Wenar, Leif. "John Rawls." *The Stanford Encyclopedia of Philosophy* (revised Spring 2017), https://plato.stanford.edu/archives/spr2017/entries/rawls/. This is a brief and reliable overview of Rawls's thought.

PART I
PUBLIC REASON

Introduction

John Rawls advances an ideal of democratic political discourse that he calls "public reason." When it comes to public discussions of basic principles of justice and constitutional essentials, Rawls contends citizens have a duty of civility to offer arguments that they believe will be found reasonable by other citizens. He holds that arguments for the foundational principles of shared society ought not depend on specific religious doctrines or controversial moral theories that one cannot reasonably expect other citizens to find acceptable. Instead, public discussions of issues of justice ought to use shared standards of reasoning, uncontroversial empirical claims, and values that can be the subject of an overlapping consensus among diverse reasonable views. Rawls calls this form of reasoning "public reason." By appealing to public reasons, one shows respect for others' views. As Charles Larmore puts it, "We respect others as ends in themselves, [Rawls] holds, when in regard to their claims and interests we act on reasons that we are prepared to explain to them in light of mutually acceptable principles."[1] The ideal of public reason is an ideal of democratic process—it is an ideal about how citizens can debate the terms of their political association in a way that is respectful of each other as free and equal. This idea of showing respect for fellow citizens through public reason plays an important role in two arguments for the use of public reason in political discourses. First, there is an argument from political legitimacy. Second, there is the argument from stability.

The first argument begins with the assumption that the exercise of political power over other people requires justification to be legitimate. In a liberal political system grounded on respect for citizens' freedom and equality, the use of political power is legitimate if and only if it can be reasonably justified to those over whom it is wielded. Rawls's ideal of public reason is a way of meeting this requirement for legitimacy. In *Political Liberalism*, Rawls argues for a principle of liberal legitimacy in which "our exercise of political power is proper only when we sincerely believe that the reasons we would offer for our political actions may reasonably be accepted by other citizens as justifications of those actions."[2] Thus,

---

[1] Charles Larmore, "Public Reason," in *The Cambridge Companion to Rawls*, ed. Samuel Freeman (Cambridge, 2003), 373.

[2] John Rawls, *Political Liberalism*, expanded ed. (Columbia University Press, 2005), xliv.

Introduction In: *John Rawls*. Edited by: Jon Mandle and Sarah Roberts-Cady, Oxford University Press (2020). © Oxford University Press. DOI: 10.1093/oso/9780190859213.003.0002.

Rawls argues that a government founded on principles of justice that are justified by public reasons is one that has political legitimacy.

A second argument for the ideal of public reason stems from the goal of creating a political system that is stable. Rawls argues that the normal exercise of human reason in a free society will inevitably result in reasonable people adopting different views. Reasonable people will hold different positions on religion, the good life, and comprehensive ethical theories. Rawls argues that achieving a stable political system in the midst of this disagreement requires more than a mere compromise in which each citizen has to give up a little of what that citizen wants in order to get something in return. Instead, stability requires a system built on principles of justice and constitutional essentials that everyone can genuinely endorse as correct, despite their disagreements on broader philosophical issues. Public reason is aimed at creating a system like this. The use of public reason in political discourse is a process aimed at resolving basic political questions among reasonable citizens with diverse views in a way that is legitimate. When it succeeds, it creates a stable foundation for a democratic society.[3]

An important point worth clarifying is that this view of public reason does not propose any limitations on the freedom of speech. Public reason is not about the government limiting what can be said in public. Civility is a moral duty, not one to be legally enforced. It serves as a guide for how citizens should engage in dialogue about justice in a public forum—a guide for discussions by candidates running for political office, discourse among public officials, and decisions by judges.[4] It's about what arguments are to be given moral weight on issues of basic justice and constitutional essentials. It is about what counts as a proper justification for policy in a liberal system.

In fact, Rawls argues that the sharing of nonpublic reasons should not only be legally permissible, but also morally permissible. In "The Idea of Public Reason Revisited," Rawls explicitly endorsed a "wide" view of public reason in contrast to an exclusive view. The contrasting "exclusive" view of public reason contends that one should only ever offer public reasons in discussing matters of constitutional essentials and justice in the public forum. This view holds that it is morally impermissible to argue publicly from nonpublic reasons, that is, reasons based on aspects of one's comprehensive doctrines that are not shared by others. Rawls argues against this exclusive view. Instead, he adopts the wide view, stating that it is morally permissible to offer arguments using nonpublic reasons, as long as "in due course" one provides a justification that appeals to public reasons, as well.[5] This allows people to be honest and open about the grounds of their beliefs, while

---

3 Rawls, *Political Liberalism*, 142–143, 391–392.
4 Rawls, *Political Liberalism*, 443.
5 Rawls, *Political Liberalism*, 462.

respecting and communicating with those who don't share those beliefs. Rawls defends this more inclusive view by arguing that openness about one's nonpublic reasons helps to foster trust. Openly discussing one's nonpublic reasons can reveal the deeper comprehensive basis for one's commitment to public reason. It can serve an explanatory and relational goal, even if these nonpublic reasons cannot play a public justificatory role.

Rawls's view of the ideal of public reason is not without critics. There are two major areas of criticisms we will examine here. First, some philosophers argue that Rawls's ideal of public reason improperly excludes certain kinds of political arguments. Second, some philosophers argue that Rawls's strict limitations on reasons will result in an inability to resolve important questions of justice.

The first concern is that Rawls's view of public reason improperly excludes certain kinds of arguments from having moral weight in the public sphere. Often this concern is expressed about the exclusion of religious beliefs from public political discourse.[6] Rawls's version of public reason is secular in the sense that it excludes controversial assumptions about religion—both theistic and atheistic. Instead, public reason appeals to arguments that would be found reasonable regardless of one's religious beliefs. Some critics argue this exclusion of religious arguments is a mistake. Sometimes this criticism is grounded in an observation about the importance of religious arguments as a powerful source for positive social change. People often point to the important role of Martin Luther King Jr.'s religious-based arguments in the civil rights movement of the 1960s. Other times the criticism is expressed as a problem of not showing adequate respect for religious perspectives. For example, Nicholas Wolterstorff states that it is disrespectful not to offer due consideration to a speaker's reasons when they are based on comprehensive religious doctrines. He writes,

> Is there not something about the person who embraces, say, the Jewish religion, that I, a Christian, should honor? Should I not honor her not only as someone who is free and equal but *as* someone who embraces the Jewish religion? Is she not worth honoring not only in her similarity to me, as free and equal, but *in* her particular difference from me—in her embrace of Judaism? Of course, I mean Judaism to be taken here as but one example among many. Are persons

[6] Christopher Eberle, *Religious Convictions in Liberal Politics* (Cambridge University Press, 2002); Kent Greenawalt, *Private Consciences and Public Reasons* (Oxford University Press, 1995); David Hollenbach, "Public Reason / Private Religion? A Response to Paul J. Weithman," *Journal of Religious Ethics* 22 (1994), 39–46; Jeffrey Stout, *Democracy and Tradition* (Princeton University Press, 2004); Kevin Vallier, *Liberalism and Public Faith: Beyond Separation* (Routledge, 2014); Paul Weithman, *Religion and the Obligation of* Citizenship (Cambridge University Press, 2002); Nicholas Wolterstorff, "The Role of Religion in Decision and Discussion of Political Issues," in *Religion in the Public Square: The Place of Religious Convictions in Political Debate*, ed. Nicholas Wolterstorff and Robert Audi (Rowman and Littlefield, 1996), 67–120.

not often worth honoring *in* their religious particularities, in their national particularities, in their class particularities, in their gender particularities? Does such honoring not require that I invite them to tell me how politics looks from their perspective—and does it not require that I genuinely listen to what they say? We need a politics that not only honors us in our similarity as free and equal, but in our particularities. For our particularities—some of them—are constitutive of who we are, constitutive of our narrative identities.[7]

This charge of improper exclusion is not limited to religious arguments. Jeremy Waldron argues the restrictions on public reason would rule out novel reasons.[8] Matteo Bonotti argues that Rawls's restrictions associated with public reason would also unjustly restrict partisan arguments (arguments based on the controversial assumptions of political parties).[9] Finally, Ben Cross also thinks Rawls's restrictions would unjustly exclude reasons of oppressed groups who hold views that are not widely shared.[10]

In defense of Rawls, many philosophers have argued that the ideal of public reason allows more expression of and respect for diverse views than is acknowledged by these critics.[11] While a full discussion of this debate cannot be offered here, three points are worth noting. First, philosophers often point to the fact that Rawls's wide view of public reason encourages the expression of nonpublic reasons (including religious reasons) as a way of fostering trust and understanding between people with diverse views. While acknowledging our differences and seeking to understand each other's unique perspectives, the ideal of public reason simply entails that we also seek some common ground for guiding the fundamental terms of our cooperation. Second, one could argue that the ideal of public reason would also encourage respect for people's unique identities—their "particularity." Part of what it means to respect people as free and equal moral beings is to respect their ability and right to affirm or endorse their own comprehensive doctrine and conception of the good. We honor and respect each other's unique perspectives not by imposing our comprehensive doctrines upon one another through our legal systems but by reasoning from

---

[7] Nicholas Wolterstorff, "Role of Religion," 110–111.

[8] Jeremy Waldron, "Religious Contributions in Public Deliberation," *San Diego Law Review* 30 (1993), 817–848.

[9] Matteo Bonotti, "Partisanship and Public Reason," *CRISPP: Critical Review of International Social and Political Philosophy* 17 (2014), 314–331.

[10] Ben Cross, "Public Reason and the Exclusion of Oppressed Groups," *Dialogue: Canadian Philosophical Review* 56 (2017), 241–265.

[11] James Sterba, "Reconciling Public Reason and Religious Values," *Social Theory and Practice* 25 (1999), 1–28; James Boettcher, "Respect, Recognition, and Public Reason," *Social Theory and Practice* 33 (2007), 223–249; Phil Ryan, "Stout, Rawls, and the Idea of Public Reason," *Journal of Religious Ethics* 42 (2014), 540–562.

mutually acceptable premises.[12] Finally, it is also worth noting that the ideal of public reason does not give extra moral weight to the assumptions of dominant views. As a guide for discourse, public reasoning acts as a limit on the views of the majority, imposing a duty on dominant groups to engage in dialogue with others and offer reasons that are reasonably expected to be acceptable to all citizens, including minorities. Further, the reasonable overlapping consensus to which Rawls refers is not discovered by examining existing beliefs and attempting to identify points of agreement. Instead, it is achieved through the process of public reasoning, perhaps only after citizens offer new, reasonable arguments that through dialogue gain the consensus of diverse, but reasonable persons.[13]

A second, distinct objection to Rawls's view of public reason is that it is incomplete. The primary concern is that Rawls's limitations on public reason result in insufficient resources for resolving important issues of justice.[14] In this volume, David Reidy explores one form of incompleteness: indeterminacy with regard to establishing eligibility for citizenship status and political relations. That is, Reidy argues that public reason cannot be used to resolve who counts as a citizen with rights. This question is at the heart of controversial issues about abortion, definitions of death, the citizenship status of severely cognitively disabled persons, and the place of higher mammals. If public reason is not sufficient for answering these key questions of justice, Reidy argues, people must appeal to their nonpublic comprehensive doctrines to resolve these issues.

In response, Jim Boettcher acknowledges the possibility of public reason resulting in this form of indeterminacy. He offers a solution in the form of a principle of wide public reason that allows citizens to appeal to nonpublic reasons if and only if public reasons are indeterminate with regard to particular issue and provided they "otherwise aim to honor public reason." What is more, he argues, contrary to an argument published previously by Reidy, that his proposed wide view of public reason is consistent with respect for political autonomy.

Suggested Reading from Rawls to Accompany These Chapters

From *Political Liberalism*, expanded edition: "Introduction to the Paperback Edition"; Lecture VI, "The Idea of Public Reason"; "The Idea of Public Reason Revisited"

---

[12] See Boettcher, "Respect, Recognition," 223–249.

[13] Rawls, *Political Liberalism*, 389.

[14] David Reidy, "Rawls's Wide View of Public Reason: Not Wide Enough," *Res Publica* 6 (2000), 49–72; Michael Sandel, *Liberalism and the Limits of Justice*, 2nd ed. (Cambridge University Press, 1998); Peter de Marneffe, "Rawls's Idea of Public Reason," *Pacific Philosophical Quarterly* 75 (1994), 232–250; Gerald Gaus, "Reasonable Pluralism and the Domain of the Political," *Inquiry* 42 (1999), 259–284.

For Further Reading

Arrell, Robbie. "Public Reason and Abortion: Was Rawls Right After All?" *Journal of Ethics* 23 (2019), 1–17. In reply to Williams ("Public Reason and Prenatal Moral Status"), this paper argues that public reason does have the resources to address the issue of abortion.

Boettcher, James. "Respect, Recognition and Public Reason." *Social Theory and Practice* 33 (2007), 223–249. This paper responds to critics of Rawls who argue that the restrictions of public reason fail to respect citizens who affirm a religious faith as part of their identity.

Quong, Jonathan. "On the Idea of Public Reason." In *A Companion to Rawls*, ed. Jon Mandle and David Reidy (Wiley-Blackwell, 2014). This contribution to a recent collection on Rawls provides an excellent overview of Rawls's idea of public reason, emphasizing the importance of the question of whether it is complete.

Reidy, David. "Rawls's Wide View of Public Reason: Not Wide Enough." *Res Publica* 6 (2000), 49–72. Reidy develops a sympathetic criticism of Rawls's account of public reason, arguing that as it stands it is importantly incomplete and often will prove inadequate to resolve fundamental political issues.

Schwartzman, Micah. "The Completeness of Public Reason." *Politics, Philosophy, and Economics* 3 (2004), 191–220. Schwartzman argues that public reason has rich enough resources to address most fundamental political issues.

Vallier, Kevin. *Liberalism and Public Faith: Beyond Separation* (Routledge, 2014). This work offers an alternative account of public reason ("convergence liberalism") that treats religious belief as falling within the scope of public political deliberation.

Weithman, Paul. *Religion and the Obligations of Citizenship* (Cambridge University Press, 2002). Weithman explores how religion can help to prepare citizens to participate in and support democratic politics.

Williams, Andrew. "The Alleged Incompleteness of Public Reason." *Res Publica* 6 (2000), 199–211. This article defends Rawls's completeness claim against Reidy ("Rawls's Wide View of Public Reason: Not Wide Enough") and supports the exclusion of comprehensive doctrines (including religious doctrines) from public reason.

Williams, Jeremy. "Public Reason and Prenatal Moral Status." *Journal of Ethics* 19 (2015), 23–52. This article provides a critique of Rawls's public reason approach to the issue of abortion based on the claim that respect for human life as such (as opposed to respect for moral persons) does not fall within the limits of public reason.

1

Public Political Reason

Still Not Wide Enough

David A. Reidy

Nearly twenty years ago I published an essay arguing that public reason as Rawls understood it was incomplete with respect to at least some constitutional essentials or matters of basic justice. This incompleteness, I maintained, placed the ideal of public reason, and so the associated values of liberal legitimacy and political autonomy, beyond the reach of democratic citizens engaged in public political deliberation and decision-making.

Scholarly inquiry into Rawls's idea and ideal of public reason has advanced a great deal over the last twenty years. James Boettcher and others have clarified and shed important light on both the Rawlsian idea and ideal and the more compelling of the rival conceptions of public reason, often themselves rooted in rival conceptions of constitutional liberal democracy. In this essay I revisit my worry that even under favorable conditions Rawlsian public reason will prove incomplete in a way or to a degree that effectively pushes the values with which it is associated beyond the reach of democratic citizens.

But I focus in this essay on a form of incompleteness unaddressed in (though I think implicit in and so consistent with) my earlier essay. As James Boettcher notes, the examples of incompleteness proffered in my earlier essay were of two sorts: cases of too many reasons and cases of too few reasons. The new cases that I proffer in what follows are cases of too few reasons. But they are of a distinctive form and it is not obvious whether they are amenable to the handling James Boettcher proposes in response to the cases identified in my earlier essay. Without taking a view on whether they are, I offer here my own proposal for how to handle them while keeping faith with the commitments undergirding public reason and the weighty goods that trail in its wake. An attractive possibility is that together Boettcher and I will have helped not only to clarify potential problems for Rawlsian public reason but also to support an optimistic assessment of its ability to meet these problems. Were this possibility to be realized, the relative gravitational force of rival conceptions of public reason drawn from rival conceptions of constitutional liberal democracy might be diminished.

David A. Reidy, *Public Political Reason* In: *John Rawls*. Edited by: Jon Mandle and Sarah Roberts-Cady, Oxford University Press (2020). © Oxford University Press. DOI: 10.1093/oso/9780190859213.003.0003.

I begin with some brief preliminary and I hope clarifying remarks about public reason and the values associated with it. I turn then to the issue of public reason's completeness or lack thereof. After a brief remark or two following up on my aforementioned paper from many years ago, I argue that justice as fairness is incomplete with respect to another important class of political issues concerning constitutional essentials or basic justice. I argue further that its incompleteness in this regard is not peculiar to it but will be widely shared by other reasonable political liberalisms. Drawing on a distinction between public reason and public political reason, I then try to show that permitting citizens to resolve these sorts of disagreements by reasoning publicly with one another as reasonable *persons* committed to diverse but reasonable *comprehensive doctrines* and not simply reasonable *citizens* committed to diverse but reasonable *political conceptions* of justice need not undermine the commitments and values served by either public reason or public political reason.

Rawls on Public Reason

In a modern democracy, citizens understand themselves each to occupy the most fundamental political office: citizenship. As its occupants, they understand themselves equally to share fundamental and so constitutive political power. Of course, as with any office, the power it makes available to those who hold it is not unlimited. Exercises of power within the limits of the office carry the presumptive authority of the office. They are right in the sense of permitted or required by the office. Those that exceed the limits do not carry the office's presumptive authority. They are wrong in the sense of forbidden or precluded by the office.

Because citizenship, at least in a modern democracy, is the fundamental political office, there is no political criterion or test of its limits, no standard of the rightful range of its authority, beyond the conscientious, reasonable, and responsible judgment of those exercising it. But there are two dimensions along which this judgment may take a different form. The first concerns the difference between the precise target optimally aimed at, on the one hand, and the general range of targets permissibly aimed at, on the other, by any exercise of the authority of the office. The second concerns a judgment made from a point of view internal to the office, on the one hand, and a judgment made from a point of view external to the office, on the other.

In *A Theory of Justice*, Rawls argued that justice as fairness was, among historically familiar candidate targets, the most reasonable, and thus uniquely the precise, target to be optimally aimed for in any exercise of the office of citizenship. His complex argument for this, launched from a point of view external to the office, rested in part on the claim that if publicly and generally adopted as the standard governing the authority of the office of citizenship, justice as fairness would uniquely bring a certain sort of stability to democracy as an ongoing form of political activity between reasonable persons. Not long after the publication of *Theory*, Rawls recognized a problem with this claim. The sort of stability he attributed to justice as fairness as a common public standard governing the authority of citizenship presupposed that the persons occupying this office would, as persons and so from a point of view external to the office, eventually embrace justice as fairness as the political part of an overall loosely Kantian but certainly liberal self-understanding and world view (including a moral, religious, and/or philosophical comprehensive doctrine). The problem Rawls recognized was that in any democracy, even one that institutionally embodied justice as fairness, it was unrealistic to think that the persons occupying and exercising the office of citizenship would ever come generally to share to the required degree any such overall self-understanding or world view, let alone the loosely Kantian and liberal one he had imagined they would. The solution to the problem, Rawls reasoned, was to trim and repackage justice as fairness as a self-standing "political" conception of justice that might be argued for from a point of view internal to the office of citizenship and embraced in different ways by reasonable persons with different but reasonable self-understandings and world views.

As Rawls pursued this solution, he came to realize also that he could not realistically expect in any democracy that citizens would ever converge fully in their conscientious, reasonable, and responsible judgments on one and the same precise target as the standard by which publicly to assess any exercise of their office as citizens. With respect to the precise target at which any exercise of their office ought optimally to be aimed, there would always be reasonable disagreement between them. This meant that there was a second problem with the stability argument given in *Theory*. It unrealistically supposed that all reasonable citizens would recognize justice as fairness as the most reasonable, and thus uniquely the precise, target to be optimally aimed at by any exercise of the office of citizenship. The solution to this problem, Rawls reasoned, was to specify a range of targets as the political criterion or test, the standard of rightful authority, by which citizens were publicly to assess any exercise of their office as citizens. While citizens might disagree over the relative reasonableness of targets within this range, they might agree that all were equally legitimate or permissible, and that those outside the range were illegitimate or impermissible. In this way they might draw on a shared sense of legitimacy rather than justice in order publicly to assure one another of their fidelity to a common commitment to democratic citizenship.

Of course, whether reasoning from within the office of citizenship or as a person who might occupy it, Rawls continued to think that justice as fairness, suitably trimmed and repackaged as a political conception of justice, was the most reasonable, and thus uniquely the precise, target at which any exercise of the office ought optimally to be aimed. But he came to see that, surprisingly, the only reasonable basis for hoping that a democratic society faithful to justice as fairness might someday be achieved and remain stable required, first, shifting the standard for publicly assessing exercises of citizenship to a family of free-standing political conceptions of justice worked up from a point of view internal to the office of citizenship and then, second, showing that while persons with different self-understandings and world views might embrace this more permissive standard in different ways and value their fidelity to it in different degrees, it was not unrealistic to think that they might still publicly know enough about one another reliably to trust one another not to exceed the rightful authority of their office in democratic political activity. In *Political Liberalism* Rawls undertakes to make the case for all this and thus to square his ambition in *Theory* with the fact of reasonable disagreement, a fact that, though permanently characterizing any democracy, he nevertheless failed fully to appreciate in *Theory*.

In *Political Liberalism* and then further in "The Idea of Public Reason Revisited," the idea of public reason is presented and clarified. The idea is that of the reason in and through which citizens in political agenda setting, deliberation, and decision collectively exercise their office as citizens, at least in the most important kinds of cases, those concerning constitutional essentials and matters of basic justice. Its content is given by the family of reasonable political liberalisms, including the public political values they interpret and express, by the common stock of noncontroversial truths of science, history, and so on, and by generally recognized standards of correct inference and sound judgment. Of course, this content will develop and change over time, even under ideal theory conditions. But, Rawls argues, it should and will be always sufficiently rich to enable citizens faithfully to exercise their office. The ideal, then, is that of citizens and other political officials actually using, at least in public political forums, the public reason they share to identify, debate, and decide fundamental political issues, at least those concerning constitutional essentials and matters of basic justice. With constitutional essentials and matters of basic justice so identified, debated, and decided, downstream exercises of political power in legislative, adjudicative, and administrative matters may be presumed consistent with fidelity to democratic citizenship provided they are pursuant to and in accord with the constitutional and other fundamental matters already determined.

Public reason plays several important roles in Rawls's revised articulation and defense of justice as fairness. It specifies how within ongoing democratic political activity citizens visibly assure one another of their common commitment to a shared standard for assessing the rightful authority of the office they exercise. In this way, it contributes to the sort of stability Rawls hopes to place within the reach of constitutional democracies. It also publicly expresses the democratic notion that irrespective of the source of the authority that citizens exercise in political life, democratic citizens recognize no public political criterion or test of its rightfulness other than that which they can together reasonably, conscientiously, and responsibly agree to. In this way, it contributes to the ideal of democratic self-governance. And it constitutes an essential part of the shared aim through which democratic citizens participate in the activity or good of civic friendship. In this way, it specifies an important part of the common good within a democracy. Though it plays these roles and is thus linked to these goods, which trail in its wake, public reason is derived from or rooted in, and so ultimately answers to, our commitment to subordinating the more important exercises of our power in creating and sustaining a shared political world to terms mutually intelligible and acceptable. It is this commitment to reciprocity in political life that is fundamental, and the idea and ideal of public reason emerge as part of Rawls's attempt to defend it, under conditions of reasonable disagreement, as reasonable, rational, and realistic.

For public reason to play the various roles Rawls assigns it, it must be complete. Or so Rawls maintains. To be complete, each of the reasonable political conceptions of justice affirmed by citizens, when combined with the other elements of public reason (e.g., noncontroversial facts of history or science), must provide enough material—facts, values, standards of inference, and so on—to yield a determinate reasonable answer for every or very nearly every fundamental political question concerning a constitutional essential or matter of basic justice. This completeness is necessary if citizens are to maintain public confidence that their political judgments are "not puppets manipulated from behind the scenes by comprehensive doctrines."[1] Without this confidence, citizens will find themselves too readily willing to use their office illegitimately, violating reciprocity in political life and thereby putting at risk stability, democratic self-governance, and civic friendship.

Rawls does not attempt to show that each member of the family of reasonable political conceptions of justice affirmed by citizens is, when combined with the other elements of public reason, complete in the sense indicated. But he does endeavor to show that his preferred political conception of justice, justice as fairness, is complete.[2] The completeness of other reasonable political conceptions of justice is presumably left for those drawn to them to work out and explain. An otherwise reasonable political conception of justice not complete in the indicated sense would fall short, at least for those issues with respect to which it was incomplete, of what reciprocity demands in political life. Relative to political conceptions complete in the relevant sense, it would be, other thing equal, less reasonable than they.

---

[1] John Rawls, *Political Liberalism*, expanded ed. (Columbia University Press, 2005), 454.
[2] Rawls, *Political Liberalism*, 207f.

Two Reasons for Thinking Public Reason Is Incomplete

There are, I continue to think, two good reasons to think that even under ideal theory conditions many reasonable political conceptions of justice, candidate political liberalisms, will prove incomplete. The first, which I do not pursue here, is that some reasonable political conceptions will inevitably lack an internal mechanism or principle sufficient to ordering internally their values with respect to all constitutional essentials or matters of basic justice. Lacking such a mechanism or principle, they generate too many reasons, to use James Boettcher's phrase, to prove complete in the required sense. Insisting that every political conception include some such mechanism or principle in order to qualify as reasonable seems to overstate the demands of the reasonable and as a result problematically to stamp intuitionist pluralist political conceptions as unreasonable. On many issues, including some concerning constitutional essentials and matters of basic justice, those who affirm intuitionist pluralist political conceptions will inevitably draw on their comprehensive commitments, because there is no other intelligent way for them to order the values belonging to their political conception, in order to reach a determinate judgment. To this extent such political conceptions are incomplete. But they are not obviously unreasonable, provided the determinate judgments reached by those who affirm them keep faith with the content common to all reasonable political conceptions: a commitment to basic liberties and their priority relative to aggregate utility and perfectionist ends, and a commitment to a social minimum adequate to the meaningful use of the basic liberties. Assuming those who affirm such political conceptions affirm also and so draw on a reasonable comprehensive doctrine to give determinate order to the values within their political conception, it seems likely that their determinate judgments on political issues will indeed keep the indicated faith with political liberalism. Whether this is sufficient tribute to reciprocity in political life to foster or at least not undermine the goods of stability of the right sort, democratic self-governance and civic friendship, I leave for another occasion to address.

What I want to focus on here is a second reason for thinking that many, perhaps all, reasonable political liberalisms will prove incomplete. This is that they will lack—indeed, notwithstanding Rawls's own claim that it is complete, justice as fairness taken as a political liberalism will lack—the resources needed to underwrite determinate judgments on some issues concerning constitutional essentials and basic justice. Though I pointed in this direction in my earlier essay, here I try to bring greater clarity and focus to what I think I had, if only hazily, in mind then. I do so by focusing on the ways in which justice as fairness, taken as an exemplary reasonable political conception, lacks the resources needed to settle some constitutional essentials or matters of basic justice regarding eligibility for citizenship and inclusion within the domain of the political. The problem here, broadly speaking, is that reasonable political liberalisms draw their content from the nature of democratic citizenship as seen from a point of view, public and political, internal to the office. Their political reasonableness is in part a function of their crediting as common currency in political deliberation all and only reasons drawn from this well. They are thus ill-equipped to generate determinate judgments on issues regarding the reasonableness of this currency. Of course, they may dogmatically refuse such challenges as unreasonable. But dogmatic refusals of this sort do not qualify as determinate judgments.

Now the bare logical possibility of such issues is not sufficient by itself to establish the incompleteness of public reason. The content of reasonable political liberalisms may prove more fecund than first meets the eye. Further, the possibility of one or more reasonable political liberalisms proving incomplete in the relevant sense is not sufficient by itself to establish the incompleteness of public reason. Other things equal, it may underwrite no more than a reason for citizens to shift their allegiance to those reasonable political conceptions that are complete. So I do not propose that what follows is any kind of knockout punch for public reason. I aim to show only that there is, prima facie, a serious worry regarding the completeness of justice as fairness as a reasonable political liberalism. After establishing the grounds for this worry, I aim to show that there is a way to meet it without abandoning the Rawlsian commitment to public reason or the conception of liberal democracy it serves.

The Boundaries of Citizenship and the Incompleteness of Public Reason

All reasonable political liberalisms identify basic structural relations between citizens as citizens as the focal concern of political justice, and possession to a requisite minimum degree of the capacities intelligently to identify and pursue one's good and to evaluate and honor terms of political cooperation as the focal criteria of citizenship. As I argued in my earlier essay, this makes it difficult to see how reasonable political liberalisms are to address challenges to the constitutional and legal permissibility of abortion when those challenges take the form of arguing that a mother's relation to her fetus is a concern of political justice or that a fetus's status as a person is politically more important than its putative nonstatus as a citizen. To be sure, reasonable political liberalisms can dogmatically refuse to address these challenges on such terms, insisting instead, as Rawls urges, that they be addressed on terms such as the value of human life, the liberty of women, and the orderly maintenance of the family. A determinate judgment on these political terms may be available. But the issue raised by many who oppose abortion concerns precisely the reasonableness of resolving the constitutional and legal permissibility of abortion on these terms alone. And it is hard to see how to reach a determinate judgment on this matter without drawing reasons from a well other than public political reason, without drawing from one or another reasonable comprehensive doctrine a premise regarding the political status of the fetus qua person or the political significance of the basic moral, psychological, and biological relation between a mother and fetus.

Another issue of this sort I now see concerns the constitutional limits on and appropriate specification of the legal definition of death. This issue arises in a variety of contexts. For example, when should it be legally permissible for a hospital to harvest the organs of an organ donor? It is typically incompatible with successful organ harvesting to wait for a period of cardiopulmonary, metabolic, and brain function cessation such that there is no longer any reasonable disagreement regarding death. Modern technologies encourage defining death to occur at a stage earlier than that which is finally noncontroversial between all reasonable persons. But where should we constitutionally and legally draw the line? This is certainly a matter of basic justice and likely at least indirectly a constitutional essential. But it is hard to see how a reasonable political liberalism will prove complete with respect to it.

Consider justice as fairness. How is one to arrive at a determinate judgment on this question working from the political conception of the person qua citizen and the political relationship as one of shared coauthorship of a basic structure? The resources available to justice as fairness are internal to the political office of citizenship. But the issue at stake is not that of defining only the end of citizenship and so exit from political relations. It is that of defining the end of personhood or of the end of citizenship qua personhood. But beyond accepting the noncontroversial truth that a person is dead when rigor mortis has set in, this is a matter with respect to which all reasonable political liberalisms aim to remain agnostic. To be sure, as with the issue of abortion, justice as fairness and other reasonable political liberalisms can draw on such political values as respect for human life in an attempt to reach a determinate judgment on the political and legal issue. But as with the abortion case, addressing the issue only in terms of such political values is, for many citizens, precisely what is at stake. To them it feels less like the reaching of a determinate judgment on and more like a dogmatic refusal to address the issue at hand: when does *a person* die?

Justice as fairness and other reasonable political liberalisms may, of course, turn to science. The noncontroversial truths of science belong to public reason. But while science may be able noncontroversially to fill in details for us regarding particular proposed criteria for marking the death of a person, it cannot noncontroversially tell us which proposed criteria to adopt. That depends on what conception of the person (not of citizenship or of the person qua citizen) we adopt, and fixing on a conception of the person lies beyond science's remit.

Science may be able to give us a clearer picture of what constitutes a persistent vegetative state. But it cannot establish that persons (rather than persons qua citizens) do not survive persistent vegetative states.

Faced with such issues, justice as fairness and other reasonable political liberalisms may look for political paths forward that appear not to entail taking a principled stand on when a person in fact dies but that nevertheless prove acceptable to all as a kind of pragmatic compromise. They might, for example, aim at some sort of policy that allows citizens to establish for themselves, within an acceptable range, their own criteria of death. I may carry a card that indicates cessation of cardiopulmonary function constitutes my death. You may carry a card that indicates cessation of brain function constitutes death. Someone else may carry a card that indicates that death is constituted only by both. And so on. But the appearance of avoiding the issue is just that, an appearance. Any such policy, which hospitals, emergency responders, insurance carriers, and so on will be required to honor, will constitute an exercise of political power for which the putative public political reason citizens give one another is that they lack adequate public political reasons to reach a determinate judgment.

In addition to issues related to the constitutional and legal permissibility of abortion and to the constitutional and legal permissibility of various definitions of death, reasonable political liberalisms are likely also to prove incomplete with respect to the political and legal entitlement claims of severely disabled human beings. Again, the problem is that reasonable political liberalisms seem unable to generate from their own resources, worked out from a point of view internal to a political conception of citizenship, more than a dogmatic refusal to take up the issues in the terms pressed by those raising them. For many parents, that their child neither has nor will ever develop the two moral powers to the requisite minimum degree or affirm a determinate conception of the good is beside the point when it comes to her entitlements as a matter of political justice within the body politic. For many parents, having their child's entitlements politically determined by reference only to her humanity or to their interests as her parents or to a kind of policy rider attached to a broad scheme of social insurance—all considerations that may be proffered from public political reason—will be an expression of the problem, not a solution.

Once seriously politically contested, the boundaries of both citizenship and the political relation, from gestation to death, are matters with respect to which reasonable political liberalisms seem ill-equipped nondogmatically to generate determinate judgments without drawing from comprehensive doctrines content not belonging to public reason as such. As noted earlier, perhaps there are internal to justice as fairness and other reasonable political liberalisms resources sufficient to generate determinate judgments on these issues. But I am doubtful. The resources internal to justice as fairness and other reasonable political liberalisms are drawn from a political point of view internal to, and reflect from that point a view, a judgment regarding the point and purpose of the office of citizenship. It is hard to see how these resources, even when combined with noncontroversial truths of science and common sense, can underwrite, except dogmatically, determinate judgments on issues that call into question the basic political status of and political relations between citizens they presuppose. So long as these issues are not politically pressed or are, if politically pressed, successfully ignored or deferred, public reason may appear to be complete. But appearance is not reality. And the issues seem likely to be politically pressed and, once pressed, unlikely to be successfully ignored or deferred for long.

The foregoing are not the only sorts of status and boundary issues regarding human persons and political relations between them with respect to which justice as fairness and other reasonable political liberalisms, and so Rawlsian public reason, will likely prove incomplete. Suppose after committing a serious criminal offense for which punishment would ordinarily be forthcoming a convicted offender suffers a permanent psychological break with her previous self. She no longer recalls who she was at the time of the offense. She lacks and presumably will never recover psychological continuity with that individual. Should it be constitutionally and legally permissible to punish her? After all, though her body remains the same in the relevant sense and though she retains the two moral powers, she is arguably a different person than she was. Her current determinate conception of the good stands for her in no obvious relation to "her" past, whether a past determinate conception of her good or past exercises by her of her two moral powers. Her history simply does not include the crime with respect to which she has been charged and convicted. How is a justice on the Supreme Court to reach a determinate judgment as to whether her punishment would be "cruel and unusual" and so constitutionally proscribed without wading into the philosophical waters of personal identity? Here the fact that it would be unreasonable according to justice as fairness and presumably all reasonable political liberalisms to hold that Paul is not the same citizen as Saul of Tarsus seems to be more a statement of the problem than a path to a solution. That citizenship survives religious conversion is too thin a reed upon which to hang a determinate judgment regarding the constitutional or legal permissibility of punishment in a case of the sort just indicated.

Incompleteness of the foregoing sorts, regarding the boundaries of basic political status and relations, may not be limited to issues involving human beings. Suppose with advanced technologies we find that it is possible to establish what appear to be sustained though minimal forms of cooperation with some higher mammals. Notwithstanding linguistic obstacles to deliberating together regarding the terms of this cooperation, we are able to discern from their behavior something more than their ready liability to being coordinated and to

feeling affection or loyalty when coordinated benevolently. Suppose their behavior suggests cooperative capacities and dispositions perhaps less developed
than those of a typical early elementary school student but more developed than
those of, say, typical toddlers. They seem to seek and value something like mutual
intelligibility and acceptability in shared activity. Suppose our advanced technologies make possible rudimentary forms of communication, not unlike those
normal adults share with toddlers. To what extent, if any, ought any such higher
mammals to have a constitutional or legal claim to political status, whether as
citizen or quasi citizen? To what extent, if any, ought our relations to them to
be included among the political relations that constitute the basic social structure of, and so fall within the scope of political justice in, society? It is worth
noting that legal challenges to the treatment of chimpanzees as property have already been and will continue to be pressed. Those pressing them do not seek for
chimpanzees the same status enjoyed by a typical adult citizen. But they do seek a
status other than property (thing), and they seek recognition of the relationship
between citizens and resident chimpanzees as political. Again, as a political liberalism, justice as fairness seems ill-equipped to deliver from its own resources
a reasoned determinate judgment here. Of course, a dogmatic speciesism is
available to all political liberalisms. But insisting on it is not well described as
reaching a judgment.

Completing Public Reason

Of course, none of the preceding proves that public reason will prove too thin
to generate determinate answers for all political issues recently or likely soon
to be pressed concerning constitutional essentials and basic justice. At best it
constitutes a reasoned basis for thinking that the bet Rawls wagers on the relative
independence and autonomy within democratic politics of the political in relation to the larger domain of reasonable comprehensive moral, religious, and philosophical commitments is perhaps riskier than he intimates. For public reason
to be complete with respect to the sorts of issues raised here, it must be able from
within its own resources to establish nondogmatically the boundary conditions
governing citizenship status and political relations. To be sure, it has proved itself
complete with respect to some issues regarding boundary conditions. As Rawls
himself points out, one did not need to draw on resources other than public
reason to reach a determinate (also correct) judgment regarding the extension of
full citizenship to previously excluded blacks and women.

But the understanding of citizenship within public reason that made it possible to reach such determinate judgments was not itself the immediate offspring
of any exercise of public political reason. Rather, it was birthed by a long history

(culminating in the first liberal constitutional republics) of often hard-fought political contestations within a field of entrenched interests and comprehensive doctrinal commitments. Our public political reason, with the conception of citizenship that has rightly been extended to include previously excluded blacks and women, is a child of this history. If the sorts of issues raised in the preceding discussion were structurally no different than those raised by earlier demands to include blacks and women, then perhaps we might reasonably ignore the genesis of the conception of citizenship found within our public reason and anticipate its ability, with respect to these more recent issues, to underwrite determinate judgments. But the issues are structurally different. The inclusion of blacks and women did not require adjudication with respect to the moral and political core of citizenship. But the issues that are raised by abortion, death, and certain forms of severe permanent disability, not to mention our relations with certain other higher mammals (e.g., chimpanzees), do. It seems likely to me, then, that we cannot ignore the probability that the path to a shared public conception of citizenship sufficiently rich to underwrite determinate judgments on these issues within public reason will necessarily begin with and pass through new sites of political contestation within a field of entrenched interests and comprehensive doctrinal commitments. Given this probability, I agree with Professor Boettcher that we continue to need an understanding of public reason wider than that which Rawls himself seems to offer. And I think that there is much to recommend Professor Boettcher's proposed principle of wide public reason as expressing the core of this much-needed understanding. What I want now to add to it here are friendly amendments or corollaries.

As belonging to the content of our public political reason we ought to recognize the distinction between fundamental but familiar and common political issues regarding the institutional relations between citizens, on the one hand, and fundamental though less common if not less familiar political issues concerning the boundary conditions of citizenship and so the domain of the political, on the other. And with respect to issues of the latter sort, we ought to recognize that while for some (e.g., the inclusion of blacks and women in full citizenship) public political reason will often if not always prove complete, for others (e.g., abortion, severe and permanent disability, the definition of death, the significance of severe and permanent psychological breaks, the status of chimpanzees, etc.) public political reason will often but perhaps not always prove incomplete.

We also ought to distinguish between public reason, on the one hand, as Rawls understands it—the authoritative reason of citizens acting officially as citizens with respect to, at least, constitutional essentials and matters of basic justice—and public reason, on the other hand, as the authoritative reason of persons (who may also be citizens) determining the nature and meaning of citizenship and so the boundary conditions on and the political relations over which the authority of *its* reason extends. The former might better be called public *political* reason and the latter a people's public reason *tout court*.

With this distinction in hand, we ought to recognize that there is a sense in which the public political reason citizens exercise as citizens may always prove incomplete once the normative core of the office they occupy is effectively politically contested such that a response from limited to the authoritative reason of the office itself would be question-begging or dogmatic. When it proves thus incomplete, reasonable persons will engage one another within public reason *tout court*. In the same way that reasonable political conceptions of justice serve as permissible reasons within public political reason, so too may reasonable comprehensive doctrines serve as permissible reasons within public reason *tout court*. And in the same way that within public political reason reasons should be offered and remain available within widely accessible public forums, so too should they be offered and remain available within public reason *tout court*. Sustained and meaningful publicity is a virtue of reasoning in and as a public. Likewise, reasons within both sorts of public reason should be responsive to widely shared standards of relevance, evidence, and sound inference.

Finally, though a people may exercise its public reason *tout court* in response to the effective political contestation of the boundary conditions of citizenship and so the political relations over which its reason is authoritative, the exercise of its public reason *tout court* ought not to threaten that which reasonable political liberalisms and so a democratic people have in fact achieved with respect to citizenship and the political. There is a difference between, on the one hand, public reason *tout court* being exercised so as to determine issues raised by abortion, severe and permanent disability, competing definitions of death, and so on, with respect to which public political reason is incomplete, and its being invoked as the exclusive basis for overturning the political settlement of an issue with respect to which public political reason is in fact complete, for example, overturning the inclusion of blacks and women in full citizenship. When the public political reason of a democratic people proves incomplete, the public reason *tout court* it permissibly exercises is still that of a people the members of which, as reasonable persons, share a commitment to the tradition of constitutional liberal democratic republicanism.

I agree with Professor Boettcher that the principle of wide public reason he proposes and that I have tried to clarify and perhaps amend remains sufficiently faithful to the ideal of reciprocity (notwithstanding its permitting citizens sometimes to resolve fundamental political issues by reasoning publicly as persons [who together share a commitment to being a people] rather than as, or from within their existing office as, citizens) so as to qualify as a friendly and helpful addition to or refinement of Rawls's treatment of public reason. The proposal recognizes that the nature and meaning and so authoritative scope of democratic citizenship is something within a tradition of constitutional liberal democratic republicanism with respect to which persons qua persons may periodically be called upon to further specify. It thereby renders the idea and ideal of public reason more realistic, without rendering it any less utopian.

If I have any reservation about the position for which I am arguing here, it rests on the fact the content of public reason, both political and *tout court*, is ultimately the offspring of effectively contesting the terms governing shared activity, that is, exercises of power that threaten to drive shared activity to a halt. Within the context bounded by citizenship and its authority as established, we call such exercises of power, in the limiting case, civil disobedience. In the larger context not bounded by citizenship and its authority as established, we call them, again in the limiting case, secession. But perhaps it is simply unrealistic to hope that we might continue to complete public reason, political and *tout court*, save through sometimes threatening in these ways to grind shared activity to a halt.

2

Just Wide Enough

Reidy on Public Reason

James Boettcher

David Reidy's "Rawls's Wide View of Public Reason: Not Wide Enough" suggests that Rawlsian public reason faces a dilemma. Requirements of public reason are based on central ideals of political liberalism, namely, liberal legitimacy and political autonomy. Citizens realize these ideals by exercising public reason, but they sometimes find that public reason is incomplete. More specifically, with respect to at least some fundamental matters of law and policy, a citizen may not be able to identify a determinate public justification from the standpoint of public reason alone. Yet to widen public reason by turning to reasons from comprehensive doctrine risks undermining the political autonomy of the democratic public and the legitimacy of its decision-making. Hence the dilemma: public reason is either incomplete or inconsistent with the animating values of political liberalism. In what follows, I call attention to several valuable interpretive insights from Reidy's article before criticizing its main thesis. I shall propose a principle for widening public reason—the Wide Public Reason principle—that responds to cases of indeterminacy while remaining consistent with political liberalism's animating values.

Public Reason and Sincerity

Reidy's recent reflection on his original article and the subsequent development of public reason liberalism emphasizes the importance of citizens being able to assure one another that their exercise of shared political power is genuinely and rightfully authoritative. Reidy now writes that at least in some cases rightful exercises of political power depend less on the completeness of public reason than on our willingness to "keep faith" with the "core content" of political liberalism. Reidy and I ultimately reach similar conclusions about the need to acknowledge some incompleteness and widen public reason, though along the way I shall argue that *aspiring* to completeness in public reason must remain a worthy and important goal for citizens. I begin, however, with what's not stressed

James Boettcher, *Just Wide Enough* In: *John Rawls*. Edited by: Jon Mandle and Sarah Roberts-Cady, Oxford University Press (2020). © Oxford University Press. DOI: 10.1093/oso/9780190859213.003.0004.

in Reidy's new contribution, namely, that sincerity in public reasoning is a necessary condition of keeping faith with the core content of political liberalism.

A brief but insightful section from the original essay pursues the question of what it means for public reason to be sincere, expounding a modest sincerity requirement and a minimal, counterfactual motivation requirement. Rawls obviously thought that public reason involves some sort of sincerity requirement.[1] But exactly what that requirement demands of citizens is not adequately spelled out, even in a paragraph that begins by asking what it means to vote "our sincere opinion."[2] Are citizens obliged always to present exactly those public reasons that, as they see it, ultimately determine matters of law and policy? Are they forbidden from offering public reasons other than those they take to be sufficiently justificatory or determinative? Must the motivation for their political activity always be based on public reason?

Reidy persuasively argues that the answer to each of these questions is no. His position, in short, is that a citizen—call her Elsa—should support constitutional essential or basic justice law L only if she deems L sufficiently justified by some public reason(s) R_1. Based on strategic considerations, she may permissibly decide not to disclose justifying reason(s) R_1 in public discourse, or she may instead offer reason(s) R_2, which she takes to be insufficient, but potentially convincing to others. Presenting reasons that are potentially convincing to others, Reidy argues, may be an important part of coalition-building around publicly justifiable laws and policies. Furthermore, Elsa's support or public advocacy for L need not be effectively *motivated* by any public reasons at all, provided that she could at least imagine herself being so motivated in her support for L.

This last element, a weak counterfactual motivation test, is a companion idea to sincerity. As a psychological matter, people are moved to political activity by all sorts of factors, including their deepest moral convictions. The idea of public reason need not include any expectations about what motivates support for laws and policies beyond measures that would aim to filter out insincere justifications. Suppose that Elsa is a member of a theologically and politically diverse American Baptist congregation. She is opposed to a proposed repeal of the Johnson Amendment, part of the US tax code that prohibits churches and other charitable organizations from contributing financially to political campaigns or explicitly advocating for or against candidates for office. Suppose further that while Elsa acknowledges a sufficient public justification for retaining the Johnson Amendment—for example, reason(s) R_1 based on fairness in taxation—the main motivation for her public defense of the amendment is fear that its

---

[1] John Rawls, *Political Liberalism*, rev. ed. (Columbia University Press, 2005), 215, 446, and 454.
[2] Rawls, *Political Liberalism*, 241. See also Kent Greenawalt, "On Public Reason," *Chicago-Kent Law Review* 69 (1994), 669–689.

repeal would do lasting damage to religious solidarity within and among Baptist congregations. Elsa does not thereby run afoul of any requirements of citizenship or civic duty.

Some political liberals who agree with this weak motivation requirement nevertheless criticize Reidy's position for allowing too much insincerity in public reasoning. Micah Schwartzman defends a stronger sincerity condition, or what he calls a principle of sincere public justification (SPJ). According to Schwartzman's principle:

> A ought to advocate proposal p if, and only if, A (i) believes that ($R_1 \rightarrow p$), and (ii) publicly asserts R_1 as sufficient to justify p.[3]

Schwartzman argues that citizens must not only disclose their reasons but should refrain from offering what they take to be insufficient reasons unless they also include their judgment that these reasons are insufficient.[4]

Schwartzman defends these requirements, and criticizes Reidy's weaker position, mainly on deliberative grounds. First, public disclosure is necessary for subjecting reasons and arguments to deliberative scrutiny. The actual reasons that citizens identify as dispositive are precisely the reasons we should be most interested in testing in public debate. Second, the practice of offering insincere, deceptive, or misleading justifications is likely to engender "political frustration, resentment, and hostility."[5] Schwartzman concludes that the mistrust associated with widely acknowledged insincere public reasoning would work against effective coalition-building.

Neither argument succeeds in demonstrating the necessity of Schwartzman's SPJ principle. If we assume robust public deliberation among citizens committed to honoring public reason, then those citizens will have access to a variety of discourses in which various reasons and arguments are examined, challenged, revised, and adapted. Even if Elsa decides not to disclose reason(s) R_1 to one of her fellow citizens, she may very well discuss it with several others. Even if she discloses R_1 to no one, it's likely that she would still have ample opportunity to reflect on criticisms of R_1 elsewhere in public political discussions. Very few reasons and arguments on fundamental political questions are so unique or obscure that a citizen would have difficulty locating criticisms of them. While the SJP principle might describe an optimal ideal, effective public deliberation depends on

---

[3] Micah Schwartzman, "The Sincerity of Public Reason," *Journal of Political Philosophy* 19 (2011), 385.

[4] On this last point, see also Micah Schwartzman, "The Ethics of Reasoning from Conjecture," *Journal of Moral Philosophy* 9 (2012), 521–544.

[5] Schwartzman, "Sincerity of Public Reason," 392, referencing Paul Weithman, *Religion and the Obligations of Citizenship* (Cambridge University Press, 2002), 110.

less, namely, reasonable citizens who are conscientiously committed to considering criticisms of their views and to revising political judgments accordingly.

The second argument, citing concerns about frustration, resentment, and hostility, wrongly assumes that Reidy's model somehow sanctions insincere reasoning, as suggested by Schwartzman's label "private sincerity, public insincerity."[6] Suppose that Elsa is unpersuaded that the Johnson Amendment is constitutionally required on nonestablishment grounds, but she believes that others might be convinced by such reasons and arguments—call them R_2—in defense of the amendment. Schwartzman's assumption is that Elsa is being insincere in presenting R_2 rather than R_1 to others, and that others will naturally recognize and object to such insincerity.

Yet whether others would interpret Elsa's suggestion that $R_2 \rightarrow L$ as insincere—where R_2 is the constitutional argument and L stands for retaining the amendment—depends on the deliberative norms and expectations of the public. Especially in ideal theory, a shared understanding of Reidy's sincerity requirement would militate against such an interpretation. Reidy's weaker sincerity requirement also fits several obvious deliberative facts. First, laws and policies are often based on a convergence of reasons, and not all of the justifications for law L will be endorsed by each supporter of L. Second, persons regularly explore arguments in conversation with others without having first made a final judgment about the cogency or soundness of those arguments. Philosophical analysis can go only so far in categorizing or guiding the conversational dynamics of political debate. Nevertheless, a reasonable and sincere citizen like Elsa would offer R_2 neither to manipulate others nor mislead them about her own judgments but either to explore its merits or to address them as fellow reasoners who may actually have sufficient grounds to endorse a law that she takes to be justified.[7]

Ordering Political Values

Suppose that with respect to law L, citizen C_1 is convinced by argument $R_3 \rightarrow L$ and citizen C_2 is convinced by argument $R_4 \rightarrow not\text{-}L$, where justifications R_3 and R_4 are both undefeated and neither is victorious.[8] Both Reidy and his critics acknowledge that public reasoning is normally *inconclusive* in this way. Reidy

---

[6] Schwartzman, "Sincerity of Public Reason," 390.

[7] I would modify Reidy's model so that any reasons presented should at least be *credible*, according to the reason-giver. This means that Elsa should not offer reasons that she deems not at all credible, e.g., that repeal would cause a religiously based civil war.

[8] See Micah Schwartzman, "The Completeness of Public Reason," *Politics, Philosophy, and Economics* 3 (2004), 193–197, and drawing on Gerald Gaus, *Justificatory Liberalism* (Oxford University Press, 1996).

concentrates instead on a different form of incompleteness, namely, the logically prior problem that, even from an individual citizen's perspective, no adequate public justifications may be available for at least some laws and policies. That is, with respect to law L citizen C_1 (or C_2) may not be able to reach *any* determinate conclusions from the standpoint of public reason alone.[9] This is the *indeterminacy problem*.

There is a distinction, then, between such first-person indeterminacy and the (third-person) inconclusiveness that normally results from multiple, determinate, but rival public justifications. Reidy concentrates on the former problem, as shall I. But even this indeterminacy may take different forms. For a citizen may fail to reach a determinate conclusion from the standpoint of public reason alone either because he finds too few public reasons to support a coherent argument, or because he finds too many reasons, yielding inconsistent or contradictory inferences. Call these the *too-few* and the *too-many* problems, respectively, where both are understood as potential forms of indeterminacy encountered from an individual citizen's first-person point of view.

This latter distinction is related to one introduced in Reidy's original essay, which identifies two main *sources* of indeterminacy, namely, the difficulty of ordering political values and the necessity of appealing to background considerations. Only the latter source presents a too-few indeterminacy problem that suggests widening public reason. In this section, however, I concentrate on the worry about ordering political values.

Reidy observes that citizens will often fail to find an ordering mechanism or criterion for the political values comprised by a reasonable political conception of justice. While values such as negative and positive liberty, equality of opportunity, economic efficiency, cultural diversity, social stability, the common good, and so on, are surely relevant to most fundamental political issues, they also regularly come into conflict with one another in difficult matters of law and policy. Some political conceptions of justice may present criteria for ranking political values, such as the original position and priority rules in justice as fairness. Yet no such method or criteria are part of liberal public reason as such, with its multiple reasonable political conceptions. The worry is that when citizens confront difficult political questions such as affirmative action, or relatively new questions such as human cloning, they will respond on the basis of either intuition or comprehensive doctrine and then adjust their view of the order of political values accordingly.

This is a *too-many* indeterminacy problem in the following sense: a citizen recognizes several determinate public justifications based on different

---

[9] David Reidy, "Rawls's Wide View of Public Reason: Not Wide Enough," *Res Publica* 6 (2000), 65 n. 18.

arrangements of the relevant political values but lacks an effective criterion for choosing among them. Yet this problem is not as serious as Reidy's original essay suggests, for two reasons. First, the examples of reasonable political conceptions cited by Rawls cast doubt on Reidy's presumption that reasonable alternatives to justice as fairness would normally encounter difficulties with ordering or ranking political values. Second, a shared aspiration to seek such ordering principles, as part of a more or less complete political conception, would be generally beneficial to the practice of public reason.

Regarding the first reason, Rawls cites Habermas's discourse theory and "Catholic views of the common good and solidarity" as permissible forms of public reason, provided they are expressed in terms of political values.[10] Both originate with and remain embedded within comprehensive doctrine, at least if we follow Rawls in understanding the Habermasian theory of communicative action as such a doctrine. Rawls's thought, presumably, is that both discourse theory and Catholic social teaching could also be formulated to satisfy both the political-domain conditions and reasonableness conditions associated with reasonable political conceptions of justice—that is, each conception supplies the normative content of public reason.[11] Both conceptions also include standards or methods for ordering and ranking various political values.

While there's no single source for or definitive statement of modern Catholic social teaching, an evolving understanding of political and economic justice can be developed out of papal encyclicals and other documents written over the last century.[12] Indeed in an earlier paper I've tried to explain how the 1986 US Catholic bishops' pastoral letter on the economy may be interpreted as a form of public reason.[13] More to the point, the letter identifies *priorities* that should inform political and economic decision-making, namely, protecting basic human rights and recognizing a preferential option for the poor.[14] With respect to the latter idea, fulfilling basic needs is the highest priority, though additional priorities include increasing active participation in the economy by those who are vulnerable or excluded, investing in social goods that benefit the poor and economically insecure, and safeguarding the strength and stability of families. These priorities are not simply stipulated. Rather, they are developed out of the more fundamental values and norms articulated in the letter, especially protecting or

---

[10] Rawls, *Political Liberalism*, 451–452.

[11] See *Political Liberalism*, 450–453 for a summary of political-domain and reasonableness conditions.

[12] Charles Curran, *Catholic Social Teaching* (Georgetown University Press, 2002), 7.

[13] James W. Boettcher, "'Political, Not Metaphysical': Reading the Bishops' Letter as a Form of Public Reason," *Proceedings of the American Catholic Philosophical Association* 77 (2004), 206–219.

[14] National Conference of Catholic Bishops, *Economic Justice for All* (United States Catholic Conference, 1997), 85 and 90–93.

promoting the dignity of the human person, solidarity with others, and full participation in social life.

The priorities articulated in the bishops' letter apply to precisely the sort of difficult political questions that might give rise to worries about indeterminacy, including taxation, public assistance, healthcare, and national service. Or, to take one of Reidy's examples, different but still important senses of equality and equal opportunity undergird arguments for and against affirmative action. Provided they are effective, however, such policies play an important role in efforts to counter the mutually reinforcing effects of racial segregation and poverty on opportunity sets. So, if we prioritize the plight of the poor and vulnerable, then we would favor what the bishops call "judiciously administered affirmative action programs in employment and education."[15]

Discourse theory also includes resources for addressing the ordering problem. According to a variant of the discourse principle, the democracy principle, legitimate laws are those that can meet with the assent of all citizens in a discursive process of legislation that in turn has been legally constituted. Democratic deliberation is informed by different forms of discourse, including *pragmatic* discourses concerning how to achieve preferences and goals, *ethical* discourses concerning the reflexively endorsed values of a context-bound community, and *moral* discourses concerning what is equally good for all.[16] When ex ante preferences and goals are challenged in deliberation, citizens should examine these goals and preferences in terms of shared values. And when citizens encounter seemingly irresolvable value conflicts connected to some fundamental political matter, they should adjust their approach by acknowledging the rights securing reasonable pluralism and by asking what is in the equal interest of all affected.[17] In other words, reasons based on this equal-interest-of-all dimension should have priority in political discourse.

While these distinctions are not always easily drawn in the context of actual legal and political controversies, they do provide a general framework for ordering values. Indeed Habermas relies on this framework in addressing one of Reidy's other main examples of the ordering problem, human cloning. Habermas concentrates mainly on certain forms of nonmedical human genetic engineering and enhancement, though his worries parallel his objection to cloning.[18] His rather complicated argument is that eugenic enhancements would undermine the capacity of those enhanced eventually to identify as free and equal persons. When the intentions and expectations of parents are imposed on a child by

---

[15] National Conference of Catholic Bishops, *Economic Justice for All*, 73.
[16] Jürgen Habermas, *Between Facts and Norms*, trans. William Rehg (MIT Press, 1996), chap. 4.
[17] Jürgen Habermas, "Reply to Symposium Participants," *Cardozo Law Review* 17 (1996), 1489.
[18] Jürgen Habermas, *The Future of Human Nature*, trans. Hella Beister and William Rehg (Polity Press, 2003).

genetic design, the child no longer enjoys "the spontaneous self-perception of being the undivided author of his own life."[19] This creates an irreversible dependence on another that is contrary to our democratic self-understanding as equals who interact freely through relations of mutual symmetrical recognition.

Many will reject this argument, which I've only sketched, just as many others will reject the position on affirmative action advanced in the bishops' letter. The goal of this section is not to defend particular policy prescriptions but rather to illustrate how different reasonable political conceptions of justice, with their distinct ordering criteria, might yield determinate arguments in public reason on complicated issues. Neither Reidy nor his critics have explored non-Rawlsian conceptions of justice in enough detail to support any final conclusions about public reasoning and the ordering problem. Their dispute is mainly about where the burden of proof lies.[20] The preceding examples provide additional evidence in support of Reidy's critics. That is, they support the assumption that political conceptions of justice normally contain enough reasons, and effective ordering criteria, to reach determinate first-person public justifications on matters of law and policy.

Of course, ordering criteria relevant to one set of issues may not apply to others. And some reasonable political conceptions may seem to lack these criteria, either altogether or at least for certain issues. Nevertheless, in these cases a reasonable citizen committed to public reason should aspire to develop and refine such criteria as part of his or her political conception's completeness. A complete political conception comprises an order of political values that is sufficient to provide an answer to nearly all fundamental political questions.[21] The effort to examine the order of political values from the standpoint of public reason alone—that is, from the standpoint of a reasonable political conception suitably ordered by the kind of mechanisms discussed earlier—is a way of disciplining our reasoning. Specifically, we should not approach fundamental questions ad hoc, as if each question bears no relation to others. Political judgments should be consistent, so that judgment about one issue should not depend on an order of values that is contrary to what is presupposed in other cases. We should be ready to apply the same order of reasons to relevantly similar matters of law and policy. This is why the readiness to explain one's position in public reason includes the ability to articulate, at least roughly, how political values are ordered by a

---

[19] Habermas, *Future of Human Nature*, 63.

[20] Schwartzman, "Completeness of Public Reason," 207.

[21] Rawls writes that the values should be ordered so that they "give a reasonable answer to all, or to nearly all, questions involving constitutional essentials and matters of basic justice." *Political Liberalism*, 454. However, if a political conception were to give a reasonable answer to *all* such questions then there would be no indeterminacy problem in the first place—hence my use of the modifiers "more or less" and "nearly all."

political conception. Aiming at consistency in judgment about ordering values across cases also helps to allay concerns, suggested in Reidy's more recent essay, that one's intuitive balancing of various considerations in a hard case is being driven simply by nonpublic commitments.

The Wide Public Reason Principle

A different source of indeterminacy is that background moral or philosophical commitments often seem essential to resolving at least some fundamental political questions. This is a *too-few* reasons form of indeterminacy. Reidy's original essay includes examples of the moral status of the fetus in debates about abortion, or the relationship between human beings and the natural world in debates about environmental regulation or the treatment of nonhuman animals. His recent essay provides even more examples. A straw man version of this concern would narrowly restrict public reason to a set of political values, but Reidy does not make this mistake. He recognizes that public reason comprises additional discursive resources such as scientific inquiry, historical reflection, probability judgments, jurisprudence, rules of inference, common sense, and other shared modes of reasoning. Some political controversies nevertheless turn on normative or evaluative questions that seem to reach beyond these resources. To the extent that citizens must turn to doctrinal or other nonpublic grounds to resolve these controversies, public reason is said to be "heteronomous and incomplete."[22]

Suppose that we do sometimes run out of public reasons. That is, suppose that, due to the background considerations problem, a citizen cannot locate a determinate public justification on some issue. One alternative would be to rely on nonpublic reasons and arguments, but doing so brings us back to the dilemma highlighted by Reidy: widening public reason to avoid indeterminacy seems to run afoul of values that are central to political liberalism, specifically, political autonomy and liberal legitimacy.

To widen public reason is to acknowledge a more expansive set of politically relevant justifying reasons than is otherwise suggested by Rawls's wide view of public political culture. According to the Rawlsian "proviso," citizens and officials may introduce nonpublic reasons into the public political forum provided that in due course they present sufficient public justifications. Rawls also encourages the introduction of nonpublic reasons for the purpose of reassuring others of one's

[22] Reidy, "Rawls's Wide View," 70. For a response, see Andrew Williams, "The Alleged Incompleteness of Public Reason," *Res Publica* 6 (2000), 199–211.

commitment to the ideal of public reason.[23] I propose the following principle for widening public reason even further:

> *Wide Public Reason (WPR):* In genuine cases of public reason indeterminacy reasonable citizens may rely on nonpublic reasons for essential justificatory purposes provided that they otherwise aim to honor public reason.

I explain the details of this principle in the remainder of this section and respond to the relevant horn of Reidy's dilemma in the next.

"Reasonable citizens" and "nonpublic reasons" refer to familiar Rawlsian ideas that need no additional elaboration. To use nonpublic reasons for "essential justificatory purposes" means that at least one such reason is a necessary part of the argument on which a citizen relies in voting on or advocating for some matter of law or policy. A citizen who believes that there is a sufficient public justification (in public reason) for law L does not rely on nonpublic reason for *essential* justificatory purposes even if he or she does in fact rely on nonpublic reason for justificatory purposes, for example, as part of some additional or complementary justification for L. The term "essential" suggests that a sufficient justification J for or against L is available to some citizen C only insofar as J includes some part of C's nonpublic reason.

Despite being implied by the idea of reasonableness, the crucial provision that citizens must otherwise "aim to honor public reason" should be spelled out in more detail.[24] Citizens honor public reason, first, by satisfying its basic requirements of seeking sufficient public justifications, deliberating with others in good faith, and avoiding exclusive appeals to nonpublic reason in their voting and advocacy. A second aspect of honoring public reason is abiding by Reidy's sincerity requirement. Third, the political conceptions of justice to which citizens appeal in their public reasoning should be more or less complete, as explained earlier. When a conception's order of political values seems inconsistent or incomplete, citizens aim to improve it.

While public reason indeterminacy takes different forms, the Wide Public Reason (WPR) principle applies mainly to the problem of encountering too few reasons. Reasonable citizens should always *attempt* to satisfy public reason's deliberation, justification, and restraint requirements, as well as its proviso, and abide by its standards of sincerity and completeness.[25] The WPR principle

---

[23] This is called "declaration." Rawls's "wide view" of public political culture includes other forms of nonpublic reasoning as well, specifically, "conjecture" and "witnessing." See Rawls *Political Liberalism*, 462–466.

[24] Here I expand upon Rawls's discussion of honoring public reason. Rawls, *Political Liberalism*, 241.

[25] The WPR principle is related and complementary to, but not equivalent to, Rawls's own "proviso." Rawls's proviso is formulated in terms of the *presentation* of reasons, while the WPR principle

suggests that if a reasonable citizen encounters a genuine case of indeterminacy based on too few reasons, despite having otherwise satisfied these requirements and standards, then his or her reliance on nonpublic reasons should be tolerated by others. Such a person generally relies on an accessible and reasonably acceptable framework of thought, that is, an ordered political conception consistent with the fact of reasonable pluralism, the burdens of judgment, and seeing others as free and equal citizens entitled to fair terms of cooperation. Recognizing this commitment to public reason's ideal and foundational values is more important than insisting on a kind of doctrinaire absolutism with respect to its alleged requirements.

Public Reason and Political Autonomy

The thesis in Reidy's original article is that widening public reason is not consistent with political liberalism's ideals of liberal legitimacy and political autonomy. While the supporting arguments are not developed as thoroughly as his analyses of sincerity and incompleteness, his original essay suggests something like the following: for Rawls, a liberal democratic public is a "body politic" that achieves and maintains its autonomy by "constituting and governing itself" according to its own reason. The body politic's reason is exercised through the reasoning of its members. Since fundamental political arrangements just are the constitutive and especially significant acts of the body politic and since members are understood as free and equal citizens, political autonomy depends on citizens settling these arrangements only in terms of what they share in common, namely, their public reason. In virtue of its political autonomy, the body politic is authorized—or, authorizes itself—to use coercion through its constitutionally regulated legal order. In this way, political decision-making through public reasoning yields legitimate law and policy.

Liberal Legitimacy

By "legitimacy" Reidy seems to have mind what public reason liberals now call public justification.[26] According to Reidy's interpretation, the constitutional

---

applies to any use of reasons for justificatory purposes. Furthermore, the WPR principle includes no "in due course" clause guaranteeing sufficient public justification.

[26] I do not claim that democratic legitimacy and public justification are equivalent, but only that in Reidy's original essay the former idea is understood primarily in terms of the latter.

structure, or any subsequent changes to it, are legitimate only if they are justified or justifiable from the standpoint of public reason alone. Other laws and policies are in turn legitimate if they are adopted according to this structure and in keeping with other requirements of public reason. Neither the constitutional structure nor the laws and policies adopted according to its rules have to be perfectly just or correct in order to be legitimate and legally (and morally) binding on citizens.

I set aside concerns about legitimacy, for two reasons. First, in light of the challenge presented to Rawlsian political liberalism from other public reason liberals, a more detailed model of legitimacy would be needed in order to evaluate the claim that widening public reason undermines legitimacy. Indeed, in contrast to the asymmetric convergence model of public justification advanced by Gaus and Vallier, much of the literature on Rawlsian public reason fails to provide a straightforward answer to the basic question: what are the necessary and sufficient conditions for a law to be publicly justified?[27] My own answer to this question is developed elsewhere.[28] With more space, I would propose that the WPR principle is consistent with a weaker and more proceduralist version of Rawlsian public justification than what Reidy may presuppose.[29] A second reason for setting aside worries about legitimacy is that they seem ultimately to depend on a particular view of political autonomy. On Reidy's interpretation, for the WPR principle to be consistent with liberal legitimacy it must first be consistent with political autonomy. Demonstrating the latter consistency is at least a first step to addressing the concerns about legitimacy.

Political Autonomy

Reidy's appeal to an autonomous "body politic" is ambiguous. The relevant paragraphs from his original essay might seem to suggest that the liberal-democratic public is a kind of macrosubject that achieves political autonomy through its reason, much as a person is thought to act autonomously in being

---

[27] For an overview of the asymmetric convergence model, see Gerald Gaus and Kevin Vallier, "'The Roles of Religious Conviction in a Publicly Justified Polity," *Philosophy and Social Criticism* 35 (2009), 51–76.

[28] James W. Boettcher, "Against the Asymmetric Convergence Model of Public Justification," *Ethical Theory and Moral Practice* 18 (2015), 191–208.

[29] The proposal would be that the WPR is consistent with honoring public reason, and so consistent with the following: Decision D about the basic institutional-structural matter L is weakly publicly justified in a public P if and only if D is generated by reasonably acceptable and widely accepted decision-making procedure, and D's success is not essentially dependent on the votes or other activity of unreasonable members i_u of P, and each reasonable member i_r of P honors requirements of public reason—or would be prepared to honor these requirements if called upon to vote or decide—in making his or her deliberative contribution to D.

guided by his or her own rationally informed choices. On this view, autonomy may be achieved only if the public's decision-making does not depart from what citizens share through their public reason. The WPR principle departs from what citizens share. So, adopting the WPR principle would, as it were, contaminate the reasoning of the body politic, thereby undermining its political autonomy. This interpretation is supported by the final sentence of Reidy's original essay, which refers to a "Rousseauian conception" of the body politic, that is, "a single unified agent guided by its own reason."[30]

Reidy is right to express concerns about the Rousseauian conception of political autonomy but wrong to attribute that conception to Rawlsian political liberalism. Nevertheless, determining what Rawls means by "political autonomy" is difficult, especially since he introduces different conditions for and formulations of the idea.[31] One theme is that political autonomy should not be confused with comprehensive ideals of personal or moral autonomy. Another is that political autonomy does not depend on seeing political activity as inherently superior to other projects or ways of life.[32] It is only in the late writings on political liberalism that we find a summary definition of political autonomy, namely, the "legal independence and assured integrity of citizens and their sharing equally with others in the exercise of political power."[33]

This definition is consistent with, though not exactly equivalent to, Rawls's earlier treatments of political autonomy. In *Political Liberalism*, Lecture III, he writes that political autonomy is realized by citizens in several ways, namely, by affirming principles of justice, enjoying rights and liberties, participating in public affairs, and "sharing in collective self-determination over time."[34] A later remark suggests that citizens realize their political autonomy by "acting from the political conception of justice guided by its public reason, and in their pursuit of the good in public and nonpublic life."[35] Yet a different formulation appears in the "Reply to Habermas," where citizens are said to "gain full political autonomy" by living under a reasonably just constitutional order, understanding and endorsing the constitution and its laws, and revising them as needed, "always suitably moved by their sense of justice and the other political virtues."[36]

Together these passages support several claims about Rawlsian political autonomy. First, political autonomy is achieved, maintained, or lost by individual citizens acting in concert with one another. To be sure, no single citizen could

---

[30] Reidy, "Rawls's Wide View," 72.
[31] See Rawls, *Political Liberalism*, xlii–xliii, 77–81, 399–403, and 455–456.
[32] Rawls, *Political Liberalism*, 420.
[33] Rawls, *Political Liberalism*, xlii and repeated at 455–456.
[34] Rawls, *Political Liberalism*, 77–78. See also Paul Weithman, "Autonomy and Disagreement about Justice in *Political Liberalism*," *Ethics* 128 (2017), 95–122.
[35] Rawls, *Political Liberalism*, 79.
[36] Rawls, *Political Liberalism*, 402.

be politically autonomous on his or her own, independent of the actions and choices of others. But ceteris paribus one citizen would enjoy less political autonomy than others insofar as he or she were denied opportunities for political participation or access to rights and liberties that the others take for granted. Political autonomy in this sense is a status attributable to citizens and not a characteristic of a single, unified body politic. Second, political autonomy is realized not only through directly "political" activity but through the pursuit of the various ways of life that liberal rights and freedoms make possible. This is implied by the Lecture III claim that enjoying rights and liberties is an aspect of political autonomy and made explicit in the later passage referring to pursuit of the good in nonpublic life. This suggestion about nonpolitical activity further validates the first point presented previously. Given the fact of reasonable pluralism, only citizens acting individually or as members of groups and associations are in a position reasonably to pursue the good in nonpublic life.

Together these claims militate against attributing the Rousseauian conception of political autonomy to political liberalism. But rejecting that conception still may not be sufficient to show that widening public reason is indeed consistent with an ideal of political autonomy. We might consider two additional questions, both deriving from the various descriptions cited earlier. First, is the WPR principle consistent with citizens "acting from a political conception of justice"? Second, is the WPR principle consistent with citizens "sharing in collective self-determination" and "sharing equally with others in the exercise of political power"? I begin with the first question.

Even acknowledging the WPR principle, citizens would normally attempt to resolve political questions from the standpoint of a reasonable political conception of justice and other shared modes of reasoning. This much is implied by the principle's "honor public reason" clause, according to which the political conception is always the starting point for public reasoning. The WPR principle does not limit citizens to reasoning from the standpoint of a reasonable political conception, but then again neither does the idea of public reason. As we have seen, public reasoning must include additional discursive resources besides political values, such as scientific inquiry.

An additional complication is Rawls's Lecture III claim that "the satisfaction of the full publicity condition . . . is necessary for the achievement of full [political] autonomy for citizens generally."[37] Satisfying this condition implies inter alia that citizens are aware of the fact that they share the same principles of justice, the full justification of which is publicly available. The concern would be that if the WPR introduces reasons that are not shareable in this way, then the

[37] Rawls, *Political Liberalism*, 78.

full publicity condition cannot be satisfied, and political autonomy cannot be achieved.

My reply is that we should discount the Lecture III claim that full publicity is necessary for political autonomy, since it is generally inconsistent with other elements of political liberalism. The first inconsistency is with the idea that a liberal society might include multiple reasonable political conceptions of justice that provide the content of public reason.[38] If so, then political autonomy cannot depend on citizens' awareness of the fact that they share the very same conception of justice. Second, and more important, Rawls clearly indicates in the "Reply to Habermas" that the full justification of a political conception of justice would be carried out by citizens from their individual or doctrinally shared perspectives.[39] The specific terms of full justification are not shared generally among citizens. The full publicity condition—or at least this particular formulation of it—should not be seen as necessary for achieving political autonomy.

Even if the WPR principle is consistent with citizens acting from a political conception, there's still the question of whether it somehow undermines or significantly works against their sharing equally in exercising political power. Perhaps equality would be compromised when some but not all rely on nonpublic reasons in political decision-making. But this is a dubious claim. To be sure, for any given law or proposed law L, one citizen might reach a determinate justification within public reason alone, while another might rely on nonpublic reasons in accordance with the WPR principle. However, the principle itself applies to all citizens equally, and it requires those who rely on nonpublic reasons to continue to deliberate and pursue public reasons for their judgments.

Recall too that part of honoring public reason is sincerity as Reidy understands it. Sincere citizens would not use the WPR as a pretext for simply deciding matters on the basis of their comprehensive doctrines. Indeed, one implication of sincerely relying on nonpublic reasons is that doing so in turn commits one to subjecting those reasons—including perhaps elements of a comprehensive doctrine—to the critical, deliberative scrutiny of political debate. Finally, the worry that the WPR might somehow compromise equality is less plausible if we follow Schwartzman in rejecting the assumption that many or most political questions are sites of public reason indeterminacy. If indeterminacy is the exception rather than the rule among sincere and reasonable citizens, or if it arises only or mainly in the kind of borderline issues discussed in Reidy's recent essay, then there is less reason to worry about deleterious effects of widening public reason on equal political opportunity.[40]

[38] Rawls, *Political Liberalism*, 164.
[39] Rawls, *Political Liberalism*, 386.
[40] Schwartzman, "Completeness of Public Reason," 209–214.

Conclusion

Reidy's "Rawls's Wide View of Public Reason: Not Wide Enough" elucidates the meaning of public reason sincerity and identifies several problems of public reason indeterminacy. Responding to these problems with a principle of Wide Public Reason is consistent with political autonomy and, I would hope later to show, liberal legitimacy. I have not attempted to reconcile the various descriptions of political autonomy in *Political Liberalism*. Nor do I address important questions about the social ontology of shared agency that may be implicated even in a politically liberal theory of political autonomy. My main goals have been to show that political autonomy is a status attributable to citizens individually and that a modest widening of public reason is consistent with the legal independence and integrity of citizens and their sharing equally with others in exercising political power.

PART II
IDEAL AND NONIDEAL THEORY

Introduction

What is the relation between political theory and political practice? In what ways can political philosophy help people to address real injustices in the world? John Rawls argues that an important role of political philosophy is to identify the ideal standards of justice at which we should aim in political practice. Other philosophers challenge this approach, arguing that Rawls's idealizations are not useful as a guide for action or, worse, that they are an impediment to addressing actual injustices in the world. They argue, instead, that political philosophy ought to be focused on theorizing about the elimination of existing injustice. Still others argue that principles of justice should be identified without any constraint concerning the possibility of implementation or regulation in the real world at all.[1] This debate about the aims and methods of political philosophy has come to be known as a debate about ideal and nonideal theory.

There is some disagreement in the literature about how to best characterize the distinction between ideal and nonideal theory. One way to define ideal theory is to describe it as aiming to identify an ideal or perfectly just social order. Rawls sometimes writes about it this way, though he is careful to specify that his ideal theory involves a "realistic utopia" in that "it probes the limits of the realistically practicable, that is, how far in our world (given its laws and tendencies) a democratic regime can attain complete realization of its appropriate political values— democratic perfection, if you like."[2] Understood in this way, ideal theory specifies the goals of political systems whereas nonideal theory examines permissible and feasible ways to get there from here. Rawls writes that ideal theory sets the goal and nonideal theory "asks how this long-term goal might be achieved, or worked toward, usually in gradual steps."[3]

But this understanding suggests a misleading picture of Rawls's goals and how he actually proceeds. Strictly speaking, in *A Theory of Justice* Rawls is primarily interested in identifying the "first principles of justice" rather than the institutions that would perfectly satisfy them. Nonetheless, it is true that once those principles are tentatively identified in Part I, Rawls goes on in Part II to

---

[1] See G. A. Cohen, *Rescuing Equality and Justice* (Harvard University Press, 2008); see also David Estlund, "Utopophobia," *Philosophy and Public Affairs* 42 (2014), 113–134.

[2] John Rawls, *Justice as Fairness: A Restatement*, ed. Erin Kelly (Harvard University Press, 2001), 13.

[3] John Rawls, *The Law of Peoples* (Harvard University Press, 1999), 89.

IIntroduction In: *John Rawls*. Edited by: Jon Mandle and Sarah Roberts-Cady, Oxford University Press (2020). © Oxford University Press. DOI: 10.1093/oso/9780190859213.003.0005.

consider which institutional arrangements might be thought to satisfy them. He does this for two reasons. First, as part of the attempt to reach reflective equilibrium, one must test the principles against one's most deeply held considered convictions. Therefore, he says, it is important "to trace out, if only in a rough and ready way, the institutional content of the two principles of justice."[4] If, for example, the principles allowed institutions that permitted religious intolerance or racial discrimination, one would properly reject the principles and the features of the choice situation that gave rise to them.[5] Second, Rawls wants to argue that these principles are more stable than rival conceptions of justice. This also requires sketching the content of just institutions in order to consider their influence on the acquisition of a sense of justice among citizens. That said, however, Rawls does not think that there is a single set of institutions that embody perfect justice for all societies at all times. Rather, he holds that which specific institutional arrangements the principles will recommend depends on a "society's historical circumstances, . . . its traditions of political thought and practice, and much else."[6] Most importantly, the choice among various possible arrangements that may be thought to satisfy the principles in given circumstances is to be made democratically. Hedged in these important ways, one could describe Rawls's theory as an ideal theory in the sense that it is aimed at identifying perfectly just institutional arrangements.

Sometimes, however, Rawls defines ideal theory in a different way. Sometimes he explains ideal theory in terms of specific idealizing assumptions that are made in his method of theorizing about justice. In *A Theory of Justice*, he describes the distinction between ideal and nonideal theory this way,

> The intuitive idea is to split the theory of justice into two parts. The first or ideal part assumes strict compliance and works out the principles that characterize a well-ordered society under favorable circumstances. It develops the conception of a perfectly just basic structure and the corresponding duties and obligations of persons under fixed constraints of human life. My main concern is with this part of the theory. Nonideal theory, the second part, is worked out after an ideal conception of justice has been chosen; only then do the parties ask which principles to adopt under less happy conditions.[7]

This passage suggests that, for Rawls, ideal theory involves two idealizing assumptions. First, in ideal theory one assumes the members of society are all

4 Rawls, *Justice as Fairness*, 136.
5 John Rawls, *A Theory of Justice*, rev. ed. (Harvard University Press, 1999), 17.
6 Rawls, *Justice as Fairness*, 139.
7 Rawls, *A Theory of Justice*, 216.

cooperating members of society who will comply with the principles of justice. He calls this the assumption of "strict compliance."[8] Second, he assumes that the historical, economic, and social conditions are such that they can sustain a just constitutional democracy. That is, he assumes favorable conditions for a well-ordered society.[9] With nonideal theory, in contrast, one theorizes about how to achieve justice in situations where some citizens do not comply with the principles of justice or in which some unfavorable conditions prevent the implementation of just principles. Accordingly, nonideal theory involves theorizing about things like fair punishments for criminals or just strategies for overcoming racial discrimination.

While these two ways of framing the distinction between ideal and nonideal theory are compatible, they are not identical. Further, each characterization raises questions both about its proper interpretation and its usefulness as a distinction. To further explore the complexity and ambiguity of the ideal/nonideal distinction see A. John Simmons, Laura Valentini, and Zofia Stemplowska and Adam Swift.[10] In this volume, the chapter by Matthew Adams adds some important insights into how to clarify these distinctions.

In addition to clarifying the nature of the ideal/nonideal theory distinction, philosophers have sought to clarify the relation between the two. Rawls argues that nonideal theory depends on ideal theory. While granting that "the problems of partial compliance theory are the pressing and urgent matters . . . that we are faced with in everyday life," he writes, "The reason for beginning with ideal theory is that it provides, I believe, the only basis for the systematic grasp of these more pressing problems [of nonideal theory]."[11] In *Justice as Fairness*, he describes the relation in more detail this way,

> Nevertheless, the idea of a well-ordered society should also provide some guidance in thinking about nonideal theory, and so about difficult cases of how to deal with existing injustices. It should also help to clarify the goal of reform and to identify which wrongs are more grievous and hence more urgent to correct.[12]

This passage suggests two different ways in which nonideal theory depends on ideal theory. First, Rawls holds that ideal theory identifies the goals at which nonideal theory should be aiming. It answers this question for nonideal theory: when

---

[8] Rawls, *A Theory of Justice*, 8, 216, *Justice as Fairness*, 13.
[9] Rawls, *A Theory of Justice*, 8, 216, *Justice as Fairness*, 13.
[10] A. John Simmons, "Ideal and Nonideal Theory," *Philosophy and Public Affairs* 38 (2010), 5–36; Zofia Stemplowska and Adam Swift, "Ideal and Nonideal Theory," in *The Oxford Handbook of Political Philosophy*, ed. David Estlund (Oxford University Press, 2012); Laura Valentini, "Ideal vs. Non-ideal Theory: A Conceptual Map," *Philosophy Compass* 7 (2012), 654–664.
[11] Rawls, *A Theory of Justice*, 8.
[12] Rawls, *Justice as Fairness*, 13.

we are working for a more just society, what is it we are working toward? Second, Rawls believes ideal theory serves as a measure by which nonideal theory may determine which injustices are most serious. It answers this question for nonideal theory: which problem of injustice ought we prioritize? Rawls argues that the most serious injustices are "identified by the extent of deviation from perfect justice."[13]

Those who criticize Rawls's ideal theory often focus on Rawls's claims about the dependence of nonideal theory on ideal theory. Some philosophers argue, contrary to Rawls, that ideal theory is not useful for guiding nonideal theory.[14] For example, Amartya Sen argues that ideal theory is neither necessary nor sufficient for doing nonideal theory. Sen distinguishes between what he calls the "transcendental approach" and the "comparative approach" to theorizing about justice. In the transcendental approach, which he attributes to Rawls, one begins with identifying "perfectly just societal arrangements."[15] In contrast, the comparative approach "concentrates instead on ranking alternative societal arrangements (whether some arrangement is 'less just' or 'more just' than another), rather than focusing exclusively—or at all—on the identification of a fully just society."[16] Sen argues that having a clear sense of transcendental justice is not sufficient for determining priorities in addressing injustices. Despite Rawls's suggestion that the most serious injustices can be recognized by "the extent of deviation from perfect justice," it is unclear how one measures or compares the distance of deviation. For example, Sen claims that if one is weighing the relative significance of two different violations of the liberty principle, Rawls's principles will not tell us which one is more pressing. Further, Sen argues that the transcendental approach is not necessary for the comparative approach. One need not have a complete theory of justice to know that slavery is unjust. One can tell that an injustice is occurring merely by comparing it to other, more just situations, without knowing what a perfectly just society would look like. He writes, "For example, we may indeed be willing to accept, with great certainty, that Everest is the tallest mountain in the world, completely unbeatable in terms of stature by any other peak, but that understanding is neither needed, nor particularly helpful, in comparing the heights of, say, Kanchenjunga and Mont Blanc. There would be something very deeply odd in a general belief that a comparison of any

---

[13] Rawls, *A Theory of Justice*, 216.

[14] Bernard Williams, *In the Beginning Was the Deed: Realism and Moralism in Political Argument* (Princeton University Press, 2005); Amartya Sen, "What Do We Want from a Theory of Justice?," *Journal of Philosophy* 103 (2006), 216; Amartya Sen, *The Idea of Justice* (Allen Lane, 2009); Raymond Geuss, *Philosophy and Real Politic* (Princeton University Press, 2008); Elizabeth Anderson, *The Imperative of Integration* (Princeton University Press, 2013).

[15] Sen, "What Do We Want?," 216.

[16] Sen, "What Do We Want?," 216.

two alternatives cannot be sensibly made without a prior identification of a supreme alternative."[17]

Rawls could respond to Sen's criticisms by arguing that while we do not need to know the details of "a supreme alternative" in order to compare the justice of two options, it will often be useful to know on what basis we are making the comparison (height in the case of mountains, or justice in the case of societies). And Rawls's primary goal, as we have seen, is to identify the principles to be used in making such assessments.

However, Charles Mills takes Sen's critique a step further, arguing ideal theory is not only useless for addressing nonideal theory, but also potentially inimical to the project. Mills is deeply troubled by the fact that Rawls, who wrote so much about justice, very rarely mentions one of the most significant issues of justice of his lifetime: racial injustice. While the causes of this silence are likely multiple, Mills attributes part of the omission to Rawls's focus on ideal theory, which abstracts away from the ugly realities of racial injustice. Mills expresses concern that the focus on ideal theory not only excuses philosophers from addressing racial injustice, but also ultimately cannot serve the role of guiding nonideal theory in addressing it. In "Rawls on Race / Race in Rawls" Mills writes,

> Ideal theory represents an unattainable target that would require us to roll back the clock and start over. So in a sense it is an ideal with little or no practical worth. What is required is the nonideal (rectificatory) ideal that starts from the reality of these injustices and then seeks some fair means of correcting for them, recognizing that in most cases the original prediscrimination situation (even if it can be intelligibly characterized and stipulated) cannot be restored.[18]

Then he adds, "But the situation is worse than that . . . it is not merely a matter of an ideal with problems of operationalization and relevance, but of an ideal likely to lend itself more readily to retrograde political agendas."[19] Mills points to the example of Chief Justice John Roberts arguing against affirmative action policies that are race-conscious on the grounds that discrimination on the basis of race cannot be overcome with more discrimination on the basis of race. Roberts's argument presumes that the standards for ideal conditions (in which racial discrimination does not exist) should also serve as the standards in our current nonideal conditions (in which racial discrimination is pervasive). In contrast, Mills argues that enacting these ideal standards would be unjust in our current

---

[17] Sen, "What Do We Want?," 222.
[18] Charles W. Mills, "Rawls on Race / Race in Rawls," *Southern Journal of Philosophy* 47 (2009), 180.
[19] Mills, "Rawls on Race," 180.

system; race-conscious policies may be necessary for repairing injustices in a deeply racist society. He writes,

> If the ideal ideal rather than the rectificatory ideal is to guide us, then a world without races and any kind of distinction drawing by race may seem to be an attractive goal. One takes the ideal to be colorblind nondiscrimination, as appropriate for a society beginning from the state of nature, and then—completely ignoring the nonideal history that has given whites a systemic illicit advantage over people of color—conflates together as "discrimination" all attempts to draw racial distinctions for public policy goals, no matter what their motivation, on the grounds that this perpetuates race and invidious differential treatment by race.[20]

In short, Mills argues that ideal theory's abstraction from the real conditions of society will lead to misguided principles that will ultimately prevent us from addressing real injustices in the world.

One way some philosophers have responded to Sen and Mills is by arguing that these critics have mischaracterized and oversimplified the relation between ideal and nonideal theory. Rawls did not claim that ideal theory was necessary for identifying each particular injustice. Instead, Rawls claimed that ideal theory was necessary for "a more systematic grasp" of the pressing problems of nonideal theory.[21] But what, exactly, does that mean? Simmons and Stemplowska and Swift argue that ideal theory is necessary for mapping the best route to justice.[22] Building on Sen's analogy, Stemplowska and Swift write:

> In mountaineering, the climber who myopically takes immediate gains in height wherever she can is less likely to reach the summit than the one who plans her route carefully. The immediate gains do indeed take her higher—with respect to altitude she is closer to the top—but they may also be taking her away from her goal. The same is true of normative ideals. To eliminate an injustice in the world is surely to make the world more just, but it could also be to take us further away from, not closer toward, a just society.[23]

This passage was intended as a response to Sen, but it also suggests a response to Mills. A Rawlsian could argue that there is a reason to be race-conscious in policies now, even if that would not be just under more ideal conditions, because

[20] Mills, "Rawls on Race," 180.
[21] Rawls, *A Theory of Justice*, 9.
[22] Simmons, "Ideal and Nonideal Theory"; Stemplowska and Swift, "Ideal and Nonideal Theory."
[23] Stemplowska and Swift, "Ideal and Nonideal Theory," 379.

that may be the best route to ultimately achieving a just society that does not discriminate on the basis of race.

The debate about what role ideal theory can and should serve in relation to nonideal theory continues in this volume. In chapter 3, Colin Farrelly argues ideal theory is problematic as a guide for nonideal theory because ideal theory inherently involves simplifying assumptions that result in value distortions. In contrast, Matthew Adams offers a defense of the value of ideal theory, arguing for a variety of ways in which nonideal theory depends on ideal theory.

Suggested Reading from Rawls to Accompany These Chapters

A Theory of Justice: §§2–3, 31, 38, 39, 48, 53–59
The Law of Peoples: §1
Justice as Fairness: A Restatement: §5

For Further Reading

Estlund, David. "Utopophobia." *Philosophy & Public Affairs* 43 (2014), 113–134. Estlund provides a powerful reply to recent critiques of ideal theory, arguing that ideal theorizing about justice is important and useful, even if the ideals can never be fully realized.

Farrelly, Colin. "Justice in Ideal Theory: A Refutation." *Political Studies* 55 (2007), 844–864. This article argues that ideal theory has inherent flaws that lead it to be unhelpful as a guide in nonideal conditions.

Gaus, Gerald. *Tyranny of the Ideal: Justice in a Diverse World* (Princeton University Press, 2016). This important book presents a formal and technical challenge to ideal theorizing about justice and a defense of nonideal theory as a practical guide in a pluralist society.

Levy, Jacob. "There Is No Such Thing as Ideal Theory." *Social Philosophy and Policy* 33 (2016), 312–333. Levy argues against the distinction between ideal and nonideal theory by claiming that all theorizing is some variation of nonideal theory.

Mills, Charles. "'Ideal Theory' as Ideology." *Hypatia* 20 (2005), 165–184. This is an influential argument for the claim that the best way to address the injustices of racism and sexism is by nonideal theorizing about justice.

Mills, Charles. "Rawls on Race / Race in Rawls." *Southern Journal of Philosophy* 47 (2009), 161–184. In this article, Mills explores how Rawls's failure to examine issues of racial injustice may be, at least in part, due to his methodological choice of ideal theory.

Sen, Amartya. "What Do We Want from a Theory of Justice?" *Journal of Philosophy* 103 (2006), 215–238. Sen develops here his influential argument for the claim that ideal theory is neither necessary nor sufficient for identifying real injustices.

Shelby, Tommie. "Race and Social Justice: Rawlsian Considerations." *Fordham Law Review* 72 (2004), 1697–1714. While acknowledging that Rawls wrote very little about race and racism, Shelby argues that several features of Rawls's ideal theory provide important contributions to thinking about how to address racial injustices in the nonideal world.

Simmons, A. John. "Ideal and Nonideal Theory." *Philosophy and Public Affairs* 38 (2010), 5–36. This is an influential interpretation and defense of Rawls's distinction between ideal and nonideal theory.

Stemplowska, Zofia. "What's Ideal about Ideal Theory?" *Social Theory and Practice* 34 (2008), 319–340. This article provides a suggestion for how to fruitfully distinguish between ideal and nonideal theory; an argument that most theories of justice (include Rawls's) do both kinds of theorizing; and a defense of the purpose of doing ideal theory.

Valentini, Laura. "Ideal vs. Non-ideal theory: A Conceptual Map." *Philosophy Compass* 7 (2012), 654–664. This article explores the different ways that people have conceptualized the ideal/nonideal distinction and the questions these conceptual distinctions raise.

Valentini, Laura. "On the Apparent Paradox of Ideal Theory." *Journal of Political Philosophy* 17 (2009), 332–355. This article develops a defense of ideal theory against the challenge that no ideal theory can be action-guiding.

Wiens, David. "Against Ideal Guidance." *Journal of Politics* 2 (2015), 433–446. This paper explores the nature of political ideals and argues that political ideals are not useful in identifying normative guidelines under nonideal conditions.

3

The "Focusing Illusion" of Rawlsian Ideal Theory

Colin Farrelly

> If ideal theory is worthy of study, it must be because, as I have
> conjectured, it is the fundamental part of the theory of justice and
> essential for the nonideal part as well.
>
> John Rawls, *A Theory of Justice*, revised edition, 343

Introduction

Since the publication of *A Theory of Justice* in 1971, John Rawls's theory of "justice as fairness" has had a profound impact on the discipline of political philosophy. One of the most significant influences Rawls has had on the discipline was *methodological*. He constructed and defended an abstract account of distributive justice founded upon hypothetical theoretical devices like the original position and the veil of ignorance, the principle of maximin, and conceptual analyses of equality of opportunity.

Rawls takes ideal theory to be the fundamental part of his account of justice, for it illuminates the "nature and aims of a perfectly just society."[1] Nonideal theory, according to Rawls and his defenders,[2] plays a secondary role, and concerns itself with the question of how the goals articulated by ideal theory might be realized. Rawls believes that, without an account of the perfectly just society, nonideal theory lacks an aim.[3]

The Rawlsian prioritization of ideal theory over nonideal theory has been the subject of much criticism. As is clear in Matthew Adams's chapter in this volume, there is often a great deal of ambiguity and misunderstanding between the defenders and critics of ideal theory. Nonideal critics take issue with the type

[1] John Rawls, *A Theory of Justice*, rev. ed. (Harvard University Press, 1999), 8.
[2] See A. John Simmons, "Ideal and Nonideal Theory," *Philosophy and Public Affairs* 38 (2010), 5–36, for a detailed defense of Rawls's position on ideal theory.
[3] John Rawls, *Political Liberalism* (Columbia University Press, 1993), 285.

Colin Farrelly, *The "Focusing Illusion" of Rawlsian Ideal Theory* In: *John Rawls*. Edited by: Jon Mandle and Sarah Roberts-Cady, Oxford University Press (2020). © Oxford University Press. DOI: 10.1093/oso/9780190859213.003.0006.

of abstract normative theorizing employed by ideal theorists like Rawls. Such a methodology places a premium on *conceptual* analyses of ideals like justice, equality, or freedom, and as such relies heavily upon abstract hypotheticals (vs. the *actual history* of injustice), and, perhaps most importantly for nonideal theorists, ideal theory "relies on idealization to the exclusion, or at least marginalization, of the actual."[4] *Idealizations* involve making claims that are actually false (like society being closed), in order to simplify an argument.[5] In this chapter I will critically exam the idealizations employed by Rawls's original theory of justice in *A Theory of Justice*.

Some critics of ideal theory, such as Charles Mills, charge that ideal theory is a form of *ideology* that contributes to perpetuating illicit group privilege. Others argue that the quest for articulating ideal justice is unnecessary[6] and/ or unhelpful.[7] I believe ideal theory is *inherently* flawed, and it is flawed because it cannot, by its very nature (especially its reliance on *idealization* that brackets many pressing concerns of justice), serve as a useful guide to nonideal theory. In this chapter I argue that Rawlsian ideal theory is inherently flawed because Rawls's idealizations make our normative theorizing prone to the *valuation distortions* that arise in what psychologists call a "focusing illusion": "When a judgment about an entire object or category is made with attention focused on a subset of that category, a focusing illusion is likely to occur, whereby the attended subset is overweighted relative to the unattended subset."[8] By assuming society is closed and filled with only fully compliant and healthy people, Rawls primes specific moral intuitions that support the choice of his serially ordered principles over intuitionism and utilitarianism. But Rawls assumes, once we oscillate back to nonideal theory, that same weighting will be an appropriate guide for the nonideal context where other societal problems, such as global poverty, institutional racism, patriarchy, and health vulnerabilities, will be abundant. This is inherently problematic because the idealizations of ideal theory create a focusing illusion that skews the vision of the moral landscape created by ideal theory. Accordingly, the weighted moral schema yielded by ideal theory will be a poor guide to invoke in the nonideal context when there will be a plurality of different types of disadvantage in need of addressing, as a matter of justice.

---

[4] Charles Mills, "'Ideal Theory' as Ideology," *Hypatia* 20 (2005), 168.

[5] Onora O'Neill, *Towards Justice and Virtue: A Constructive Account of Practical Reasoning* (Cambridge University Press, 1996), 41.

[6] Amartaya Sen, *The Idea of Justice* (Harvard University Press, 2009).

[7] Colin Farrelly, "Justice in Ideal Theory: A Refutation," *Political Studies* 55 (2007), 844–864.

[8] David Schkade and Daniel Kahneman, "Does Living in California Make People Happy? A Focusing Illusion in Judgments of Life Satisfaction," *Psychological Science* 9 (1998), 340.

Ideal Theory as a Solution to the Problems of Intuitionism and Utilitarianism

My case for interpreting Rawls's account of ideal theory as the (unwitting) positing of a focusing illusion begins by highlighting the central concerns that motivate Rawls's invocation of the original position in chapter 1 of *A Theory of Justice*. In this first chapter Rawls addresses the two main rivals to "justice as fairness": intuitionism and utilitarianism.

Rawls defines intuitionism as the doctrine "that there is an irreducible family of first principles which have to be weighed against one another by asking ourselves which balance, in our considered judgement, is most just."[9] Rawls then claims that intuitionism consists of a plurality of principles, which often conflict, and there are no priority rules for weighing these principles. Herein lies the problem, according to Rawls, with intuitionism, namely, its failure to assign priority rules for the first principles of justice. Rawls remarks:

> The assignment of weights is an essential and not a minor part of a conception of justice. If we cannot explain how these weights are to be determined by reasonable ethical criteria, the means of rational discussion will have to come to an end. We should do what we can to formulate explicit principles for the priority problem, even though the dependence on intuition cannot be eliminated entirely.[10]

To help resolve the priority issue, Rawls invokes a number of "simplifying assumptions" (i.e., idealizations) that in effect help him prime a subset of moral intuitions while bracketing or ignoring others. And it is this desire to achieve some determinacy concerning the weighting of principles, without which Rawls fears rational discussion will come to an end, that explains why he invokes ideal theory. The latter offers determinacy concerning the weight to be attributed to fundamental principles. Intuitionism is unwieldly as a moral theory because it endorses a plurality of principles that cannot be serially ordered. But justice as fairness can yield serially ordered principles precisely *because* it invokes a limited set of intuitions for a contrived context (namely a closed society, filled with fully compliant, healthy people) that support serially ordering Rawls's two principles of justice.

Until Rawls's *A Theory of Justice*, utilitarianism was the dominant tradition in ethics. Utilitarianism maintains that "society is rightly ordered, and therefore just, when its major institutions are arranged so as to achieve the greatest

---

[9] Rawls, *A Theory of Justice*, 30.
[10] Rawls, *A Theory of Justice*, 37.

net balance of satisfaction summed over all the individuals belonging to it."[11] Like his criticism of intuitionism—namely that it undermines what he thinks the proper ordering of the principles of justice should be (because it cannot yield any ranking)—Rawls rejects utilitarianism because it also fails to adequately cohere with the priority rules Rawls believes would be endorsed in the original position.

Unlike "justice as fairness," utilitarianism is what Rawls calls a *teleological* theory. This means it is a theory that interprets the right as *maximizing* the good. The latter is objectionable, claims Rawls, because it treats the correct decision about allocations as essentially questions "of efficient administration."[12] In doing so utilitarianism does not take seriously the distinction between persons.[13]

These two concerns, to resolve the priority problem that intuitionism cannot resolve, and to take seriously the separateness of persons that utilitarianism fails to do, lead Rawls to construct the hypothetical choice situation where specific "considered judgments" can be primed to lend support for his two principles of justice and their priority rules.

In "Rawls on Justification," Thomas Scanlon argues that there are three ideas of justification in Rawls's work—the method of reflective equilibrium, the derivation of principles in the original position, and the idea of public reason. Because of space constraints I will limit my critique of Rawls and ideal theory to the first two justifications. These two justifications are, in my opinion, the most foundational justifications to Rawls's *A Theory of Justice*, and to his defense of the need for ideal theory.

Scanlon describes reflective equilibrium as an intuitive, "inductive" method. "On one natural interpretation, it holds that principles are justified by their ability to explain those judgements in which we feel the highest degree of confidence."[14] This can be contrasted with the deductive justification offered by the choice situation of the original position: "Principles of justice are justified if they could be derived in the right way, institutions are just if they conform to these principles, and particular distributions are just if they are the products of just institutions."[15]

While the two methods of justification are distinct, both employ interrelated considered judgments concerning justice as a virtue. These considered judgments are not arrived at via an extensive analysis of the actual injustices that permeated the world in the early 1970s, such as poverty, racism, war, patriarchy, and consideration of how to prioritize the duty to mitigate the full range of

[11] Rawls, *A Theory of Justice*, 20.

[12] Rawls, *A Theory of Justice*, 24.

[13] Rawls, *A Theory of Justice*, 24.

[14] Thomas Scanlon, "Rawls on Justification," in *The Cambridge Companion to Rawls*, ed. Samuel Freeman (Cambridge University Press, 2006), 139.

[15] Scanlon, "Rawls on Justification."

vulnerabilities and injustices that plague actual societies. Instead, various elements of Rawls's account of the original position, like the veil of ignorance and formal constraints of the right, and the "circumstances of justice," invoke specific moral sensibilities, and only a very limited range of empirical factors (e.g., limited altruism, moderate scarcity). To put it bluntly, in order to elicit "judgements in which we feel the highest degree of confidence," Rawls engages in a focusing illusion by getting the participants in the original position to consider a limited range of concerns of distributive justice in isolation from other concerns.

Cass Sunstein explains how distortion valuations arise when problems are considered in isolation:

> Suppose that you are asked to say, without reference to any other problem, how much you would be willing to pay to protect certain threats to coral reefs. Now suppose that you are asked to say, without reference to any other problem, how much you would pay to protect against skin cancer among the elderly. Suppose, finally, that you are asked to say how much you would be willing to pay to protect certain threats to coral reefs and how much you would be willing to pay to protect against skin cancer among the elderly. Empirical evidence suggests that people's answers to questions taken in isolation are very different from their answer to questions when they are asked to engage in cross-category comparisons.[16]

Rawls's idealizations help isolate the problem of distributive justice to a very limited set of concerns—namely, the priority of liberty and mitigating the social and natural lotteries of life for persons who fall within "normal species functioning" and live in a closed society. When we are instructed to consider judgments of justice for a closed society, that means we will not invoke judgments about justice that arise for societies that have a legacy of colonialism and slavery, or those posed by the challenges of immigration. When we assume citizens are fully compliant, we will not invoke valuations about the importance of tackling crime, sexism, racism, and so on. And when we assume everyone is healthy and productive, we will not invoke those judgments likely to arise when considering the problems posed by disease, disability, and aging. These idealizations help Rawls resolve the "priority problem" intuitionism cannot resolve precisely because Rawls brackets many considered judgments from the thought experiment deployed with the original position by isolating competing, or at least potentially conflicting, "moral intuitions."

---

[16] Cass Sunstein, "Cognition and Cost-Benefit Analysis," *Journal of Legal Studies* 29 (2000), 1071.

Any considered judgments the participants in the Rawlsian exercise of ideal theory might have—about the urgency and importance of tackling gender, race, cultural inequality, or health disparities are cast aside so that only specific moral sensibilities are primed for cohering with the choice of principles on offer in the original position. At best Rawls's theory of justice only offers first principles that match a small subset of our "general" considered judgments. All other judgments are thus relegated to the secondary role of nonideal theory, when "real world" complications like people getting sick, institutional racism, or a patriarchal family are addressed. To understand why ideal theory cannot function as an adequate guide to nonideal theory, we must delve more deeply into the psychology of the focusing illusion.

The "Focusing Illusion"

Rawlsian ideal theory aspires to attribute weights to serially ordered moral principles—liberty over fair equality of opportunity, and fair equality of opportunity over the difference principle—and these two principles are, according to Rawls, to be preferred over intuitionism and the principle of utility. For Rawls the former fails because it doesn't yield determinate priority rules, and the latter because it fails to take seriously the separateness of persons. The interpretation of Rawls I am advancing in this chapter is one in which the central motivation for Rawls making the idealizations he does is not, contrary to what Rawls speculates, that it helps provide nonideal theory with a useful end to strive for (since he says little to establish this point). But rather it was his desire to champion a moral theory that he thought was superior to both intuitionism and utilitarianism, in particular his desire to champion a moral theory that assigns weights because, if theory failed to do so, Rawls feared that "the means of rational discussion will have come to an end."[17]

If the primary value of ideal theory is, as Rawls and his defenders claim, its ability to provide an objective or aim that we can use as a guide when we turn to nonideal theory, one might have expected there to be some extensive discussion, and numerous examples, of how this could be done in a book as lengthy as A Theory of Justice (at well over five hundred pages in length). And yet, surprisingly, there is not. The only treatment of a nonideal topic in domestic justice is civil disobedience, and it is only briefly addressed toward the end of part II of A Theory of Justice in the chapter "Duty and Obligation."

[17] Rawls, A Theory of Justice, 37.

In addition to its scant treatment, what is also surprising is that even the "non-ideal topic" of civil disobedience is discussed within the parameters of what we might call *partial* ideal theory. Rawls tells us that the account of civil disobedience he develops is for a "nearly just society," that is, "a society that is well-ordered for the most part but in which some serious violations of justice nevertheless do occur."[18]

In the following passage, which I think is both revealing but also puzzling concerning the relationship Rawls thinks his ideal account of justice has to nonideal theory, Rawls states:

> By way of a comment, these principles and priority rules are no doubt incomplete. Other modifications will surely need to be made, but I shall not complicate the statement of the principles. It suffices to observe that when we come to nonideal theory, the lexical ordering of the two principles, and the valuations that this ordering implies, suggest priority rules which seem to be reasonable enough in many cases. . . . In the more extreme and tangled instances of nonideal theory this priority of rules will no doubt fail; and indeed, we may be unable to find any satisfactory answer at all. But we must try to postpone the day of reckoning as long as possible, and try to arrange society so that it never comes.[19]

There are two parts of this passage I wish to expand upon: first, the assertion that Rawls's priority rules "seem to be reasonable enough *in many* cases"; and second, that in the "more extreme and tangled instances of nonideal theory this priority of rules will no doubt fail."

I would reject the first assertion because Rawls's idealizing assumptions rule out the test that his serially ordered principles are "reasonable enough *in many* cases." Rawls does not subject the priority rules to an examination "in many cases." Indeed, the only case he considers is the choice situation of the hypothetical idealized original position. And by doing so only a very limited set of considered judgments—concerning impartiality, the importance of liberty, mitigating bad brute luck, and so on—are primed by devices like the veil of ignorance and formal constraints of the right. But Rawls does not test his principles in the cases of a society plagued by institutional racism and patriarchy, or societies with the health and healthcare challenges typical of developed liberal democracies, or the quandary of societal issues open (vs. closed) societies face, such as dealing with the legacy of colonialism and slavery or with immigration.

Rawls does not consider if his priority rules are reasonable in less than idealized circumstances. Is it reasonable to serially order liberty over fair equality of

---

[18] Rawls, *A Theory of Justice*, 319.
[19] Rawls, *A Theory of Justice*, 267.

opportunity in a society with historical racial injustice and patriarchy? The contentious topics of censoring hate speech and pornography speak precisely to this issue. In ideal theory, where there are no neo-Nazis wanting to march in Skokie, Illinois (1977) or Charlottesville, Virginia (2017), it might sound reasonable to prioritize free speech protection over restrictions that seek to promote equality between races or sexes by restricting the distribution of hate propaganda or pornography that glorifies the degradation of women. The priority rules Rawls invokes in ideal theory fail to provide adequate guidance for real, nonideal societies where trade-offs between the values of liberty, equality, and priority are inevitable.

Insights from psychology and the phenomenon known as the "focusing illusion" provide grounds for remaining sceptical about the suitability of ideal theory as a guide for nonideal theory. The focusing illusion occurs when certain valuations are primed to exaggerate their overall importance, and such an exaggeration in valuation occurs because the deliberation about the appropriate weight to attribute to the factors under consideration is not made with an eye to "the big picture" in terms of what else is valued or important in the case under examination.

Numerous psychological experiments make certain aspects of life satisfaction salient, which then skew how people rank either their current life satisfaction or predictions about their future states of well-being. For example, in a study of students' general happiness, researchers found that the answers to this general question had little correlation to how happy students were with their dating life when this more specific question came immediately *after* the general happiness ranking question on a questionnaire.[20] But if the specific question about their dating life preceded the general happiness question, then the correlation significantly increased. Priming certain information, like how many dates you had in the past month, can distort our general assessment of our happiness because it brings certain specific information to the fore (e.g., how happy or unhappy am I with my love life) while ignoring other relevant information (e.g., how happy am I with my career, family life, etc.).

Studies have also demonstrated that we are not good at predicting how certain events (e.g., becoming paraplegic, winning the lottery, or moving to California) will impact our well-being. For example, if healthy people are asked to predict how their happiness would be impacted if they became paraplegic, they are likely to answer that it would have a serious, adverse impact on their well-being. Conversely, if asked to predict how happy they would be if they won the lottery,

---

[20] Fritz Strack, Leonard L. Martin, and Norbert Schwarz, "Priming and Communication: Social Determinants of Information Use in Judgments of Life Satisfaction," *European Journal of Social Psychology* 18 (1988), 429–442.

most people assume this event would substantially increase their happiness. And yet, "in a famous study, the happiness of people 1 year after developing paraplegia was almost indistinguishable from the happiness of people 1 year after winning the lottery."[21] When it comes to predicting how happy you would be living in California,[22] or if you were richer,[23] the actual reports of life satisfaction from people in those circumstances are very different from what people predict the life satisfaction of people in those circumstances must be. When fixating on how the weather or money will impact our well-being, we tend to exaggerate the importance of these factors and ignore other important factors (e.g., the commute to work, relationships, a sense of fulfillment by work). "The psychological explanation of the illusion is that it is difficult or impossible to simultaneously allocate appropriate weights to considerations that are at the focus of attention and to considerations that are currently in the background."[24] The illusion has been studied extensively in the context of life satisfaction, but it is not restricted to that context.[25] These findings from life satisfaction studies have relevance for the ideal/nonideal debate in political philosophy. Ideal theory involves deriving the fundamental principles of justice with many nonideal factors bracketed, ignored, or relegated to the background because of the ideal theorist's *idealizations*; thus the distributive principles yielded from an ideal analysis are prone to exaggerate the moral weighting of the few considered judgments it primes.

The exaggeration Rawls places on the importance of serially ordering the principle of fair equality of opportunity over the difference principle is critiqued by Richard Arneson, and Arneson's example is a nice illustration of how the focusing illusion can be revealed once nonideal considerations are addressed.[26] Arneson considers the radical implications the principle of fair equality of opportunity has for social policies in modern democracies. His example is a good test for the ideal theorist's claim that ideal theory provides an appropriate aim for nonideal theory.

Arneson's example is as follows. Suppose two identically talented individuals are born into privileged households—one is born into an affluent upper-middle-class household and the second into the very richest household. Rawls's second principle dictates that these individuals should have the same prospects of success in the competition for jobs. But suppose this is not the case. The child born

---

[21] Peter Ubel et al. "Do Nonpatients Underestimate the Quality of Life Associated with Chronic Health Conditions Because of a Focusing Illusion?," *Medical Decision Making* 21 (2001), 190.

[22] Schkade and Kahneman, "Living in California."

[23] Daniel Kahneman et al. "Would You Be Happier If You Were Richer? A Focusing Illusion," *Science* 312 (2006), 1908–1910.

[24] Schkade and Kahneman, "Living in California," 345.

[25] Schkade and Kahneman, "Living in California," 345.

[26] Richard Arneson, "Against Rawlsian Equality of Opportunity," *Philosophical Studies* 93 (1999), 77–112.

into the richest household has a slight advantage over the equally talented child born into the upper-middle-class household. According to Rawlsian equal opportunity, we must redress this inequality. Furthermore, because this principle is serially ordered over the difference principle, we are to redress such an inequality independently of any concerns we might have about how such action will deplete efforts and/or public funds away from goals that might help those with less skills. So, for example, if redressing the inequality between the affluent (yet unequal) and talented individuals proves to be so costly that there is less of a cooperative surplus left to invest in the prioritarian aspirations of the difference principle, then this does not contravene Rawlsian justice.

By saying the principle of fair equal opportunity has lexical priority over the difference principle, Rawls assumes we would not be prepared to trade any amount of "inequality among the well-off with equal talents" for a benefit to the least advantaged. Such a judgment loses any intuitive attraction it might have when placed within the context of the real world, rather than the abstract thought experiment of the original position, where *any* inequality of opportunity among the equally talented might appear as the most egregious of injustices. And this suggests that the uncompromising appeal the principle of fair equality of opportunity (arguably) has in the original position stems from the device's focusing illusion. If we focus, in isolation, on the importance of people with equal talents having equal opportunities, we might be inclined to accord it lexical priority over the difference principle. But when asked to consider the importance of fair equality of opportunity in a scenario with more details, as in Arneson's real-world example, the suggestion that we prioritize mitigating *all* inequalities of opportunity over the prioritarian concerns of the difference principle can seem perverse. The weight we ought to place on the equality or priority of different goods and opportunities is thus *context dependent*. When we ignore important, relevant information (like the vulnerability of the disadvantaged) we can end up with skewed weighted judgments. And this is why I believe Rawlsian ideal theory is inherently flawed as a guide to nonideal theory. Far from providing an appropriate aim for nonideal theory, the idealizations of ideal theory end up distorting the proper weighting to be placed on the different demands of justice because they impede, rather than facilitate, adopting the "big picture" perspective of the moral landscape.

Conclusion

Since its initial publication in 1971, Rawls's *A Theory of Justice* has been the subject of extensive critique and debate. Many of the most pressing objections can, I believe, be understood as concerns that arise because of Rawls's reliance on idealizations. For example, in his original domestic theory of justice, Rawls assumed society was "closed." This "simplifying assumption" permits Rawls to posit a falsehood, but one that helps Rawls advance, and defend, a domestic theory of justice that highlights the moral duties we have to compatriots. But this ignores completely the question of what our duties are to noncompatriots living in circumstances that are less advantaged than our own society.[27] Rawls's idealization that society is closed thus results in what Sen calls "closed impartiality," which obstructs our ability to engage with the "eyes of mankind."[28]

In addition to neglecting the duties we have to noncompatriots, the assumption that society is closed creates a second problem for a theory of justice—it distorts the account of the obligations we have to compatriots. This is so because an account of justice appropriate for a society like the United States ought to highlight, rather than bracket, the importance of historical realities that shape real injustices, such as the legacy of colonialism and slavery. Colonialism and slavery are important historical events that dramatically impact the moral landscape in terms of understanding what justice requires us to do in the real world. To bracket or ignore such considerations, in order to derive determinate, serially ordered principles, is to obfuscate rather than clarify our deliberations concerning "what needs to be done" to mitigate injustice in the real world. This gives rise to critics like Charles Mills, who, in *The Racial Contract*, remarks: "So John Rawls, an American working in the late twentieth century, writes a book on justice widely credited with reviving postwar political philosophy in which not a single reference to American slavery and its legacy can be found."[29]

A further idealization that Rawls presumes in his original theory is that, at least in the choice situation of the original position, sex and the institution of the family are irrelevant. Rawls treats the parties in the original position as "heads of families," and as Carole Pateman notes in *The Sexual Contract*, the representatives in the original position are "sexless," and "their bodies can be dispensed with."[30] By drawing our attention to a hypothetical "sexless" choice situation, we ignore the historical injustices of patriarchy.

And finally, by employing the idealization that all people in society are healthy, the Rawlsian exercise skews our valuation of the weight of different distributive principles. This is so because Rawls chose to ignore the distribution of natural primary goods (e.g., health and vigor, intelligence and imagination) and focused

[27] See Charles Beitz, *Political Theory and International Relations* (Princeton University Press, 1979), for an example of extending Rawls's difference principle globally. Rawls eventually did extend his theory to the international arena in *The Law of Peoples* (Harvard University Press, 1999), but the fact that societies are "open" rather than "closed" did not lead him to revise the principles of justice or their priority rules.

[28] Amartya Sen, *The Idea of Justice* (Harvard University Press, 2009), 130.

[29] Charles Mills, *The Racial Contract* (Cornell University Press, 1997), 77.

[30] Carol Pateman, *The Sexual Contract* (Stanford University Press, 1988), 43.

instead on the social primary goods. The "least advantaged" members of society are defined by reference solely to the social primary goods: that is, those with approximately the income and wealth of the unskilled worker, or less; or, alternatively, all persons with less than half of the median income and wealth. If ideal theory defines the least advantaged in such a limited fashion, then, once we turn to nonideal theory and a theorist considers "dictating the route" to that objective of justice for an aging population or persons with disability, the route will be a very limited one. In most cases the focus will be on the redistribution of wealth and income, not healthcare provisions or health itself. In *Just Healthcare* Norman Daniels attempted to redress this shortcoming of Rawls's original theory by extending the principle of fair equality of opportunity to healthcare.

The abstract method of justice Rawls employed inspired many political philosophers to follow Rawls's example of theorizing about justice in the abstract. In the three decades following *A Theory of Justice* many conceptual-level analyses of justice and equality dominated the discipline. Debates such as the "equality of what?" debate could progress for many years with discussions of clam-shell auctions among persons on a deserted island, and debates about whether Malibu surfers who chose not to work should be fed.[31] Such discussions and debates were largely devoid of historical understanding of the causes of different types of inequality and injustice, or the real-world complexities of treating inequality as a problem of disentangling instances of "bad brute luck" from those that are the result of personal responsibility.[32] As the years went on, the voices of discontent with the Rawlsian methodology grew louder, culminating in what is now loosely known as "nonideal" theory.

What unites nonideal theorists is the commitment to *theorize the nonideal*, whether it be racism, patriarchy, global poverty, climate change, or health vulnerabilities. Are nonideal theorists immune to the focusing illusion? No. A nonideal analysis of the demands of justice can also exaggerate the importance of particular moral interests when it fails to adopt a "big picture" perspective on the demands of justice. But unlike ideal theory, which I believe is inherently prone to this problem because it relies on idealization (which requires assuming falsehoods in order to simplify the moral landscape so that first principles and priority rules can be derived), nonideal theory will yield more provisional and contextual conclusions precisely because it takes the *actual* more seriously than ideal theory.

---

[31] See Elizabeth Anderson, "What Is the Point of Equality?," *Ethics* 109 (1999), 287–337.
[32] Jonathan Wolff, "Fairness, Respect, and the Egalitarian Ethos," *Philosophy and Public Affairs* 27 (1998), 97–122.

4

The Value of Ideal Theory

Matthew Adams

> Obviously the problems of partial compliance theory [i.e., nonideal
> theory] are the pressing and urgent matters . . . The reason for begin-
> ning with ideal theory is that it provides, I believe, the only basis for
> the systematic grasp of these more pressing problems.
>
> —John Rawls, *A Theory of Justice*, 8

Introduction

Throughout his writing career John Rawls focused on ideal theory, and he thought
that he did so with good reason. As the epigraph conveys, he argued that nonideal
theory depends on ideal theory: in nonideal conditions we should transition to the
realization of perfect justice, and this transition should be orientated by ideal theory.[1]

Unfortunately, in Rawls's work—and in the Rawlsian tradition in general—
this alleged relation of dependence is rather obscure and underdefended.[2] Some
of this obscurity no doubt springs from the fact that philosophers have failed to
reach a consensus about how to explicate the term "ideal theory."

In this chapter I have two central aims: first, to propose a helpful definition of
ideal theory; second, to clarify and defend Rawls's central claim that nonideal
theory depends on ideal theory.

What Is Ideal Theory?

The Current Status of the Literature

An array of competing conceptions of ideal theory is scattered through the literature. Ideal theory has been defined in a number of different ways including

---

[1] See John Rawls, *The Law of Peoples* (Harvard University Press, 2001), 89. Cf. Ingrid Robeyns,
"Ideal Theory in Theory and Practice," *Social Theory and Practice* 34 (2008), 341–362; and A. John
Simmons, "Ideal and Nonideal Theory," *Philosophy & Public Affairs* 38 (2010), 5–36.

[2] Following Michael Phillips, "Reflections on the Transition from Ideal to Non-ideal Theory,"
Noûs 19 (1985), 551.

Matthew Adams, *The Value of Ideal Theory* In: *John Rawls*. Edited by: Jon Mandle and Sarah Roberts-Cady, Oxford
University Press (2020). © Oxford University Press. DOI: 10.1093/oso/9780190859213.003.0007.

the following: (i) a conception of perfect justice,[3] (ii) theory constructed using the method of idealization,[4] (iii) a top-down approach to theorizing,[5] (iv) fact-insensitive theorizing.[6] This has led David Schmidtz to make the reasonable observation that the contrast between ideal and nonideal theory has proved to be elusive.[7]

At the very minimum an adequate definition of ideal theory must satisfy the following two conditions: (1) the conception must be clear and determinate (2) the conception should be illuminating, in the sense that it can facilitate fruitful philosophical discussion.

Simply combining the different conceptions of ideal theory that are scattered across the literature into a single unified conception would violate (1). Such a unified conception would not be determinate because these different conceptions can either come apart from one another or cut against one another. Sharon Dolovich's theory of punishment, for example, is ideal according to definition (ii) because it is constructed using a Rawlsian contractualist framework and, therefore, uses the method of idealization. It is *not*, however, ideal according to definition (i) because it is a theory for a liberal democracy that is not fully just.[8]

A number of philosophers have defined ideal theory in a way that violates (2). Jacob Levy, for instance, writes:

> The hope for a normative political theory that is ideal in some absolute sense is a conceptual mistake, the equivalent of taking the simplifying models of introductory physics ("frictionless movement in a vacuum") and trying to develop an ideal theory of aerodynamics. Like aerodynamics, political life is *about* friction: no friction, no politics or justice.[9]

Consequently, Levy concludes, all political theory is nonideal.

Levy, however, just stipulatively defines ideal theory in a *particular* sense and uses this definition to argue that it is inappropriate for philosophers to classify their theorizing as ideal in *any* sense. Levy's argument merely shows that

---

[3] See Simmons, "Ideal and Nonideal Theory," 7; Phillips, "Reflections on the Transition," 551; Amartya Sen, "What Do We Want from a Theory of Justice?," *Journal of Philosophy* 103 (2006), 216.

[4] See Onora O'Neill, *Towards Justice and Virtue: A Constructive Account of Practical Reasoning* (Cambridge University Press, 1996), 40.

[5] See Elizabeth Anderson, "Towards a Non-ideal, Relational Methodology for Political Philosophy: Comments on Schwartzman's 'Challenging Liberalism,'" *Hypatia* 24 (2009), 135.

[6] See G. A. Cohen, "Facts and Principles," *Philosophy & Public Affairs* 31 (2003), 211–245.

[7] David Schmidtz, "Nonideal Theory: What It Is and What It Needs to Be," *Ethics* 121 (2011), 773.

[8] See Sharon Dolovich, "Legitimate Punishment in Liberal Democracy," *Buffalo Criminal Law Review* 7 (2004), 307–442.

[9] Jacob T. Levy, "There's No Such Thing as Ideal Theory," *Social Philosophy and Policy* 33 (2016), 313–314.

there is no ideal theory in the sense that he has stipulatively defined the term. This stipulative definition makes his conclusion come out as uncontroversially true. No (reasonable) philosopher who defends ideal theory assumes that ideal theory should regulate absolutely perfect people who disagree about absolutely nothing.[10] Ideal theory of such a sort would indeed idealize away the "friction" that generates the phenomenon of politics.

Levy's argument is irrelevant for the work of other philosophers such as Rawls who define ideal theory as a conception of justice that is perfect in the sense that it is "realistically utopian" and, consequently, do not idealize away all of the friction that generates the need for politics.[11] The dispute between Levy and philosophers who choose to label their work as ideal concerns the question of how it is appropriate to label types of theorizing. Levy clearly thinks, using analogies from science, that the label is inappropriate. Levy's conception of ideal theory is not, however, illuminating: it is incapable of facilitating productive discussion about whether a certain type of theorizing is valuable. Rather, it simply leads to a verbal dispute about how to define the term "ideal theory": both Levy and his opponents agree about the relevant facts about the theoretical domain and disagree about the language used to describe this domain.[12]

My Proposal

Given my present purposes, I will follow the lead of Laura Valentini and delineate two types of theorizing that have standardly been lumped under the single heading of ideal theory:[13]

Ideal-content theory: criteria for evaluating whether or not something is a perfectly just institution.

Ideal-method theory: theory that is constructed using the method of idealization; essentially, theory built on assumptions that do not directly correspond with the actual world.[14]

---

[10] See David Estlund, "What Is Circumstantial about Justice?," *Social Philosophy and Policy* 33 (2016), 292–311.

[11] David Estlund defends a more idealized conception of justice than Rawls. Even he, however, does not completely idealize away, for instance, the phenomenon of disagreement. See David Estlund, "Prime Justice," in *Political Utopias: Contemporary Debates*, ed. Kevin Vallier and Michael Weber (Oxford University Press, 2017), 35–56.

[12] Following David Chalmers, "Verbal Disputes," *Philosophical Review* 120 (2011), 515–566.

[13] Following Laura Valentini, "Ideal vs. Non-ideal theory: A Conceptual Map," *Philosophy Compass* 7 (2012), 654–655.

[14] Following O'Neill, *Towards Justice and Virtue*.

In Rawls's work there is a tight connection between these two types of theorizing. The former is constructed using the latter: when selecting ideal principles of justice behind the veil of ignorance, the contracting parties assume, for example, that actual people will strictly comply with the principles of justice that they select.[15] This assumption does not, of course, correspond with how actual people will in fact behave.

There is, however, no essential connection between these two types of theorizing. Martha Nussbaum's capability approach is an ideal-content theory because it treats the achievement of ten central human capabilities as a necessary condition for realizing perfect justice. Her theory is not, however, an ideal-method theory because—in contrast to Rawls's theory of justice—it is not built on any idealizing assumptions, such as strict compliance.[16]

This two-part definition of ideal theory satisfies condition (1). It is clear. Furthermore, the distinction between the two types of ideal theorizing makes the definition determinate: we can distinguish theorizing that falls into just one of the categories of ideal theory from theorizing that falls into both. It also satisfies condition (2) because it illuminates a number of important questions. Most significantly, it allows us to assess Rawls's claim that both types of theorizing are valuable for nonideal theory: a conception of what we ought to do in conditions that fail to realize perfect justice.[17]

A Final Comment

In the current literature on the topic, the question of how to define ideal theory is clearly contested. This contestation is symptomatic of a deeper point: philosophers are experimenting with the conceptual space in order to determine which way of defining ideal theory will allow them to explore the most substantive and interesting philosophical questions. Such experimentation

---

[15] John Rawls, A Theory of Justice, rev. ed. (Harvard University Press, 1999), 215.

[16] Following Robeyns, "Ideal Theory." See also Martha C. Nussbaum, "Capabilities as Fundamental Entitlements: Sen and Social Justice," Feminist Economics 9 (2003), 33–59.

[17] One interesting question is whether nonideal theorizing should be partial or complete. Plato suggests a partial conception of nonideal theory in the following passage of The Laws: "It looks as if we have a choice: either we can examine ideal laws, if we want to, or again, if we feel like it, we can look at the minimum standard we are prepared to put up with." Plato, The Laws, trans. Trevor J. Saunders (Penguin Classics, 1975), 858a. This latter partial conception instructs theorists to articulate minimal, necessary conditions of permissibility, rather than a complete account of what ought to be done in nonideal conditions. Rawls's discussion of decent hierarchical societies in The Law of Peoples is arguably an attempt to pursue Plato's suggestion of articulating the minimum standards—such as the nonviolation of human rights—that we should be prepared to tolerate. See Rawls, The Law of Peoples, 71–85.

seems reasonable because the literature on the ideal theory debate is still emerging. However, some of the literature seems haunted by the impulse to produce a definitive answer to the question "What *is* ideal theory?"[18] This is unfortunate, because the idea of some ultimate best way of defining terms of art is a chimera. At best, definitions of such terms can be clear, illuminating, and sensible; at worst, unclear, confusing, and eccentric. I think that my conception of ideal theory has some obvious theoretical virtues and is in keeping with the Rawlsian tradition. It seems highly plausible to me, however, that there are alternative, coherent ways of defining both ideal and nonideal theory that would facilitate the exploration of other interesting questions.

Distinguishing the Question of Whether Ideal Theory Is Valuable from Other Questions

In order to defend the Rawlsian method of ideal theory, I will provide two independent justifications: one for ideal-content theory and one for ideal-method theory. An independent justification for each type of theorizing is required because, as I clarified earlier, there is no essential connection between these two types of theorizing.

Before proceeding to defend ideal theory, I must confront the unfortunate tendency in the literature to conflate the methodological debate about the value of ideal theory with other distinct debates. In his accompanying piece in this volume, for example, Colin Farrelly notes that Rawls uses a specific set of idealizing assumptions. These include the assumptions that each society is closed and all people are healthy. Farrelly argues that this specific set of idealizing assumptions make Rawls's defense of priority rules artificially appealing and the rival theories of utilitarianism and intuitionism artificially implausible.

Assuming that this argument succeeds, it establishes that the specific set of idealizing assumptions that Rawls uses for a specific set of purposes is problematic. This argument, however, is not sufficient to establish that there is a problem with either ideal-content theory or ideal-method theory per se. Indeed, there is a vast literature that challenges some of the specific idealizing assumptions that Rawls makes—and the substantive normative conclusions that he reaches on the basis of such assumptions—that nevertheless retains the Rawlsian method of ideal theory.[19]

[18] See, for instance, Gerald Gaus, *Tyranny of the Ideal: Justice in a Diverse World* (Princeton University Press, 2016), 3–41.

[19] In the context of debates about global justice, for instance, see Charles Beitz, *Political Theory and International Relations* (Princeton University Press, 1979); Thomas Pogge, "Cosmopolitanism

Relatedly, the methodological debate about the value of ideal theory must be distinguished from a debate about Rawls's character. Charles Mills has extensively attacked Rawls for his failure to address pressing topics of nonideal theory, in particular, his inability to "find the time to write even *one essay* on racial justice."[20] However, as Tommie Shelby in his response to Mills argues, the pertinent philosophical question is whether ideal theory can be harnessed to address pressing topics of nonideal theory such as the legacy of racial injustice in the United States. This philosophical question is independent of whether Rawls's silence on the topic of racial justice is blameworthy.[21]

The Value of Ideal-Method Theory

A. John Simmons suggests that the use of ideal-method theory is justifiable because idealizations are sometimes required in order to simplify problems and, thereby, to make the results of theorizing determinate.[22]

Simmons's argument is plausible. All theorizing—whether of an ideal or nonideal variety—must make certain simplifying assumptions.[23] For if it did not, it would merely consist in a complete description of social reality, which would have no explanatory value.

Despite the plausibility of Simmons's line of argument, I think that it is insufficient to provide an adequate justification for ideal-method theory. As Alexander Rosenberg argues—with respect to the idealizing assumption of strict compliance—if the justification for such an assumption is merely that it simplifies the problem under consideration, then this would open the door to a number of wildly implausible idealizing assumptions. The assumption of sufficiently great material abundance, for example, would simplify the problem even further because problems of distributive justice would neither arise nor need to be solved.[24] The upshot of Rosenberg's argument is that certain idealizations can, of course, have the utility of simplifying the problems that we face as theorists. We require, however, some further account as to why we are licensed to simplify

and Sovereignty," *Ethics* 103 (1992), 48–75; A. John Simmons, *The Boundaries of Authority* (Oxford University Press, 2016). For a helpful attempt to distinguish between good and bad idealizations in political philosophy see Laura Valentini, "On the Apparent Paradox of Ideal Theory," *Journal of Political philosophy* 17 (2009), 332–355.

[20]   Charles W. Mills, "Rawls on Race / Race in Rawls," *Southern Journal of Philosophy* 47 (2009), 178.
[21]   Tommie Shelby, "Racial Realities and Corrective Justice: A Reply to Charles Mills," *Critical Philosophy of Race* 1 (2013), 148.
[22]   See Simmons, "Ideal and Nonideal Theory," 8–9.
[23]   For related discussion see Gaus, *Tyranny of the Ideal*, 38.
[24]   Alexander Rosenberg, "On the Very Ideal of Ideal Theory in Political Philosophy," *Social Philosophy and Policy* 33 (2016), 59.

our problems in some particular way and to what degree; otherwise, we would face the absurd result that we can simply idealize away our problems completely.

At least with respect to the assumption of strict compliance, I suggest that this further account can be supplied by appealing to the value of a conception of justice that is constructed against the backdrop of such an assumption. First, it allows the contracting parties to select principles of justice that specify what justice simpliciter requires, without that selection being tainted by actual people's expected noncompliance. The fact that such an assumption is not realistic is unproblematic: justice after all need not reflect how actual people will in fact behave—rather it is a normative standard that identifies how they should behave and that allows us to judge appropriately actual people's noncompliance with the demands of justice.

Second, the assumption of strict compliance is valuable because it helps to clarify the distinction between distributive justice and retributive justice. As Rawls notes, in conditions in which actual people strictly complied "There would be no need for the penal law except insofar as the assurance problem made it necessary."[25] Essentially, because no one would break the criminal law, it would be required only insofar as penal sanctions were necessary for the stability of social cooperation—so that everyone could act with the confidence that noncompliance with the penal law would be punished.[26] In contrast, even if all actual people strictly complied, central questions of distributive justice—such as how to arrange tax schemes—would arise. This is because actual agents' strict compliance with the demands of justice is not sufficient to obviate the need for just political institutions that ensure that the background "rules of the game" are fair. For distributive justice depends (at least primarily) on the arrangement of political institutions rather than the actions of actual agents.[27]

In this section I have presented a piecemeal justification for one idealizing assumption—the assumption of strict compliance. This defense is sufficient to vindicate the value of ideal-method theory at least under certain parameters. It

[25] Rawls, A Theory of Justice, 277.

[26] Rawls, A Theory of Justice, 211. For related discussion, see Carlisle Ford Runge, "Institutions and the Free Rider Problem: The Assurance Problem in Collective Action," Journal of Politics 46 (1984), 154–181.

[27] Rawls elaborates this point in Political Liberalism. He explains that economic conditions can be unjust even if no agent consciously acts wrongly. This is because whether economic agreements are just cannot be determined by examining the conduct of agents at a particular time. Rather, it depends on underlying social conditions—such as fair opportunity—that extend backward in time well beyond the finite viewpoint of a single situated agent. See John Rawls, Political Liberalism, expanded ed. (Columbia University Press, 1993), 266–267. I thank Jon Mandle and Sarah Roberts-Cady for suggesting this point.

allows me to remain neutral about whether all of the idealizations that Rawls uses for his specific philosophical purposes are defensible.

The Value of Ideal-Content Theory

Rawls advances the bold claim that ideal-content theory is valuable because what we ought to do in our actual nonideal world depends on such theory.[28] This claim has been extensively challenged. Amartya Sen argues that an array of counterexamples to this claim can be produced: we know, for instance, that slavery and human sex trafficking are wrong independently of ideal-content theory.[29]

In this section I will respond to Sen's influential objection. In doing so, I will defend Rawls's claim that nonideal theory depends on ideal theory in a qualified form.

Clarifying the Relation of Dependence

In order to assess Sen's objection, it is crucial to distinguish between the following two ways in which nonideal theory could depend on ideal-content theory:

A guidance relation of dependence: ideal-content theory plays an essential role in guiding the actions of political actors in nonideal conditions; consequently, without such theory the actors would not be able to determine what should be done.

A theoretical relation of dependence: the best theoretical account of what should be done in nonideal conditions requires ideal-content theory, regardless of whether such theory plays an essential role in guiding the actions of political actors.

This distinction reveals that Sen's objection is ambiguous. Clearly, at the minimum, the former relation of dependence must be denied: it is possible for political actors to muddle along quite reliably without being guided by the content of an antecedently determined ideal-content theory. A stronger version of the charge that ideal-content theory is redundant would also deny the latter relation of dependence: in order to give the best account of what should be done in

[28] Following Simmons, "Ideal and Nonideal Theory."
[29] Sen, "What Do We Want?"

nonideal conditions, it is not necessary to appeal to ideal-content theory; consequently, the content of such theory is irrelevant.

Defending the Relations of Dependence

In what follows I will begin by arguing that the theoretical relation of dependence always holds. I will then, more tentatively, suggest that the guidance relation of dependence holds in a qualified form.

The theoretical relation of dependence appears to be prima facie plausible. Imagine, for instance, that removing an injustice in our actual nonideal world would set back (to a sufficiently great degree) the long-term realization of perfect justice, as specified by ideal-content theory. Assuming that it would be possible to achieve perfect justice in the future, this would seem to supply a reason—under some empirical conditions, a decisive reason—to oppose immediately removing this injustice. Consequently, one salient consideration in all nonideal conditions is how what we do will impede or enable the long-term realization of perfect justice—as specified by ideal-content theory. Therefore, the theoretical relation of dependence holds. This is because the best account of what should be done in nonideal conditions makes essential reference to ideal-content theory.

Some philosophers who work on nonideal theory, however, oppose this conclusion. In her recent work on racial injustice, for instance, Elizabeth Anderson argues that a theoretical account of how and why we should ameliorate racial injustice can be presented without ideal-content theory. The following passage provides a good overview of her central argument:

> Segregation is the linchpin of unjust systematic race-based disadvantage. . . .
> Integration helps dismantle these underlying causes of race-based injustice. . . .
> Integration is also needed to advance a democratic culture, by providing opportunities for citizens from all walks of life to communicate on matters of public interest. . . . This is a forward-looking rationale: it views the integration of mainstream institutions as essential to advancing justice and democracy.[30]

Anderson's conception of nonideal theory—like Rawls's conception of nonideal theory—is transitional. The transitional target that she proposes is integration. This target is not a conception of perfect justice that is specified by an ideal-content theory. Rather, it is a transitional step forward that falls short of perfect justice.

[30] Elizabeth Anderson, *The Imperative of Integration* (Princeton University Press, 2013), 136.

From a Rawlsian perspective I think that it is reasonable for nonideal theorists such as Anderson to approach exigent problems in nonideal theory without waiting around for ideal theory to be completed. That having been said, I argue that the theoretical relation of dependence still holds. For, the *best* theoretical account of whether a particular transitional step such as integration should be pursued will require taking a position on ideal-content theory. Suppose, for instance, that a libertarian ideal-content theory of "upholding people's negative rights" is true.[31] Then what Anderson presents as the target of certain policies—transitioning toward greater social integration—should be rejected. On such a libertarian theory this is not the right transitional step forward because integration is not an essential part of their ideal-content theory of justice. More generally, even if this libertarian theory were rejected and integration were construed as a component of justice, we would require some further account as to how the goal of integration should be weighed against other political values; for instance, perhaps, how it should be weighed against the value of providing compensation for historic state-based injustice. Essentially, Anderson assumes that integration should be prioritized; however, this proposal cannot be conclusively assessed without building up a more determinate sense of our ultimate goals and political values.

I think that this result generalizes. Conclusively establishing that a particular transitional step is acceptable depends on our ultimate goal: on ideal-content theory. We cannot assess a proposed transitional step without considering its broader context—without considering whether it is, in addition to being *a* step forward, *the right* step forward given our long-term aims and complete set of political values. Therefore, the theoretical relation of dependence holds.

In his work on healthcare and global justice, Gopal Sreenivasan develops an argument against the guidance relation of dependence. He writes:

> There exists a kind of non-ideal theory for which the priority assumption fails. On this conception, non-ideal theory functions as an anticipation of ideal theory. Its prescriptions anticipate the ideal requirements of justice rather than presupposing them. To do so, non-ideal theory has to make assumptions about the minimum requirements that *any plausible and complete* ideal theory of justice will include. In this vein, it can define targets for practical action *before* a complete ideal has been worked out, even in outline.[32]

[31] See Jan Narveson, *The Libertarian Idea* (Temple University Press, 1988).
[32] Gopal Sreenivasan, "Health and Justice in Our Non-ideal World," *Politics, Philosophy, & Economics* (2007), 221.

As Sreenivasan goes on to explain, he has in mind the following example of non-ideal theorizing that can anticipate the results of ideal-content theory:

> Any plausible and complete ideal theory of international distributive justice will minimally include an obligation on the richest nations to transfer *1 percent* of their GDP to the poorest nations.[33]

Sreenivasan is clearly correct that an array of counterexamples can be produced against the claim that ideal-content theory always performs an essential role in guiding the actions of political actors. But it is worth noting—as philosophers such as Sreenivasan and Sen do not—that this conclusion should not be all that surprising for Rawlsians. It is, in fact, entailed by a commitment to a reflective-equilibrium methodology. As Rawls himself explains, the purpose of a contractualist procedure is to model and extend our intuitions about justice, which we take as provisional fixed points.[34] Consequently, of course it is possible—in an array of actual cases—to determine what should be done in independence of ideal-content theory. After all, ideal-content theory is, itself, constructed (at least partially) by obdurate intuitions about an array of actual cases.

I think that the best response to this line of objection is to argue that the guidance relation of dependence cannot be as crude as Sen and Sreenivasan implicitly presuppose. Interestingly, a careful reading of Rawls reveals that he is sensitive to the very concerns that animate Sen's and Sreenivasan's objections. Rawls explains that he begins with ideal-content theory because he believes that it provides "the only basis for the *systematic* grasp of these more pressing problems"[35] of non-ideal theory. Here the caveat of "systematic" is important: he is not suggesting that it is essential in all cases, just that it is necessary to obtain a systematic grasp of the subject matter of nonideal theory.

The crucial question, therefore, is whether the guidance relation of dependence holds in this qualified systematic sense. Isolated counterexamples produced by philosophers such as Sen and Sreenivasan are insufficient to refute this systematic relation of dependence.

Establishing that this systematic relation of dependence holds would be a massive task that I do not have the space to undertake in this chapter: it would require developing an account of each topic of nonideal theory and examining the extent to which the guidance offered by ideal-content theory was necessary.

---

[33] Sreenivasan, "Health and Justice," 221.
[34] Following Rawls, *A Theory of Justice*, 18.
[35] Rawls, *A Theory of Justice*, 8, emphasis added.

I will close this section by suggesting that this systematic relation of dependence is at least plausible. When we are confronted with easy cases such as whether slavery should be abolished, we do not need the best theoretical account of why slavery is wrong to know that it is wrong. With respect to such easy cases, therefore, ideal-content theory plays no essential guidance function. Nonideal theory, however, does not just consist of such easy cases. It also encompasses difficult—greatly contested—cases such as whether certain affirmative action policies should be adopted and how progressive rates of taxation should be determined. With respect to such difficult cases, one may well not be able to know how to act justly without the guidance of ideal-content theory. For such vexing and contested cases will plausibly require the long-term and complete picture of political values that ideal-content theory provides. If my suggestion that ideal-content theory plays an essential guidance role in such difficult cases is correct, then it seems reasonable to claim that the guidance relation of dependence holds in the sense that it is necessary to gain a systematic grasp of the whole domain of nonideal theory.

Coda: The Specter of Distortion

Some philosophers' objections to ideal theory are not couched in purely theoretical terms. Rather, they object to the role that such theorizing allegedly performs in actual social practice. Most famously, Mills argues that ideal theory is ideological because it performs the distorting social role of distracting our attention away from the pressing topics of nonideal theory.[36] In a similar vein, Farrelly argues in his accompanying piece in this volume that ideal theory is a focal illusion.

My arguments in this chapter point toward a provisional response to this type of concern. This response is partially concessive. Some idealizations that Rawls uses—such as the assumption that each domestic society is closed—give rise to the objection that they conceal rather than illuminate some central questions of global justice. Furthermore, some of Rawls's remarks about the way in which nonideal theory depends on ideal-content theory may understandably engender misunderstanding. Even if, as I have suggested, Rawls is correct that a systematic grasp of nonideal theory presupposes ideal theory, he should have been more explicit that there is room within his framework for plenty of provisional nonideal theorizing prior to the determination of ideal-content theory.

---

[36]   Charles W. Mills, "'Ideal Theory' as Ideology," *Hypatia* 20 (2005), 165–184.

This response, however, insists that ideal-method theory can be valuable at least in certain instances, and that ideal-content theory is an essential part of a complete theoretical conception of justice. Taken at face value, Mills's claim that ideal theory somehow distracts away from or is even blind to actual injustice is misleading.[37] For, ideal-content theory does not just consist in a distant dream about how a perfectly just society should be arranged. It provides evaluative criteria that highlight the wrongness of actual injustice. From a Rawlsian perspective, for example, race-based slavery is an abhorrent wrong because it is a gross violation of Rawls's ideal liberty principle that *everyone* should have access to the most extensive scheme of basic liberties.

Acknowledgments

For very helpful feedback I would like to thank Colin Bird, Talbot Brewer, Jeffrey Carroll, Jon Mandle, Nicholas Rimell, Sarah Roberts-Cady, A. John Simmons, and Rebecca Stangl.

---

[37] Mills, "'Ideal Theory' as Ideology," 168, 172. I challenge Mills's attempt to undermine the value of ideal theory further in my, "An Ideology Critique of Nonideal Methodology," *The European Journal of Political Theory*, forthcoming.

PART III
LIBERTY AND ECONOMIC JUSTICE

Introduction

One of the most influential and enduring responses to *A Theory of Justice* was written by Rawls's Harvard colleague Robert Nozick. While certainly not the first defense of libertarianism, *Anarchy, State, and Utopia* is the founding philosophical text of modern libertarianism. Nozick expresses high praise for *A Theory of Justice*, commenting that "political philosophers now must either work within Rawls' theory or explain why not."[1] In ostensible opposition to Rawls, however, Nozick rejects all "patterned principles" of distributive justice in favor of what he calls an "entitlement theory." In this, he is typical of libertarians who reject a commitment to any kind of distributive equality in favor of an emphasis on individual rights, especially property rights. Notwithstanding Rawls's prioritizing his first principle of equal liberty and his claim that the principles allow "a reconciliation of liberty and equality,"[2] it is commonly assumed that Rawls's fundamental commitment is to equality while Nozick's is to individual rights and liberty and that these are in tension if not completely opposed.[3] Thus, Rawls and Nozick are often taken to represent the extreme poles of liberalism's commitment to freedom and equality.

Nozick begins *Anarchy, State, and Utopia* with the famous assertion that "individuals have rights, and there are things no person or group may do to them (without violating their rights)."[4] Nozick takes these rights to be practically absolute.[5] But the content and the foundation for these rights is notoriously obscure, with Nozick himself noting that "this book does not present a precise theory of the moral basis of individual rights."[6] One influential libertarian argument is that self-ownership is the foundation of all individual rights. Some philosophers interpret Nozick as holding this position.[7] But while Nozick thinks there is such

---

[1] Robert Nozick, *Anarchy, State, and Utopia* (Basic Books, 1974), 183.

[2] John Rawls, *A Theory of Justice*, rev. ed. (Harvard University Press, 1999), 179.

[3] See, for example, Alasdair MacIntyre, *After Virtue*, 2nd ed. (University of Notre Dame Press, 1984), 244–249.

[4] Nozick, *Anarchy, State, and Utopia*, ix.

[5] Nozick, *Anarchy, State, and Utopia*, 30n: "The question of whether these side constraints are absolute, or whether they may be violated in order to avoid catastrophic moral horror, and if the latter, what the resulting structure might look like, is one I hope largely to avoid."

[6] Nozick, *Anarchy, State, and Utopia*, xiv.

[7] See, for example, Jonathan Wolff, *Robert Nozick* (Stanford University Press, 1991), 7–8; Will Kymlicka, *Contemporary Political Philosophy* (Oxford University Press, 1990), 103; G. A. Cohen, *Self-Ownership, Freedom, and Equality* (Cambridge University Press, 1995), 13.

Introduction In: *John Rawls*. Edited by: Jon Mandle and Sarah Roberts-Cady, Oxford University Press (2020). © Oxford University Press. DOI: 10.1093/oso/9780190859213.003.0008.

a right, it is far less clear that it plays any special role in justifying other rights. On the other hand, he does apparently believe all rights are rights over *things* conceived of as property rights.[8] Rejecting purported rights to "equality of opportunity, life, and so on," he writes: "The particular rights over things fill the space of rights, leaving no room for general rights to be in a certain material condition."[9] For Nozick, there are two important features of property rights that are worth noting. First, these rights are "negative"; they prohibit others from acting in various ways, rather than requiring any particular actions. Second, they are prepolitical; they exist in a state of nature without being authorized by any political process. In fact, Nozick holds that the only proper role for the political state—the "minimal state," as he calls it—is to enforce these prepolitical property rights.

Nozick's entitlement theory—or more precisely, his outline of such a theory—is apparently straightforward. It depends on specifying a principle "of justice in acquisition" of holdings, a principle "of justice in transfer" of holdings, and in case of violation of either of these principles, a "principle of rectification of injustice in holdings."[10] Once these principles are specified, "Whatever arises from a just situation by just steps is itself just."[11] Because how individuals will actually utilize these principles is unpredictable, the resulting just distribution will conform to no antecedently identifiable pattern. "Any favored pattern would be transformed into one unfavored by the principle, by people choosing to act in various ways."[12] Nozick makes this point vivid with his well-known "Wilt Chamberlain example" in which he imagines fans paying to watch Chamberlain play basketball. Over the course of a season, what started out as a particular distribution—for example, equality—becomes quite different—unequal—with Chamberlain profiting from his rare and valuable skill. If the initial distribution was just, which we assume by stipulation, then the resulting unequal distribution is also just if each of the ticket purchases was in accordance with the principle of just transfer. The only way to maintain any particular pattern of distribution, for example, by some form of taxation, would violate the just property rights of some individuals.

Nozick presents this as a criticism of Rawls's theory.[13] He interprets Rawls's difference principle as a patterned principle of distributive justice that requires maximizing the share of primary goods to the least advantaged.[14] In order to

---

[8] As Peter Vallentyne observes, "Nozick implicitly assumes *proprietarianism*, the view that all enforceable rights are moral property rights (rights over things)." "Nozick's Libertarian Theory of Justice," in *The Cambridge Companion to Nozick's Anarchy, State, and Utopia*, ed. Ralf Bader and John Meadowcroft (Cambridge University Press, 2011), 151.

[9] Nozick, *Anarchy, State, and Utopia*, 238.

[10] Nozick, *Anarchy, State, and Utopia*, 151–152.

[11] Nozick, *Anarchy, State, and Utopia*, 151.

[12] Nozick, *Anarchy, State, and Utopia*, 163.

[13] Nozick, *Anarchy, State and Utopia*, section II.

[14] Nozick, *Anarchy, State and Utopia*, 209.

maintain that pattern, the state would have to be constantly interfering with people's free transactions and/or violating people's property rights by taxation and redistribution. One cannot maintain this distributive pattern without massive interference with individual liberty. In short, Nozick holds that Rawls cannot maintain his commitment to the difference principle while also respecting the priority of liberty.

In response to this objection, one can argue that since Rawls intends the difference principle to underwrite a system of pure procedural justice, it is not a patterned principle of distributive justice. The principles of justice are intended to guide the design of basic social systems, not individual economic choices. Rawls holds that once a just basic structure is in place (with its rules of transfer and much else), then individuals may freely pursue their permissible ends, and "the distribution that results will be just (or at least not unjust) whatever it is."[15] Although Nozick assumes that the payments from fans to Chamberlain are just, strictly speaking this depends on the specification of the principle of justice in transfer, and Nozick never specifies or defends any such principle. Because Rawls holds that specific entitlements are matters of pure procedural justice, he would agree that if resources are transferred to Chamberlain *in accordance with the rules of a just basic structure*, then he is entitled to his income. And while Rawls does not directly specify the principles of just transfer either, his principles of justice, including the difference principle, are to be used precisely to evaluate and select those institutions and rules.[16] Thus, the difference between Nozick's libertarianism and Rawls's justice as fairness is not that one relies on procedural justice and the other involves a patterned principle of justice. Instead, the disagreement is perhaps best understood as a disagreement about what are—or how to identify—just rules for economic institutions and property rights.

Libertarians such as Nozick recognize a close connection between property rights and freedom. They raise an important challenge to Rawls, arguing that he gives insufficient weight to the importance of economic rights such as the right to personal property and the right to own capital. These rights, they argue, are essential to our ability to live autonomously. Of course, one can recognize the importance of the connection between economic rights and liberty without going to the extreme that Nozick does when he asserts that "taxation of earnings from labor is on a par with forced labor."[17] Rawls, for his part, recognizes that

---

[15] Rawls, *A Theory of Justice*, 267.

[16] Nozick is simply incorrect, at least with regard to Rawls's application of the difference principle, when he says that "the difference principle fixes how the ongoing process is to turn out and provides an external patterned criterion it must meet" (*Anarchy, State, and Utopia*, 208). Rawls directly replies in *Political Liberalism*: "Again, the two principles of justice do not insist that the actual distribution conform at any given time (or over time) to any observable pattern." *Political Liberalism*, expanded ed. (Columbia University Press, 2005), 283.

[17] Nozick, *Anarchy, State, and Utopia*, 169.

"among the basic rights is the right to hold and to have the exclusive use of personal property. One ground of this right is to allow a sufficient material basis for personal independence and a sense of self-respect."[18] While Rawls includes this *formal* right under the control of the first principle of justice, the specification of its particular content depends on the second principle and, indeed, the more specific choice of economic institutions. Rawls explicitly leaves aside two "wider conceptions of the right to property," asserting that neither is a *basic* right: "the right to private property in natural resources and means of production generally... [and] the right to property as including the equal right to participate in the control of the means of production and of natural resources."[19] Whether rights to natural resources and rights to controlling capital are justified depends on "existing historical and social conditions" and the democratic political decision of a particular society.[20] This, of course, is precisely what concerns libertarians, who believe these economic rights are fundamental.

While libertarians typically advocate for laissez-faire economic policies, Rawls holds that even welfare state capitalism does not go far enough to ensure that all citizens are "in a position to manage their own affairs on a footing of a suitable degree of social and economic equality."[21] Rawls calls his model of a just economic system (in which private ownership of the means of production is allowed but is widely dispersed) a "property-owning democracy." Whereas welfare state capitalism aims to provide a safety net below which no individual will fall, it "permits a small class to have a near monopoly of the means of production."[22] In contrast, a property-owning democracy "work[s] to disperse the ownership of wealth and capital... not by the redistribution of income to those with less at the end of each period, so to speak, but rather by ensuring the widespread ownership of productive assets and human capital (that is, education and trained skills) at the beginning of each period, all this against a background of fair equality of opportunity."[23]

Much as Rawls has served as the baseline liberal theory of justice against which rival theories define themselves, Nozick has played an analogous role for more recent libertarians.[24] Of particular note are so-called left libertarians who argue

---

[18] John Rawls, *Justice as Fairness: A Restatement*, ed. Erin Kelly (Harvard University Press, 2001), 114.

[19] Rawls, *Justice as Fairness*, 114.

[20] Rawls, *Justice as Fairness*, 114.

[21] Rawls, *Justice as Fairness*, 139.

[22] Rawls, *Justice as Fairness*, 139.

[23] Rawls, *Justice as Fairness*, 139.

[24] See, for example, Jeffrey Paul, ed., *Reading Nozick: Essays on "Anarchy, State, and Utopia"* (Blackwell, 1982); Jan Narveson, *The Libertarian Idea* (Temple University Press, 1988); Jacob Levy, "Toward a Non-Lockean Libertarianism," in *The Routledge Handbook of Libertarianism*, ed. Jason Brennan, Bas van der Vossen, and David Schmidtz (Routledge, 2017).

for "a plausible form of liberal egalitarianism"[25] by combining the idea of self-ownership with some kind of collective ownership of natural resources. Exactly how self-ownership and collective ownership of natural resources are to be understood is disputed, but they generally hold that self-ownership entails a property right in the product of one's labor. However, they emphasize that labor is almost always exercised on natural resources (or on goods that themselves have been produced from natural resources) and in a social context. This means that in the typical case, contrary to "right libertarians," society as a whole has some legitimate claim on the product of production, and this share is available to be distributed for egalitarian ends. Again, the exact nature of this social claim is disputed, but the aim generally is to establish that some kind of egalitarian system of taxation is consistent with full self-ownership.[26]

In this volume, Jeppe von Platz examines three different libertarian arguments challenging Rawls. While he ultimately argues that none of them succeed, he argues that they are right to hold that Rawls's account "underestimates the importance of economic agency and, therefore, fails to give economic rights their proper role and priority."[27] He offers his own account of why economic rights are important. In the companion essay, Alan Thomas argues that libertarians are wrongly focused exclusively on protecting citizens from domination by the state. Thomas holds, in contrast, that we also ought to be concerned about protecting citizens from domination by each other, as well. Since one important way we dominate each other is through the control of capital, he argues citizens will be best protected from domination by protecting a right to fair and universal access to capital. Further, he claims this right is best protected by property-owning democracy.

Suggested Reading from Rawls to Accompany These Chapters

A Theory of Justice: Chapters 2 and 5
Political Liberalism: Lectures VII and VIII
Justice as Fairness: §§14, 20–22, 39, 41–43, 52

---

[25] Peter Vallentyne, Hillel Steiner, and Michael Otsuka, "Why Left-Libertarianism Is Not Incoherent, Indeterminate, or Irrelevant," *Philosophy and Public Affairs* 33 (2005), 201.

[26] See, for example, Hillel Steiner, *An Essay on Rights* (Blackwell, 1994); Michael Otsuka, *Libertarianism without Inequality* (Oxford University Press, 2003). For criticisms, see Barbara Friedman, "Left-Libertarianism: A Review Essay," *Philosophy and Public Affairs* 32 (2004), 66–92; and Mathias Risse, "Does Left-Libertarianism Have Coherent Foundations?" *Politics, Philosophy, and Economics* 3 (2004), 337–364.

[27] Von Platz, this volume.

For Further Reading

Edmundson, William. *John Rawls: Reticent Socialist* (Cambridge University Press, 2017). Edmundson defends the view that given nonideal, empirical circumstances, the choice left open by Rawls between a "property-owning democracy" and "liberal democratic socialism" should be resolved in favor of the latter.

Freeman, Samuel. "Illiberal Libertarians: Why Libertarianism Is Not a Liberal View." *Philosophy and Public Affairs* 30 (2001), 105–151. Freeman presents a provocative argument that since libertarianism rejects a role for public political power that is impartially exercised for the common good, it has more in common with the doctrine of private political power that underlies feudalism than it does with liberalism.

Friedman, Barbara. "Begging the Question with Style: *Anarchy, State and Utopia* at Thirty Years." *Social Philosophy and Policy* 22 (2005), 221–254. This paper examines the rhetorical style of *Anarchy, State, and Utopia* in order to explain the influence of the book despite the numerous gaps and undefended assumptions in its arguments.

Mandle, Jon. "Wealth Should Be Redistributed" and "Response to Narveson." In *Problems in Value Theory*, ed. Steven Cowan (Bloomsbury Publishing, 2020). Paired with a defense of libertarianism by Jan Narveson, this chapter (and response) contrasts a Rawlsian egalitarianism with libertarianism by arguing that while they both focus on procedural justice, egalitarianism offers a superior way to evaluate possible distributive procedures.

Nozick, Robert. *Anarchy, State, and Utopia* (Basic Books, 1974), chap. 7. Nozick's book is by far the most influential defense of the libertarian approach to distributive justice.

Thomas, Alan. *Republic of Equals: Predistribution and Property-Owning Democracy* (Oxford University Press, 2017). Thomas defends property-owning democracy in a framework of liberal-republican freedom that is focused on the conditions of nondomination.

Tomasi, John. *Free Market Fairness* (Princeton University Press, 2012). Tomasi emphasizes the importance of economic liberty to individual autonomy and democratic legitimacy while defending the justice of free markets.

von Platz, Jeppe, and John Tomasi. "Liberalism and Economic Liberty." In *The Cambridge Companion to Liberalism*, ed. Steven Wall (Cambridge University Press, 2015). This chapter provides a clear introduction comparing different conceptions of economic liberty and its significance.

5

Rawls's Underestimation of the Importance of Economic Agency and Economic Rights

Jeppe von Platz

1. Introduction: Rawls on Economic Rights

Rawls's list of basic rights leaves out economic liberties such as rights to own productive property and freedom of contract. Libertarians take issue with this exception, arguing that it reveals insufficient concern for economic agency, and that proper concern for economic agency would give such economic liberties high priority. I argue that, even if we accept Rawls's theory of basic rights, this libertarian complaint is true; economic agency is more important than Rawls makes it, and some economic rights *are* basic. However, I also argue that the libertarian critique is wrong about *how* we should care about economic agency and *which* economic rights are basic.

Rawls's theory of basic rights is complicated. The rights protected and given priority by the first principle are all and only the rights necessary for the adequate development and exercise of the moral powers of democratic citizenship.[1] Rawls conceives of democratic citizenship as social cooperation between free and equal persons; these powers, therefore, are those that enable citizens to participate in and benefit from this sort of cooperation. Rawls identifies two such powers:[2] first, the power to make up one's mind about and pursue a determinate conception of the good life, or the capacity for a conception of the good; second, the power to think about, pursue, offer, and abide by fair terms of cooperation, or the capacity for a sense of justice.

---

[1] For the full story see John Rawls, *Political Liberalism*, expanded ed. (Columbia University Press, 2005), Lecture IX. For my attempts to clarify Rawls's theory of basic rights see "Are Economic Liberties Basic Rights?," *Politics, Philosophy, and Economics* 13 (2014), 23–44; "Social Cooperation and Basic Economic Rights: A Rawlsian Route to Social Democracy," *Journal of Social Philosophy* 47 (2016), 288–308.

[2] E.g., John Rawls, *Justice as Fairness: A Restatement*, ed. Erin Kelly (Harvard University Press, 2001), 18–24; *Political Liberalism*, 18–20, 73–75, 81–82, 302.

Jeppe von Platz, *Rawls's Underestimation of the Importance of Economic Agency and Economic Rights* In: *John Rawls*. Edited by: Jon Mandle and Sarah Roberts-Cady, Oxford University Press (2020). © Oxford University Press. DOI: 10.1093/oso/9780190859213.003.0009.

The capacity for a conception of the good is exercised in our ethical agency and explains *why* we cooperate, namely, to produce the many social goods that will allow us to pursue our conception of the good life, whatever it may be.[3] These goods include material goods such as comfortable shelter, food, means of transportation, and so on, but also, and more importantly, immaterial goods such as peace, social stability, the accumulation of knowledge and progressively more powerful technologies, vibrant and diverse cultural experiences, and so on. It is by and through cooperating that we create all of these things, to the benefit of all.

The sense of justice is exercised in our political agency and involves articulating, offering, and abiding by fair terms of social cooperation. It is an understanding of the norms that ought to govern cooperation and a willingness to take these norms as directive. The sense of justice explains *how* we cooperate; our cooperation is governed by justice both internally (by our willingness to cooperate on fair terms) and externally (by the rules we legislate that define the terms of fair cooperation).

To secure the development and exercise of these two sorts of agency, the first principle secures three sets of rights.[4] Ethical agency is protected and enabled by rights that protect the person, and by liberties of religion, thought, and association that allow people to freely make up their minds about and pursue their own conceptions of the good life.[5] Political agency is protected and enabled by a set of political rights—freedom of speech and assembly; rights to join, form, leave, and criticize political parties; rights to participate in regular, free, and fair elections; and so on. The political rights also enjoy a fair-value guarantee to ensure that similarly talented and motivated citizens have roughly equal prospects for influencing government policies and gaining political power.[6] Rawls's first principle also covers a set of supporting rights that secure background conditions for the rights established as basic in one of the first two ways. These include the rule of law, privacy, and security of personal property.[7]

Economic rights enable and protect the exercise of economic agency.[8] These rights include rights governing ownership of productive property, rights related to working and contracting, rights related to transfer of goods and services, rights governing economic associations (corporations, unions, and so on), and

[3] I here use the term "ethical" in the broad sense of "concerning the good life" rather than the narrow sense of "morally permissible."

[4] Rawls, *Political Liberalism*, 310–324, 334–335, 409–419; *Justice as Fairness*, 45, 112–113. See also James Nickel, "Rethinking Rawls's Theory of Liberty and Rights," *Chicago-Kent Law Review* 69 (1994), 763–785, esp. sections 2 and 3.

[5] Rawls, *Political Liberalism*, 310–314.

[6] Rawls, *Political Liberalism*, 358.

[7] Rawls, *Political Liberalism*, 291; *Justice as Fairness*, 112–113.

[8] The following list builds on James W. Nickel, "Economic Liberties," in *The Idea of Political Liberalism: Essays on Rawls*, ed. Victoria Davion and Clark Wolf (Rowman & Littlefield, 2000), 156–157.

rights to public supports for one's development and exercise of the powers of economic agency. Other than personal property (and perhaps free choice of occupation), Rawls does *not* include economic rights on the list of rights protected by the first principle.[9] Generally speaking, then, economic rights are not, by Rawls's theory, necessary for the development and exercise of the moral powers of democratic citizenship, and so do not serve the same role or enjoy the same priority as the basic rights.

There is a division of labor between the two principles of justice in Rawls's theory, and the place and role of economic rights can be understood in terms of this division. Justice divides into enabling and distributive justice. *Enabling justice* deals with the preconditions of social cooperation; it requires that we secure for all citizens the conditions necessary to empower them to participate in social cooperation as free and equal persons. In Rawls's theory, enabling justice is governed by the first principle and a sufficientarian guarantee that all have "adequate all-purpose means to make effective use of their liberties and opportunities."[10] Of course, the first principle has distributive implications, for example, through the aforementioned sufficientarian guarantee and the fair-value requirement for political rights, but these requirements, again, aim to empower citizens to cooperate as free and equal. The distribution of the benefits and burdens of the social cooperation that takes place between citizens thus empowered is the subject of *distributive justice*. Distributive justice requires that these benefits and burdens are distributed fairly, which, in Rawls's theory, means subject to the requirements of the second principle of justice.

For Rawls, the system of economic rights that regulate economic agency is part of distributive justice. This leaves open the choice between capitalist and socialist systems, and it allows society to design property rights, labor laws, and the laws that define contracts to serve social concerns for efficiency and distributive justice.[11] The Rawlsian view of the role and (low) priority of economic rights thus leaves democratic governments free to design the economic system, subject only to the requirements of fairness stated by the second principle.

In the following section I sketch three libertarian critiques of Rawls's theory of economic rights. In section 3, I discuss the critique I believe is most worrying for Rawlsians, that is, the critique offered by Tomasi and like-minded thinkers.

[9] John Rawls, *A Theory of Justice*, rev. ed. (Harvard University Press, 1999), 42, 43, 82; *Political Liberalism*, 228, 232, 298, 335, 338, 363; *Justice as Fairness*, 114. Notably, Rawls often sets freedom of occupation apart from the list of basic liberties (e.g., *Political Liberalism*, 181, 308).

[10] Rawls, *Political Liberalism*, 6; see also *Lectures on the History of Political Philosophy*, ed. Samuel Freeman (Harvard University Press, 2008), 12; "The Idea of Public Reason Revisited," in *The Law of Peoples* (Harvard University Press, 2001), 141.

[11] There is substantial disagreement about how open Rawls's theory leaves this choice of economic systems. See Alan Thomas's entry in this volume for an overview and discussion of this site of disagreement.

This critique is most worrying because it accepts the Rawlsian approach to thinking about justice, but aims to show that this approach leads to a libertarian system of economic rights. If sound, Tomasi's argument shows that Rawlsians should be libertarians. In section 4, I argue that while Tomasi's argument fails in the detail, the general version of the libertarian complaint hits home, for some (nonlibertarian) economic rights are basic. In section 5, I indicate how economic agency and economic rights should be appreciated in justice as fairness.

2. Three Libertarian Critiques

A straightforward critique of Rawls's theory of economic rights can be built on the assumption that economic rights are natural rights that must be protected and respected by the state; a state serving the principles of justice as fairness does neither. Nozick, for example, begins *Anarchy, State, and Utopia* with the claim that "individuals have rights. . . . So strong and far-reaching are these rights that they raise the question of what, if anything, the state and its officials may do."[12] In particular, the state may not interfere with property or contract, except to protect rights: "Any state more extensive violates people's rights."[13]

To Nozickian libertarians, the most important economic rights are original: they are powers to acquire rights either by original acquisition of something previously unowned or by contracting with other persons. By exercising these powers, persons acquire property rights and rights to the services of other people.

The moral powers that this sort of libertarian theory cares about are thus not Rawls's two moral powers, but rather the powers that enable acquisition and transfer of property and other contractual obligations. Moreover, the basic rights are not those that *enable* the exercise of these powers; instead they simply *are* the rights to exercise these powers. Economic agency is the source of all interpersonally acquired rights and is, accordingly, a central concern of justice. The economic rights, including property rights that persons can acquire by dealing with each other, are thus theoretically and normatively prior to the authority of the state—to secure these rights is the source, end, and limit of state authority.

Theft, breach of contract, violence, and other forms of aggression are impermissible, but any exchange that exercises the relevant powers without violating the rights of other persons is permissible, and the distribution of acquired rights that results from permissible acquisitions and exchanges is just, no matter what else is true about it: "A distribution is just if it arose from another just

---

12 Robert Nozick, *Anarchy, State, and Utopia* (Basic Books, 1974), ix.
13 Nozick, *Anarchy, State, and Utopia*, 149.

distribution by legitimate means."[14] So when Rawlsians delegate the design of the system of economic rights to second-principle concerns, they commit the state to gross rights violations on a massive scale. For the pursuit of fairness through regulations or taxation violates basic economic rights: "Holdings to which these people are entitled may not be seized, even to provide equality of opportunity for others."[15] Indeed, Nozick says that taxation is "on par with forced labor,"[16] for people need to work and so have no alternative to working and paying taxes; they are forced to work and pay taxes.

Rawlsians need not worry much about this sort of libertarian critique, for it assumes a theory of the nature and sources of rights and political authority that Rawlsians reject. Rawlsians start from an idea of democratic society as a system of fair social cooperation between free and equal citizens and construct justice as fairness from the resources this idea makes available (social cooperation, fairness, free and equal citizens). The question is how we can enable social cooperation and distribute its burdens and fruits fairly among citizens. The Nozickian libertarian critique of Rawls amounts to a wholesale rejection of this starting point, and the particular critiques of distributive justice as rights-violating assumes that distributive justice is satisfied by the permissible exercise of the powers of property and contract. Since Rawlsians reject this assumption, they remain unconcerned by the critique leveled from it.

The second sort of libertarian critique assumes an indirect utilitarian framework. While Hayek did not target Rawls's theory directly, his discussion of distributive justice offers a clear illustration of this sort of critique. The argument starts from the view that the aim of society is social prosperity, and justice is the set of norms that best achieves this aim.

This indirect utilitarian view of the nature of justice turns libertarian once it is combined with the view that the best tool for creating maximal social prosperity is to unleash what Hayek calls the "creative powers of a free civilization,"[17] that is, to allow individuals as much economic liberty as possible, while preventing market failures and providing for public goods. Any limitation of economic agency beyond this tends to frustrate or destroy the productive powers of society at the expense of social prosperity and is, therefore, unjust. Justice consists in the marriage of economic liberty and social utility: the free exercise of economic agency is the primary means of utility, and we should, therefore, take the economic liberties of a laissez-faire economy as basic requirements of justice.

[14] Nozick, *Anarchy, State, and Utopia*, 150.
[15] Nozick, *Anarchy, State, and Utopia*, 235.
[16] Nozick, *Anarchy, State, and Utopia*, 169.
[17] Friedrich Hayek, *The Constitution of Liberty* (University of Chicago Press, 1960), 22.

In this perspective, the Rawlsian pursuit of distributive justice is counter-productive and inefficient and, therefore, unjust.[18] The pursuit of equality of opportunity requires government interference with liberty and leads to less opportunities for the average person. The pursuit of a fair distribution of the benefits and burdens of cooperation requires micromanagement of resources and individual choices. Thus, "Within the limits set by the rule of law, a great deal can be done to make the market work more effectively and smoothly; but within these limits, what people now regard as distributive justice can never be achieved."[19]

Justice, accordingly, permits (and legitimates) whatever distribution arises from the free market working its productive magic; not, as Nozick thought, because justice is concerned exclusively with transactions, or because economic liberties are basic rights, but because economic liberty produces the best overall outcome.[20] In a free society the distribution of wealth and income is the result of everybody playing the same economic game in accordance with the rules of liberty, and "There is no need morally to justify specific distributions (of income or wealth) which have not been brought about deliberately but are the outcome of a game that is played because it improves the chances of all."[21]

As with the first sort of libertarian critique, this Hayekian critique is of limited concern to Rawlsians. The point of justice as fairness is to offer a contractualist alternative to utilitarian theories of justice, so the fact that those who assume a utilitarian framework for thinking about justice find fault with justice as fairness is unsurprising and unconcerning.

These critiques derive from fundamental disagreements about the subject and role of justice. They are, at bottom, *inter*framework disagreements; disagreements about how we should think about justice in the first place. Nozickian libertarians believe that justice is about natural rights; Hayekians believe that justice is about social prosperity; Rawlsians believe that justice is about fair social cooperation. Because they disagree about this choice of framework, they disagree about what justice requires. Rawlsians are comfortable with their choice of framework and thus have little to fear from those who attack them based on the assumptions of other frameworks.

The third sort of libertarian critique accepts the Rawlsian framework for thinking about justice, but argues that this framework supports libertarian

[18] Cf. Hayek, *The Constitution of Liberty*, 231–233; *Law, Legislation, and Liberty*, vol. 2: *The Mirage of Social Justice* (University of Chicago Press, 1976), chap. 9.

[19] Hayek, *The Constitution of Liberty*, 232–233.

[20] Hayek, *Mirage of Social Justice*, 70, 140–141; *Law, Legislation, and Liberty*, vol. 3: *The Political Order of a Free People* (University of Chicago Press, 1979), 141, 142.

[21] Hayek, *Mirage of Social Justice*, 11; cf. 33; 64–65, 69–70, 83, 96, 117; and *The Constitution of Liberty*, 232–233.

conclusions about the status and priority of economic liberties. Here, then, is an *intra*framework disagreement that should worry Rawlsians, for if the charge is true, then Rawlsians should be libertarians.

Tomasi offers one version of this critique. He argues, first, that Rawls fails to provide justification for excepting the economic liberties of classical liberalism from protection by the first principle of justice.[22] This omission is puzzling, for including or omitting these liberties in the first principle has dramatic implications for what the state is required to do in terms of enabling justice, and what it is permitted to do in pursuit of distributive justice. Moreover, the economic liberties were central to the history of liberalism; given Rawls's insistence that he is working from and within this history, one would expect him to include them.

The second part of Tomasi's critique aims to show that economic liberties of property and contract should be basic rights, by Rawls's own criterion, for these economic liberties are no less important for the development and exercise of the moral powers than the liberties Rawls includes in the list. Take, for example, the rights of work and freedom of contract for work. Rawls allows for free choice of occupation, but

> One is defined by one's workplace experience not simply by *what* profession one pursues. One is also defined by *where* one chooses to work, by the *terms* that one seeks and accepts for one's work, by the *number of hours* that one devotes to one's work, and much more besides. . . . The particular pattern of decisions one makes in response to these questions about working often goes a long way to defining what makes one person's life distinct.[23]

Similarly, with the activities of ownership; for many, their identity as owners of productive property is crucial to their conception of the good life.[24] More generally, economic identity is no less essential to who we are than our religious or political identities, and so should enjoy no less protection than these.[25] Thus, the economic liberties are basic for the same reason that liberties of conscience and the political rights are basic.

This critique should worry Rawlsians. If it is true that the economic liberties are basic rights, then justice as fairness prescribes an economy along the laissez-faire capitalist lines that Hayek envisioned. In the next section, I offer an incomplete reply to Tomasi. My reply is incomplete, for it shows that we may doubt that the economic liberties are basic rights, but it also agrees with Tomasi's

[22] John Tomasi, *Free Market Fairness* (Princeton University Press, 2012), especially chap. 4.
[23] Tomasi, *Free Market Fairness*, 77.
[24] "For many people the ownership of productive property plays a profound role in the formation and maintenance of self-authored lives. (Tomasi, *Free Market Fairness*, 78).
[25] Tomasi, *Free Market Fairness*, 80.

charge of unjustified exceptionalism. The libertarians are right about this: economic agency is no less central to justice than ethical and political agency, and Rawls should include economic rights on the list of rights protected by the first principle.

3. A Partial Defense of Rawls

Tomasi argues that the economic liberties of classical liberalism are basic rights, since the exercise of economic agency for many people involves engaging in economic activities that require private property as the means of production or unrestricted freedom of contract. Such economic activities express who they are as persons, and government regulation of them hinders their expression of who they are and frustrates their ability to develop as "responsible self-authors."[26]

However, even if we grant that economic activities are central to persons' identities in this manner, it is unclear that this has the desired implication for the rights that would protect these activities.[27] To establish that it does not, I will distinguish between two versions of Tomasi's argument and show why neither of these yields the conclusion he draws.

The first version focuses on the criterion of basic rights that aim to secure the *exercise* of the capacity for a conception of the good. Here Tomasi's argument is that the first principle aims to secure people in the pursuit of their determinate conceptions of the good; since people have or could have conceptions of the good that cannot be exercised without, say, property rights in productive property, this right should be protected as a basic liberty.[28] However, Rawls's theory of basic rights is unconcerned with the expression of personal identities or determinate conceptions of the good as these are or could be found in this or that society. The first principle's concern is for the capacity for developing and exercising the moral powers, including the capacity for a conception of the good. Freedom of religion, for example, is not protected because people are religious or to protect people in the exercise of the religion they may happen to have, but because freedom of religion is necessary for people to make up their own minds about religious matters. The same cannot be said for, say ownership of productive property (or, maybe it could, but it hasn't).

[26] Tomasi, *Free Market Fairness*, 82.

[27] For extended discussions of Tomasi's argument see Melenowsky and Bernstein discussing a variety of market democratic arguments in "Why Free Market Rights Are Not Basic Liberties," *Journal of Value Inquiry* 49 (2015), 47–67; Alan Patten, "Are Economic Liberties Basic?," *Critical Review* 26 (2014), 362–374; von Platz, "Economic Liberties"; "Social Cooperation."

[28] Cf. Tomasi's example of Amy and her shop in *Free Market Fairness*, 81. Tomasi likewise suggests that the exercise of the liberties of the person as consumer is an ingredient in the identities of many persons (*Free Market Fairness*, 79–81).

Relatedly, the Rawlsian theory of basic rights does not aim to maximize the set of determinate conceptions of the good that people could pursue, nor to minimize the legal hindrances to pursuing such conceptions. What matters is not the size of the choice set of conceptions of the good that members of society can choose from, but that they are empowered to choose freely. Of course, the choice set cannot be zero or one (or some other low number), but Rawls argues that there will be a plurality of ways of life available in a society that secures the liberties of conscience.[29]

Tomasi might object that the moral power of ethical agency is the capacity to design and *pursue* a conception of the good, and the economic liberties are necessary to enable this pursuit. This objection misunderstands Rawls's criterion. For Rawls, the capacity to pursue a conception of the good is the capacity to order one's preferences into a coherent scheme, lay plans, and make choices based on one's conception of the good.[30] Exercising one's conception of the good thus requires rationality and strength of will so that one can act prudently in light of one's material and legal circumstances; it does not require that the material or legal circumstances are hospitable to one's pursuits.

The second version focuses on the *development* of the moral powers. In this version, Tomasi argues that that the first principle aims to secure optimal conditions for the development of the powers of responsible self-authorship and that security of economic liberties is part of these optimal conditions.[31] Yet there are no maximizing tendencies in the first principle, but only the satisficing concern for the development of the moral powers *adequate* to enable free and equal cooperation. Of course, society may (and perhaps should) aim to provide the most hospitable environment for responsible self-authorship, but this is not the aim sought by the first principle.

Each of Tomasi's renditions of the two aims of the first principle is sensible, but neither is Rawls's. Rawlsians are thus off the hook; Tomasi's argument does not show that Rawlsians must be libertarians.

However, while Tomasi's critique fails in this particular regard, the general challenge to Rawls's view on economic rights is intact. Rawls offers no argument for why economic rights are excluded from protection by the first principle. Even worse, Rawls treats the development and exercise of economic agency as a matter of distributive rather than of enabling justice; but economic agency is no less central to social cooperation than the ethical and political forms of agency that the first principle protects and enables. In the following I elaborate on this concern.

---

[29] This is, of course, the "fact of reasonable pluralism"; cf. Rawls, *Political Liberalism*, 36–37.
[30] For details, see Rawls's account of deliberative rationality, *A Theory of Justice*, 361–372.
[31] "In seeking the most appropriate specification of the basic rights and liberties, we seek the specification that most fully allows citizens to develop themselves as responsible self-authors" (Tomasi, *Free Market Fairness*, 82).

4. Enabling Economic Agency

Enabling justice, the first principle, aims to provide the necessary institutional conditions for the development and exercise of the moral powers and, thereby, to enable all citizens to participate freely and equally in social cooperation. Distributive justice, the second principle, sets the basic terms by which the burdens and benefits of cooperation are distributed. For social cooperation is burdensome as well as beneficial—it involves *work*, the investment of time and effort, and the distribution of that work is as central a subject of distributive justice as is the distribution of benefits produced by the work of society as a whole.

Rawls deals with the exercise of economic agency—its opportunities for exercise, burdens, and benefits—as a matter of distributive rather than enabling justice; a matter for the second rather than the first principle of justice. This is odd, and not only for the reasons articulated by Tomasi; for our economic agency and the development and exercise of the moral powers of economic agency seem no less essential to participating in social cooperation as free and equal persons than the powers of ethical and political agency that are Rawls's focus. Though the first principle secures the conditions for developing the capacity for a conception of the good and the sense of justice, this interest and willingness are insufficient to empower members of society to participate in the cooperative relationship as free and equal, for that requires also an ability to perform productive work—the ability to carry one's fair share of the burden in the production and distribution of the benefits of social cooperation. If the capacity for a conception of the good explains why we cooperate, and the sense of justice explains how we cooperate, we still must posit a further capacity to explain our cooperation, our capacity to work productively with others.

There is, then, a third moral power that I claim is missing from Rawls's theory of justice: the capacity to *work*, to be a productive participant in social cooperation.[32] This too is not a power we are born with, but one that we develop over time, and the adequate development and full exercise of this power is no less institutionally preconditioned than are the other two moral powers.

Why and in what sense do I claim that the power to work is *fundamental*?[33] The power to work is fundamental for the same reason and in the same sense that the other two moral powers are fundamental; without it, citizens cannot cooperate as free and equal citizens. Rawls at times describes the moral powers as the capacities necessary to engage in, benefit from, and comply with fair terms of cooperation.[34] The capacity for a conception of the good explains how we *benefit*

---

[32] For a more detailed argument that Rawlsians should recognize this moral power, see my "Social Cooperation."

[33] I'm grateful to the editors for nudging me to respond directly to this question.

[34] E.g., Rawls, *Political Liberalism*, 18–20; *Justice as Fairness*, 18–19, 24, 169.

from cooperation, for cooperation allows us to access the various means that we might need to pursue our conceptions of the good (recall, the products of social cooperation are immaterial as well as material goods). The sense of justice explains our capacity to *comply with* fair terms of cooperation, for it allows us to cooperate on terms that all could reasonably agree to from a situation of freedom and equality. The capacity for working explains how we *engage in* cooperation, for cooperation consists in *working together* on fair terms.

The moral powers are also fundamental in the sense that they are the bases of equal citizenship.[35] This invites the worry that adding the capacity to work to the list of moral powers exacerbates the degree to which justice as fairness implies that persons with disabilities are denied equal standing as citizens.[36] To answer this worry would take a separate essay, and I am unsure that an adequate answer is readily available. This problem is general to any theory of justice that takes the notion of cooperation between free and equal persons as its starting point. I believe that this is the right starting point, but it might carry costly commitments.

Another worry is that my proposal turns justice as fairness into a liberal perfectionism.[37] I do not believe that it does. I am not arguing with Marx that work is essential to the human existence (I don't mean to deny that it is, but my argument does not take this as premise nor try to establish it as conclusion), nor that conceptions of the good that do not include working are inferior. Recall that my focus is on enabling justice. The idea, again, is that the first principle requires that all citizens are institutionally empowered to cooperate as free and equal persons. My claim is simply that to be thus empowered, citizens must enjoy the institutional preconditions for the development and exercise of their capacity to work no less than the other two moral powers. The capacity for a conception of the good makes social cooperation meaningful (or rational), the sense of justice makes fair cooperation possible, and the capacity for work enables us to share in the burden of producing all the good things. There is no perfectionism in my argument not already present in justice as fairness.

In summary, economic agency is as central to Rawls's theory of justice as are ethical and political agency; and the moral power corresponding to the exercise of economic agency, the power to work, is as important as the capacity for a conception of the good and the sense of justice. It follows that the first-principle concern for enabling justice extends to economic agency, and that the first principle

---

[35] Rawls, *Political Liberalism*, 79, 86, 183, 272 n. 10, 301–303, 370.

[36] E.g., Gregory Kavka, "Disability and the Right to Work," in *Philosophy and the Problems of Work*, ed. Kory Schaff (Rowman and Littlefield, 2001), 249–264; and Martha Nussbaum, *Frontiers of Justice: Disability, Nationality, Species Membership* (Harvard University Press, 2007), chaps. 1 and 2. For a Rawlsian reply, see Samuel Freeman, "Contractarianism vs. the Capabilities Approach: Review of Martha Nussbaum's Frontiers of Justice," *Texas Law Review* 85 (2006), 385–430.

[37] Thomas in this volume. See also Thomas's critique of Tomasi in *Republic of Equals: Predistribution and Property-Owning Democracy* (Oxford University Press, 2017).

ought to secure the institutional preconditions for its adequate development and exercise.

5. Appreciating Economic Agency

One might question the significance of this conclusion. What, exactly, would be the changes a Rawlsian should make, if she accepts the argument so far? Would not the system of economic rights be the same as that favored by Rawls?

I believe that my proposed amendment has important implications for both the theory and pursuit of justice as fairness. First, and most obviously, my proposed amendment will add to the list of rights covered by the first principle, insofar as there are institutional preconditions for the development and exercise of the capacity for working. Such rights could include rights to access to productive work, to the education required in order to engage in such work, and to the healthcare and other supports adequate to maintain one's productive powers throughout one's adult life.

Though the concern for economic agency as a matter of distributive justice could yield similar rights, it could not give them priority as *basic* rights. It is a very different thing to care for, say, job training, workplace conditions, and healthcare as second-principle concerns, and to care for them as first-principle concerns. Suppose, for example, a conflict between freedom of association and providing adequate access to productive work for all. If the concern for adequate access to productive work is a second-principle concern, then the concern for freedom of association should get priority, and we should sacrifice access to work. If access to work is a first-principle concern, then we should try to find a compromise or balance where we fit both rights into a coherent scheme of rights. For the same reasons, a first-principle concern makes the relevant economic rights a constitutional matter that defines and restricts what democratic legislation must and may do, rather than a legislative matter that can be left for determination through the democratic process.

In justice as fairness, the basic needs that must be met for all citizens are defined as the means adequate to develop and exercise the moral powers. Since my proposed amendment adds rights to the list of basic rights, it also adds content to the sufficientarian basic needs principle of justice as fairness. Adding a moral power and the corresponding rights thus defines an additional set of basic needs that must be met; needs for the means required to engage in productive work.

The different kinds of concerns also have implications for what the rights require (i.e., to their content in addition to their status and level of priority). If, as I propose, all have a right to access to productive work, then this right would impose limits on how we should distribute ownership of productive property.

A distribution of productive property that would make access to productive work for some members of society a matter left to the discretion of others would be prohibited (for a *right* to productive work corresponds to *duties* to provide access to productive work, and the satisfaction of such entitlements cannot then depend on the discretion of capitalists). So certain types of capitalism would be impermissible, since they do not provide adequate access to the development and exercise of the productive powers of all.[38]

Of course, Rawls also thought that such types of capitalism were impermissible, but he never fully explained why. Rawls favored two regimes, property-owning democracy and liberal socialism—presumably because both prevent the accumulation of productive property in the hands of a few capitalists; the first by dispersing ownership of productive property into the hands of producers, the second by maintaining public ownership of productive property. Yet Rawls does not, I think, explain why the accumulation of productive property in the hands of the few is so worrisome. It might be that such accumulation is unfair because it makes it harder to provide fair equality of opportunity or to satisfy the difference principle, or because it undermines the fair value of political rights, but I am unsure why we should think this would be true in general. It seems possible that accumulated capital can exist without undermining the fair value of political rights or fair equality of opportunity. The amended theory I have proposed offers a straightforward and, I think, intuitive complaint about capitalist accumulation (which need not serve instead of, but can serve alongside, worries about fairness): that the accumulation of capital in the hands of a few means unequal access to the conditions for the adequate development and exercise of the economic agency of all. This is, I think, the deeper Marxist and social democratic worry about capitalism—that it fails to provide access to all to participate as free and equal persons in the productive and distributive functions of society—a worry that Rawls seems to share.

Note how easy it is to state the preceding worry about capitalism in terms of freedom and equality, once we include economic agency as one of the dimensions of democratic citizenship. Since we ought to enable citizens to cooperate as free and equal, we ought to create an economic environment where all have access to a free and equal cooperative relationship; to assuming their role as equal and productive members of society. Once they are in that relationship, there are, of course, further questions about how the benefits and burdens of their cooperation should be distributed—questions of distributive justice proper—and to ensure a fair distribution presumably requires careful design of the rights and opportunities attendant upon economic agency. But the more basic concern with

---

[38] In his contribution to the present volume Thomas suggests that this sort of reasoning actually rules out capitalism as such and not just some varieties of capitalism.

economic agency is that of enabling justice; namely, that all citizens enjoy access to the preconditions for the development and exercise of economic agency itself.

6. Conclusion

The libertarian critique is true: Rawls underestimates the importance of economic agency and, therefore, fails to give economic rights their proper role and priority. However, the problem is not, as Nozick thought, that economic rights are natural rights that determine and constrain the role of political authority; nor, as Hayek thought, that economic liberties are the basic tools of prosperity. The problem rather is, as Tomasi argues, that economic rights are basic rights by Rawls's own understanding of the role and justification of basic rights. I have argued, however, that Tomasi's argument justifying the economic rights of classical liberalism as basic rights fails; Rawlsians need not be libertarians. Rather, Rawlsians might be a bit more Marxist, in that they should take the development and exercise of the powers of economic agency, understood as the powers involved in productive work, as a primary concern of justice. Amended accordingly, justice as fairness would stand stronger as alternative to both libertarianism and Marxism—defending a clear alternative to both *laissez-faire* capitalism and socialism.

Acknowledgments

I am grateful to the editors of this volume and Alan Thomas for several suggested improvements and to Lauren McGillicuddy for expert editorial assistance.

6

Rawls on Economic Liberty
and the Choice of Systems
of Social Cooperation

Alan Thomas

Comparatively little attention has been paid, in the Rawls literature, to that which he called our "choice of a social system."[1] In addition to deciding upon principles of justice, we must compare the different ways in which they might be implemented·in generic social forms:[2]

> It is important to trace out, if only in a rough and ready way, the institutional content of the two principles of justice. We need to do this before we can endorse these principles, even provisionally.[3]

Analogous to Weberian "ideal types," such social forms as laissez-faire capitalism, welfare state capitalism, liberal market socialism, command socialism, and a property-owning democracy are all candidates for this choice from a closed list of options.

There were two surprising aspects of Rawls's own verdict on this choice: first, he vindicates no single option, rather the disjunctive choice between liberal market socialism and a property-owning democracy. Second, while nearly all the options on Rawls's closed list can claim to have some basis in historical fact, one of his chosen options does not.[4] In formulating such a list we draw on our

---

[1] John Rawls, *Justice as Fairness: A Restatement*, ed. Erin Kelly (Harvard University Press, 2001).
[2] Although Rawls is equally explicit that only one of the four questions to be asked about such a choice is raised at this point: whether any such regime can be effectively and workably maintained (Rawls, *Justice as Fairness*, 136–137). Three other questions require full information: the effectiveness of the implied institutional design, compliance (corruption), and whether the roles assigned by the structure can be competently performed.
[3] Rawls, *Justice as Fairness*, 136.
[4] Paul Weithman, "Review of Property-Owning Democracy: Rawls and Beyond," *Notre Dame Philosophical Reviews*, https://ndpr.nd.edu/news/property-owning-democracy-rawls-and-beyond/ (August 7, 2013).

Alan Thomas, *Rawls on Economic Liberty and the Choice of Systems of Social Cooperation* In: *John Rawls*. Edited by: Jon Mandle and Sarah Roberts-Cady, Oxford University Press (2020). © Oxford University Press.
DOI: 10.1093/oso/9780190859213.003.0010.

knowledge of sociological and historical facts, even if our knowledge must be regimented into relatively abstract generic forms.

While there may be historical examples of approximations to command socialism, or laissez-faire capitalism, or welfare state capitalism, there is no historical example of a property-owning democracy. Unlike the other candidates, it seems to be stipulated, rather than derived from historical examples. Yet it is one of two Rawls's preferred (disjoined) options—perhaps hardly surprisingly given that it seems to be stipulated as the private property form that would uniquely realize the values of Rawls's theory of reciprocal fairness.[5] One candidate on his list seems to be favored from the start given that this is a test it could hardly fail.

This anomalous treatment has been one of the motives for a close examination in a series of recent studies not only of this option, but of Rawls's methodology as a whole.[6] In this chapter I will draw on this material to exposit both Rawls's own views and the recent criticism to which his answer has been subject.

Rawls's Principled Agnosticism

Rawls's own answer to the question of which social system we should choose is subtle: we can eliminate laissez-faire capitalism, welfare state capitalism, and command socialism from his list as incompatible with justice. However, while that leaves two candidates, we cannot choose between *them*. Rawls's answer is disjunctive: our verdict should be the choice of either a property-owning democracy or liberal market socialism. He vindicates the disjunction, and neither disjunct, because he believes that this is as far as the kind of reflection characteristic of political philosophy can take us.

Given its location in Rawls's architectonic, immediately after the choice of principles, but before we have proceeded any further in his "four-stage sequence," Rawls implies that we do not have enough information to resolve this disjunction one way or another at this level of abstraction.[7] The decision will be taken when more information about the history and sociology of actual societies is known to its citizens and their legislators:

---

[5] Weithman, "Property-Owning Democracy."

[6] Martin O'Neill and Thad Williamson, *Property-Owning Democracy: Rawls and Beyond* (Wiley-Blackwell, 2012); John Tomasi, *Free Market Fairness* (Princeton University Press, 2012); Alan Thomas, *Republic of Equals: Predistribution and Property-Owning Democracy* (Oxford University Press, 2017); William A. Edmundson, *John Rawls: Reticent Socialist* (Cambridge University Press, 2017); Gavin Kerr, *The Property-Owning Democracy* (Routledge, 2017).

[7] After the choice of principles comes a constitutional stage, a legislative stage, then, finally, an administrative-cum-judicial stage. John Rawls, *A Theory of Justice*, rev. ed. (Harvard University Press, 1999), 171–176.

When a practical decision is to be made between property-owning democracy and a liberal socialist regime, we look to a society's historical circumstances, to its traditions of political thought and practice, and much else. Justice as fairness does not decide between these regimes but tries to set out guidelines for how the decision can reasonably be approached.[8]

When we make the choice, we will be guaranteed to have implemented the values of justice as reciprocal fairness either way.

Rawls's answer therefore has three features: (i) it is agnostic—we lack the information to decide the issue at a high level of reflection; (ii) it is noncommittal—it vindicates a disjunction and neither disjunct taken alone; (iii) it is nonconstitutional—the issue is resolved beyond the stage of the constitutional convention, and so this choice of social form cannot be constrained by the constitution. Rawls's critics, as we shall see, are unhappy with each of these three claims.

What other parts of Rawls's view rationalize his answer? Both of his options are species of the genus "private property system." Yet he seems to take the question of "capitalism versus socialism" to be an issue deferred to the later stage of reflection when an individual society has knowledge of its own history and traditions. Is this not inconsistent? By choosing a private property system are you not, automatically, thereby committed to capitalism?

Not for Rawls: he splits the issue of private property into two parts. One issue about personal private property can be resolved at this level of abstraction: it is required to protect the development of the moral powers of the individual. Parties in the choice situation that Rawls calls "the original position" are guaranteed

> the right to hold and to have the exclusive use of personal property . . . to allow a sufficient material basis for a secure sense of personal independence and self-respect, both of which are essential for the development and exercise of the moral powers.[9]

However, the wider question of the ownership of major means of production can be deferred until the later stages of the four-stage sequence because settling that question is not necessary to protect the individual's moral powers.

> These wider conceptions of property are not used because they cannot, I think, be accounted for as necessary for the development and full exercise of the

---

[8] Rawls, *Justice as Fairness*, 139.

[9] John Rawls, *Political Liberalism*, expanded ed. (Harvard University Press, 2005), 298; see also Rawls, *Justice as Fairness*, 114.

moral powers. The merits of these and other conceptions of the right of property are decided at later stages when much more information about a society's circumstances and historical traditions is available.[10]

So for Rawls it is an open question how far his unwavering commitment to personal private property can further vindicate ownership of the major productive means of a society. For him, the crux of this decision is how widely dispersed such ownership can reasonably be constrained to be.

Furthermore, Rawls's two preferred choices are shaped by his "anticapitalism." As Arthur DiQuattro pointed out, the word "capitalism" did not appear in the first edition of A Theory of Justice.[11] In both of Rawls's preferred social systems there is no capitalist class. Each exemplifies what he calls a "private property system," but there is no identifiable class of individuals with monopoly control of the major means of production. There is no distinct social class who exploit this monopoly control to give them the social power to dictate the terms on which other people labor. This is more than a verbal point: you might say that in his two preferred schemes every citizen is a capitalist. Speaking loosely, that might well be true. However, Rawls is using the term strictly, following Marx's use of the term "capitalism." So his two preferred forms of social system are both private property systems, neither of which are capitalist.

This anticapitalism consists in widely dispersing ownership of capital. A property-owning democracy is continually involved in the circulation of capital and with pre-emptively preventing its excessive accumulation. Rawls described its aim as being

to prevent a small part of society from controlling the economy and indirectly, political life as well. . . . Property-owning democracy avoids this, not by the redistribution of income to those with less at the end of each period . . . but rather by ensuring the widespread ownership of productive assets and human capital (that is, education and trained skills) at the beginning of each period, all of this against a background of fair equality of opportunity.[12]

Similarly, in liberal market socialism, the state owns all capital and leases it out to productive enterprises that may, or may not, take the form of worker cooperatives.[13] Some liberal socialists insist that a society that is democratic at

[10] Rawls, Political Liberalism, 298; Rawls, Justice as Fairness, 114.

[11] Arthur DiQuattro, "Rawls and Left Criticism," Political Theory 11 (1983), 53–78.

[12] Rawls, Justice as Fairness, 139.

[13] In Justice as Fairness, Rawls makes it clear that his conception of liberal market socialism was strongly influenced by the views of John Stuart Mill, Principles of Political Economy and Chapters on Socialism, ed. Jonathan Riley (Oxford University Press, 2008). However, for my purposes here Mill's work has been valuably supplemented by the work of David Schweickart and David Ellerman, who

the macro level must instantiate democratic values in the micro-level institutional forms of the economy. It is an interesting question whether that goal can only be secured by being made legally mandatory and, if it is, whether the view remains liberal.[14]

For Rawls the key issue is that either all citizens own capital in a property-owning democracy, or democratic citizens are the "principal" and the democratic state their appointed "agent" in leasing out capital to productive enterprises. In that sense, even in a liberal market socialist society, ownership of capital is fully dispersed (even if control is not). Either way, we have a private property system, a market, and the liberal basic liberties realized in social forms that are noncapitalist private property systems.

That, then, is Rawls's answer to the question of our choice of a social system. I turn now to expositing the views of three critics of his answer: John Tomasi, William A. Edmundson—and myself. It will emerge that in spite of disagreement between our respective outlooks, there is remarkable agreement between us over the way in which we think Rawls's answer ought to be criticized.

The "Fact of Domination"

Rawls was always sensitive to the Marxist charge that his liberal theory gave citizens formal equality before the law, but that its toleration of material inequality undermined the fair value of those same liberties. His response to this challenge was twofold: all and only the political liberties were to receive a "fair value guarantee." Primarily, that took the form of an "insulation strategy" that tried, as far as possible, to keep money out of politics.[15]

One way to understand Rawls's recent critics is that each of them believes that Rawls was right, as his career developed, to take Marx's charge ever more seriously. It is the central concern addressed by his last substantive monograph, *Justice as Fairness: A Restatement*. However, his critics also allege that Rawls failed to review every aspect of his system: he nowhere explicitly says that he no

---

have independently comprehensively worked out of the details of liberal market socialist scheme. See David Schweickart, *Against Capitalism* (Cambridge University Press, 1993); David Ellerman, *The Democratic Worker-Owned Firm* (Routledge Reprints, 2016).

[14] This "congruence" requirement is prominent defended by Joshua Cohen, "The Economic Basis of Deliberative Democracy," *Social Philosophy and Policy* 6 (1989), 25–50. I critique this view in *Republic of Equals*. The term is taken from Nancy Rosenblum, *Membership and Morals* (Princeton University Press, 1998).

[15] Richard Krouse and Michael Macpherson, "Capitalism, 'Property-Owning Democracy' and the Welfare State," in *Democracy and the Welfare State*, ed. Amy Gutmann (Princeton University Press, 1988), 86.

longer views an insulation strategy as sufficient to guarantee the fair value of political liberty, nor does he explain how his preferred social systems address a key problem, namely, the "fact of domination."[16]

I take this useful phrase from Edmundson's recent book; but while the phrase is novel, the phenomenon it captures is not. It is also at the forefront of a complementary book by me and of Tomasi's *Free Market Fairness*.[17] It is the tendency, in a social democratic state that is also capitalist, for concentrations of capital to be leveraged via what John Stuart Mill calls the "fact of combination" into pressure on the democratic process.[18] In a similar phrase, Thomas Piketty called this the "drift to oligarchy."[19] Piketty's historical work demonstrates how, over the long run, the social democratic state has failed to prevent concentrated capital from shaping policy in the interests of capital holders. This underlying structure of wealth inequality exhibits a tendency toward self-reinforcing and self-perpetuating wealth inequality and oligarchic governance.

Plural interests can combine in different ways to produce the fact of domination; as Edmundson notes, we need postulate neither conspiracy theories nor the agency of specific classes.[20] The fact of domination is one of those "laws and tendencies of the social world" that Rawls draws on throughout his work. It claims to be nothing more than a well-grounded empirical generalization about a tendency, or capacity, not always fully realized and in some cases impeded by explicit safeguards. Rawls described it as follows:

> The liberties protected by the principle of [political] participation lose much of their value whenever those who have greater private means are permitted to use their advantages to control the course of public debate. For eventually these inequalities will enable those better situated to exercise a larger influence over the development of legislation. In due time they are likely to acquire a preponderant weight in settling social questions, at least in regard to those matters upon which they normally agree, which is to say in regard to those things that support their favored circumstances.[21]

That which worries Edmundson, Tomasi, and me is that while Rawls is explicit about the threat, he is less explicit about whether he has retained his confidence in an insulation strategy to contain it.[22] Nor, if he takes the very choice of a social

---

16　Edmundson, *John Rawls*, 103.
17　Thomas, *Republic of Equals*; Tomasi, *Free Market Fairness*.
18　, Mill, *Principles of Political Economy*.
19　Thomas Piketty, *Capital in the Twenty-First Century* (Harvard University Press, 2014), 514.
20　Edmundson, *John Rawls*, 108; Rawls, *Justice as Fairness*, 125.
21　Rawls, *A Theory of Justice*, 198.
22　Or, as I would prefer to put it, Rawls is "reticent" about announcing that the only effective, preemptive insulation strategy is nothing less than the selection of a property-owning democracy itself as the only way to guarantee the fair value of political liberty.

system to be the ultimate, successful, pre-emptive strategy of capital dispersal offering the strongest protection against the fact of domination, did he revise the architectonic of his system to reflect that fact.

This group of critics is certainly internally disparate. Philip Pettit has drawn a distinction between *dominium* and *imperium*: the former is the "private power of interference" that some private agents enjoy over others; the latter is the "imperium of the state" or "public power."[23] Tomasi's form of neoclassical liberalism is primarily concerned with the abuse of *imperium*: his view is that Rawls failed to develop a sufficiently robust defense of individual economic liberty and that the primary threat to such liberty is the overreaching power of the affirmative welfare state. In their (laudable) attempts to secure the joint freedom of all, such states misguidedly aim to reduce *dominium*—a lack of individual freedom—only to subject us all to overreaching *imperium*.

Tomasi's solution is to give individual economic liberty as strong a degree of protection as a citizen's other basic liberties. The immediate consequence is that such a liberty receives constitutional protection. Tomasi predictably downgrades the importance of Rawls's further principles, namely the fair equality of opportunity and difference principles, to defend a weakened interpretation of both. Economic institutions are to be so arranged as to maximally benefit the worst off and as to provide a decent safety net justified in terms of justice—not mere pragmatism. In addition, there is some concern with a formal sense of equality of opportunity. This is not the case for a full assessment of Tomasi's views, which I have discussed elsewhere, but the key point for present purposes is that Tomasi is concerned with one form of the fact of domination—*imperium*—and his remedy is constitutional.[24]

Similarly, Edmundson makes his analysis of the fact of domination central to his interpretation of Rawls's work.[25] He claims that this interpretation is one Rawls could have endorsed if only he had fully drawn out explicit inferences from his implicit commitments. Edmundson argues that Rawls ought to have included the fact of domination among the basic circumstances of justice that constrain the theorizing about its nature. Unlike Tomasi, Edmundson is as sensitive to threats from *dominium* (private power) to the same degree that he is concerned with the threat of *imperium* (public power). His is a slippery-slope argument: given that Rawls permits personal private property, there is no natural stopping point from that position to the ownership of productive means. But the category of productive means is a broad one, ranging from the sphere of

[23] Philip Pettit, *Republicanism: A Theory of Freedom and Government* (Oxford University Press, 1997), 152.

[24] Thomas, *Republic of Equals*, chap. 10.

[25] Edmundson, *John Rawls*.

"petty production" to those *major* productive means that supply the goods that any person needs in the ordinary course of life.

Yet, Edmundson continues, we know that what Rawls sought to justify was a value connected to ownership, yet distinct from it. The entrepreneurial component is to be distinguished from that which the Cambridge economist Joan Robinson called "pure ownership":

> Rawls conceived the entrepreneurial or control aspects of ownership as inhering not in capital assets, but in the acquired skills and "natural assets" exercised in marshaling and managing capital assets. To say that a doctor has a basic right to own a stethoscope is to obscure what is important, namely, the excellence that a competent doctor manifests in skillfully making use of a stethoscope and other tools of the trade. A right to have use of a stethoscope in this sense is an aspect of the basic right to occupational choice, which choosers in the original position already recognize as a basic liberty. The right to profit from the sale or lease of medical instruments is another matter.[26]

As Edmundson notes, Rawls quotes Robinson's phrase to characterize the "pure ownership" that grounds rent-seeking.[27] So while Rawls wants to vindicate personal private property, he does not want to vindicate "pure ownership," whether by public or private agents, because either will engage in rent-seeking unless the public agency is owned by all and controlled by a delegated management subject to democratic oversight.

Edmundson therefore revises Rawls's view in this way: to make his overall commitments consistent, and to accommodate the fact of domination, we have to revise his noncommittal choice of a property-owning democracy or liberal market socialism and replace the latter with what I will call "liberal democratic socialism"—and only with that.

The difference between Mill's liberal market socialism and Edmundson's liberal democratic socialism is that Edmundson sees no principled requirement for workplaces to be democratic, nor is he committed to associational pluralism. But I would argue that, on any workable conception of Mill's scheme, it can be seen to share Edmundson's aim: for the major means of production, a democratic citizenry appoints the state to own those assets on their behalf with control being delegated to appointed management. There is one sense, then, in which this is also the dispersal of ownership of capital: all citizens own nationalized (publicly owned) industry via an agent they appoint to do so.

---

[26] Edmundson, *John Rawls*, 47.
[27] Edmundson, *John Rawls*, citing Rawls, *Lectures on the History of Political Philosophy*, ed. Samuel Freeman (Harvard University Press, 2007), 350.

Edmundson's liberal democratic socialism is the traditional socialism of the British Labour Party until the rise of "New Labour." The Labour Party of Sidney and Beatrice Webb, and of Clement Attlee's post–World War II Labour government, was committed to the public ownership of what Edmundson calls the "commanding heights" of the economy. Edmundson functionally defines the commanding heights as those industries with the capacity to extract rents from the provision of those goods and services that any person needs to lead a flourishing life.[28] The major difference between Edmundson's view and its historical precedents is that his view, like Tomasi's, is constitutionally underwritten.

Edmundson therefore revises Rawls's noncommittal view to being committal: as the endorsement of liberal democratic socialism (to the exclusion of a property-owning democracy). Edmundson is a stringent critic of the latter, which he is happy to see relegated to the sphere of petty production.

This is an ironic reversal of my view.[29] While I also disagree with Rawls's agnostic proposal and argue for a "committal" view, it is the mirror image of Edmundson's. My claim is that a property-owning democracy is uniquely expressive of the values of liberal republicanism. (Liberal market socialism, by contrast, is not.) Once again, however, my proposal is constitutional. To be precise, it is not that we place the difference principle in the constitution, as it fails the test of "justiciability," but we do place in the constitution a task specification for the wide dispersal of capital that a property-owning democracy is well placed to meet.[30]

So my views, and those of Tomasi and Edmundson, share intersecting concerns and patterns of argument. Edmundson and I view Tomasi as too focused on *imperium* and inadvertently neglectful of *dominium*: a Tomasian society is likely to see some private agents acquire a capacity to dominate, and extract rents, that will lead his ideal regime type to become unstable over time because of its neglect of the "background conditions" to individual transactions.[31] Tomasi presumably views Edmundson and me as committing the opposite error: of reducing *dominium* only by giving excessive power to *imperium*. The internecine dispute between myself and Edmundson is over whether we resolve Rawls's noncommittal choice for a property-owning democracy or socialism in

---

[28] "Under socialism, citizens, whether working in an enterprise that makes use of socially vital means of production or not, enjoy all the incidents of joint ownership—in particular, an equal say in how the rents that accrue to this means of production are to be distributed. Those incidents of ownership that are rents, and thus not the fruit of productive activity, are not for private accumulation.... [R]ents may be set at zero, as when essential services are provided without charge to the public and are subsidized by revenues otherwise generated and collected" (Edmundson, *John Rawls*, 88).

[29] Thomas, *Republic of Equals*.

[30] Thomas, *Republic of Equals*, chap. 5.

[31] Exactly as Rawls predicted would happen for all neo-Lockean "Ideal Social Process" views that neglect the background conditions for fairness in this way (Rawls, *Justice as Fairness*, 52–55).

favor of the former (my view) or reverse that choice and uniquely select liberal democratic socialism (Edmundson's view).

We all share the view that Rawls's increasing focus on the fact of domination, and his explicit concern to address Marx's critique, may have hit upon the right form of a solution (at least, from my and Edmundson's point of view). What Rawls did not do—and here Tomasi agrees—was revise the architectonic of his position to acknowledge that the level of protection afforded the basic liberties had to be extended to the fair value of political liberty. The fair-value guarantee requires constitutional protection. It cannot be left, as Rawls leaves it, to the later stages of the four-stage sequence where a society has acquired sufficient information about its own history and sociology to come to an informed decision on the question of "capitalism versus socialism." I share Edmundson's and Tomasi's view that the fair value of the political liberties cannot be held hostage by the majoritarian democratic process; the measures taken to protect fair value have to be put in place to constrain that process so that it operates in the right way and for the right reasons.

How Do We Choose?

Rawls believes that the question of the choice of social system is secondary, in its importance, only to the selection of the principles that ground that choice. It seems to me that there are three choice points: is our choice committal to one option, or noncommittal across two or more disjuncts? If we are to be committal, committed to what? Finally, how does the important fact that Rawls calls "the burdens of judgment" bear on the two prior questions?

The first point to be made is that all four of us—Tomasi, Edmundson, Jeppe von Platz (in this volume), and myself—are engaged in what Phillipe van Parijs has memorably called "social-justice-guided constitutional engineering."[32] In doing so, I think, we need to be very careful about the overall impact on liberty (not, I would hope, a distinctively libertarian thought). Take Edmundson's option first: given that which Rawls called the "burdens of judgment," there is very little uncontroversial evidence about the economic merits of nationalized as opposed to privately owned industry on which to base the decision to remove the whole issue from democratic debate.

Edmundson advertises it as an advantage of his own view that it is "reconciliatory" to place a contested issue beyond the remit of democratic politics. Edmundson reports an objection to his proposal from Kevin Vallier as follows: "A

---

[32] Philippe van Parijs, *Just Democracy: The Rawls and Machiavelli Programme* (ECPR Press, 2011), 38 n.b19; cited also in Edmundson, *John Rawls*, 13 n. 2.

structure cannot be stabilized . . . by the mere expedient of taking things that are in fact reasonably contentious out of the realm of ordinary politics."[33] But while he reports this objection, he does not supply much of an answer to Vallier—who seems to me to raise a serious problem. Given the burdens of judgment, it is a hasty measure to place this controversial issue beyond the ambit of democratic politics.

Anyone who engages in constitutional engineering has to be aware of the risk of unwarranted restrictions on liberty: I think Edmundson is not sufficiently sensitive to this risk when he runs together three questions. One is whether a measure to address the fact of domination has to have a constitutional robustness. The second is what its content is: ought it to reproduce Rawls's agnosticism, or ought it to be committal? The third is, if committal, committal to what?

In my view it is only a property-owning democracy that steers the appropriate middle course between two alternatives. When it suits him, Edmundson borrows arguments from Tomasi. As we have seen, in Tomasi's neoclassical liberalism, a robust individual economic liberty is given the same status as a basic liberty; in other words, constitutional protection. Von Platz follows him in this.[34] My concern about this version of a committal strategy is that when we seek to implement a fully adequate scheme of such liberties compossibly for all, the overall view will be unstable (particularly if it rests on a controversial ethical perfectionism).[35] By contrast, in Edmundson's alternative, we are also committal in the wrong way: given the burdens of judgment, we ought not to be deciding the extent of state ownership of industry prior to a wholly pragmatic legislative decision that takes into account any given society's history and traditions. We risk Vallier's objection that our proposal will not be "reconciliatory"—far from it.

By contrast with both Tomasi's and Edmundson's proposals, consider a constitutional specification of *a right to fair and universal access to capital*—a functional requirement well met by a property-owning democracy. It permits private property in all productive means (major and minor), but as Edmundson concedes, it does not guarantee it. It is a committal version of the fair-value guarantee, but less committal than Tomasi's, von Platz's, or Edmundson's proposals. A constitutionally guaranteed property-owning democracy threatens the least restriction to liberty overall. The republican hope is that when we correctly identify the correct regime of law, it will be freedom enabling and no restriction at all. But given the burdens of judgment, the constitutional engineer ought to proceed with caution. Edmundson denies at one point that a property-owning democracy could be constitutionally guaranteed; he does not say why. I think he believes that it

[33] Edmundson, *John Rawls*, 143.
[34] Tomasi, *Free Market Fairness*; von Platz, this volume.
[35] Thomas, *Republic of Equals*, chap. 10.

fails the test of justiciability. But I have already noted that this is not the proposal: a functional requirement, expressed as a right, goes into the constitution. A property-owning democracy is tailored uniquely to satisfy this requirement.[36]

Rawls Redux

Sadly, Rawls in no longer with us to contribute to this debate; but, if he could, what might he say? Surely he would enjoy the irony of seeing his noncommittal disjunction resolved in one way by Edmundson and in the diametrically opposed one by me; might this suggest *to Rawls* that we should be happy with disjunction itself? Given the epistemically soft and shifting sands of political philosophy, do either Edmundson or I have such confidence in our conclusions to advance each of our conflicting proposals at the expense of the other?

Perhaps it matters here that we are engaged in different projects: Edmundson seeks a view that Rawls ought to have endorsed, but did not, while I am engaged in an openly revisionary appropriation of elements of Rawls's view at the service of an avowedly hybrid liberal republicanism. Yet Rawls may nevertheless observe that since I take advantage of his own argument from the burdens of judgment to advantage my position over Edmundson's, might the very same burdens not favor any noncommittal proposal (such as Rawls's) over any committal one such as mine?

Yet Rawls can go further: as I have emphasized in this chapter, all of Rawls's critics share a concern with domination and rent-seeking, and all share the general form of a solution to address it.[37] We all see the dispersal of capital as the dispersal of power; not just of market power but of the political power into which capital accumulation is leveraged. Edmundson's program of nationalization, Tomasi's and von Platz's dispersal of economic power to individuals each of whom is empowered on the market, Mill's system of worker cooperatives understood (Schweickart-style) as lessees of state capital, and my version of a property-owning democracy all share the same aim at this level of abstraction. So, of course, does Rawls's *Justice as Fairness*—another point of convergence, then, between all of the views I have discussed here—including Rawls's own.

---

[36] Thomas, *Republic of Equals*, chap. 5.

[37] There is, nevertheless, a difference between Edmundson and myself on the one hand, and Tomasi on the other: while I think it is reasonable to read Tomasi as not in favor of rent-seeking, in practice it is not clear how his view is going to avoid it over the long run. So while Tomasi shares my, and Edmundson's, goals, I do not think either of us is convinced that a Tomasian commercial republic will be able to avoid the fact of private domination arising over the long run in a way that threatens its stability. I am grateful to the editors of this volume for asking me to clarify this point.

The irreconcilable difference, then, remains the strategy of constitutionaliza-tion to which Edmundson, Tomasi, and I are committed. The issues then, are complex, and in light of the burdens of judgment, good conscience counsels us to admit that perhaps they are difficult to resolve. What is undoubtedly true is that in the light of Rawls's work it is at least much clearer to us what the issues are. Rawls ought to have the last word:

> Even if by some convincing philosophical argument—at least convincing to us and a few likeminded others—we could trace the right of private or social own-ership back to first principles or basic rights, there is a good reason for working out a conception of justice which does not do this.[38]

The good reason is that it is more advisable "to look for bases of agreement im-plicit in the public political culture and therefore in its underlying conceptions of the person and of social cooperation."[39] In lieu of a conclusion, then, let me say this: perhaps those pursuing this issue via a spiral of reflection may find, as they ascend, that Rawls not only started them on this journey, but may be waiting to greet them, as they complete it, with a suitably cautious answer.

---

[38] Rawls, *Political Liberalism*, 338.
[39] Rawls, *Political Liberalism*, 339.

PART IV
LUCK EGALITARIANISM

Introduction

Many people share a strong intuition that it is unjust when one child is born into severe poverty with limited life prospects while another is born into affluence with many more opportunities. But what's unjust about it? One might say it is unjust because there is nothing that either child did to *deserve* her initial social position. Their social positions are merely a matter of luck, and inequalities that are grounded on luck alone are unfair. This is the basic thought that underwrites the philosophical position of "luck egalitarianism." An alternative perspective is that what is wrong with these very unequal starting positions and prospects is that they are likely to undermine the ability of individuals to relate to one another as equals. This is the concern that is the foundation of "relational egalitarianism." While both approaches would condemn such a case as unjust, there are other cases where they diverge—for example, when inequalities due to luck do not undermine the relational equality of individuals or when individuals are responsible for choices that do undermine such relations. There is no doubt that Rawls's principles of justice would condemn the case as unjust, but over the course of defending his principles in *A Theory of Justice*, Rawls says various things that have been taken to support both interpretations of why it is unjust. And in the years since *A Theory of Justice* was published, both luck egalitarianism and relational egalitarianism have been developed into ever-more sophisticated forms that, despite their differences, trace their origins back to Rawls.

Some luck egalitarians point out that Rawls drew a connection between luck and injustice in his defense of the difference principle. But Rawls himself writes that his argument for the principles of justice is based on the original position. He introduces the choice from the original position as a device to help us achieve reflective equilibrium concerning principles of justice for the basic structure of society. The strategy is to identify the features of "the most philosophically favored interpretation of this initial choice situation for the purposes of a theory of justice. . . The idea here is simply to make vivid to ourselves the restrictions that it seems reasonable to impose on arguments for principles of justice, and therefore on these principles themselves."[1] It is important not to lose sight of the fact that this construction is embedded within the project of reflective equilibrium. Thus,

---

[1] John Rawls, *A Theory of Justice*, rev. ed. (Harvard University Press, 1999), 16.

Introduction In: *John Rawls.* Edited by: Jon Mandle and Sarah Roberts-Cady, Oxford University Press (2020). © Oxford University Press. DOI: 10.1093/oso/9780190859213.003.0011.

if the principles chosen from the choice situation conflict with our pretheoretical considered convictions about justice, "We can either modify the account of the initial situation or we can revise our existing judgments."[2] In *A Theory of Justice* itself Rawls does not "actually work through this process" of making such adjustments.[3] Rather, he explains the features of the original position, considers which principles would be chosen there, explores some possible implications of those principles, and then considers the stability of a society that realizes them.

In chapter 2 of *A Theory of Justice*, Rawls covers a variety of topics, but "the aim is to explain the meaning and application of the principles."[4] There is no discussion of the features of the original position or the considerations that would lead the parties there to make their choice. As he explains, "Not until the next chapter do I take up the interpretation of the initial situation and begin the argument to show that the principles considered here would indeed be acknowledged [from the original position]."[5] And he later repeats the point: "None of the preceding remarks are an argument for this conception, since in a contract theory all arguments, strictly speaking, are to be made in terms of what it would be rational to agree to in the original position. But I am concerned here to prepare the way for the favored interpretation of the two principles so that these criteria, especially the second one, will not strike the reader as extreme."[6] The thought, apparently, is that while there is considerable pretheoretical agreement between our considered convictions and the first principle, the second principle, and especially the difference principle, may appear to conflict with these initial judgments. Thus, Rawls offers some considerations intended to explain this principle more clearly and to bring it into closer agreement with our pretheoretical intuitions before presenting the argument from the original position. For example, someone might think that justice requires no more than equality of opportunity, that is, eliminating or mitigating unequal prospects that are due to unequal initial social position. But, Rawls claims, if justice requires that we interrogate the dependence of distributive shares on unequal initial social positions, it also requires that we interrogate the dependence of distributive shares on unequal natural endowments: "Once we are troubled by the influence of either social contingencies or natural chance on the determination of distributive shares, we are bound, on reflection, to be bothered by the influence of the other. From a moral standpoint the two seem equally arbitrary."[7]

[2] Rawls, *A Theory of Justice*, 18.
[3] Rawls, *A Theory of Justice*, 18.
[4] Rawls, *A Theory of Justice*, 47.
[5] Rawls, *A Theory of Justice*, 47.
[6] Rawls, *A Theory of Justice*, 65.
[7] Rawls, *A Theory of Justice*, 64–65.

Some commentators claim that these preliminary considerations, emphasizing the influence of arbitrary factors on distributive shares, actually amount to an "informal" or "intuitive" argument for the principles that is more compelling than the "official" argument from the original position. In an influential textbook from 1990, for example, Will Kymlicka argued that the argument from the original position "adds little to Rawls's theory" and that "the intuitive argument is the primary argument, whatever Rawls says to the contrary."[8] This intuitive argument, Kymlicka claims, is grounded in the following thought: "It is fair for individuals to have unequal shares of social goods if those inequalities are earned and deserved by the individual, that is, if they are the product of the individual's actions and choices. But it is unfair for individuals to be disadvantaged or privileged by arbitrary and undeserved differences in their social circumstances."[9] Similarly, G. A. Cohen, while acknowledging that it is not the "official argument," reconstructs Rawls's egalitarianism in two steps: "The first thought is that true equality of opportunity is achieved only when all morally arbitrary causes of inequality are eliminated. . . . And the second thought . . . is that there exist no causes of inequality that are not arbitrary in the specified sense."[10] Focusing on the difference principle in particular, Thomas Nagel writes that it "depends on the moral claim that it is unfair if people suffer or benefit differentially because of differences between them that are not their fault."[11]

In her influential 1999 article "What Is the Point of Equality?" Elizabeth Anderson introduced the term "luck egalitarianism" to describe theories of justice that identify "the fundamental injustice to be natural inequality in the distribution of luck."[12] The substantive merit of luck egalitarianism is, of course, quite independent of whether Rawls himself endorsed the position. But since this position initially developed as an interpretation of his theory, it is worth noting that there is at least as much evidence against this interpretation as in support of it. Anderson herself notes that "this conception of justice can be traced to the work of John Rawls, and has been (I believe mistakenly) attributed to him."[13] For one thing, in A Theory of Justice, Rawls writes explicitly that "the natural distribution [of abilities and talents] is neither just nor unjust."[14] And while noting some similarities, he distinguishes the difference principle from what he calls "the principle of redress," which holds that "undeserved inequalities call for redress; and since inequalities of birth and natural endowment are undeserved, these inequalities

---

[8] Will Kymlicka, Contemporary Political Philosophy (Oxford University Press, 1990), 69.
[9] Kymlicka, Contemporary Political Philosophy, 56.
[10] G. A. Cohen, Rescuing Justice and Equality (Harvard University Press, 2008), 89.
[11] Thomas Nagel, "Rawls and Liberalism," in The Cambridge Companion to Rawls, ed. Samuel Freeman (Cambridge University Press, 2003), 71.
[12] Elizabeth Anderson, "What Is the Point of Equality?," Ethics 109 (1999), 289.
[13] Anderson, "What Is the Point," 290.
[14] Rawls, A Theory of Justice, 87.

are to be somehow compensated for."[15] In "A Kantian Conception of Equality" (1975), he was even more explicit: "The aim is not to eliminate the various contingencies."[16] Even defenders of this interpretation typically recognize that Rawls doesn't fully embrace it. Kymlicka writes that the difference principle "still allows too much room for people's fate to be influenced by arbitrary factors."[17] And Cohen points to "a radical tension between the Rawlsian *case* for the difference principle . . . and the *content* of the difference principle."[18]

But, to repeat, many philosophers have embraced this doctrine quite independently from any interpretation of Rawls, and it has developed into an advanced research program, with numerous variations articulated and defended. The underlying intuition is well put by G. A. Cohen, who states that his "animating conviction in political philosophy with respect to justice" is that "an unequal distribution whose inequality cannot be vindicated by some choice or fault or desert on the part of (some of) the relevant affected agents is unfair, and therefore, *pro tanto*, unjust, and that nothing can remove that particular injustice."[19] In other words, when individuals suffer from bad luck, justice requires that they receive compensation for their loss. On the other hand, when an individual suffers a loss that is the result (in some appropriate sense) of a choice that is deliberate (in some appropriate sense), the individual is properly held responsible and compensation is not owed. One key dispute concerns the metric of loss and gain. In one early and influential formulation, what must be equalized are "opportunities for welfare,"[20] while in another it is resources,[21] and in still others it is "real freedom."[22] A second fundamental question is how the "cut" between luck and responsibility is to be made. It seems appropriate to hold people responsible for some outcomes that are partially a matter of luck—for example, if someone chooses to gamble. For that reason, luck egalitarians typically distinguish between "option luck," which is the result of a "deliberate gamble" for which

---

[15] Rawls, *A Theory of Justice*, 86. He notes that although they are different, "the difference principle gives some weight to the considerations singled out by the principle of redress," and they both turn away from an emphasis on "social efficiency and technocratic values" (86, 87).

[16] John Rawls, "A Kantian Conception of Equality" (1975) in *Collected Papers*, ed. Samuel Freeman (Harvard University Press, 1999), 263. Compare: implicit in the difference principle is the idea "that social institutions are not to take advantage of contingencies of native endowment, or of initial social position, or of good or bad luck over the course of life, except in ways that benefit everyone, including the least favored." John Rawls, *Justice as Fairness: A Restatement*, ed. Erin Kelly (Harvard University Press, 2001), 124.

[17] Kymlicka, *Contemporary Political Philosophy*, 71.

[18] Cohen, *Rescuing Justice and Equality*, 17.

[19] Cohen, *Rescuing Justice and Equality*, 7.

[20] Richard Arneson, "Equality and Equal Opportunity for Welfare," *Philosophical Studies* 56 (1989), 77–93.

[21] Ronald Dworkin, *Sovereign Virtue: The Theory and Practice of Equality* (Harvard University Press, 2000). The relevant material was first published in 1981.

[22] Philippe van Parjis, *Real Freedom for All* (Oxford University Press, 1995).

individuals are held responsible, and "brute luck," which is not the result of deliberately chosen risks and therefore for which individuals are not responsible.[23] Another issue concerns whether or not to hold people responsible for their values, tastes, and preferences. If these are a matter of (brute) luck, then they are subject to compensation. Dworkin makes a "distinction between a person and his circumstances, and assigns his tastes and ambitions to his person [for which he is held responsible] and his physical and mental powers to his circumstances [for which he is not held responsible]."[24] Cohen disagrees. He holds that justice requires that "we should compensate for disadvantage beyond a person's control, as such, and that we should not, accordingly, draw a line between unfortunate resource endowment and unfortunate utility function."[25] In other words, justice requires that we compensate people not only if they have lower than average natural abilities (which they did not choose), but also if they have expensive preferences, as long as they were not chosen. In his example,

> Paul loves photography, while Fred loves fishing. Prices are such that Fred pursues his pastime with ease while Paul cannot afford to. Paul's life is a lot less pleasant as a result: it might even be true that it has less meaning than Fred's does. I think the egalitarian thing to do is to subsidize Paul's photography.[26]

Other disputes concern whether the luck egalitarian standard applies comprehensively to individual conduct[27] or only to institutions,[28] and how responsibility is related to free will and determinism.[29]

In her 1999 article, Anderson presents a litany of objections to luck egalitarianism, but she also defends an alternative, a "relational theory of equality,"[30] which she calls "democratic equality," not coincidentally the same name that Rawls gives his interpretation of the second principle. It holds that justice aims at "the construction of a community of equals. . . . Democratic equality guarantees all law-abiding citizens effective access to the social conditions of their freedom at all times."[31] The fundamental contrast, as she sees it, between luck egalitarianism and democratic equality is as follows:

---

[23] See Dworkin, *Sovereign Virtue*, 73–74; and Peter Vallentyne, "Brute Luck, Option Luck, and Equality," *Ethics* 112 (2002), 529–557.

[24] Dworkin, *Sovereign Virtue*, 81.

[25] G. A. Cohen, "On the Currency of Egalitarian Justice," *Ethics* 99 (1989), 922.

[26] Cohen, "Currency of Egalitarian Justice," 923.

[27] Cohen, *Rescuing Justice and Equality*.

[28] Kok-Chor Tan, *Justice, Institutions, and Luck* (Oxford University Press, 2012).

[29] Cohen: "We may indeed be up to our necks in the free will problem" ("Currency of Egalitarian Justice," 934). See also Saul Smilansky, "Egalitarian Justice and the Importance of the Free Will Problem," *Philosophia* 25 (1997), 153–161.

[30] Anderson, "What Is the Point," 313.

[31] Anderson, "What Is the Point," 289.

[Luck egalitarianism] regards two people as equal so long as they enjoy equal amounts of some distributable good—income, resources, opportunities for welfare, and so forth. Social relationships are largely seen as instrumental to generating such patterns of distribution. By contrast, democratic equality regards two people as equal when each accepts the obligation to justify their actions by principles acceptable to the other, and in which they take mutual consultation, reciprocation, and recognition for granted. Certain patterns in the distribution of goods may be instrumental to securing such relationships, follow from them, or even be constitutive of them. But democratic egalitarians are fundamentally concerned with the relationships within which goods are distributed, not only with the distribution of goods themselves.[32]

Anderson explores some implications of her conception of democratic equality, but she does not pursue the comparison to justice as fairness beyond a few remarks, at one point suggesting that her conception would not require a "policy as demanding as Rawls's difference principle."[33]

Samuel Scheffler is another influential defender of the "relational" interpretation of Rawls. He comments, "If luck egalitarianism is to be supplied with a compelling motivation, that motivation will need to come from somewhere else [besides Rawls]."[34] And in language that echoes Anderson, he writes that, on Rawls's view,

equality is understood as a social and political ideal that governs the relations in which people stand to one another. The core value of equality does not . . . consist in the idea that there is something that must be distributed or allocated equally. . . . Instead, the core of the value is a normative conception of human relations.[35]

To be sure, there are distributive implications of establishing equal relations among individuals. But these implications are not fundamental, and more to the point, there is no reason to believe that all of the effects of brute luck on distributive shares must be undone in order to establish such relations.

It's a testament to the richness of Rawls's work that such diverse research agendas, both for and against luck egalitarianism, trace their origins to him. In this volume, Kasper Lippert-Rasmussen and Rainer Forst develop this debate

---

[32] Anderson, "What Is the Point," 313–314.
[33] Anderson, "What Is the Point," 326.
[34] Samuel Scheffler, "What Is Egalitarianism?," *Philosophy and Public Affairs* 31 (2003), 30.
[35] Scheffler, "What Is Egalitarianism?" 31.

between luck egalitarians and relational egalitarians about how to conceive the fundamental issues of distributive justice. Lippert-Rasmussen explores and evaluates different interpretations the philosophers have offered about the role that luck plays in Rawls's conception of justice. Moving beyond exegetical questions, he offers an argument for the role luck *should* play in a theory of justice such as Rawls's. In the companion chapter, Rainer Forst argues against a luck egalitarian interpretation of Rawls's work. He argues that the main focus of Rawls's conception of justice is a Kantian concern for the standing of citizens as moral and political equals. Accordingly, the main task of a theory of justice is to identify basic social structures that prevent legal, political, and social forms of domination.

Suggested Reading from Rawls to Accompany These Chapters

A Theory of Justice: chapter 1, §3; chapter 2, §§12–15, 17; chapter 5
Justice as Fairness: §§18–22

For Further Reading

Anderson, Elizabeth. "What Is the Point of Equality?" *Ethics* 109 (1999), 287–337. This is a highly influential paper that offers a litany of criticisms of "luck egalitarianism" (and is where the term is first introduced) and develops and defends a "relational egalitarianism" alternative.

Arneson, Richard. "Luck Egalitarianism Interpreted and Defended." *Philosophical Topics* 32 (2004), 1–20. This paper consolidates and defends what Arneson takes to be the core of various formulations of luck egalitarianism (including a revision to his previous formulation of the theory).

Cohen, G. A. *Rescuing Justice and Equality* (Harvard University Press, 2008), chap. 4. Cohen shows that despite how it is most commonly interpreted, the difference principle cannot be defended on luck egalitarian grounds since it allows distributive shares to be influenced by morally arbitrary factors.

Forst, Rainer. "Two Pictures of Justice." In his *Justification and Critique: Towards a Critical Theory of Politics* (Polity Press, 2014). This chapter distinguishes between theories of justice oriented toward goods to be distributed and theories of justice oriented toward relations among persons and possible structures of domination, defending the latter.

Kymlicka, Will. *Contemporary Political Philosophy* (Oxford University Press, 1990; 2nd ed., 2002), chap. 3. Kymlicka's introduction is a widely read survey of contemporary political philosophy, including an influential luck egalitarian interpretation of Rawls.

Lippert-Rasmussen, Kasper. *Luck Egalitarianism* (Bloomsbury, 2015). This book provides a clear and careful overview and defense of luck egalitarianism.

Scheffler, Samuel. "What Is Egalitarianism?" *Philosophy and Public Affairs* 31 (2003), 5–39. Scheffler argues against luck egalitarianism and offers an interpretation of Rawls grounded in an ideal of social and political relations similar to that of Anderson ("What Is the Point of Equality?").

Tomlin, Patrick. "Can I Be a Luck Egalitarian and a Rawlsian?" *Ethical Perspectives* 19 (2012), 371–397. This article aims to provide a kind of reconciliation between luck egalitarianism and justice as fairness by recognizing how they purport to answer different questions.

7

Rawls and Luck Egalitarianism

Kasper Lippert-Rasmussen

1. Introduction

Rawls's theory of justice has occupied the center stage of political philosophy for more than forty years. Far from everyone accepts it, but even those who do not are often occupied with how their favored theory of justice relates to Rawls's. Luck egalitarians are no exception. One common view among them is that Rawls saw the truth of luck egalitarianism through a glass darkly and sought to articulate his theory of justice in recognition of this truth, but failed to do so adequately. In this chapter, I argue (1) that this slightly self-congratulatory interpretation is not entirely warranted; (2) that even if it is not warranted to interpret Rawls as a luck egalitarian *malgré lui*, there is an important luck egalitarian strain in his motivation of his theory of justice; and (3) that, despite the tensions in his theory this generates, this is an attractive strain in Rawls's account of justice, since it captures part of the truth about justice.

Section 2 sets out some main differences between Rawls's theory of justice and luck egalitarianism. Section 3 scrutinizes Kymlicka's reading of Rawls—notably his intuitive argument for the difference principle—as one who aspired to construct a luck egalitarian account of justice, but failed to do so. Section 4 takes a critical look at some arguments for why the luck egalitarian reading of Rawls is unwarranted. Section 5 surveys some recent relational egalitarian criticisms of luck egalitarianism and, in the light thereof, briefly addresses the question of whether luck egalitarians offer an attractive account of distributive justice. To lay the cards on the table, I think they do. Section 6 briefly sums up the main claims of this chapter.

2. Rawls's Principles of Justice Are Not Luck Egalitarian

According to Rawls, the basic structure of society is just if, and only if,

each person has "an equal right to the most extensive total system of equal liberties compatible with a similar system of liberty for all" (the liberty principle);

Kasper Lippert-Rasmussen, *Rawls and Luck Egalitarianism* In: *John Rawls.* Edited by: Jon Mandle and Sarah Roberts-Cady, Oxford University Press (2020). © Oxford University Press. DOI: 10.1093/oso/9780190859213.003.0012.

"social and economic inequalities" are "attached to offices and positions open to all under conditions of fair equality of opportunity" (the principle of fair equality of opportunity); and

social and economic inequalities are "to the greatest benefit of the least advantaged, consistent with the just saving principle" (the difference principle).[1]

The liberty principle is lexically prior to the principle of fair equality of opportunity, and the latter is in turn lexically prior to the difference principle. For example, justice forbids introducing a tiny amount of unfair inequality of opportunity even if this is to the greatest benefit of the least advantaged. The "just savings principle" implies, inter alia, that one generation cannot justly promote the position of its worst off if that jeopardizes just institutions otherwise enjoyed by later generations.[2]

According to luck egalitarians:

A distribution is just if, and only if, it is ambition-sensitive and endowment-insensitive.[3]

A distribution is ambition-sensitive if, and only if, it reflects people's differential option luck, where "Option luck is a matter of how deliberate and calculated gambles turn out—whether someone gains or loses through accepting an isolated risk he or she should have anticipated and might have declined."[4] Suppose you win at the casino and I lose. In that case, justice requires that you get to keep your win. We were both aware of the risks involved and could reasonably have refrained from gambling. A distribution is endowment-insensitive if, and only if, no one is worse off than others as a result of bad brute luck, where this is a matter of how risks fall out that are not in the option luck sense deliberate gambles.[5] If I am worse off than you are, because, unfortunately for me, I am naturally less talented than you are, or because, unlike you, I was born paralyzed, then I am worse off than you through bad brute luck.[6]

---

[1] John Rawls, *A Theory of Justice*, rev. ed. (Harvard University Press, 1999), 266.

[2] Samuel Freeman, *Rawls* (Routledge, 2007), 136–139.

[3] Cf. Ronald Dworkin, *Sovereign Virtue: The Theory and Practice of Equality* (Harvard University Press, 2000), 89.

[4] Dworkin, *Sovereign Virtue*, 73.

[5] Dworkin, *Sovereign Virtue*, 73.

[6] Dworkin, *Sovereign Virtue*, 73–74. There are other ways of articulating the core luck egalitarian commitment. See Richard Arneson, "Equality and Equal Opportunity for Welfare," *Philosophical Studies* 56 (1989), 85–86; G. A. Cohen, *On the Currency of Egalitarian Justice and Other Essays in Political Philosophy* (Princeton University Press, 2011), 13, 117; Larry S. Temkin, *Inequality* (Oxford

The two displayed statements of Rawlsian justice and luck egalitarianism, respectively, make clear that Rawls and luck egalitarians make different claims about justice. First, the site of Rawls's theory is social institutions, whereas the site of luck egalitarianism is distributions.[7] Luck egalitarians might see a distribution across hermits living outside any social structure as unjust, whereas Rawls's theory of justice does not speak to that situation.[8] Also, a basic structure might be just on Rawls's view, even if the resulting unequal distribution is unjust on luck egalitarian grounds.

Second, Rawls's theory of justice speaks to the issue of liberty. A tyranny in which the distribution is perfectly ambition-sensitive and endowment-insensitive is unjust according to Rawls's liberty principle, but it might be just according to luck egalitarians. Similarly, a society in which offices and positions are not open to all under conditions of fair equality of opportunity—for example, a lottery determines who ends up in which offices and positions—but which realizes an ambition-sensitive and endowment-insensitive distribution of primary goods, is unjust according to Rawls, even though it might be just according to luck egalitarians.

Third, even if we restrict our attention to the difference principle, it diverges from luck egalitarianism in several ways. It ascribes no significance to whether the least advantaged are so because of deficient ambitions or deficient endowments. Also, it permits unequal distributions provided these are to the greatest benefit of the least advantaged, whereas luck egalitarians condemn unequal distributions reflecting differential endowments as unjust.[9] The difference principle concerns the expectations of the group of worst-off (employed) people—for example, "the class of minimum wage workers"[10]—whereas, generally, luck egalitarians are concerned with equality across individuals.[11] The currency of the difference principle is expectations of social primary goods—to wit, social goods that "any rational man is presumed to want"[12]—whereas luck egalitarianism as stated

University Press, 1993), 17. Arguably, being "deliberate and calculated" is a matter of degree and, thus, the distinction between option and brute luck a matter of degree. Cf. Kasper Lippert-Rasmussen, "Equality, Option Luck, and Responsibility," *Ethics* 111 (2001), 548–579.

[7] Cf. Freeman, *Rawls*, 125–127.

[8] Richard Arneson, "Egalitarianism and Responsibility," *Journal of Ethics* 3 (1999), 226.

[9] Pluralist luck egalitarians care about things other than egalitarian justice, e.g., welfare, and, thus, might think that inequalities are morally permissible, all things considered. Unlike Rawls, many luck egalitarians do not think justice is "the first virtue of social institutions" such that unjust institutions "no matter how efficient and well-arranged must be reformed or abolished." Rawls, *A Theory of Justice*, 3; cf. G. A. Cohen, *Rescuing Justice and Equality* (Harvard University Press, 2008), 302–307, 323–327, 367.

[10] Freeman, *Rawls*, 106.

[11] The quoted passage does not manifest this commitment, but it shows elsewhere. Rawls, *A Theory of Justice*, 56.

[12] Rawls, *A Theory of Justice*, 54.

previously is neutral on the currency issue.[13] Finally, unlike the difference principle the luck egalitarian principle is not constrained by a just saving principle,
which captures a concern for intergenerational justice. Indeed, on the most natural interpretation of luck egalitarianism, it implies that inequalities across generations that are due to differential bad luck are unjust.[14]

Rawls's principles of justice are not luck egalitarian principles!

3. The Luck Egalitarian Reading of Rawls

Despite the conclusion of the previous section, some see Rawls as a proto-luck
egalitarian, who, while ending up defending a non-luck-egalitarian theory of
justice, harbored considerable luck egalitarian sympathies and at various points
appealed to considerations more congenial to luck egalitarianism than to his own
theory of justice. On this interpretation—call it *the luck egalitarian reading of
Rawls*—in several important places, Rawls either embraces luck egalitarian principles of justice or makes judgments about the moral qualities of distributions
that are best explained by a commitment to luck egalitarian principles of justice.

The most important reason why some see Rawls as a proto-luck egalitarian is his
so-called intuitive argument for the difference principle. This is one of his two main
arguments for the difference principle, the other being the hypothetical contractualist
argument, which asserts that the parties behind the veil of ignorance will select his
principles of justice. The contractualist argument is the one Rawls presents as his real
argument for his theory of justice, whereas the intuitive argument mostly serves a
heuristic function.[15] However, the considerations that the intuitive argument appeals
to also play a role in motivating the contract situation, which in turn plays the central
role in the contractualist argument. Hence, some think Rawls is too modest on behalf
of the intuitive and too immodest on behalf of the contractualist argument.[16]

The intuitive argument starts with the idea that justice requires equality of opportunity. That can mean quite different things. On what Rawls calls the system
of natural liberty, equality of opportunity obtains when all have "at least the same
legal rights of access to all advantaged social positions."[17] While the system of

---

[13] While social primary goods could be the metric of luck egalitarian justice, luck egalitarians
could not focus on *expected* distributions predictably generated by the basic structure, since presumably differences between the expected and the actual distribution will reflect some people's suffering
differential bad brute luck. Also, given the most plausible rationale for luck egalitarianism—the un-
fairness of differential luck—a metric that excludes natural goods would seem incoherent.

[14] Kasper Lippert-Rasmussen, *Luck Egalitarianism* (Bloomsbury, 2015), 156–161.

[15] Rawls, *A Theory of Justice*, 65.

[16] cf. Brian Barry, *Theories of Justice* (University of California Press, 1989), 217–234; Will Kymlicka,
Contemporary Political Philosophy: An Introduction, 2nd ed. (Oxford University Press, 2002), 67.

[17] Rawls, *A Theory of Justice*, 62.

natural liberty is better justice-wise than situations where some are denied access by law to advantaged social positions, for example, because some positions are reserved for men, Rawls rejects this interpretation of equality of opportunity: "Intuitively, the most obvious injustice the system of natural liberty is that it permits the distributive shares to be improperly influenced by these factors [i.e., natural and social contingencies] so arbitrary from a moral point of view."[18]

In view of this, one might instead favor a liberal interpretation, which corrects for differences in social contingencies. On this view and on the assumption that there is a distribution of natural talents, equality of opportunity obtains only if "those who are at the same level of talent and ability, and have the same willingness to use them, have the same prospects of success regardless of their initial place in the social system."[19]

While equality of opportunity on the liberal interpretation represents an improvement relative to the system of natural liberty, it too is flawed, because it "permits the distribution of wealth and income to be determined by the natural distribution of abilities and talents" and there "is no more reason to permit the distribution of income and wealth to be settled by the distribution of natural assets than by historical and social fortune."[20] This warrants moving from liberal to Rawls's favored democratic equality of opportunity, which combines fair equality of opportunity and the difference principle.[21] On this view, the basic structure should be such that the worst off cannot be better off. Thus, the advantaged social positions to which there is fair equality of opportunity are part of a basic structure, which is to the greatest advantage of the worst off. Hence, realizing fair equality of opportunity on Rawls's interpretation has much more egalitarian consequences than fair equality of opportunity on the liberal interpretation.

On the luck egalitarian interpretation, the intuitive argument manifests the view that justice requires neutralizing differences in luck.[22] After all, does Rawls not say that intuitively the most obvious injustice of the system of natural liberty is the extent to which distributions reflect differential luck? As we saw in the previous section, Rawls ends up embracing a theory of justice that does not propose to neutralize all forms of luck, namely, differential brute luck the

---

[18] Rawls, *A Theory of Justice*, 63.
[19] Rawls, *A Theory of Justice*, 63.
[20] Rawls, *A Theory of Justice*, 64.
[21] Rawls, *A Theory of Justice*, 64.
[22] At most, Rawls's intuitive argument supports the view that inequalities reflecting differential option luck are not unjust, not that eliminating them is unjust. In relation to this aspect of luck egalitarianism, luck egalitarians often appeal to how Rawls thinks citizens should be held consequentially responsible being disadvantaged by expensive tastes. See John Rawls, "Social Unity and Primary Goods," in *Collected Papers*, ed. Samuel Freema (Harvard University Press, 1999), 369; cf. Samuel Scheffler, "What Is Egalitarianism?," *Philosophy and Public Affairs* 31 (2003), 10.

nonneutralization of which benefits the worst off, and which does not enjoin the worst off being even worse off than they could be, when their so being reflects bad option luck. However, this might reflect a failure of Rawls to realize "the full implications of his own argument."[23]

In a widely used introduction to political philosophy Kymlicka reads Rawls as one who offers his principles of justice as a theory of justice that is meant to incorporate the luck egalitarian requirements that distributions should be "ambition-sensitive" and "endowment-insensitive," but fails to do so. As Kymlicka's particularly strong version of the luck egalitarian reading of Rawls has it:

> While Rawls appeals to [the] choices-circumstances distinction, his difference principle violates it in two important ways. It is supposed to mitigate the effect of one's place in the distribution of natural assets. But because Rawls excludes natural primary goods from the index which determines who is least well off, there is in fact no compensation for those who suffer undeserved natural disadvantages. Conversely, people are supposed to be responsible for the cost of their choices. But the difference principle requires that some people subsidize the costs of other people's choices. Can we do a better job being "ambition-sensitive" and "endowment-insensitive"? This is the goal of Dworkin's [luck egalitarian] theory.[24]

On this view, Rawls's theory of justice is deficient and inferior to luck egalitarianism by the lights of his own goals, that is, to construct a theory of justice that is "supposed" to be ambition-sensitive and endowment-insensitive. While this interpretation underwrites a nice narrative about progress in political philosophy, it also attributes a fairly obvious mistake to Rawls. Perhaps this is some reason to think Rawls's aim was not luck egalitarian theory construction, even if, consistently with that being so, he also appealed to views supportive of luck egalitarianism.

4. The Anti-Luck-Egalitarian Reading of Rawls

Several political philosophers have argued that we should not accept the luck egalitarian interpretation of Rawls. In this section I briefly survey and assess two of their arguments. One important critic of the luck egalitarian interpretation is Samuel Scheffler. He accepts that considerations about moral luck—or to put the same point differently on the assumption that what is a matter of moral luck is

---

23 Kymlicka, *Contemporary Political Philosophy*, 71.
24 Kymlicka, *Contemporary Political Philosophy*, 74–75.

that for which we are not responsible—and considerations about responsibility play an important role in Rawls's theory of justice. However, he distinguishes between two such roles: a limited and negative role and an ambitious and positive role.[25] On the luck egalitarian interpretation, luck plays the latter role in Rawls, whereas, according to Scheffler, it only plays the former role.

On the reading Scheffler favors, Rawls only appeals to luck to undermine arguments for inequality based on appeal to certain factors that might seem to justify inequality but which, in the light of the fact that the degree to which people are favored in terms of these factors is a matter of luck, do not. An illustration of this negative strategy is Rawls's argument that desert in the ordinary sense does not justify inequalities, since how deserving one is depends on "happy family and social circumstances."[26] The crucial point is that this negative point is one Rawls can make without committing himself to the view that any brute luck inequality is unjust. In sum:

The negative view: for a certain set of putatively justice making features, for example, desert, to the degree variations across persons in terms of these features are a matter of luck, these features are not justice-making features after all.

The positive view is more ambitious than that. This view holds that inequalities, for example, under a system of natural liberty, are unjust because they reflect differential luck. Hence, when Rawls writes that, intuitively, the most obvious injustice of this system is the way it permits distributive shares to be improperly influenced by moral and social contingencies (see section 3), on the positive reading this reflects an embrace of the view that failure to eliminate differential luck is an injustice-making feature.[27] In sum:

The positive view: if a certain unequal distribution is a matter of differential luck across persons, then that distribution is unjust.[28]

---

[25] Samuel Scheffler, "Choice, Circumstance, and the Value of Equality," *Politics, Philosophy and Economics* 4 (2005), 7.

[26] Rawls, *A Theory of Justice*, 64.

[27] On the negative reading, one can either emphasize that "intuitively" might signal a contrast to "really" or emphasize that "improperly influence" might signal a contrast to "properly influence," where that would involve inequalities conforming to Rawls's democratic equality of opportunity. Cf. Scheffler, "What Is Egalitarianism?," 9. However, these readings go against Rawls's claim that "the principle of fair opportunity can only be imperfectly carried out . . . as long as the institution of the family exists," since it implies that perfection involves complete neutralization of differential social luck (Rawls, *A Theory of Justice*, 74; cf. 88).

[28] The "positive version" of the positive view, i.e., the part that reflects the ambition-sensitivity of luck egalitarianism, says: "If it is not the case that a distribution involves inequalities that are a matter of differential luck across different persons, then that distribution is just."

These two views are quite different. Only on the positive view, differential luck is an injustice-making feature. Only on the latter view, differential luck is merely something that deprives other features of their justice-making capacity. Because the negative view is silent on what makes distribution (un)just, it is compatible with the view that the fact that a distribution has the feature that it is the distribution that makes the worst off as well off as possible is a justice-making feature of that distribution. The negative view says that, for a certain set of putatively justice-making features, their justice-making capacities are undermined by luck, and it is open for a proponent of the negative view to say that the feature of being such that for the worst off to be as well off as possible, one must be better off than others, does not belong to that set.

In response, Kymlicka might observe that Rawls could consistently both embrace the negative and the positive views. Indeed, a natural explanation of why equalities resulting from differential luck are not justified is that such inequalities are unjust.[29] Scheffler comes close to attributing such a view to Rawls: "[The degree to which the system of natural liberty allow people's prospects to be influenced by luck] is indefensible because it is incongruous with people's status as equals and because the distribution of those contingencies does not in itself have any moral status."[30] But if so, does it not follow that justice requires that the prospects of people who are equals should only depend on factors that have moral status and that to the extent that people's prospects does not depend on such factors, that is unjust?

In response, Scheffler might stress that it is only the *large degree* to which the system of natural liberty allows prospects to depend on morally arbitrary factors that is incompatible with our status as equals. It seems odd, however, that moral equality should be "incongruous" with a high as opposed to a low degree of dependence on moral contingency. Why not say instead that moral equality is "strongly incongruous" with a high degree of dependence on luck and "weakly incongruous" with a low degree of dependence? Possibly, what Scheffler should say is that what matters here is not the *degree* to which moral contingency influences outcomes. Rather, it is the *nature* of that influence that matters—if that influence promotes the prospects of the worst off, then even a huge degree of dependence on moral contingency is just, whereas if it does not, then even a tiny degree of dependence is unjust.

Friends of the anti-luck-egalitarian reading often submit that not only can Rawls's intuitive argument for the difference principle be read in a way that

---

[29] Friends of the negative view must also explain why moral contingencies undermine differential desert's ability to justify inequality, while moral contingencies do not undermine the fact that there is no alternative to arrange the basic structure, which improves the expectations of the worst-offs' ability to justify inequalities.

[30] Scheffler, "What Is Egalitarianism?," 26.

avoids any commitment to luck egalitarianism. Rawls actually discusses a principle that is entailed by luck egalitarianism and which he rejects as "the sole criterion of justice, as the single aim of the social order"—this is what I referred to as the second anti-luck-egalitarian interpretation argument in the beginning of this section. However, Rawls does accept this principle, but "only as a prima facie principle, one that is to be weighed in the balance with others," for example, "the principle to improve average standard of life, or to advance the common good."[31] This principle—the principle of redress—says that

> undeserved inequalities call for redress; and since inequalities of birth and natural endowment are undeserved, these inequalities are somehow to be compensated for.[32]

Luck egalitarians might agree that the principle of redress has to be weighed in the balance with other principles, but, presumably, these will be principles other than principles of distributive justice, whereas for Rawls the outcome of the weighing is the correct principle of justice. Still, Rawls claims that his theory of justice "gives some weight to the considerations singled out by the principle of redress."[33] On a natural reading of Rawls, he thinks the principle of redress has some intuitive force and that it is a reason that speaks in favor of his own different account of justice that it gives some weight to this principle (but not more than is warranted given that weight should be given to other principles as well).[34]

In response, friends of the anti-luck-egalitarian reading might argue that Rawls "explicitly rejects the principle of redress" at least when that principle is understood as a principle that applies directly to distribution across individuals and not as a principle that motivates specifying the veil of ignorance in a certain way.[35] Relatively early on in his book Rawls suggests that "once we decide to look for a conception that nullifies the accidents of natural endowment and contingencies of social circumstances as counters in quest for political and economic advantage, we are led to" his principles of justice.[36] While, strictly speaking, this passage, and others like it, does not say what luck egalitarians say—for example,

---

[31] Rawls, A Theory of Justice, 86. The principle is entailed by, but is different from, luck egalitarianism because it does not enjoin leaving inequalities reflecting choice to stand. Luck egalitarians are likely to dispute that their principle states "the single aim of the social order" (cf. note 2).

[32] Rawls, A Theory of Justice, 86.

[33] Rawls, A Theory of Justice, 86.

[34] Rawls appears to treat the judgments reflected by the principle of redress not as intuitions of moral truth, as luck egalitarian are likely to do, but more like a desideratum among others that a principle of justice should satisfy to the degree compatible with the satisfaction of other desiderata.

[35] Jon Mandle, Rawls's "A Theory of Justice": An Introduction (Cambridge University Press, 2009), 25–26; cf. Thomas Nagel, "Rawls and Liberalism," in The Cambridge Companion to Rawls, ed. Samuel Freeman (Cambridge University Press, 2003), 71.

[36] Rawls, A Theory of Justice, 14.

it does not say that inequalities due to accidents of natural endowment are unjust—the spirit of it may seem congenial to luck egalitarianism. However, on the anti-luck-egalitarian reading, the decision referred to in the quotation earlier in this paragraph refers to the process of describing a choice situation suitable for identifying the correct principles of justice and not directly to distributions.

In response, luck egalitarians might ask why there is something worrisome about "using accidents of natural endowment and contingencies of social circumstances," or, along the line suggested by the interpretation just proposed, something worrisome about describing a choice situation that allows individuals to use good luck to press for principles that make them better off than others. In particular, would there be any reason to think that such a use is unjust, if we do not think that inequalities reflecting differential luck are unjust? Rawls could not, for instance, think that such use is worrisome, because it reduces human welfare. Nothing in Rawls's works suggests that a worry like that lies behind these reservations, and such a worry would in any case seem unwarranted. He could stress that his account of justice is a matter of pure procedural justice, that is, it is one that "within a certain range" implies that any distributive outcome might be just provided that the outcome is a result of a social system that is fair.[37] But to justify the relevant fair procedure, Rawls relies on intuitions such as those reflected by the principle of redress, and it is unclear how Rawls could justify doing that if these intuitions are not at least prima facie plausible intuitions about the justice of distributions.[38] That in turn means that luck egalitarians can derive some support from Rawls's arguments even if his aim was different from those attributed to him by Kymlicka, since luck egalitarianism is supported by the relevant intuitions and, indeed, does not conflict with them in a way Rawls's principle of justice does.

Rawls thinks that it is a considered moral judgment of ours that slavery is unjust.[39] Accordingly, if it turns out that, given a certain specification, the hypothetical contract situation is such that under some standard circumstances parties will favor slavery, this is a reason for revising the description of the choice situation. If that considered judgment is not a prima facie reason to think that slavery is unjust and, thus, an intuition that supports a free-standing antislavery principle, then how could it be so? Similarly, if Rawls appeals to the principle of redress to support his own theory of justice—as he does when he notes how

---

[37] Rawls, A Theory of Justice, 74–75.
[38] "The idea [behind the veil of ignorance] . . . is to make vivid to ourselves the restrictions that it seems reasonable to impose on arguments for principles of justice, *and therefore on those principles themselves*" (Rawls, A Theory of Justice, 16, my italics). One of the restrictions Rawls mentions is that "no one should be advantaged or disadvantaged by "natural fortune or social circumstances" (A Theory of Justice, 16).
[39] Rawls, A Theory of Justice, 42–43, 218.

his principles of justice accommodate the principle of redress—how can he deny that the intuition captured by the principle of redress is some prima facie reason to accept luck egalitarianism?[40] Accordingly, I think that luck played a greater role in Rawls's work than that implied by the negative view and, thus, embrace a version of the luck egalitarian reading, though one that is more modest than Kymlicka's.

5. Should We Be Relational Egalitarians or Luck Egalitarians?

Rawls is a towering figure in twentieth-century philosophy, and so, from the point of view of history of philosophy, it is an important question whether Rawls not at all or through a glass darkly subscribed to luck egalitarianism. Still, to address the following nonexegetical, substantive question is at least as important: should we, unlike Rawls, be luck egalitarians? Here I return to Scheffler's anti-luck-egalitarian reading of Rawls and the way in which it ties up with relational egalitarianism—a view that presently is influential and is seen as a rival to luck egalitarianism and which, while distinct from Rawls's theory, draws on central themes in Rawls.

Scheffler thinks that there are two ways of thinking about the ideal of equality broadly construed. We can, as luck egalitarians do, think of it as a purely distributive ideal, or we can think of it as an ideal about how citizens should relate to one another. If we think about it in the former way, we are naturally led to think that there is some good, be it resources or welfare, such that justice requires that everyone has equal amounts of that good. However, this, Scheffler contends, is not a crucial question if, roughly like Rawls, we think that justice basically is about relating to one another as equals.[41] Doing so might in some cases favor an equal distribution over an unequal one. It might even favor a distribution that ascribes some consequential responsibility to people for their choices. But in many cases we can relate as equals even if we are not equally well off, and in many cases we do not relate as equals if we ascribe full consequential responsibility to people

---

[40] Rawlsians might appeal to his method of reflective equilibrium at this point. The method involves mutual adjustment of our considered moral views about particular cases and our moral principles, inter alia, until they form the most coherent set of commitments. While, initially, the principle of redress is a considered moral belief of ours, it is one of those commitments that is discarded in the process of reaching reflective equilibrium. In that case, however, it cannot provide a reason to accept his theory of justice. Alternatively, Rawlsians might say that during the process of reaching reflective equilibrium, we retain the principle of redress but clarify or revise our belief about its status such that it applies only when providing redress benefits the worst off.

[41] cf. Mandle, Rawls's "A Theory of Justice", 169.

for their choices. To relate to one another as equals is, inter alia, to be prepared to take into account one another's interests and attitudes on an equal footing.[42]

This contrast aligns well with a distinction made by Elizabeth Anderson:

> Democratic equality [Anderson's favored theory of relational equality] . . . is a relational theory of equality: it conceives equality as a social relationship. Equality of fortune [i.e., luck egalitarianism] is a distributive theory of equality: it conceives of equality as a pattern of distribution. Thus, equality of fortune regards two people as equal as long as they enjoy equal amounts of some distributable good. . . . Social relations are largely seen as instrumental to generating such patterns of distribution. By contrast, democratic equality regards two people as equal when each accepts the obligation to justify their actions by principles acceptable to the other. . . . Certain patterns in the distribution of goods may be instrumental to securing such relationships, follow from them, or even be constitutive of them. But democratic egalitarians are fundamentally concerned with the relationships within which goods are distributed, not only with the distribution of goods themselves.[43]

This contrast contains an important objection to luck egalitarianism because, like Scheffler, Anderson believes that many injustices cannot be captured in distributive terms. Take the injustice of gays and lesbians not being able "to publicly reveal their identities without shame or fear."[44] This injustice is a matter of unjust social relations, not a matter of distributive injustice, and we cannot address it by, for instance, compensating gays and lesbians for their relevant deficient ability by making them better off moneywise. Indeed, when considered in isolation, a concern for making people equally well off in terms of some overall currency of justice appears fetishistic: "Unless distributive egalitarianism is anchored in some version of that ideal, or in some other comparably general understanding of equality as a moral value or normative ideal, it will be arbitrary, pointless, fetishistic: no more compelling than a preference for any other distributive pattern."[45]

In response to these criticisms, I offer five luck egalitarian replies. The first and simple reply is to play the pluralism card (note 9): justice is more than distributive

---

[42] Samuel Scheffler, "The Practice of Equality," in *Social Equality: On What It Means to Be Equals*, ed. Carina Fourie, Fabian Schuppert, and Ivo Wallimann-Helmer (Oxford University Press, 2015), 21–44.

[43] Elizabeth Anderson, "What Is the Point of Equality?," *Ethics* 109 (1999), 313–314.

[44] Anderson "What Is the Point," 320.

[45] Scheffler, "What Is Egalitarianism?," 23. Relational egalitarians also criticize luck egalitarians for ascribing too large a role to considerations about responsibility. I set aside this criticism here, because it is an open question what role relational egalitarians should ascribe to responsibility qua relational egalitarians, and because friends of distributive equality too might ascribe no role to responsibility. Cf. Kasper Lippert-Rasmussen, *Relational Egalitarianism* (Cambridge University Press, 2018), chap. 1.

justice, and a situation can involve relational injustice even if it involves no distributive justice.

Second, luck egalitarians might argue that while luck egalitarian theorists have not considered relational goods as part of the egalitarian *equalisandum*, nothing in luck egalitarianism prevents them from doing so. Return to the inability of gays and lesbians to reveal their identity in public without fear and shame. It is a disadvantage to have this disability and an advantage not to have it. But then luck egalitarians can agree that a certain good is at stake and indeed that this good is distributed unequally across gays and lesbians on the one hand and heterosexuals on the other. Admittedly, the relevant good is not like money in that one can take it away from one person and then give what one has taken away to another. Also, there might be nothing more to enjoying equal amount of the relevant presentational good "than standing in certain types of symmetrical social relations with others."[46] But, clearly, the luck egalitarian principle introduced in section 2 leaves open which goods the value of equality is concerned with.[47]

Third, the two previous replies leave Scheffler's fetishism charge unaddressed. However, luck egalitarians can offer a strong reply here, appealing to the issue of intergenerational justice, which was mentioned previously in connection with Rawls's just savings principle. Most agree with Rawls that there is such a thing as intergenerational justice and that, say, we act unjustly if we act in such a way that future generations fall below a certain sufficiency threshold, thereby rendering just institutions impossible in the future. But this view cannot be grounded in our social relations with future generations. While our actions might affect their conditions, they cannot affect us, and that is sufficient for our not being socially related to them. Hence, if there is such a thing as intergenerational justice and these requirements can be cashed out in part in terms of distributive principles, we can discuss the plausibility of distributive principles independently of how distributions are instrumental to or constitutive of certain desirable social egalitarian relations obtaining. Why cannot we then similarly discuss such principles in the intragenerational case?

Fourth, luck egalitarians might also offer a *tu quoque* reply to the fetishism objection. Why is it so important, they might ask, that we relate as equals? Of course, if the alternative is that we relate as masters and slaves, this question is disingenuous. But suppose that the alternative is a slight deviation from the ideal

---

[46] Elizabeth Anderson, "Equality," in *Oxford Handbook of Political Philosophy*, ed. David Estlund (Oxford University Press, 2012), 41.

[47] cf. Kasper Lippert-Rasmussen, "(Luck and Relational) Egalitarians of the World, Unite!," *Oxford Studies in Political Philosophy* 4 (2018), 81–109. Luck egalitarians could adopt a Walzerian view that justice is compartmentalized such that, for any individual type of good, e.g., the ability to reveal one's sexual identity in public without fear or shame, people should be equally well off unless differences in choice warrants deviations from equality.

of relating to one another as equals. Suppose, for instance, that we are marginally more concerned to justify ourselves to some people, for example, friends and family, than to others, for example, strangers. We treat some as only nearly equals in a way, which violates the relational ideal. But why is a concern to avoid this not fetishistic—an odd arithmetic obsession—if the concern that people are not unequally well off through bad luck is fetishistic?

Fifth and finally, luck egalitarians might reply that, even if distributive ideals must be grounded in some wider social and moral ideal, it is unclear why luck egalitarianism cannot be so grounded. Luck egalitarianism, as stated earlier, says nothing about what *makes* a luck-neutralizing distributive pattern one that is required by justice.[48] Hence, luck egalitarian might point to the fact that Anderson in the block quotation notes that distributions might be "constitutive" of attractive social relations. One way to flesh this out is to say that justice requires that citizens can justify their relative distributive positions to one another, where that in turn requires equality of opportunity on some luck egalitarian understanding thereof. On the view proposed here, the attractiveness of luck egalitarian equality of opportunity is grounded in a certain social ideal and thus meets, in principle at least, Scheffler's challenge to friends of the distributive ideal of equality.

Suppose luck egalitarianism can be defended against the challenges from relational egalitarians. This merely means that certain objections to the view can be defeated, and this leaves open whether there is any positive reason to accept it. Is there? Something like Rawls's principle of redress captures an important influential intuition, to wit, that is unfair that some people end up worse than others through no choice or fault of their own. In support of the intuitive force of this idea consider the phenomenon of survivor guilt. According to Michael Otsuka:

> Survivor guilt is a feeling that it is not fair that one was spared over others who were no less worthy. "Why me and not them?" . . . survivor guilt does not arise when everyone is spared. Nobody, for example, would feel survivor guilt if an asteroid whose impact would have obliterated all of humanity were unexpectedly to veer from a collision course with our planet. People would, however, feel survivor guilt if a meteor shower killed neighbors while sparing them. When some are randomly killed and others spared, this is bad not only because it is bad to be killed but also because it is unfair that some are killed and others spared. It would have been better in one respect because fairer, even though of course not all things considered better, if everyone had been killed.[49]

---

[48] As Scheffler notes, for Dworkin, the distributive ideal of equality is grounded in a wider, but hierarchical, and, for that reason, unattractive ideal about how the state should relate to its subjects, to wit, that it should treat citizens with equal concern and respect, albeit as objects of administration.

[49] Michael Otsuka, "Equality, Ambition and Insurance," *Proceedings of Aristotelian Society*, suppl. vol. 78 (2004), 151–152.

This is the sort of basic intuition that underpins luck egalitarianism and which makes scattered, disputed appearances in Rawls's *A Theory of Justice*.

It is, admittedly, a further question what we owe to one another in light of the fact that, in all sorts of ways, we are unequally well off due to differential brute luck. However, as suggested, one response is to say that we should relate to one another in such a way that we can justify our relative distributive positions to one another and that, ceteris paribus, we can do so only to the extent that we have eliminated the differential influence of brute luck on our lives to the greatest extent possible. Such a view, even if it does not condemn pure natural inequality—by definition, we cannot do anything about these differences (though we can mitigate or eliminate the disadvantages they typically involve)—is clearly luck egalitarian in spirit.[50] Moreover, it is grounded in a certain ideal of how we should relate to one another.

6. Conclusion

In this chapter, I have argued that Rawls's theory of justice is incompatible with luck egalitarianism. However, I have also argued that Rawls in his justification for his theory of justice ascribes a greater role to considerations about neutralizing differential luck than that implied by the negative view proposed by Scheffler. In closing, I submitted that some of the main objections to luck egalitarianism recently canvassed by relational egalitarians can be defused and, indeed, that luck egalitarianism is firmly grounded in strong intuitive responses such as those captured by Rawls's principle of redress and the phenomenon of survivor guilt.

Acknowledgments

I thank Jon Mandle and Sarah Roberts-Cady for useful comments on a previous version of this chapter.

---

[50] Rawls, *A Theory of Justice*, 88.

8

The Point of Justice

On the Paradigmatic Incompatibility between Rawlsian "Justice as Fairness" and Luck Egalitarianism

Rainer Forst

John Rawls famously claimed that we need to look for a "conception of justice that nullifies the accidents of natural endowment and the contingencies of social circumstance as counters in quest for social and economic advantage," as these aspects are "arbitrary from a moral point of view."[1] Luck egalitarians believe that a conception of justice that eliminates the effects of circumstance but not of choice, or, in Ronald Dworkin's words, that is "endowment-insensitive" and "ambition-sensitive,"[2] captures that intuition better than Rawls's own principles of justice. G. A. Cohen even went so far as to say that Rawls "was not (really) investigating the nature of justice as such"[3] when he stopped pursuing his luck egalitarian intuition and went into the business of constructing "rules of social regulation"[4] that took many other things into account besides pure justice.[5]

In what follows, I argue that the opposite is the case. As I show in section 1, we can learn from Rawls that one cannot overcome moral arbitrariness in social life by using or implementing a morally arbitrary distinction between choice and circumstance or between ambition and endowment, which is why he never made use of such a distinction in his conception of justice. Rather, he argued that principles of justice should be *chosen* (or constructed) in an "original position" that "ensures that no one is advantaged or disadvantaged in the choice of principles by the outcomes of natural chance or the contingency of social circumstances."[6] That does not mean that these principles eradicate such chances

---

[1] John Rawls, *A Theory of Justice* (Harvard University Press, 1971), 15. In this chapter, references will be to the original edition of *A Theory of Justice*, as this was the version that the debates I discuss refer to.

[2] Ronald Dworkin, *Sovereign Virtue: The Theory and Practice of Equality* (Harvard University Press, 2002), 89.

[3] G. A. Cohen, *Rescuing Justice and Equality* (Harvard University Press, 2008), 301.

[4] Cohen, *Rescuing Justice and Equality*, 285.

[5] See also Will Kymlicka, *Contemporary Political Philosophy: An Introduction* (Oxford University Press, 1991), chap. 3.1.

[6] Rawls, *A Theory of Justice*, 12.

Rainer Forst, *The Point of Justice* In: *John Rawls*. Edited by: Jon Mandle and Sarah Roberts-Cady, Oxford University Press (2020). © Oxford University Press. DOI: 10.1093/oso/9780190859213.003.0013.

or circumstances or compensate persons for "brute luck" and honor their "option luck";[7] rather, it means that the chosen principles deny that persons have any prerogative in virtue of "natural" or "social" luck, *whatever* such luck is based on, whether it be chance or choice.

In section 2, I argue that the incompatibility between these two approaches points to a deeper difference between a deontological and a teleological paradigm that is relevant for the debate between relational and non-relational notions of political and social justice.

1. The Impossibility of Overcoming Moral Arbitrariness in a Morally Arbitrary Way

One of the major points of Rawls's theory is that there are no valid claims of justice *before* a properly constructed conception of justice is in place that is justifiable between persons without regard to natural luck or social contingency. This is what libertarian critics like Robert Nozick[8] took issue with, especially with Rawls's claim "to regard the distribution of natural talents as a common asset and to share in the benefits of this distribution whatever it turns out to be. Those who have been favored by nature, whoever they are, may gain from their good fortune only on terms that improve the situation of those who have lost out."[9] In the eyes of these critics, this would amount to expropriating individuals and would turn them into the servants of society. And indeed, for Rawls there is no presocial ground—or, better, no ground prior to the construction of a suitable conception of justice—for any claim to what is justly "yours" or what you deserve. According to Rawls, "[n]o one deserves his greater natural capacity nor merits a more favorable starting place in society. But it does not follow that one should eliminate these distinctions. There is another way to deal with them."[10] This "other way" is the way of justice, and Rawls does not argue for this way as a practical concession to what is feasible in human society; rather, his idea is to construct a system of social cooperation in which talents can develop and claims of entitlement can be raised, but only on the basis of a conception of justice that follows a strict imperative of reciprocal and general justification between moral and political equals.

So luck egalitarianism, as seen from a Rawlsian perspective, commits a number of errors.

---

[7] Dworkin, *Sovereign Virtue*, 73.

[8] Robert Nozick, *Anarchy, State, and Utopia* (Basic Books, 1974).

[9] Rawls, *A Theory of Justice*, 101. On this point, see also Rawls's more extensive discussion in *Justice as Fairness: A Restatement*, ed. Erin Kelly (Harvard University Press, 2001), 75–78.

[10] Rawls, *A Theory of Justice*, 102.

1.1 First, it starts either from a presocial notion of "brute bad luck" that serves as a basis for claims to compensation or from a presocial notion of "ambition" that serves as a prepolitical ground of justice claims. But that runs counter to Rawls's essentially social perspective on both phenomena. He argues that the "natural distribution is neither just nor unjust; nor is it unjust that persons are born into society at some particular position. These are simply natural facts. What is just and unjust is the way that institutions deal with these facts."[11] There are no "natural" justice claims—neither for compensation nor that ambition or choice should be honored. Will Kymlicka, for example, argues that people with "natural handicaps," such as people born into a "disadvantaged class or race,"[12] should be compensated for their disadvantage. But there is nothing "natural" about handicaps when it comes to matters of justice. A just society does not compensate persons for a natural injustice; rather, it removes the socially established barriers and (ideally) the assumptions that put people in a descriptive box of the "handicapped." "Natural" differences are an issue for justice because society turns them into social disadvantages; but then the persons affected are not owed compensation for "natural" bad luck but are instead owed the means to be a participating member of society to the greatest extent possible.[13]

The other side of the coin of the presocial and prepolitical view of the grounds of justice claims found in luck egalitarianism is the idea that the choices or ambitions of individuals should be sufficiently honored, assuming that there is some objective measure of "sufficiently." Kymlicka, for example, raises the issue that the difference principle, which states that all inequalities must be justifiable to the worst off as contributions to their greatest benefit, does not take into account the claim of a person who says: "What if I was not born into a privileged social group, and was not born with any special talents, and yet by my own choices and effort have managed to secure a larger income than others?"[14] According to an "ambition-sensitive" luck egalitarianism, this larger income is justified. But according to Rawls it is not, because the claim this person makes falls under the verdict of the moral arbitrariness of any desert or entitlement claim that is raised outside the context of a system of fair social cooperation.

Luck egalitarians try to adopt and use a libertarian argument for egalitarian purposes[15]—but in fact they fall prey to a libertarian idea that gives a prerogative to individual claims as naturalized asocial claims to be rewarded for one's own

---

[11] Rawls, *A Theory of Justice*, 102.

[12] Kymlicka, *Contemporary Political Philosophy*, 72f.

[13] This does not imply that the way Rawls dealt with disabilities was adequate; for a critique, see Martha Nussbaum, *Frontiers of Justice: Disability, Nationality, Species Membership* (Harvard University Press, 2007).

[14] Kymlicka, *Contemporary Political Philosophy*, 58.

[15] G. A. Cohen, *On the Currency of Egalitarian Justice and Other Essays in Political Philosophy* (Princeton University Press, 2011), 32.

efforts unaided by circumstance. In Rawls's view, this is a natural desert claim that has no status as a justice claim—not only because there are no "natural" justice claims of such a kind but also because the distinction between "pure" effort (and choice) and the benefit from personal or social advantage (as circumstance) is, to use Samuel Scheffler's apt phrase, "philosophically dubious and morally implausible."[16] Which brings me to the next point: the distinction is morally arbitrary in Rawls's sense.

1.2 Luck egalitarian writers such as Dworkin are well aware of the difficulties in distinguishing between "choice" and "circumstance." Choices, Dworkin argues, reflect a person's ambition and character: the ambitions "include all his tastes, preferences, and convictions as well as his overall plan of life,"[17] while someone's character includes personality traits that affect the pursuit of ambitions such as "energy, industry, doggedness, and ability to work now for distant rewards."[18] Someone's circumstances, on the other hand, "consist of his personal and his impersonal resources," such as, among the personal ones, "physical and mental health and ability—his general fitness and capacities, including his wealth-talent, that is, his innate capacity to produce goods or services that others will pay to have."[19] According to Dworkin, persons are responsible for their choices as well as for their character traits, but not for their circumstances. And he adds that there are often "formidable difficulties in deciding whether someone's failure to find employment at a decent wage is a consequence of his lack of wealth-talent or his lack of industry and application, for example."[20]

This raises a number of questions. The most important is: Can one ever reliably make such distinctions? How have my tastes, preferences, and convictions been formed, and are they really not just grounds of my choices but *chosen* grounds of my choices, such that I am responsible for these choices and the character traits they are based on? And is talent an "innate" force within me, such that the way it has been formed and developed is pure circumstance and not part of my character, reflecting certain choices? If one traces decisions as choices back to their sources, will one not find many circumstances, and if one traces someone's circumstances, will one not find many choices? And the more one traces both, the more the line between them gets blurred to the point of becoming effaced altogether. And the more one tries to draw the distinction in spite of the never-ending mixtures of the two, the more arbitrary it becomes. And since the distinction does a lot of work in moral and political assessments, its application

---

[16] Samuel Scheffler, *Equality and Tradition: Questions of Value in Moral and Political Theory* (Oxford University Press, 2010), 187.
[17] Dworkin, *Sovereign Virtue*, 322.
[18] Dworkin, *Sovereign Virtue*, 322.
[19] Dworkin, *Sovereign Virtue*, 322f.
[20] Dworkin, *Sovereign Virtue*, 324.

becomes morally arbitrary in Rawls's sense by attaching moral value to a distinction that arbitrarily carves out a space of "pure" choice within an inextricable genealogical combination of personality and social context in a given case. According to Rawls, "character depends in large part upon fortunate family and social circumstances for which [one] can claim no credit."[21] There is no place in Rawls's theory for the idea of pure choice or ambition or character for which one is solely responsible, "since the initial endowment of natural assets and the contingencies of their growth and nurture in early life are arbitrary from a moral point of view. . . . Once again . . . , it seems clear that the effort a person is willing to make is influenced by his natural abilities and skills and the alternatives open to him."[22] Thus, the distinction between "energy" and "industry" as choice-related character traits and endowment and talent as circumstance breaks down, because persons are not "unencumbered" agents of free choice.

This does not mean that Rawls did not hold persons responsible for their choices, since he stresses the autonomy of persons as having two moral powers, namely the capacity for a conception of the good and the capacity for a sense of justice. But Rawls was aware that ascribing responsibility is a matter of a practical attitude of respect toward the other as an equal moral agent, and that this normally means not considering whether a person is guided in her acts by choice or circumstance but assuming that she takes responsibility for her ends, whether chosen or inherited, as in cases of what has been called "expensive tastes": "[T]hat we can take responsibility for our ends is part of what free citizens may expect of one another. Taking responsibility for our tastes and preferences, whether or not they have arisen from our actual choices, is a special case of that responsibility."[23]

1.3 Following Elizabeth Anderson and Jonathan Wolff,[24] I also think that it would be disrespectful, and to some extent unjust, to establish a social order on the distinction between choice and circumstance if—on a counterfactual assumption—we could make it.

A luck egalitarian society could be a veritable dystopia of control and mistrust involving the administration of harsh sanction or broad compensation schemes. All of this violates basic norms of equal respect. First, think of the level and degree of information needed to discover whether some action with consequences relevant for social justice was due to choice or circumstance. That would entail "insulting levels of scrutiny," as Wolff argues,[25] since it would require a panopticon-like institution of social analysis that tracked the actions of persons

---

[21] Rawls, *A Theory of Justice*, 104.

[22] Rawls, *A Theory of Justice*, 311f.

[23] John Rawls, *Political Liberalism*, expanded ed. (Columbia University Press, 2005), 185.

[24] Elizabeth Anderson, "What Is the Point of Equality?," *Ethics* 109 (1999), 287–337; and Jonathan Wolff, "Fairness, Respect, and the Egalitarian Ethos," *Philosophy and Public Affairs* 27 (1998), 97–122.

[25] Wolff, "Fairness, Respect," 112.

as regards their motives and deeper causes. The state might have to enforce a daily protocol on persons to list their reasons for doing this and that and the risks as they saw them, but these protocols would have to be checked by authorities with profound knowledge of the person, the situation, and so on. Such a state would be authoritarian in two respects—on the one hand, because of the intrusion into people's lives, and on the other hand because of the sanctioning and punitive implication with which this was being done.

This leads to the second reason why such a system would be far from establishing justice as based on mutual respect. If the disciplining administration found out that you were reckless or careless in your actions and as a result had an accident that, for example, caused you severe health damage, the luck egalitarian system would regard this as a consequence of your choices, provided that you could not show why your decision really had deeper causes you could not control, such as a bad upbringing or a risk gene. The state would have to differentiate, as Anderson criticizes,[26] between cases of people with severe health problems according to their responsibility for those problems, so that an active smoker would be treated differently from a passive smoker if they both developed lung diseases. Society would turn into a system of blame or excuse, guilt or innocence, with respect to every relevant instance of distribution. For the blameworthy, this would be a very bad combination of an authoritarian and a libertarian state.

That has an implication for the rewarding side of a libertarian-plus-luck-egalitarian system. If persons are successful in their economic activities without being aided by circumstance (another huge counterfactual), as in Kymlicka's aforementioned example, then according to the luck egalitarian view they deserve their special gains as claims of justice. But that could establish social reward systems and hierarchies that are not acceptable from a Rawlsian perspective, because they honor desert claims of dubious justifiability.

A third reason for why such a system would fail to show appropriate respect for individuals as autonomous sources of claims is that it turns claims of justice into claims to compensation, either for the lack of certain personal endowment or for social circumstances that had negative consequences. As Anderson convincingly shows,[27] state agencies explaining to persons why they should be compensated for being physically disabled, less intelligent, or less beautiful than dictated by social norms would be demeaning and reproduce exclusive stereotypes. With respect to the negative effects of social circumstances, the language of compensation is also the wrong language, because it turns social mechanisms like class or racial domination into cases of "bad luck," thereby anonymizing structures of domination and exploitation as if they were mere contingencies whose results

---

[26] Anderson, "What Is the Point," 296.
[27] Anderson, "What Is the Point," 305.

need to be corrected, as is especially apparent in the welfare-oriented versions of luck egalitarianism.[28]

1.4 At this point, luck egalitarians might be inclined to have recourse to Rawls's discussion of what he calls the "principle of redress."[29] The principle states that "undeserved inequalities call for redress; and since inequalities of birth and natural endowment are undeserved, these inequalities are to be somehow compensated for."[30] Rawls regards this as a plausible "prima facie principle."[31] But he argues that better than to try to "eliminate"[32] these personal differences is to use the difference principle, which "is not of course the principle of redress. It does not require trying to even out handicaps as if all were to compete on a fair basis in the same race."[33] Rather, it allows all persons to enjoy their benefits only on the condition that the principles of justice are met, that is, that the principle of equal opportunity and the difference principle especially are satisfied.

The structuring idea behind this notion of social cooperation is that of *reciprocity*.[34] It implies that the "social order can be justified to everyone, and in particular to those who are least favored; and in this sense it is egalitarian."[35] This is connected to a particular aspect of Rawls's theory that luck egalitarianism neglects, namely the idea of what he calls "pure procedural justice." The conception of democratic equality Rawls favors implies that the combination of equal opportunity and the difference principle establishes a basic structure of institutions guided by public rules such that "pure procedural justice" exists, that is, a kind of justice for which no independent criterion for just results exists apart from a notion of just procedures. "The intuitive idea is to design the social system so that the outcome is just whatever it happens to be."[36] The basic structure is one of procedural and reciprocal justice if it is set up in such a way that it establishes a form of social cooperation based on the two principles of justice; and if that is the case, distributive justice is realized in comparison to what Rawls calls "allocative justice." The latter abstracts from "what individuals have done in good faith in the light of established expectations" and asks "whether one distribution of a given stock of things to definite individuals with known desires and preferences is better than another."[37] In the case of justice as fairness, by contrast, "the great practical advantage of pure procedural justice is that it is no longer

---

[28] See, for example, Richard Arneson, "Luck Egalitarianism Interpreted and Defended," *Philosophical Topics* 32 (2004), 1–20.
[29] See Kasper Lippert-Rasmussen, "Rawls and Luck Egalitarianism," in this volume.
[30] Rawls, *A Theory of Justice*, 100.
[31] Rawls, *A Theory of Justice*, 101.
[32] Rawls, *A Theory of Justice*, 102.
[33] Rawls, *A Theory of Justice*, 101.
[34] Rawls, *A Theory of Justice*, 102.
[35] Rawls, *A Theory of Justice*, 103.
[36] Rawls, *A Theory of Justice*, 85.
[37] Rawls, *A Theory of Justice*, 88.

necessary in meeting the demands of justice to keep track of the endless variety of circumstances and the changing relative positions of particular persons. One avoids the problem of defining principles to cope with the enormous complexities which would arise if such details were relevant."[38]

Rawls's argument here is not just a practical one, as luck egalitarians tend to think. Rather, it is based on a certain idea of cooperation as reciprocity within a system of institutionalized public rules that makes it unnecessary to establish individual protocols of transactions and desert or ambition or failure. According to Rawls it is a mistake to aim at such protocols, for only the general features of the basic structure ought to be judged according to principles of justice, but not the situation that individuals occupy within it as a result of chance or choice. Again, we see an important incompatibility between Rawlsian and luck egalitarian accounts of justice, incompatibilities that, I think, point to a deeper disagreement about the point of justice.

2. Two Paradigms of Justice

2.1 There is a fundamental difference between two paradigmatic ways of thinking about political and social justice.[39] The first—and in my view a deficient one— is the result of a particular interpretation of the ancient principle *suum cuique*, which is taken to mean that the primary issue of justice is what goods individuals justly receive or deserve—in other words, who "gets" what. This then leads either to comparisons between people's sets of goods, and thus to relative conclusions, or to the question of whether individuals have "enough" of the essential goods, regardless of comparative considerations. Such goods- and distribution-centered, *recipient-oriented* points of view have their merits, for distributive justice is, of course, concerned with the goods individuals can appropriately claim.

Nevertheless, this paradigm obscures essential aspects of justice. In the first place, the question of how the goods to be distributed come into existence is neglected in a purely goods-focused view; hence issues of production and its just organization are largely ignored.[40] Furthermore, there is the second problem that the *political* question of who determines the structures of production and distribution and in what ways is disregarded, as though a great distribution machine—a neutral "distributor"[41]—could exist that only needs to be

---

[38] Rawls, *A Theory of Justice*, 87.

[39] In the following, I adapt some sections of my "Two Pictures of Justice," in *Justification and Critique: Towards a Critical Theory of Politics* (Polity Press, 2014), chap. 1.

[40] Not all luck-egalitarian theories are guilty of that charge; G. A. Cohen, for example, in a number of his writings, addresses questions of the organization of production. See his *Currency of Egalitarian Justice*, chap. 7.

[41] In a telling phrase from Cohen, *Currency of Egalitarian Justice*, 61.

programmed correctly using the right "metric" of justice.[42] But according to a more thoroughly political understanding of justice, it is not only essential that there should not be such a machine, because this would mean that justice would no longer be understood as a political accomplishment of the subjects themselves but would turn them into passive recipients of goods—but not of justice. This is a point where the often-made distinction between "pure" distributive and political justice[43] has to be problematized, for according to the second paradigm of justice, social justice can only come about through political institutions that are politically just. A benevolent distributive dictator in this view could not establish distributive justice, even if he or she used the right metric, for justice is about the standing you enjoy within the institutional scheme to which you are subject—which necessarily includes your standing as a politically autonomous member who codetermines the basic structure.

The goods-oriented view also neglects, third, the fact that justified claims to goods do not simply "exist" but can be arrived at only through discourse in the context of corresponding procedures of justification in which—and this is the fundamental requirement of political as well as social justice—all can in principle participate as free and equal individuals.

Finally, in the fourth place, the goods-fixated view of justice largely leaves the question of injustice out of account; for, by concentrating on overcoming deficiencies in the distribution of goods, it deems someone who suffers want as a result of a natural catastrophe to be equivalent to someone who suffers want as a result of economic or political exploitation. Although it is correct that assistance is required in both cases, according to my understanding of the grammar of justice it is required in the one case as an act of *moral solidarity*, but in the other as an act of *justice* conditioned by the nature of one's involvement in relations of exploitation and injustice and of the specific wrong in question.[44] Hence there are different grounds for action as well as different kinds of action that are required. Ignoring this difference can lead to a situation in which—in a dialectic of morality, as it were[45]—what is actually a requirement of justice is seen instead as an act of generous assistance or "aid," thus adding insult to injury.

[42] For the first two points, see esp. Iris Young, *Justice and the Politics of Difference* (Princeton University Press, 1990).

[43] For this see Simon Caney, "Justice and the Basic Right to Justification," in Rainer Forst, *Justice, Democracy and the Right to Justification: Rainer Forst in Dialogue* (Bloomsbury, 2014).

[44] Here a whole series of cases would have to be distinguished: direct participation in or (joint) causation of injustice; indirect participation in injustice by profiting from it without oneself actively contributing to relations of exploitation; and the ("natural") duty to put an end to unjust relations, even if one does not benefit from them but possesses the means to overcome them.

[45] See my *The Right to Justification: Elements of a Constructivist Theory of Justice* (Columbia University Press, 2012), chap. 11.

For these reasons, it is especially important when dealing with questions of *distributive* justice to recognize the *political* point of justice and to liberate oneself from a one-sided and truncated notion fixated on quantities of goods (or on a measure of well-being to be produced by them). On a second, fuller, and more apt paradigm, by contrast, justice must be geared to *intersubjective structural relations*, not to *subjective* or *putatively objective states* of the provision of goods or of well-being. Only in this way, by taking into consideration the first question of justice—namely, the question of the justifiability of social relations and, correspondingly, how much "justification power" individuals or groups have in a political context—can a critical conception of justice be developed, one that gets at the roots of relations of injustice. In short, the basic question of justice is not *what you have* but *how you are treated*.[46] Thus, we see that the real difference between the two paradigms of justice is one of teleology versus deontology.

2.2 When it comes to how to decide between the two rivaling paradigms, we need to consider the concept of justice itself. This concept possesses a core meaning to which the essential contrasting concept, as Rawls argued,[47] is that of *arbitrariness*. The second paradigm understands arbitrariness in a social and political sense—that is, as assuming the form of arbitrary rule by individuals or by a part of the community (for example, a class) over others, or of the acceptance of social contingencies that lead to social subordination and domination. A metaphysical conception of arbitrariness in the context of social justice would go further, as luck egalitarianism does, and aim to eradicate or compensate for all differences between persons that give some an advantage over others due to brute luck, regardless of whether the differences in question lead to social domination.

The term "domination" is important in this context, because it signifies the arbitrary rule of some over others—that is, rule without proper reasons and justifications and (as a higher-order form of domination) without proper structures of justification existing in the first place.[48] When people engage in struggles against injustice, they are combating forms of domination of this kind. The basic impulse that opposes injustice, according to the second paradigm, is not primarily one of wanting something, but is instead that of not wanting to be

---

[46] Derek Parfit's distinction between a "telic" and a "deontic" egalitarian view captures important aspects of these different ways of thinking about justice, and it is interesting to note that—without commenting explicitly on this—he uses the term "justice" only in connection with the deontic view. See his "Equality or Priority?," in *The Ideal of Equality*, ed. Matthew Clayton and Andrew Williams (Palgrave, 2002), 90.

[47] See Rawls's definition: "Those who hold different conceptions of justice can, then, still agree that institutions are just when no arbitrary distinctions are made between persons in the assigning of basic rights and duties and when the rules determine a proper balance between competing claims to the advantages of social life" (*A Theory of Justice*, 5).

[48] I explain the difference between such a discourse-theoretical understanding of domination and a neorepublican one based on freedom of choice in Rainer Forst, *Normativity and Power: Analyzing Social Orders of Justification* (Oxford University Press, 2017), chap. 10.

dominated or overruled in one's claim to a *basic right to justification*.[49] This moral right of persons as equal normative authorities expresses the demand that no political or social-economic relations should exist that cannot be adequately justified toward those involved. This constitutes the profoundly *political* essence of justice, which is not captured, but rather is suppressed, by the recipient-focused interpretations of the principle *suum cuique*, whether of a luck egalitarian or sufficientarian kind.

2.3 Since Nozick's influential critique, Rawls's theory has often been interpreted as belonging to the first, allocative-distributive and recipient-oriented, paradigm of justice. Nozick criticizes Rawls's principles of justice as "end-state principles" that correspond to pregiven patterns that illegitimately constrain the liberty of market participants.[50] Even Thomas Pogge regards Rawls's as a "purely recipient-oriented approach," because it concentrates on comparisons between distributive results as regards basic goods.[51] This assessment has a certain justification, given the importance of primary goods in Rawls's theory. Nevertheless, Rawls does not share the first but rather the second paradigm of justice, the one that accords priority to social structures and relations and the social status of the individual within such a scheme of cooperation. The main reason for this is the Kantian character of his theory, based on the idea that persons are equal normative authorities when it comes to the construction of principles for a basic structure of society.

In the first place, the Kantian character of Rawls's theory implies that the autonomy of free and equal persons, which is at the normative heart of the approach, is not the autonomy of individuals who are primarily conceived as recipients of goods that they would need in order to lead a "good life." It is rather the *constructive autonomy* of free and equal subjects of justification that manifests itself in the fact that individuals are able to regard the principles of justice as morally self-given; hence, the citizens view the social basic structure as the social expression of their self-determination.[52] The relevant conception of autonomy is that of the autonomy to actively determine the basic structure, not that of the autonomy to enjoy its goods. The emphasis on public reason in the later works underscores this, because public reason represents the medium of discursive justification in which an autonomous conception of justice that all can accept as free and equal individuals is grounded: "In affirming the political doctrine as a whole we, as citizens, are ourselves autonomous, politically speaking."[53]

---

49   I explain this more fully in Forst, *The Right to Justification*.

50   Nozick, *Anarchy, State, and Utopia*, 149ff. Young, *Justice*, 28, agrees with Nozick in criticizing end-state theories (to which in her view the Rawlsian belongs).

51   Thomas Pogge, "The Incoherence between Rawls's Theories of Justice," *Fordham Law Review* 72 (2004), 1739.

52   Rawls, *A Theory of Justice*, §40.

53   Rawls, *Political Liberalism*, 98.

An important aspect of the Kantian background of the theory consists in the aim of excluding the aspects of the social world that seem "arbitrary from a moral point of view" both in justifying the principles and in the institutions of the basic structure, as shown previously. In this way differences in natural endowments and social inequalities should not lead to advantages that cannot be legitimized, especially toward the worst off. This is a criterion for social relations between citizens of a "well-ordered society," not primarily a criterion for determining the amounts of goods to which everyone can lay claim as an independent metric of justice.[54]

With this we arrive at the most important concept as regards the Kantian character of the theory, namely that of social cooperation as a system of reciprocity. As we saw in the context of the discussion of the principle of redress, Rawls's conception of "procedural justice" is geared to social relations and structures. It leads to a system of social cooperation that expresses the "sociability of human beings" in such a way that they complement each other in productive ways and participate in a context of cooperation that includes all as politically and socially autonomous members—think of the picture of the orchestra employed by Rawls as an ideal of social cooperation.[55] In the *Restatement* of his theory, he comes back to the contrast between his conception of justice as fairness and a conception of "allocative justice":

> The problem of distributive justice in justice as fairness is always this: How are the institutions of the basic structure to be regulated as one unified scheme of institutions so that a fair, efficient, and productive system of social cooperation can be maintained over time, from one generation to the next? Contrast this with the very different problem of how a given bundle of commodities is to be distributed, or allocated, among various individuals whose particular needs, desires, and preferences are known to us, and who have not cooperated in any way to produce those commodities. This second problem is that of allocative justice. . . . We reject the idea of allocative justice as incompatible with the fundamental idea by which justice as fairness is organized. . . . In a well-ordered society . . . the distribution of income and wealth illustrates what we may call pure background procedural justice. The basic structure is arranged so that when everyone follows the publicly recognized rules of cooperation, and honors the claims the rules specify, the particular distributions of goods that result are acceptable as just . . . whatever these distributions turn out to be.[56]

---

[54] See also Scheffler, *Equality and Tradition*, 195f.
[55] Rawls, *A Theory of Justice*, §79.
[56] Rawls, *Justice as Fairness*, 50.

The overriding issue within such a context of production and distribution is who the individuals "are," and not primarily what they receive according to an independent yardstick that theories such as luck egalitarian ones provide. The point is that the institutions function in accordance with justified principles, such as the difference principle, and do not involve any social privileges, and that they do not lead to the creation and cementing of groups that are excluded from the system of cooperation and permanently depend on allocative transfers of goods. This is also what underlies Rawls's criticism of the capitalist welfare state model, because this, in contrast to a "property-owning democracy," does not ensure that the ownership of wealth and capital is sufficiently dispersed and as a result cannot prevent "a small part of society from controlling the economy, and indirectly, political life as well."[57]

2.4 At this point, however, we can ask whether Rawls's theory sufficiently accommodates the principle that social asymmetries are in need of justification and provides for corresponding institutional practices of justification. I have my doubts about that and would argue for a discourse-theoretical conception of justice that differs from Rawls's theory in central aspects while nevertheless remaining true to its deontological spirit. However, I will have to leave this argument for another occasion.[58]

Acknowledgments

I am grateful to Sarah Roberts-Cady, Jon Mandle, Amadeus Ulrich, Felix Kämper, and Ciaran Cronin for their helpful comments and questions.

[57] Rawls, *Justice as Fairness*, 139.
[58] See especially my *Right to Justification* and *Justification and Critique*.

PART V
THE CAPABILITY CRITIQUE

Introduction

Any egalitarian theory of justice must have some measure by which one can determine whether a system of social cooperation is fair or not. In particular, one must have some metric by which to tell if a system is working to the advantage or disadvantage of a citizen, or as John Rawls puts it, we need "an idea of each participant's rational advantage, or good."[1] One important debate among political philosophers is about how to conceive of this metric. Rawls relies on the idea of "primary goods" as a measure of advantage, but other philosophers have argued for other measures such as welfare or capabilities. This section of the book will explore this debate.

A central assumption of justice as fairness is that reasonable individuals have a wide variety of comprehensive values, so they do not share any particular conception of the good. Since they disagree about how to measure overall success in life, this presents a problem for measuring when individuals are being treated fairly. Rawls introduces the idea of "social primary goods" to respond to this problem. The idea is to have a measure that is not dependent on any one particular conception of the good. Rawls's list of social primary goods includes "a. basic rights and liberties . . . b. freedom of movement and free choice of occupation . . . c. powers and prerogatives of offices and positions of responsibility . . . d. income and wealth . . . e. the social basis of self-respect."[2]

There are two basic (and related) roles that the idea of primary goods plays in justice as fairness. First, the veil of ignorance prevents the parties in the original position from assessing conceptions of justice on the basis of their own particular conception of the good. They fall back, therefore, on the idea of primary goods, which they assume will be valuable no matter which (reasonable) conception of the good they turn out to hold. So the parties in the original position are motivated to select principles that will secure primary goods. Second, in a well-ordered society, citizens will use the principles of justice to evaluate publicly the justice of their basic institutions. In order to apply the principles, and specifically in order to identify the least advantaged position in society, they will measure and compare people's positions by expected shares of social primary goods over a complete life.

---

[1] John Rawls, *Political Liberalism*, expanded ed. (Columbia University Press, 2005), 16.
[2] Rawls, *Political Liberalism*, 181.

Introduction In: *John Rawls*. Edited by: Jon Mandle and Sarah Roberts-Cady, Oxford University Press (2020). © Oxford University Press. DOI: 10.1093/oso/9780190859213.003.0014.

Although these roles and the core list of primary goods have not changed significantly over the course of Rawls's writing, the justification for them has been revised. In *A Theory of Justice*, Rawls writes that the primary goods are "things that every rational man is presumed to want. These goods normally have a use whatever a person's rational plan of life."[3] In other words, the primary goods have an instrumental value for a wide range of conceptions of the good, and possibly intrinsic value for some. Thus, the parties in the original position can rely on them because "The preference for primary goods is derived . . . from only the most general assumptions about rationality and the conditions of human life."[4] Starting in 1982,[5] and continuing through *Political Liberalism* in 1993, there was an important development. In the "Preface to the Revised Edition" of *A Theory of Justice*, Rawls observes that the original account "left it ambiguous whether something's being a primary good depends solely on the natural facts of human psychology or whether it also depends on a moral conception of the person that embodies a certain ideal."[6] Rawls favors the latter in his more recent work. Looking for a possible empirical overlap of existing conceptions of the good would make justice as fairness "political in the wrong way."[7] Instead, justice as fairness relies on a certain model of the person (or citizen), which includes two "higher-order interests" in developing and maintaining their capacity for a sense of justice and capacity for a conception of the good (their two "moral powers"). These interests are viewed as "normally regulative and effective" because without them an individual "cannot be a normally and fully cooperating member of society over a complete life."[8] Social primary goods are necessary not only to achieve the contingent ends that individuals happen to have, but more importantly they are necessary to realizing these higher-order interests that are tied to a normative ideal of the person.

If all egalitarian theories of justice require a measure of individual advantage, why not directly measure it in the form of happiness, preference satisfaction, or utility, for example? Consistent with the diversity of conceptions of the good, this would have to be a formal measure, not assuming any particular content. This may seem appealing since individuals want primary goods, in the typical case, not for their own sake but for the sake of realizing their higher-order interests and their particular conception of the good. Furthermore, an equal share of primary goods by no means ensures citizens an equal level of success

---

[3] John Rawls, *A Theory of Justice*, rev. ed. (Harvard University Press, 1999), 54.

[4] Rawls, *A Theory of Justice*, 223.

[5] See "Social Unity and Primary Goods," in *Collected Papers*, ed. Samuel Freeman (Harvard University Press, 1999).

[6] Rawls, *A Theory of Justice*, xiii.

[7] Rawls, *Political Liberalism*, 39–40.

[8] Rawls, *Political Liberalism*, 74.

in achieving their ends. For example, other things equal, an individual with expensive preferences will require a larger share of resources to achieve a level of satisfaction equal to one whose preferences can more easily be satisfied. Rawls has two objections to such a proposal. First, recall that the measure of primary goods is to be used by citizens in assessing the fairness of their institutions. Thus, it is important to "find workable criteria for interpersonal comparisons that can be publicly and, if possible, easily applied."[9] An individual's share of social primary goods is public in a way that a measure of subjective satisfaction is not. The information necessary to make such judgments "is difficult if not impossible to obtain, and often there are insuperable problems in reaching an objective and agreed assessment."[10] Second, Rawls rejects the idea that those with preferences that are difficult or expensive to satisfy are necessarily entitled to a greater share of social resources. Justice as fairness does not "view citizens as passive carriers of desires."[11] Rather, as part of "the moral power to form, to revise, and rationally to pursue a conception of the good," for purposes of political justice they "assume responsibility for their ends."[12] Justice as fairness relies on "a social division of responsibility" where "society, citizens as a collective body, accepts responsibility for maintaining the equal basic liberties and fair equality of opportunity, and for providing a fair share of the primary goods for all . . . ; while citizens as individuals and associations accept responsibility for revising and adjusting their ends and aspirations in view of the all-purpose means they can expect, given their present and foreseeable situation."[13]

In 1979, Amartya Sen delivered his "Tanner Lecture" (published in 1980) titled "Equality of What?,"[14] in which he is critical both of theories that rely on utility and of Rawls's reliance on primary goods. "Primary goods," he writes, "suffers from fetishist handicap in being concerned with goods . . . rather than with what these good things *do* to human beings. Utility, on the other hand, *is* concerned with what these things do to human beings, but uses a metric that focuses not on the person's capabilities but on his mental reaction."[15] Reliance on primary goods neglects the fact that "people seem to have very different needs varying with health, longevity, climatic conditions, locations, work conditions, temperament, and even body size (affecting food and clothing requirements)."[16] "What is missing," he suggests, "is some notion of 'basic capabilities': a person

---

[9] Rawls, *Political Liberalism*, 186.
[10] Rawls, *Political Liberalism*, 162.
[11] Rawls, *Political Liberalism*, 186.
[12] Rawls, *Political Liberalism*, 186.
[13] Rawls, *Political Liberalism*, 189.
[14] Amartya Sen, "Equality of What?," in *The Tanner Lectures on Human Values*, vol. 1, ed. Sterling McMurrin (University of Utah Press, 1980).
[15] Sen, "Equality of What?," 218.
[16] Sen, "Equality of What?," 215–216.

being able to do certain basic things."[17] This alternative is perhaps most compelling in the case of an individual with a disability requiring significant medical or social support for whom an equal share of resources might not translate into an equal ability to pursue one's ends. A focus on capabilities would respond to the differential needs in a way that a focus on resources would not. As Ingrid Robeyns puts the point: "Since ends are what ultimately matters when thinking about well-being and the quality of life, means can only work as reliable proxies of people's opportunities to achieve those ends if they all have the same capacities or powers to convert those means into equal capability sets."[18]

More recently, the capabilities approach has been developed by Martha Nussbaum. She is far more specific than Sen in listing ten "central human functional capabilities," including, among others, life, bodily health, bodily integrity, "being able to use the senses, to imagine, think, and reason," "being able to live with concern for and in relation to animals, plants, and the world of nature," and play.[19] Nussbaum intends the list to be endorsed "by people who otherwise have very different views of what a complete good life for a human being would be."[20] In other words, although she presents this as a rival to the primary goods of justice as fairness, like justice as fairness, it is a form of political liberalism.[21] On the other hand, she recognizes that it is not "a complete theory of justice." Rather, it is designed to identify a threshold of "a decent social minimum in a variety of areas."[22] This is not inappropriate, as both Sen and Nussbaum focus primarily on societies where large numbers of people fall below this threshold. Still, as Robeyns points out, Nussbaum's "theory is partial and simply leaves unaddressed the question what social justice requires once those thresholds are met."[23]

Rawls has several replies to this challenge, but most importantly he indicates that the contrast is perhaps not as deep as his critics have suggested. In fact, he says: "I agree with Sen that basic capabilities are of first importance and that the use of primary goods is always to be assessed in the light of assumptions about those capabilities."[24] Elsewhere he notes that "the account of primary goods does take into account, and does not abstract from, basic capabilities: namely, the capabilities of citizens as free and equal persons in virtue of their two moral

---

[17] Sen, "Equality of What?," 218.

[18] Ingrid Robeyns, "The Capability Approach," *Stanford Encyclopedia of Philosophy*, https://plato.stanford.edu/entries/capability-approach/, sec. 2.3, accessed January 16, 2019.

[19] Martha Nussbaum, *Women and Human Development: The Capabilities Approach* (Cambridge University Press, 2000), 78–80. See also *Creating Capabilities* (Harvard University Press, 2011), 33–34.

[20] Nussbaum, *Women and Human Development*, 74.

[21] Nussbaum, *Creating Capabilities*, 89–93.

[22] Nussbaum, *Women and Human Development*, 75. See also *Creating Capabilities*, 40.

[23] Robeyns, "The Capability Approach," sec. 3.3.

[24] Rawls, *Political Liberalism*, 183.

powers."[25] Rawls also stresses the flexibility of primary goods, indicating the possibility of expanding the list "to include other goods, for example, leisure time, and even certain mental states such as freedom from physical pain."[26] In addition, the integration of the various primary goods into a single "index" occurs not a priori, or even from the point of view of the original position, but rather at the "legislative stage" of the four-stage sequence when specific information (economic, social, historical, etc.) about the particular society is available.[27] Thus, Rawls believes that a proper understanding of primary goods allows for the flexibility necessary to respond to the more concrete forms of deprivation that Sen and Nussbaum highlight.

As Robeyns points out, however, it remains true that people will have different abilities to convert their primary goods into well-being and the quality of their lives. The question is what significance this has for political justice. For relatively small variations that do not affect persons' ability to be "fully cooperating members of society,"[28] Rawls holds that justice does not require that we equalize prospects for well-being. In part, this is related to his rejection of the "principle of redress"[29]—see the discussion of luck egalitarianism in Part IV of this volume— as well as his skepticism that there can be a practical, public measure that is sufficiently fine-grained to respond to differences in such capabilities. In the case of larger variations in capabilities, in which some individuals are not able fully to participate in social cooperation, he holds that justice requires taking steps to restore them to that level.[30]

In his more recent discussions of the provision of healthcare, which is barely mentioned in A Theory of Justice, Rawls follows the work of Norman Daniels. One obvious possibility for addressing healthcare would be to identify it as a social primary good, but Daniels argues this is unnecessary.[31] Instead, he focuses on the fact that the provision of healthcare is necessary in order to achieve fair equality of opportunity, as Rawls's second principle requires. The distribution of material resources governed by the difference principle is subordinated to the fair (and not merely formal) equality of opportunity, and both are at the service of the broader goal "to put all citizens in a position to manage their own affairs and to take part in social cooperation on a footing of mutual respect under

[25] John Rawls, Justice as Fairness: A Restatement, ed. Erin Kelly, (Harvard University Press, 2001), 169.
[26] Rawls, Political Liberalism, 181–182. See also Justice as Fairness, 172, where Rawls mentions healthcare and "measures ensuring public health (clean air and unpolluted water, and the like). All of these items can (if necessary) be included in the index of primary goods."
[27] Rawls, Political Liberalism, 185.
[28] Rawls, Justice as Fairness, 170.
[29] Rawls, A Theory of Justice, 86.
[30] Rawls, Political Liberalism, 184, 186.
[31] See Just Health Care (Cambridge University Press, 1985), 45, 57. Thanks to Jenny Tillman for discussion of this point.

appropriately equal conditions."[32] When this is recognized, Daniels argues, "There is more convergence than difference between an account of justice and health that focuses on opportunity, properly construed, and one that sees the target of justice as protecting human capabilities."[33] This is not to say that there are no differences between these approaches, but only that they are close relatives in the family of liberal theories of justice.

In this volume, Christopher Lowry explores Sen's capability critique, carefully specifying the nature of the disagreement between Rawls and Sen and the implications of Sen's criticisms for Rawls's theory. Lowry offers a solution to the disagreement by way of a modification of Rawls's theory that he calls "public value perfectionism." Offering a different perspective, Tony Fitzpatrick argues that both the capabilities approach and the primary goods approach face an "elasticity problem" to which he does not think there is an ideal solution. In short, he argues that neither view has the flexibility to address all the types of problems one may want a theory of justice to address. He offers up a multiperspectivist way of moving forward.

Suggested Reading from Rawls to Accompany These Chapters

A Theory of Justice: §§11, 15, 28, 60, 63, 67
Political Liberalism: Lecture V, §§1–4
Justice as Fairness: §§17, 45, 46, 51–53

For Further Reading

Brighouse, Harry, and Ingrid Robeyns, eds. *Measuring Justice: Primary Goods and Capabilities*, (Cambridge, 2010). This collection includes a variety of perspectives comparing the use of primary goods and capabilities in theories of justice.

Claassen, Rutger. "Making Capability Lists: Philosophy versus Democracy." *Political Studies* 59 (2011), 491–508. This article addresses a question internal to the capabilities approach: whether the list of capabilities should be drawn up through democratic deliberation or by relying on a philosophical theory.

---

[32] Rawls, *A Theory of Justice*, xv.
[33] Norman Daniels, "Capabilities, Opportunity, and Health," in *Measuring Justice*, ed. Harry Brighouse and Ingrid Robeyns (Cambridge University Press, 2010), 131. Compare Erin Kelly, "Equal Opportunity, Unequal Capability," in Brighouse and Robeyns, *Measuring Justice*, 78: "When a capabilities approach appeals to shared political values and avoids comprehensive conceptions of the good, it would appear not to differ much from a primary goods approach."

Kaufman, Alexander, ed. *Capabilities Equality: Basic Issues and Problems* (Routledge, 2006). This collection of essays addresses fundamental issues and objections concerning the capabilities approach.

Nussbaum, Martha. *Creating Capabilities: The Human Development Approach* (Harvard University Press, 2011). Nussbaum is one of the most important defenders of the capabilities approach, and this is her most complete statement of her view.

Robeyns, Ingrid. "The Capability Approach: A Theoretical Survey." *Journal of Human Development* 6 (2005), 93–117. Focusing on the work of Sen and Nussbaum, this is a valuable overview of the issues facing the capabilities approach.

Sen, Amartya. "Justice: Means vs. Freedoms." *Philosophy and Public Affairs* 19 (1990), 111–121. Along with Nussbaum, Sen is the most influential defender of the capabilities approach, and this is an early and influential argument for relying on capabilities rather than primary goods.

9

Sen's Capability Critique

Christopher Lowry

Rawls takes citizens to be *normal and fully cooperating participants* in social cooperation—where the first part of this conjunction means having "physical needs and psychological capacities within the normal range."[1] By rejecting Rawls's bracketing of disability, Sen's capability approach is able to widen the range of inequalities it can acknowledge. A theory must first give us the tools to acknowledge inequalities before it can help us determine whether they are unfair. I will provide an interpretation of the disagreement between Rawls and Sen that departs somewhat from how they and others typically present it. My view is that the disagreement can best be understood by focusing on Rawls's remarks about the value of liberties and Sen's remarks about a public ranking of valuable functionings.

Rawls and the Value of Liberties

Consider this passage from *Theory*:

> The inability to take advantage of one's rights and opportunities as a result of poverty and ignorance, and a lack of means generally, is sometimes counted among the constraints definitive of liberty. I shall not, however, say this, but rather I shall think of these things as affecting the worth of liberty, the value to individuals of the rights that the first principle defines. . . . [T]he worth of liberty to persons and groups depends upon their capacity to advance their ends within the framework the system defines. . . . Taking the two principles together, the basic structure is to be arranged to maximize the worth to the least advantaged of the complete scheme of equal liberty shared by all. This defines the end of social justice.[2]

---

[1] John Rawls, *A Theory of Justice*, rev. ed. (Harvard University Press, 1999), §16: 83–84.
[2] *A Theory of Justice*, §32: 179; cf. John Rawls, *Justice as Fairness: A Restatement*, ed. Erin Kelly (Harvard University Press, 2001), §45: 149.

Christopher Lowry, *Sen's Capability Critique* In: *John Rawls*. Edited by: Jon Mandle and Sarah Roberts-Cady, Oxford University Press (2020). © Oxford University Press. DOI: 10.1093/oso/9780190859213.003.0015.

The point of justice as fairness is to secure people's basic liberties and then give worth, or value, to those liberties. The first principle has two parts: equal basic liberties and fair value of political liberties. The second principle also has two parts: fair equality of opportunity and the difference principle. The first of these four parts—equal basic liberties—secures people's basic liberties. The other three parts give value to those liberties. I will explain.

Equal basic liberties provide people with, among other things, formal equality for political participation, which means an absence of discriminatory legal obstacles, such as voting restrictions based on gender or race or personal wealth. It is not enough, however, that all members of society have the same political liberties; Rawls is also concerned with people's ability to make use of them—in other words, the value political liberties have for them. The government is required to take action to increase the likelihood that people's level of success in politics will correlate only with their talent for and dedication to politics. For example, to prevent people from buying political influence, Rawls argues that political campaigns must be publicly funded and that the government must use taxes and inheritance laws to prevent excessive concentrations of wealth.[3]

To determine whether the government has done enough to achieve fair value of political liberties, society would need to measure people's success in politics and then examine whether inequalities in success correspond to such factors as gender, race, wealth, and so on. The government might therefore collect data on voting participation, candidates, elected representatives, appointed political officials, and other indicators of success in politics. Whenever there is excessive correlation between patterns of success and a factor other than talent for or dedication to politics, the government must consider whether to take further action toward achieving fair value of political liberties.

Next, consider fair equality of opportunity. Rawls enters into discussion of opportunity in order to specify the meaning of "open to all" in the sentence "Social and economic inequalities are to be arranged so that they are . . . attached to positions and offices open to all."[4] He notes that "open to all" might be interpreted to mean "careers open to talents," according to which the opportunity to compete for jobs is only formally equal (as guaranteed by equal basic liberties). Since the competitive process related to careers begins at school, school-related opportunities are also relevant here. (Later on, we will consider an expanded reading of opportunity.) I will refer to liberties related to work and school as *occupational liberties*. Rawls is concerned not only with whether everyone has the same occupational liberties, but also with people's ability to make use of them. Fair equality of opportunity aims makes sure that the value occupational liberties have for you

---

[3] Rawls, *Justice as Fairness*, §§45 and 49.4.
[4] Rawls, *A Theory of Justice*, §11: 53.

is not affected by factors such as your gender, race, parents' wealth, and so on.[5] The government is required to take action to increase the likelihood that people's level of occupational success will correlate only with their talent for and dedication to the career(s) they pursue.

To achieve fair equality of opportunity, the government must, for example, either prohibit private schools or make sure that public schools are of equivalent educational quality. To decide between these two actions, the government would need to measure people's success in school and work, and then examine whether inequalities in success correspond only to people's talent and dedication, and not to such factors as familial wealth, gender, race, and so on. The government might therefore collect data on high school graduation, postsecondary graduation, income, unemployment, leadership positions, and other indicators of success. Whenever there is excessive correlation between patterns of success and a factor other than talent and dedication, the government must consider whether to take further action toward achieving fair equality of opportunity.

Finally, consider the difference principle. Since political and occupational liberties are addressed by prior principles, the difference principle, in effect, concerns only inequalities in the value of other liberties, which I will refer to as *civil liberties*.[6] Civil liberties are about leading your life outside of school, work, and politics, in pursuit of your conception of the good. Justice as fairness does not guarantee the fair value of civil liberties.[7] Greater income and wealth give you greater ability to make use of your civil liberties by giving you a wider range of valuable options in your social and personal life. Instead of aiming to give fair value to civil liberties, the difference principle permits (and demands) inequality in the value civil liberties have for different people in order to maximize the value civil liberties have for the least advantaged.

To determine whether the government has done enough to satisfy the difference principle, society would need to measure changes over time in the value civil liberties have for the least advantaged. One way to do this would be to identify indicators of success in social and personal life. Justice as fairness is designed to avoid this. Instead, Rawls explicitly assumes, as an idealization, that all citizens have physical and mental abilities "within the normal range" and then concludes, since money is an all-purpose means, that a given amount of money gives the same value to civil liberties for any two people. On that basis, justice as fairness takes your level of income and wealth to be adequate evidence of the value civil

---

[5] *Fair value of political liberties* could just as easily be called *fair equality of political opportunity*. Likewise, *fair equality of (occupational) opportunity* could just as easily be called *fair value of occupational liberties*. To guarantee the fair value of a certain type of liberties is to secure fair equality of the corresponding opportunity, and vice versa.

[6] My usage may not match the ordinary usage of the term *civil liberties*.

[7] Rawls, *Justice as Fairness*, §46.

liberties have for you. For example, freedom of movement has greater value for wealthier persons, because their money gives them a better set of travel options. To evaluate implementation of the difference principle, the question then becomes whether the government has done all it can to increase the income and wealth of the least advantaged (without running afoul of the prior principles).

It is worth reflecting on why civil liberties are approached differently by Rawls. To measure success in social and personal life, we would need to appeal to ideas of the good that are beyond what could be included in a political, rather than comprehensive, conception of justice. (Rawls uses the term *political* in a technical sense here, rather than the ordinary sense it has when he writes about political liberties.) The political conception of society views a society as a fair system of social cooperation, and views a person as a citizen who is able to be a fully cooperating participant therein by working with others and being fair to them. Societies and persons are obviously much more than this, but the political conception of society can be agreed upon without needing to reach agreement on the complete nature and value of humans and society. Ideas of the good can "worked up" from the political conception of society and then included in a political conception of justice as political values—political in the technical sense. The value of occupational and political liberties can be judged using political values; but the value of civil liberties cannot. I will explain why.

Consider how we might think about success in school, work, and politics. One way would be to use a complete conception of the good to assess how *occupational goods* and *political goods* contribute to your well-being. Surely they do. This approach is not open to Rawls, because he does not seek to defend a comprehensive conception of justice, and so must appeal only to political values. Concerning occupational goods, being able to develop skills and use them in the labor market is something people need *as citizens* when society is understood as a fair system of social cooperation. The same is true for the ability to be fair and to do one's part to create and sustain just institutions. This is how a significant part of the value of occupational and political goods can be explained without appeal to a complete view of well-being.

In contrast, the entire importance of *civil goods* comes from their contribution to your well-being. Civil goods are not meant to help you be able to be a fully cooperating participant. Rather, you participate in social cooperation in order to earn resources for enjoying civil goods in pursuit of your conception of the good. This is why the value of civil liberties cannot be judged using political values. And that is why justice as fairness is designed to avoid the need to identify indicators of success in social and personal life.

Some things that can be valued as a civil good can also be valued as a political or occupational good. For example, consider a café. It is a place where you can (i) be employed, (ii) have a business meeting, (iii) meet to politically organize, or

(iv) enjoy leisure time. In the first two respects it is an occupational good, in the third a political, and in the fourth a civil. Justice as fairness can value a café qua occupational good or political good, but not qua civil good, because this would involve taking a stand about its importance for well-being. The theory is also unable to value things that are *mere* civil goods—whose value comes entirely from their contribution to your well-being.

Sen and a Public Ranking of Valuable Functionings

Sen offers the idea of capability as way to think about *the extent of freedom*. As we will see, this is essentially the same as Rawls's idea of the value of liberties. To explain the idea of capability, we should start with *functionings*.

Functionings are *doings* or *beings*. A *doing* is any action; a *being* is any physical or mental state. These are descriptive terms. A trivial action, like bending your finger, is just as much a doing as a monumental action, like giving birth. A harmful state, like starving or being homicidal, is just as much a being as beneficial state, like being well-nourished or having self-respect.

To have a complete description of the kind of life people lead, you would need to have a complete record of the functionings they achieve—that is, all their physical and mental states and everything they do. Sen uses the term *achieve* broadly to include functionings that happen with or without assistance from other people. For example, infants who are fed well by their parents are said to *achieve* the functioning of being well-nourished.[8]

To turn a record of a person's achieved functionings into an assessment of well-being, you would need to judge how valuable each functioning is. Sen uses the term *valuation function* for one set of such judgments. If you are evaluating one person's well-being, the valuation function would be the person's own judgments about the value of the person's functionings. To do interpersonal comparisons of well-being, there must be an agreed-upon valuation function. Sen argues that it is impossible to do "inter-valuation-functional" comparisons of well-being involving two or more valuation functions at once.[9]

It is humanly impossible to have a valuation function that lists and ranks all valuable functionings. An incomplete valuation function can have significant practical implications. That being said, we will see later on that there is reason to include more, rather than fewer, valuable functionings.

---

[8] Amartya Sen, "Capability and Well-Being," in *The Quality of Life*, ed. Martha Nussbaum and Amartya Sen (Oxford University Press, 1993), 43.

[9] Amartya Sen, *Commodities and Capabilities* (North-Holland, 1985), 58.

We are now in a position to examine Sen's idea of *capability*. He describes it as *the freedom to achieve well-being* or *the freedom to lead the kind of life you have reason to value.*[10] Suppose you knew not only the combination of functionings a person actually achieves, but also all the other possible combinations of functionings that person could have achieved instead. This is called a *capability set*. A person's capability is about the alternative combinations of functionings the person has the freedom to achieve. How do we assess how good the set of alternatives is? Sen rejects the *count method*, according to which a larger set is always better, because there is an obvious and compelling sense in which people are given more freedom by a smaller number of options they judge to be valuable than by a larger number of options they judge to be detrimental or worthless.[11] The evaluation of capability sets requires judging the value of the options themselves.[12] In order to use the idea of capability to inform government action, we would need a public list of valuable functionings and a public ranking of those functionings.

How would all of this work? It is difficult to gather information about people's capability set directly, because it is hard to know what functionings they *could have but chose not to* achieve. Instead, a society can examine information about achieved functionings in order to reach conclusions about capability. For example, if a particular functioning is achieved by a significant number of people, and if no social group is disproportionately represented among the people who do not achieve it, this indicates that all people have the capability related to this functioning. If, instead, a social group is overrepresented among people who do not achieve this functioning, this suggests that there may be a group-linked obstacle blocking this capability. The government must then consider whether to take action to address this obstacle.

It is important to note that a society's ability to put the idea of capability into practice is made possible—and, at the same time, is limited—by the content of the public ranking of valuable functionings. This is because a larger capability set is judged to be better (i.e., to give more freedom) than a smaller capability set only if the functionings that are found in the larger one and are missing in the smaller one are recognized as valuable. Recall Sen's rejection of the count method. If those extra functionings are not on the public list, then the larger set is judged to be merely numerically larger, but not better. If a group-linked inequality manifests only in terms of functionings that are not on the public list, then capability theory would be unable to acknowledge that inequality. This can be a reason in favor of a longer, rather than shorter, public list.

---

[10] Amartya Sen, *Development as Freedom* (Anchor Books, 1999).
[11] Amartya Sen, *Rationality and Freedom* (Harvard University Press, 2002), 13.
[12] Sen, "Capability and Well-Being," 35.

Rawls and a Public Ranking of Valuable Functionings

Is justice as fairness opposed to a public ranking of valuable functionings? Rawls does not address this explicitly. I will argue that justice as fairness could support a public ranking of valuable functionings related to political and occupational goods, but not civil goods.

In our discussion of fair value of political liberties we saw that society would need to gather information about indicators of success and then look for patterns that suggest that the value of political liberties is affected by wealth, gender, race, and so on. Those indicators simply are valuable functionings in politics. The patterns in question are about inequality in achieved political functionings, which may indicate inequality in the freedom to achieve valuable political functionings. Talking about how much value political liberties have for different people is the same as talking about people's capabilities related to political participation.

Much the same is true of occupational liberties. When we identify indicators of success in school or work, what we are doing is making a list of valuable occupational functionings. Fair equality of opportunity is about capabilities related to school and work.

In contrast, Rawls's view is opposed to a public ranking of valuable civil functionings. Justice as fairness is designed to avoid the need to identify indicators of success in social and personal life. Civil functionings are valuable because of their importance for a person's well-being, and so cannot be identified and ranked by appealing only to political values. Civil functionings that can be valued qua occupational or political functionings could be included on a Rawlsian list, although they might be ranked lower than they would have been if their full value were acknowledged. Functionings that are about *mere* civil goods could not be included on a Rawlsian list. Justice as fairness assumes that people's income and wealth is adequate evidence of their freedom to achieve valuable civil functionings.

An Expanded Reading of Fair Equality of Opportunity?

Let us consider whether fair equality of opportunity should be given an expanded reading, according to which it includes some civil goods.[13] This would allow justice as fairness to value some things qua civil goods, which means some valuable civil functionings could be included on a Rawlsian public list. I will consider

---

[13] I thank Sarah Roberts-Cady and Jon Mandle for raising these points.

whether there is support for this in Tommie Shelby's work on race and Norman Daniels's work on health and disability.

Shelby writes that in order to fully achieve fair equality of opportunity in the United States in a way that addresses racial injustice, especially as experienced by African Americans, institutional reforms would have to include, among other things, "aggressive measures to address discrimination in . . . housing and lending."[14] Shelby is surely right, but I do not think he is advocating for *fair* equality of opportunity in housing and lending, because this would require the government to take steps to make sure that people's success in housing is determined only by their talent for and dedication to housing, and is unaffected by, among other things, their income and wealth. Perhaps the best houses would go to the best architects regardless of money. This is not Shelby's position. Instead, what is needed is formal equality in housing and lending—which ought to be guaranteed by equal basic liberties—in combination with fair equality of occupational opportunity. Such formal equality, Shelby notes, would place demands not only on the content of rules that regulate institutions related to housing and lending, but also to those institutions *as realized*.

When the distorting effects of racial prejudice and bias pervade the operation of an institution, the institution as realized is itself unjust, notwithstanding the justice of its rules and procedures when viewed abstractly.[15]

Fair equality of occupational opportunity ensures that people's income and wealth are not influenced by their racial identity; and formal equality in housing and lending ensures that people's ability to secure loans and acquire housing depends only on their finances and is unaffected by their racial identity.

Daniels aims to improve Rawls's ability to address illness and disability.[16] Rawls cites Daniels favorably.[17] Daniels broadens fair equality of opportunity, so that it requires society to meet people's health needs when doing so will help them have a fair share of the *normal opportunity range*, which is "the array of life plans reasonable persons are likely to develop for themselves."[18] He argues that guaranteeing people fair opportunity shares is a vital part of what they need in order to be "normal, fully functioning members of society."[19] If, for example, social meetings in cafés or in private homes play an important social role in a

---

[14] Tommie Shelby, "Race and Social Justice: Rawlsian Considerations," *Fordham Law Review* 72 (2004), 1711.

[15] Shelby, "Race and Social Justice," 1706.

[16] Norman Daniels, *Just Health: Meeting Health Needs Fairly* (Cambridge University Press, 2008).

[17] Rawls, *Justice as Fairness*, §51.6: 175 n. 58.

[18] Daniels, *Just Health*, 43.

[19] Norman Daniels, *Justice and Justification: Reflective Equilibrium in Theory and Practice* (Cambridge University Press, 1996), 216.

particular society, then we might say that these civil goods should be included in the normal opportunity range; and this could provide support for requiring the accessibility of these and other socially significant spaces for the sake of making sure everyone has the ability to participate as a free and equal citizen.[20]

One question this raises is how a civil good would be identified as being one that has an important social role. On the one hand, we could say that a civil good has an important social role if it makes an important well-being contribution to social or personal life. If we do this, then we are identifying indicators of success in social and personal life. This is what the use of primary goods is supposed to allow justice as fairness to avoid. If we take this route, the normal opportunity range becomes equivalent to the idea of capability, which, indeed, Daniels acknowledges.[21] On the other hand, the civil good might be valued qua political or occupational good, and not qua civil good. We might say, for example, that having access to socially significant spaces is an occupational and political good, because social networks grow out of social events, and such networks have importance in politics, work, and school. This takes us back to my reading of fair equality of opportunity as involving only occupational goods.

Conversion Factors

Sen argues that justice as fairness is insensitive to the fact that there is significant *interindividual variation* with respect to people's ability to convert resources into the freedom to achieve well-being. We can rephrase Sen's objection as being precisely about Rawls's approach to measuring the value of civil liberties. The key claim in the objection to Rawls is, then, that a given level of income and wealth does not give the same value to civil liberties for different people. Such interindividual variation exists among the members of the least advantaged (as well as at every other level of income and wealth). It therefore affects society's ability to accurately measure the value civil liberties have for the least advantaged. This, in turn, affects society's ability to determine whether its government has done enough to satisfy the difference principle. This variation can be explained using the idea of *conversion factors*.

Ingrid Robeyns distinguishes between three types of conversion factors: *personal, environmental,* and *social*.[22] To illustrate, imagine you are a wheelchair user in a society that makes no effort to be inclusive of people with disabilities.

---

[20] I thank Sarah Roberts-Cady and Jon Mandle for this point.
[21] Daniels, *Just Health*, 66–71.
[22] Ingrid Robeyns, "The Capability Approach: A Theoretical Survey," *Journal of Human Development* 6 (2005), 99.

You must pay out of pocket for your wheelchair and related expenses, which reduces your ability to convert your income into the freedom to achieve valuable civil functionings. This is a personal conversion factor. Your ability to make use of civil liberties is further reduced by the inaccessible design of many public spaces. This is an environmental conversion factor. The prevalence of ableist attitudes further shrinks the range of valuable civil functionings you have the freedom to achieve. This is a social conversion factor. Your *conversion ability* (i.e., your ability to convert resources into the freedom to achieve well-being) is affected by the interaction between all three types of conversion factors. If you are nondisabled, your income gives more value to your civil liberties, or, in other words, opens up a larger range of valuable civil functionings. Not all conversion factors are related to disability, but the importance of giving justice to disabled members of society is enough by itself to fuel the capability critique; and so I will focus on disability-related conversion factors.

Disability

The disadvantage that is attached to disability can be lessened by addressing any or all of the three types of conversion factors. For example, consider the capability to participate in a recreational basketball league with a $60 registration fee at a community center that lacks accessible design. If you are a wheelchair user, then you would not be able to convert $60 into this functioning. Some actions society could take to change this are

(i) Offering publicly funded medical treatments to restore the use of your legs (if such treatments exist),
(ii) Offering publicly funded assistive devices or technologies that allow you to stand, walk, run, and jump (if such devices or technologies exist),
(iii) Making the community center physically accessible,
(iv) Introducing a recreational wheelchair basketball league,
(v) Purchasing a set of basketball wheelchairs for public use, and
(vi) Doing outreach to change attitudes so that the wheelchair basketball league is enjoyed by good numbers of nondisabled players as well as wheelchair users.

The last of these addresses social factors, (iii)–(v) address environmental factors, and the first two address personal factors.

What if playing in a recreational basketball league is not a functioning that is included in the public ranking of valuable functionings? Recall Sen's rejection of the count method. The mere fact that one capability set is numerically larger than another tells us nothing about whether it is better. We must know whether the extra functioning in the larger set is valuable. If the public ranking does not recognize playing in a recreational basketball league as a valuable functioning, then adding that functioning to a capability set would make it merely larger, not *better*. Only a theory that can first acknowledge an inequality can help us argue that society should take action to reduce that inequality. Capability theory's ability to do this is made possible—and, conversely, is limited—by the content of the public ranking of valuable functionings. If disability shrinks a person's capability set, capability theory is able to count this as disadvantageous only insofar as the lost functionings are recognized as valuable by the public ranking.

This brings into focus the practical significance of the disagreement between Rawls and Sen. That disagreement is best thought of as being about how to value civil functionings. Rawls seeks to avoid generating a public ranking of valuable civil functionings; Sen shows the importance of doing so. And so, if disability shrinks a person's capability set in a way that blocks valuable civil functionings, Rawls's view cannot help us argue that society should take any of the actions (i)–(vi) in cases where what is at stake are mere civil goods—that is, those that are important only for social and personal life.

Consider personal conversion factors. Imagine that you, by birth, illness, or injury, are able to walk but not run. A medical treatment exists that could allow you to run. It is unlikely that Rawls's view could recognize running as a valuable functioning, because you need not run in order to fully participate in school, work, or politics. And so, the treatment would not be publicly funded; although treatments that provide a level of mobility that is important for school, work, or politics would be. For similar reasons, there would be public funding for standard prosthetics and assistive devices, but not for prosthetics or assistive devices that are specially designed for allow people to participate in recreational activities (unless, of course, this is valued qua occupational or political good). In short, a Rawlsian government could be called on to take action to address personal conversion factors only if they affect people's occupational or political life.

Concerning environmental conversion factors, consider the question of how many spaces should be accessible. One might well want to argue that all spaces that could be made accessible, should be. A Rawlsian public ranking could not support this. In order to recognize the inaccessibility of a given space as disadvantageous to people who cannot access it, the functionings that are blocked by the inaccessibility must be recognized as valuable. If a space is important only for civil goods, then having access to it is a civil functioning that would not be on a Rawlsian list.

What all this shows is that Rawls's desire to avoid the need to identify valuable civil functionings (i.e., indicators of success in social and personal life) makes his theory unable to address disability-related inequalities in the value that civil liberties have for people. The severity of this limitation in the theory depends on (a) how often civil goods can be valued qua occupational or political goods and (b) to what extent this results in an underappreciation of the importance of civil goods so valued.

Public Value Perfectionism

Rawls's desire to avoid identifying valuable civil functionings is motivated by his antiperfectionism—that is, his desire to avoid appealing to ideas of the good that are not political values. The worry can be thought of as follows. A public ranking of valuable civil functionings is likely to excessively reflect ideas of the good from the dominant group in society. If such a ranking were put to use in the implementation of the difference principle, the outcome would favor the dominant group's conception of the good. This goes directly against Rawls's requirement that a reasonable person or group shall not use political power to advance their own conception of the good. The worry is avoided when the value of civil liberties is measured in terms of income and wealth.

As we have seen, avoiding this worry in this way renders the theory unable to adequately address conversion factors related to civil functionings. Is this cost too great? My view is that at least when the conversion factors are related to disability, it is.

A compromise position is possible. I call it *public value perfectionism*. I propose to leave the two parts of Rawls's second principle as is—including the use of income and wealth to measure the value of civil liberties for the sake of implementing the difference principle—and to add third part. This third part, which I will call *the inclusion principle*, would require society to take action to reduce disability-related inequalities in conversion ability related to civil functionings. To implement the third part—and only this part—there would be a public ranking of valuable civil functionings.[23] Such a ranking could not be generated using political values. Instead, a society would use what I call *public values*. I will explain the difference.

Political values have two key features. First, citizens are asked to affirm political values *for political purposes* without also being asked to affirm them for other purposes, such as forming and pursuing a complete conception of the good. Second, political values are "worked up" from the political conception of society. Public values lack the second feature, but have a restricted version of the first—namely, citizens are asked to affirm them *for one political purpose* without

---

[23] Public rankings of political and occupational functionings would already be needed because of fair value of political liberties and fair equality of opportunity.

also being asked to affirm them for other purposes (including other political purposes). The purpose in question is to reduce the disadvantage attached to disability.

For public values to have this feature, the right question must be asked when generating the public list of valuable civil functionings. The question is not "Is it important for me to achieve this functioning?" This focuses too narrowly on what you think contributes to your good. The question is not "Is it important for people to have the freedom to achieve this functioning?" This focus is too broad, because it suggests that society might seek, as a general aim, to promote the civil functionings on the public list. The risk of advancing the dominant group's conception of the good would be too great. The question should be "Is it important that disability not block people from having the freedom to achieve this functioning?" This question makes it clear that the public ranking is used only to guide government action to address disability-related conversion factors. You could support government action to reduce disability-related barriers to a recreational activity, while at the same time being opposed, on antiperfectionist grounds, to the idea that the activity should be generally encouraged using government power. For example, you could support accessibility requirements for ski hills and public funding for sit-skis, and so support a public ranking that includes alpine skiing as a valuable civil functioning; and at the same time, you could oppose the idea that the government should provide a general subsidy to reduce the cost of skiing for all skiers.

The use of public values to implement the inclusion principle would be a constrained form of perfectionism. The alternative is a theory that is unable to see—and therefore unable to address—disability-related inequalities in the value of civil liberties. This is the key question raised by Sen's capability critique: should such inequalities be ignored in order to avoid (even a constrained form of) state perfectionism?

10

Specters of Democracy

Detouring the Limitations of Rawls and the Capabilities Approach

Tony Fitzpatrick

The apparently simple question that Amartya Sen posed in the late 1970s—equality of what?—spawned numerous philosophical discussions. The one we are concerned with here, Rawls and the capabilities approach (CA), is also incredibly vast.

According to the CA, people's well-being is shaped not simply by what they have (resources) but by what they are realistically capable of doing and being. A resource-based approach is charged with tending toward a "single metric"; as if justice merely requires a fair distribution of income or property. And by excluding disabled people from what he called the "normal range of functionings," Rawls implied that justice for those outside that range was somehow supplementary to questions of justice for those within it. For CA advocates, justice actually implies improving *all* individuals' ability to do and to be.[1]

By contrast, Rawls himself seemed adamant that there was nothing about the concept of capabilities that was not already encompassed within that of the primary social goods—called "primary goods" here.[2] The primary goods were what everyone needed to be fully functioning citizens in the first place.

As a way of getting to grips with this debate, I am going to explore how those interested in policy studies (analysis of the making, implementation, and effects of government policies) might approach it. To this end, the exploration will invoke another fundamental question: what do we want a theory of justice to do? I will propose that policy studies should want any theory to do lots of different, possibly incommensurable, things. To illustrate this point, I will argue that both Rawls and the CA wrestle with an "elasticity problem" to which there is no final, ideal solution. That being the case, there is no all-purpose, one-size-fits-all

---

[1] Martha Nussbaum, *Frontiers of Justice* (Harvard University Press, 2006); Amartya Sen, *The Idea of Justice* (Allen Lane, 2009).

[2] John Rawls, *Justice as Fairness: A Restatement*, ed. Erin Kelly (Harvard University Press, 2001), 168–176.

Tony Fitzpatrick, *Specters of Democracy* In: *John Rawls*. Edited by: Jon Mandle and Sarah Roberts-Cady, Oxford University Press (2020). © Oxford University Press. DOI: 10.1093/oso/9780190859213.003.0016.

theory, and instead we ought to imagine the existence of an intellectual space I call the "manifold." I will sketch this manifold and the "spectral traits" needed to navigate it. The implication of this, in relation to policy studies, is a *permanent redemocratization* of the policy process.

The Elasticity Problem

How should that debate be addressed? Since there are good things to be said about both Rawlsian and CA accounts, where might this take us? In the absence of an overarching, grand narrative, there seem to be two realistic options: we either choose sides or imagine a hybrid alternative.

Nelson suggests that the apparent pluralism of the CA masks significant similarities between it and Rawls.[3] It does not matter where you draw the line—three primary goods/capabilities or thirty?—because there is a weakness underpinning both perspectives:

Neither primary goods nor "central capabilities" are things we all want no matter what else we want; the act of making a list is therefore inherently sectarian.[4]

Sectarianism is ultimately inevitable, Nelson suggests, because moral egalitarianism (all persons should be able to pursue their version of the good life without coercion) and economic egalitarianism (a more equal distribution of wealth, requiring coercion) cannot coexist in the same theory. We cannot have everything we might want.

Rawls was arguably sensitive to this problem and that is perhaps why he later reframed his as a "political" conception and, years later, refused to apply the difference principle (his version of economic egalitarianism) to the "law of peoples."[5] This shift was regretted by those who thought the difference principle made a vital contribution to our understanding of justice.[6]

Advocates of the CA are also sensitive. Robeyns acknowledges that a list of capabilities imposes a comprehensive view of the good life that will inevitably exclude some views.[7] Sen takes a step back, therefore, thinking that the solution

---

[3] Eric Nelson, "From Primary Goods to Capabilities: Distributive Justice and the Problem of Neutrality," *Political Theory* 36 (2008), 93–122.

[4] Nelson, "Primary Goods," 115.

[5] cf. Martha Nussbaum, "Introduction," in *Rawls's "Political Liberalism"*, ed. Thom Brooks and Martha Nussbaum (Columbia University Press, 2015), 18.

[6] Thomas Pogge, "The Incoherence between Rawls's Theories of Justice," *Fordham Law Review* 72 (2004), 1739–1759.

[7] Ingrid Robeyns, "Equality and Justice," in *An Introduction to the Human Development and Capability Approach*, ed. Severine Deneulin and Lila Shahani (Routledge, 2009), 100–112; Andrew Williams, "Dworkin on Capability," *Ethics* 113 (2002), 39.

is to invoke "freedom," some aspects of which may not even be covered by the vocabulary of capabilities.[8]

If Nelson is correct, the traditional framing of the debate—primary goods versus capabilities—is misleading. It is idle to characterize the former as restrictive and the latter as flexible and pluralistic. A list of each can arguably be expanded or contracted as needs must. For example, those attracted to primary goods and a resources-based approach are not necessarily bound by Rawls's own restrictions. Though they may be *primary* goods, our account of them does not have to assume narrowness and inflexibility.

Instead, the real framing is about how extensive or restrictive our list (of goods/capabilities) ought to be. The more fundamental question, then, is this: should our conception of justice be parsimonious or nonparsimonious? This brings us to the elasticity problem.[9]

Although in doing so we are trying to be inclusive, the more items we place on our list, the more conceptually, methodologically, and empirically imprecise our formulation risks becoming.

For instance, when formulating her "central capabilities" Nussbaum says that they must be "pluralist about value" but do "not tell us what to value" because "freedom has intrinsic value."[10] Yet there are ineliminable tensions here between pluralism, nonprescription, and intrinsicality.

Let's say we favor pluralism. This means, for instance, permitting Muslim women to wear niqabs and burkas. Such dress may be freely chosen reflections of religious devotion, and so consistent with the intrinsic value of women. Or they may deny Muslim women the same intrinsic rights and dignity accorded to Muslim men.[11] If the latter, then we have favored pluralism at the cost of intrinsicality, yet, either way, surely we cannot help but prescribe. Is a ban discriminatory or likely to amend religious discrimination?

Now, Nussbaum is aware of these tensions.[12] She denotes them as "tragic choices" and says that they can only be resolved "on the ground," within each context, so that "we create a future in which this sort of choice does not confront people." Yet this builds a utopian aspiration on top of a standard recourse. If our job really is to create a minimal threshold of justice, then surely some pluralisms must be ruled out; that is, there are inevitable limits to inclusivity, and some ways

---

[8] Amartya Sen, "Human Rights and Capabilities," *Journal of Human Development* 6 (2005), 152–153.

[9] See Robeyns, "Equality and Justice"; also Rutger Claassen and Marcus Düwell, "The Foundations of Capability Theory: Comparing Nussbaum and Gewirth," *Ethical Theory and Moral Practice* 16 (2013), 496.

[10] Martha Nussbaum, *Creating Capabilities* (Harvard University Press, 2011), 18, 25, 28.

[11] Prohibitions on Islamic face veils came into force in France and Denmark in 2010 and 2018 respectively.

[12] Nussbaum, *Creating Capabilities*, 37–39.

of living must be prescribed above others. If so, the distinction between "central capabilities" and a Rawlsian "single metric of justice" appears less important than Nussbaum insists.

Yet if we go to the opposite extreme, if we are too restrictive in our list's formulation, then we potentially miss things of importance to considerations of justice, equality, and whatever makes for a good life.

For example, Rawls formulates a "thin theory of the good" in that, while there are ends at which all rational people should aim (such as good health and education), for the most part we should we concerned with *deliberative means* rather than with advocating a particular version of the good life.[13] Rawls then combines this with an "Aristotelian principle" whereby it is rational to cultivate and realize our "higher capacities."[14] We might term this combination a "thin perfectionism": human flourishing implies nurturing and mastering the higher capacities made possible through the exercise of deliberative reason.

This may explain why Rawls was subsequently amenable to the idea that only those who performed—or at least wished to perform—an eight-hour working day could count as members of the "least advantaged" and so receive the benefits distributed according to the difference principle.[15] Laboring for a wage is more rational and more conducive to flourishing than surfing all day.

What this thereby rules out are both nonthin and nonperfectionist versions of the good. Nonthinness implies having available to us—from a socioeconomic shelf of possibilities—substantive opportunities to pursue a wider range of versions of the good life.[16] Leisure time could thus be reconceived as a "real freedom" rather than the waste of potential characterized by Rawls. Nonperfectionism implies that there are many ways of realizing the capacities of human nature and that aiming at flourishing is not always necessary. We may surf to become good surfers or we may just want to mess around and have fun.

Hence, a nonthin, nonperfectionism might lead us to conceptions of justice, equality, and the good based upon some form of hedonic utilitarianism.[17]

In short, according to the elasticity problem, there are significant problems with having a long list *and* a short list of goods/capabilities. Can we, somehow, have both? Can we retain the precision of a short list while incorporating

---

[13] e.g. John Rawls, *A Theory of Justice*, rev. ed. (Harvard University Press, 1999), 395–399.

[14] Rawls, *A Theory of Justice*, 424–433.

[15] John Rawls, *Political Liberalism*, expanded ed. (Columbia University Press, 2005), 15–22; Rawls, *Justice as Fairness*, 179.

[16] Philippe van Parijs, *Real Freedom for All* (Oxford University Press, 1995).

[17] Tony Fitzpatrick, *How to Live Well: Epicurus as a Guide to Contemporary Social Reform* (Edward Elgar, 2018).

what a long list aims for, the "thick and deep" complexities and diversities of social life?

To address this possibility, let us now assume that Nelson is wrong and that it is possible and desirable to develop a nonsectarian hybrid model.[18] Have attempts at rapprochement between Rawls and the CA successfully addressed the elasticity problem?

Rapprochement 1

What of those who start with Rawls and work toward the CA? Here, attempts have been made to refine the content and scope of primary goods.

Daniels has attached opportunities, liberties, rights, income, and wealth to health needs and healthcare.[19] So, rather than equality across *all* capabilities, we should protect "individuals from certain impairments of their capabilities."[20] Being flexible about the meaning of the "normal range" means that the concept of primary goods "provides people with the capabilities required of free and equal citizens."[21] Far from being unduly restrictive, therefore, Rawls is committed to a political and therefore pluralistic reading of what it means to be a citizen.

So Daniels does not extend the list of primary goods—since this might undermine consensus about what all people need to be citizens—but he does seek to enhance the meaning of "fair equality of opportunity."

Capabilities theorists may well bristle at this.[22] Though Sen and Nussbaum disagree about what it implies, both start with a "thicker," more contextualized account of the capabilities than that provided by Rawls's abstract conceptualizations and highly formalized treatment of political and social institutions. Advocates of the CA revel in the experiential and in the methodological challenges presented by social life as it is lived.[23] It makes more sense to start from where we are, they might argue, than to abstract yourself and then work back to the places we

---

[18] Martin Binder and Alex Coad, "Disentangling the Circularity in Sen's Capability Approach: An Analysis of the Co-evolution of Functioning Achievement and Resources," *Social Indicators Research* 103 (2011), 328.

[19] Norman Daniels, "Equality of What: Welfare, Resources, or Capabilities?," *Philosophy and Phenomenological Research* 50 (1990), 273–296; Norman Daniels, *Just Health* (Cambridge University Press, 2008).

[20] Daniels, "Equality of What," 283.

[21] Daniels, *Just Health*, 66, 70–71.

[22] Sridhar Venkatapuram, *Health Justice: An Argument from the Capabilities Approach* (Polity Press, 2011).

[23] Tania Burchardt, "Incomes, Functionings and Capabilities: The Well-Being of Disabled People in Britain," PhD diss., London School of Economics, 2005; Solava Ibrahim, "Introduction," in *The Capabilities Approach: From Theory to Practice*, ed. Solava Ibrahim and Meera Tiwari (Palgrave Macmillan, 2014).

already occupy. Daniels's rapprochement therefore begins from the wrong point, they could claim.

As an alternative to Daniels's approach, Blythe refines the content and scope of the primary goods themselves.[24] He makes a distinction between those capabilities most directly relevant to free and equal citizenship and those that are related to well-being and flourishing more generally. "Citizenship capabilities" therefore become folded into the domain of primary goods and debates about society's basic structure. A "known range" of disadvantages—including those deriving from differing physical and mental abilities—can now be more firmly integrated into deliberations about principles of justice.[25] "Well-being capabilities" remain important, but more in terms of how those principles should be applied in practice.

One possible criticism is that Blythe retains an underlying bias toward an homogenized, highly generalized notion of rationality and reasonableness that risks becoming thin, abstract, and therefore banal. If well-being implies flourishing, then for someone's citizenship capabilities to flourish we must appreciate that well-being and citizenship are entangled from the outset. To separate them out is to neglect this entanglement. Flourishing for Jamie, a young, transgender activist, is profoundly different than for Kurt, a white, culturally conservative nationalist. Only in a trite sense can we abstract from their particularities to specify the citizenship capabilities they share. Their well-being is thus not a post-original position appendage; instead, their flourishing *constitutes who they are*—their rationalities are always embodied.

Hence, Blythe's "known range" arguably reproduces Rawls's partition between what lies inside and outside the "normal range." Even if we invite more capabilities into the former, Blythe's distinction between two types of capabilities may be inherently debilitating, potentially undermining what made the concept so valuable in the first place. We are always citizens in the context of particular locations and identities.

A strict defender of the CA, then, might complain that both Daniels and Blythe have acknowledged the importance of the CA but, in order to claim that the Rawlsian framework can accommodate it, have only skimmed the surface of the CA's critique. They aim at something nonparsimonious but fall short. For Sen and Nussbaum, being a free and equal citizen could imply that the meanings of "free," "equal," and "citizen" are far less restrictive than Rawlsians imagine.

---

[24] Mark Blythe, "The Means to Social Justice: Accounting for Functional Capabilities in the Rawlsian Approach," *Canadian Journal of Political Science* 41 (2008), 1010–1013.
[25] Blythe, "Means to Social Justice," 1014.

Rapprochement 2

Instead, therefore, should we start with the CA and work our way toward some modified version of Rawls?

Nussbaum and Sen accuse Rawls of unjustly excluding from view those who do not lie within the normal range.[26] Better to begin with the dignity of every human, respect for which means recognizing and valuing the pluralisms through which they come to be themselves. This means making room for those who do not fall within the normal range, including disabled people. We might expand the index of primary goods, but if our inclination is to retain Rawls's initial formulation, then we risk casting a net too small to capture the full scale of the moral community and the panoply of activities that make a life worth living.

So Nussbaum seeks to preserve what is valuable about Rawlsian justice within an alternative (Aristotelian) framework. Does this rapprochement succeed?[27]

According to Nussbaum, those who prefer a resources-based approach tend to emphasize the thinglike properties of resources.[28] The CA has therefore contributed to the increasingly popular view that GDP is an imperfect measure of national prosperity and household income an imperfect measure of a person's capacity to flourish. Yet, in doing so, advocates of the CA risk downgrading the importance of income and wealth, a risk carrying with it two potential costs: political and methodological.

The political cost is in part extraneous to the CA. The CA was surely inspired by the politics of diversity that increasingly characterized political and philosophical debate in the 1970s and 1980s.[29] Given the hole into which class politics and the material-distributive paradigm had dug themselves, this new politics was initially a breath of fresh air. Yet while we are more sensitive than we once were to intersections of various identities and diversities, the cross-sectional zones of relative stability—the hubs and nodes in the structural stratification of dis/advantages—have all too often been neglected. To put it simply, class-specific disadvantages and political strategies of disempowerment have been disregarded.[30] Some intersections remain more important than others, particularly in an era of capitalist globalization. Yet you will struggle to find much reference in Sen and Nussbaum to "class" and "capital" (however, see footnote 33 below).

---

[26] Nussbaum, *Frontiers of Justice*, 108–127; and Sen, *The Idea of Justice*, 260–262.

[27] See Tony Fitzpatrick, "From Contracts to Capabilities and Back Again," *Res Publica* 14 (2008), 83–100; and Tony Fitzpatrick, *Climate Change and Poverty* (Policy Press, 2014), 21–35, for longer accounts of the following critique.

[28] Nussbaum, *Frontiers of Justice*, 50–51.

[29] Robeyns, "Equality and Justice."

[30] Hartley Dean, "Critiquing Capabilities: The Distractions of a Beguiling Concept," *Critical Social Policy* 29 (2009), 271–273.

Of course, there are hardly many references in Rawls either. Yet his critics cannot have it both ways. You cannot consistently criticize someone for over-emphasizing income and wealth while denying that the subject of criticism articulated a stronger approach to distributive justice in socioeconomic relations.

The potential methodological cost is as follows. It is now widely accepted that well-being depends upon much more than the cash or cash equivalents available to you. Hence the need to go "beyond income" when researching the causes of, symptoms of, and solutions to poverty and social exclusion.[31] This is partly why Sen and Nussbaum accuse Rawls of seeking a "list of things," including income and wealth.[32]

Their case is poorly evidenced, however.[33] Hence, regardless of whether Rawls thought in such terms or not, the CA risks adopting this characterization as its own. Income and wealth sometimes become fixed in CA arguments either as objects (notes, coins, or numbers in an account) or as a rigid tool of statisticians and economists. Yet income and wealth are not "things," they are social relations: symbols of, and weapons deployed within, structured systems of social class power that shape not only external endowments (opportunities and liberties) but also our internal sense of worth in relation to others.

If this criticism is reasonable, then the accusations of rigidity that the CA throws at the Rawlsian primary goods might be unfounded or at least underdeveloped. Hence, like Daniels and Blythe, Nussbaum falls short of the hybridity for which she aims.

Sectarians After All?

So have any of these attempts at rapprochement between Rawls and the CA addressed the elasticity problem? Not successfully, because there is no way in

---

[31] Tania Burchardt, "Time, Income and Substantive Freedom: A Capability Approach," *Time and Society* 19 (2010), 318–344.

[32] See also David Levine and S. Rizvi, *Poverty, Work, and Freedom* (Cambridge University Press, 2005).

[33] See Fitzpatrick, "Contracts to Capabilities." This claim as criticism of Rawls can stand. However, Burchardt and Hick have recently said that "income and wealth must be retained as measures of economic inequality, but supplemented by measures of achievements and power in other dimensions as well." Tania Burchardt and Rod Hick, "Inequality, Advantage and the Capability Approach," *Journal of Human Development and Capabilities* 19 (2018), 38–52. Yet although they say a few things about socioeconomic power, their claim to offer "an analysis of power that goes beyond purely economic means" implicitly treats "the economic" as a distributional matter rather than as a political strategy of disempowerment (Burchardt and Hick "Inequality," 39). Interestingly, Robeyns has more to say on this score. Ingrid Robeyns, "Having Too Much," in *Wealth (NOMOS LVI)*, ed. Jack Knight and Melissa Schwartzberg (New York University Press, 2017), 6–10. Hopefully, such interventions will influence future research and commentary.

which any all-purpose, one-size-fits-all list (of goods/capabilities) can fulfill every role that we should want a theory of justice to fulfill.

Daniels and Blythe are not wrong in proposing that the concept of primary goods is more flexible than its critics allow while insisting that, without a stable core of enduring goods, it is difficult to see how people can flourish and function in the ways that CA advocates stress. Yet, as indicated previously, the risk of their approaches is that they fail to drill down into the thicker, social contexts of life and well-being.

Nussbaum is not wrong in seeking to reconfigure Rawls without the restrictions of the normal range. Flourishing is not something we can properly envision if our map of the territories across which people live their lives is divided between the normal and the nonnormal. Yet there are political and methodological costs to diluting a distributive, resources-based approach in favor of the vaguer, more Aristotelian tenets that she favors.[34]

The essential elasticity problem remains, therefore. The more you stretch the elastic to encompass particularities and the thicker entanglements of social life, the more you risk losing its cross-contextual reach and universal applicability.[35] Yet if you decline to stretch it sufficiently far, you perhaps lose many of the social specifics—the everyday clutter and contingencies of interrelationships and practices—that may be relevant to considerations of justice.

Is Nelson correct, then? Must we simply pick a sectarian position and stick to it? For a Rawlsian, for instance, it may be that some exclusion from the normal range is a necessary price to pay if we are to create the best possible systems of freedom and justice. We can try to incorporate the doings and the voices of those with severe mental disabilities, but, even with the best will in the world, it is the perspectives and the understandings of the nondisabled that will predominate.

Perhaps so, and perhaps sectarianism more generally is indeed unavoidable. However, it seems debilitating to restrict the horizons of our ambition in this way, to confine ourselves to a single locale. The instincts of hybridists are laudable, even if the execution is often lacking. Therefore, in the continued absence of some grand, all-encompassing theoretical framework, let me outline a hypothetical alternative approach.

Living with Incommensurability

Any answer to the question "What is justice?" presupposes another one: What do we want a theory of justice to do? Do we want it to do one thing or many things?

---

[34] As argued in the last section; see also the earlier critique of her "tragic choices" argument.
[35] S. Charusheela, "Social Analysis and the Capabilities Approach: A Limit to Martha Nussbaum's Universalist Ethics," *Cambridge Journal of Economics* 33 (2009), 1135–1152.

The elasticity problem arises because of two impulses: first, the *desire* to be focused and streamlined in some respects, while embracing flexibility, expansiveness, and open-endedness in others; second, a *recognition* that our list of justice-enhancing goods/capabilities cannot be both parsimonious and nonparsimonious simultaneously if it is to be meaningful.

The hybrid models described previously broadly agree we should want justice to realize three dimensions: havings, doings, and beings. By "havings" we mean material-distributive resources of one form or another, such as those implied by Rawlsian primary goods. By "doings" we mean the capacity of individuals and groups to translate resources into meaningful activities and practices. The CA takes root here since the resource-based approach does not tell us enough "about how people are really doing."[36] And when individuals *do*, they are trying to realize some state of *being* (or functioning). Welfarist philosophies are also concerned with states of being, and Nussbaum highlights certain similarities between utilitarianism and the CA.[37]

Since social and political philosophers give varying accounts of havings, doings, and beings, philosophy has something of a dual personality. The partisanship of each ("I come to defend my theory") evolves into a noisy, communal bipartisanship of the many (a dialogue among those willing to acknowledge the limitations of their favored theory). The desires and recognitions of the elasticity problem are folded into an intellectual space, or "manifold." I may think we ought to focus on a few key resources—perhaps because liberalism emphasizes individuals' right to choose their version of the good life—but I cannot easily dismiss those who highlight the multifaceted range of what people do, or those who argue that even liberalism implies a comprehensive view of the good. Hence, a particular perspective contributes to a multiperspective dialogue.

The Policy Problem

Policymakers, professionals, administrators, practitioners, activists, and user groups do not possess a similar luxury. For understandable reasons, that is, the imperative to get things done, they habitually prioritize some *ideas* over others, favor some *interests* over others, and bias certain *institutional* cultures, rules, and norms over others. This both reflects and perpetuates a partisanship, whether of ideology and rule by political parties ("our ideas, our interests, our norms are the best") or of technocratic managerialism that treats decision-making and

---

[36] Nussbaum, *Creating Capabilities*, 58.
[37] Nussbaum, *Frontiers of Justice*, 338–346.

government as so highly specialized that it must be closed away from genuine consultation, user involvement, pluralism, and participatory governance.

This characterization is clearly broad-brush. The policy process is more open and democratic in some nations and some sectors than others.[38] Nonetheless, what Fung calls the "minimal representative policy process" tends to predominate, and so the allegation that most government systems are top-heavy, overcentralized, and inaccessible is hardly a controversial one.[39]

Consequently, that process tends to embody centers of power, guarded by gatekeepers, whose doors swing open only infrequently. If you don't like existing legislative and policy reforms, then, according to conventional understanding, wait until the next election, after which you may acquire the power to change things. The notion that those offices should continue to be open, during interelection periods, to those who were not voted into power is not one that many electoral winners have embraced. "It's our turn now" is the prize, and "It may be our turn next time" is the consolation. The expectations in which we have been schooled (a winner-takes-all mentality) derive from and perpetuate hierarchical systems of power. The aim is to occupy the apex, rather than collapse the hierarchy's floors. With the democratic ideal pointing in one direction and systems of bureaucratic power in another, the lifeblood of civic participation is thus always at risk of ossifying.

This therefore represents a system of minimal empowerment only, in which many more decisions are made *for* rather than *by* the populace. The political and policymaking process often seems to disempower. This gap—between democratic ideal and reality—has become starker in the very post-1989 era when democratic victory over communism was repeatedly heralded:

- A globalization dominated by corporate governance and financial mobility has led to the ascendency of markets over politics and capital (asset holders) over labor (the wage-dependent). The deregulation of markets has accompanied the reregulation of people.
- An unrestrained capitalism has generated runaway inequalities that threaten the solidarities and mutualities upon which civic society depends.
- The business model of social media platforms and tech giants restricts the communicative capacities of individuals by encouraging closed, self-reinforcing reality-bubbles, by commercializing information flows, and by facilitating the subversion of open and fair elections.

---

[38] Maija Setälä and Theo Schiller, eds., *Citizens' Initiatives in Europe* (Palgrave, 2012).
[39] Archon Fung, "Democratizing the Policy Process," in *The Oxford Handbook of Public Policy*, ed. Michael Moran, Martin Rein, and Robert Goodin (Oxford University Press, 2008), 669–670.

- The impulse to reassert national self-control and cultural nostalgia has led to a resurgence in authoritarian, populist, and fascistic nationalisms.

With fewer antidemocratic communist nations to contrast themselves against, the deficiencies of actually existing liberal democracies have been exposed.

The policymaking deficit has undoubtedly contributed to that wider democratic stagnation. If the policy process looks closed, then why spend time and effort trying to access it? Why even take an interest? In short, the policymaking process cannot be rescued by wider democratic systems, not when the failings in the former have contributed to failings in the latter.

You may think all of this is a world away from philosophical debates about justice. You may be wrong.

Permanent Redemocratization

Our task should be to engineer a revitalization of the impulse toward democratic, participative justice, embodying the moral values and respect for public goods that neoliberal markets abjure.[40] Insofar as it is possible, we have to find and cultivate institutional arrangements and practices that replicate the openness and communal bipartisanship of the manifold, capable of rupturing the distant and opaque centers of policymaking and political power that currently prevail.

The imperative to *get things done* remains. People need to have their bins emptied and their schools run effectively. Professionalization and technocratic expertise must not only inform decision-making but must sometimes predominate. Yet, if the preceding characterization is reasonable, a system of minimal empowerment prevails because of the assumption that democratization crowds out efficiency, that participation by many voices slows down decision-making and dilutes the efficacy of the resulting decisions.

It is this assumption that needs to be continually challenged. An alternative assumption is that the quality and legitimacy of decisions is improved if people can see the fairness and participative openness embodied in the means through which they were reached. Anyone who works in even a small institution knows that reorganizations are most effective when, to the greatest extent possible, they are shaped by the members of said institution[41]—"To the greatest extent possible" because democratic participation still has to be consistent with good

---

[40] Such a political revitalization was promised in the early days of the internet (assurances we would live in a "global town hall" of rational debate). Still, a restructured architecture for the internet and smart regulation of tech giants could yet fulfil some of that potential.

[41] Juliette Summers and Jeff Hyman, *Employee Participation and Company Performance: A Review of the Literature* (Joseph Rowntree Foundation, 2005).

governance. Yet what this means and how it works will itself be subject to deliberative debate. Sometimes considerations of efficiency must dominate; at other
times, institutions need to be messy, cacophonous, experimental, and creatively
inefficient. There is no way of determining which is appropriate, and why, prior
to that participative debate in that local context.

In short, reforms come and go. Actors come and go. But the process must remain constant and must aim at the democratic ideal: deliberative, transparent,
open, diverse, egalitarian.

Now, this is not offered as an original insight. The literature is replete with
recommendations on how to democratize policymaking and contemporary government.[42] Indeed, Rawlsians and the CA have both made important
contributions to such debates.[43] What I am concerned with here is how and
why such democratization might traverse the considerations of justice that
we explored earlier. If the preceding narrative is reasonable—if the import of
the elasticity problem has been missed by both camps—then this suggests a
distinct angle.

Any bureaucracy, any rule-based system of decision-making, any policy process will gravitate toward rigidity and elitism. Cultures tend to calcify, and institutional structures tend to petrify. Democratization requires a permanent effort
and a willingness to recognize that the shortest distance between two points is
not always the best route, that is, administrative competence should not occlude
participative legitimacy. Therefore, if the democratic ideal is to prevail, the democratic impulse has to be to break things open constantly. To agitate, to shake up.
The ideal implies both rule-taking and rule-remaking. The good citizen follows
the rules while also being a good enough troublemaker to challenge them.
Accordingly, those gravitational tendencies must be resisted through an impulse
toward permanent *re*democratization. So for future social reforms to embody
a progressive politics of social justice, policymaking may have to mimic a communal dialogue, the noises and diverse domains of the crowd.[44]

We earlier considered two approaches to justice: the sectarianism of Nelson and
the hybridity of Daniels et al. The redemocratization being urged here may imply

[42] Fung, "Democratizing the Policy Process"; Dena Freeman, "De-democratisation and Rising Inequality: The Underlying Cause of a Worrying Trend," Working Paper 12, London School of Economics, 2017.

[43] Samuel Freeman, "Deliberative Democracy: A Sympathetic Comment," *Philosophy and Public Affairs* 29 (2000), 371–418; David Crocker, *Ethics of Global Development* (Cambridge University Press, 2008).

[44] All of which begs the question of how to initiate a permanent redemocratization when this implies the kind of participation and transparency that our closed, distant, opaque systems are likely to resist. I suspect the solution lies in starting wherever power is less closed, less distant, and less opaque; e.g., in many territories this will be local government and building new models of democracy that can spread out from there. This is another story, however.

another approach, one of *living with incommensurability* if doing so assists the ethos of democratic vandalization. If our systems are ossifying toward havings (e.g., over-emphasizing the distributive paradigm), then even Rawlsians need to demolish and disrupt them. Likewise, if there is a deficiency of justice in resource distribution, then the CA needs to emphasis those nodes (like social class and capital ownership) that frequently underpin the capabilities.

This could imply that all services (public, charitable, and commercial) that impact significantly upon social well-being should be latticed via a constitution or charter designed to articulate and preserve an equilibrium of havings, doings, and beings. Such services would thus be subject to a periodic and bipartisan "well-being audit," a process designed to appraise the distribution of resources and capabilities and recalibrate where necessary. This would not simply be an evaluation made by experts but by "well-being practitioners," users and laypeople too.

Precedents for such audits exist. The UK's 2008 Climate Change Act instituted a system of five-yearly carbon budgets and established a Committee on Climate Change, an independent body of experts, to make recommendations on said budgets so that emission reduction targets could be met. The system has been poor at engaging the public, but there is no reason why both ecological and well-being audits could not be informed by wider, deliberative democratic processes.

Yet such processes are only as good as the ethos that informs them. Even when authority must be wielded behind closed doors by professionals and experts, they should always understand—and respectfully demonstrate their understanding—that it has been delegated *to* them by *all* those (especially the disadvantaged) to whom they remain accountable. In all cases, then, the ethos involves an impulse to self-critique, to think against oneself and one's habits. If professionals and laypeople, experts and users, sit around the same table without trying to inhabit each other's perspectives, then the result has the appearance but not the substance of consultation and democratic appraisal.

In short, living with incommensurability implies "spectral traits" in which we haunt diverse roles across a landscape of multiple perspectives, as ghosts in a permanent state of mobility. Rawlsians should be willing to mutate into advocates of the CA and the latter to mutate into Rawlsians.

Therefore, in Figure 10.1, we ought to resist our inclination to stabilize the justice loop ("doings predominate over havings and beings," or whatever). It is the circularity itself that is important and which needs to be kept in a state of dynamic flow.

That landscape, or manifold, therefore implies the multiple lines of sight and the fluctuating interrelationships embodied in Figure 10.2.[45]

---

[45] For the sake of completeness I have added a welfarist sector but not incorporated this into the narrative.

Figure 10.1 The justice loop

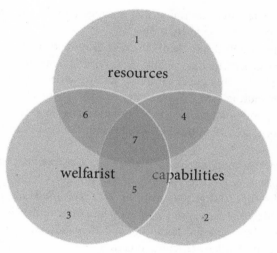

Figure 10.2 Policymaking using multiple perspectives

Because it is static and flat, Figure 10.2 is an imperfect representation of something more dynamic and multidimensional. The lines of sight come from imagining yourself in any number of positions—just seven of them have been inserted—and panning out over the surrounding scape. The sense of fluctuating interrelationships is given by understanding that the content of each of the main zones and shaded areas is never fixed.

Though we can look down on Figure 10.2, in the manifold itself there is no omniscience, and so movement within it resembles a parallax jolt. The thumb you hold before you shifts against the background as you first close one eye, keeping the other open, and then reverse the process. But, in the absence of a God's-eye view, there is no way of keeping both eyes open at the same time.

To sum up. In their different ways, Rawls, Sen, and Nussbaum all observe that democracy and justice matter but disagree over whether this implies primary goods and a parsimonious list, or capabilities and a nonparsimonious one. An ethos of living with incommensurability suggests something subtly different. *Every elasticity matters and matters so much that the impulse to fix everything into a single concept of justice should be resisted. The social and political institutions designed to realize justice must therefore be subject to a permanent redemocratization in which policymaking processes are not allowed to ossify.*

Spectral Traits

There are three features, or traits, that I suggest underpin and drive that ethos: appearing, appealing, fluctuating.

First, it is spectral in the sense of ghostlike. Multiperspectivism implies that which is multilocatory, that is, capable of appearing in several places simultaneously. It implies a willingness to uproot and unsettle yourself, for example, Rawlsians transmuting into CA advocates or experts empathizing with users. Re the latter, a good policymaking process will enable the relevant actors to inhabit plural roles and identities by guaranteeing the necessary resources and procedures.

Second, it means having appeal to diverse identities, interests, and ideas across a range of political, moral, and social spectra. Consensus-building remains important, not by suppressing pluralism but by accommodating it. The shared public spaces of liberal democracy, currently said to be under threat by illiberal movements and "strong man" authoritarians, demand constant attendance to similarities *and* dissimilarities, commonalities *and* discords. The alternative is the kind of homogenized space dominated by the interests of the usual suspects (white, male, affluent, heteronormative).

Finally, if we are eschewing single frameworks and solves-all-problems systems, the implication is that we have to get used to flux and fluidity. This does not mean giving up on progress but—in contrast to the progressive politics of the past—embracing something more protean, where elements are reshuffled into ever-changing mosaics.[46]

In short, whether our list is long or short, whether it leans toward resources/primary goods or capabilities, a spectral approach means appealing as widely as possible and circumnavigating those who police boundaries too rigidly. Both philosophers and students of policy studies should be less willing than previous generations to, as Wittgenstein (1981) had it, plant their flags in just one community of ideas.

---

[46] Fitzpatrick, *How to Live Well.*

Conclusion

My suggestion is that neither the CA nor Rawlsians are sufficiently panoramic and peripatetic. The latter's limitations lie in trying to make capabilities adjuncts to the primary goods; the former's are in allowing capabilities to occlude the material-distributive characteristics of resources and the political strategies of capitalism.

This leaves four possibilities: first, that we have yet to devise an overarching, grand narrative; second, that we are condemned to sectarianism, that is, to make a choice that will only ever be partial; third, that we can opt for a hybrid model, whether one of those presented earlier or some alternative.

The fourth and final possibility is the one sketched previously and which has been described in terms such as the manifold, permanent redemocratization, and the spectral traits needed to navigate the restless contours of the era in which we now live.

The task will be to find practical, institutional forms for this multi-perspectivism. For our era seems to be one in which we must either start to practice democracy better or we risk being left, at best, with a shell of democracy; one making it less likely we can defend the systems of social and political justice we already have, let alone implement and embolden new ones. For the interior of any postdemocratic shell would likely be occupied by demagogues, trolls, conspiracy theorists, irrationalists, and extremists, aided by corporations obsessed with profits and electorates lulled by dreamlike incantations promising them forms of social identity and belonging constructed around fantasies of cultural exclusivity and moral purification.

In short, we ought to mobilize Rawlsian and CA ideas in order to avoid this nightmare scenario. Debates about which perspective triumphs over the other may be ones we can no longer afford.

PART VI
THE DEPENDENCY CRITIQUE

Introduction

Liberal political philosophers, including John Rawls, often ground their theories in a model of citizens as free and equal individuals engaging in cooperation with each other. In starting with that model of citizens, little attention is given to the reality of inevitable human dependence. We all begin our lives as infants in a state of complete dependence on others. Many of us will end our lives that way as well. For people with certain significant disabilities, this dependence may continue throughout life. In contemporary societies, the dependence experienced by some people with disabilities can result in substantial social disadvantages. Further, the disadvantages associated with dependency do not just impact the dependent, but also those who care for them. Caring for dependents involves personal and economic costs that can negatively affect caregivers' ability to pursue their own opportunities or to exercise their rights. How ought our institutions be designed to ensure equal respect for those who are significantly dependent and for their caregivers?

To be clear, the issues of justice for dependents and the issues of justice for people with disabilities are not identical. Many people with disabilities are not dependent on others and many people who are dependent are not disabled (e.g., infants and children). Further, the dependence experienced by some people with disabilities is not the result of some inherent feature of their bodies but the result of socially constructed systems that exclude or marginalize them for their differences. As such, justice certainly requires changes to those institutions and systems that marginalize people with disabilities. On the other hand, it does not follow that justice requires the elimination of dependence. Some human dependence is inevitable and can be a healthy part of human life. The key is to sort out how institutions can ensure that these inevitable dependencies do not create unfair disadvantages for people.

At first glance, it seems John Rawls's theory of justice offers some valuable resources for thinking about justice for both dependents and their caregivers. Certainly Rawls intended the principle of equal opportunity to afford dependent children with the care they need to develop their talents and nurture their moral powers. What's more, the difference principle could be used to criticize many disadvantages faced by dependents and caregivers, who often could be appropriately categorized as the least advantaged. However, Rawls quite explicitly declined to address justice for people with significant disabilities. His thought

Introduction In: *John Rawls*. Edited by: Jon Mandle and Sarah Roberts-Cady, Oxford University Press (2020). © Oxford University Press. DOI: 10.1093/oso/9780190859213.003.0017.

was that "if we can work out a viable theory for the normal range [of human needs and capacities], we can attempt to handle these other cases later."[1] But can his theory provide an adequate framework for identifying the requirements of justice for those who are severely dependent and their caregivers?

In 1999, Eva Kittay published *Love's Labor: Essays on Women, Equality and Dependency*, in which she argues that Rawls gives too little attention to dependents and dependency workers. Rawls begins with the idea that "citizens are equal in virtue of possessing, to the requisite minimum degree, the two moral powers and the other capacities that enable us to be normal and fully cooperating members of society."[2] Kittay argues that, in beginning with this idealization, Rawls fails to address the requirements of justice with respect to those who do not fit this description. "The point of the dependency critique is to show that, as long as the bounds of justice are drawn within reciprocal relations among free and equal persons, dependents will continue to remain disenfranchised, and dependency workers who are otherwise fully capable and cooperating members of society will continue to share varying degrees of the dependents' disenfranchisement."[3]

In the essay that appears in this volume, Kittay lays out her argument that revisions of the liberal concept of equality are needed in order to include dependents and dependency workers. She argues that there are five areas where Rawls's conception of equality is inadequate for addressing dependency. First, Rawls accepts Hume's account of the circumstances of justice, which omits inevitable human dependency. Second, Rawls accepts the assumption that "all citizens are fully cooperating members of society over the course of a complete life."[4] Third, the theory of justice presumes that all people are free in the sense that they are a "self-originating" or "self-authenticating source of valid claims,"[5] which perhaps pays insufficient attention to those people who are not self-originating sources of valid claims, but depend on others to make those claims. Fourth, the realization of equality presumes some common measure of equality—primary goods or capabilities. Yet Kittay argues that Rawls's list of primary goods is not adequate for meeting the needs of those giving and receiving care. Fifth, Rawls begins with a concept of social cooperation that presumes equality among those who cooperate. Kittay argues that with each of these assumptions, important concerns about dependency are omitted.

[1] John Rawls, *Political Liberalism*, expanded ed. (Columbia University Press, 2005), 272 n.10.
[2] Rawls, *Political Liberalism*, 79.
[3] Eva Kittay, *Love's Labor: Essays on Women, Equality and Dependence* (Routledge, 1999), 76–77.
[4] John Rawls, "Kantian Constructivism in Moral Theory," in *Collected Papers*, ed. Samuel Freeman (Harvard University Press, 2001), 332.
[5] Eva Kittay, this volume.

Amy Baehr agrees with Kittay's claims about the importance of integrating justice for people who are dependent, but aims to think through how to develop a Rawlsian liberal theory that acknowledges "a just society is . . . a fair care-giving and care-receiving society" and avoids "dependency-related injustice."[6] Baehr argues that if caregiving is conceived as a primary good, then there are reasons, broadly accepted in public culture, for adding principles of justice in caregiving, including protecting access to caregiving for those who need it and avoiding disadvantages for those who provide care.

Suggested Reading from Rawls to Accompany These Chapters

A Theory of Justice: §§16, 77

Political Liberalism: Lecture I, §5; Lecture III; Lecture VIII, §3; and "The Idea of Public Reason Revisited," §5

Justice as Fairness: A Restatement: §§4, 18, and 50

For Further Reading

Bhandary, Asha. *Freedom to Care: Liberalism, Dependency Care and Culture* (Routledge, 2019). This book develops a neo-Rawlsian liberal theory of justice for evaluating different social approaches to dependency care.

Kittay, Eva. *Love's Labor: Essays on Women, Equality and Dependency* (Routledge, 1999). This pathbreaking book examines relationships of dependency and their implications for conceptualizing justice and equality.

Nussbaum, Martha. *Frontiers of Justice: Disability, Nationality, and Species Membership* (Harvard University Press, 2006). This book explores issues of justice for persons with disabilities, justice across political borders, and justice across species, in which Nussbaum argues that Rawls's theory of justice cannot adequately address justice for people with disabilities, but that the capabilities approach to justice can.

Okin, Susan Moller. *Justice, Gender and the Family* (Basic Books, 1989). In this highly influential book, Okin argues that modern political philosophers' inattention to injustices in the family leads to theories of justice that cannot adequately address injustices women face outside the family in the social, political, and economic realms.

---

[6] Amy Baehr, this volume.

11

The Dependency Critique of Rawlsian Equality

Eva Feder Kittay

Just societies are to treat all persons as free and equal.[1] This is a view shared by different theories within the liberal tradition. While white men of a certain class at first delimited the scope of *all*, that scope has been expanded to include the formerly disenfranchised, for example, black men and black and white women. The dependency critique means to extend the scope still further. It calls attention to the neglect of human dependency and the consequences of that omission in theories of equality and social justice. To be fully inclusive, the principles of equality, freedom, and just treatment must also be extended to persons who are dependent upon others in basic ways, that is to say, children, the disabled, and the frail elderly. To include dependent persons in the community of equal citizens, however, dependency needs require special consideration. Moreover, as adult rational agents who possess the two moral powers, dependency workers turn their interests and attention to the well-being of a vulnerable person, often at the expense of their own needs and interests. As a result, dependency workers, whom we might think are covered by the theory are, in fact, situated unequally with respect to those not similarly obligated to care for dependents. The claim of the dependency critique is that dependents and dependency workers cannot be included within the scope of a liberal conception of equality without a serious revision of the liberal conception of equality and the many notions that contribute to the view of society as an association of equals.

For all its comprehensiveness and power, John Rawls's theory of justice, like those that have come before it, fails to attend to the fact of human dependency and the consequences of this dependency on social organization. He joins those who have omitted responsibility for dependents from (or relegated it to the periphery of) the political.[2] The presumption has been that these responsibilities belong to

---

[1] This chapter is a composite and a reworking of the ideas originally presented in Eva Kittay, *Love's Labor: Essays in Women, Equality and Dependency* (Routledge, 1999), especially chaps. 3 and 4.

[2] See, for example, John Rawls, *Political Liberalism*, expanded ed. (Columbia University Press, 2005), xxviii–ix, for the characterization of his project. Rawls acknowledges that a conception of justice "so arrived at may prove defective" (*Political Liberalism*, xxix). My claim is that it is defective because it is so arrived at.

Eva Feder Kittay, *The Dependency Critique of Rawlsian Equality* In: *John Rawls*. Edited by: Jon Mandle and Sarah Roberts-Cady, Oxford University Press (2020). © Oxford University Press.
DOI: 10.1093/oso/9780190859213.003.0018.

citizens' nonpublic, rather than public, concerns—a dichotomy that appears reasonable only by virtue of the neglect of dependency in delineating the political. The particular situation of dependents and of those who care for dependents becomes invisible in the political domain—the domain in which parties are to be reckoned as equals. The liberal ideal of equality casts its light in this public domain and so fails to illuminate the nether world of human dependency.

Some dependencies are a consequence of socially prescribed roles, privileges, or distribution policies, for example, the dependency of slaves and serfs on masters, and the economic dependency of women on men in patriarchal societies. These are injustices that a liberal theory of justice such as Rawls's will have ruled out of a well-ordered society. I, however, throw the spotlight on *inevitable dependencies*, those times in our lives when we are dependent by virtue of infancy, frail old age, and incapacitating illness or disability.

In the case of utter and inevitable dependency certain features are inexorably linked. First, the dependent requires care and caring persons to meet fundamental needs for survival and basic thriving. Second, while in the condition of dependency, the dependent is unable to reciprocate in kind the benefits received. Third, the intervention of another (or more likely others) is crucial to meet the needs of the dependent and ensure that the interests of the dependents, and those who care for them, are socially recognized.[3] And fourth, dependency, so understood, underscores not only the limitations of an individual's capability, but also the necessary labor of a dependency worker.

That dependency concerns do not make an appearance in Rawls's theory accords with Rawls's belief that his theory ought to rest on a "few main and enduring classical problems"[4] of political philosophy. Yet these traditional theories for the most part have cast the political actor as male. In so doing they have occluded certain problems that have, generally been the domain of women, particularly those that concern inevitable dependencies and care. Such issues have thus been excluded from the list of the "few main and enduring classical problems." In *Political Liberalism*, Rawls defends his theory's reliance on these enduring classical problems, especially the liberal characterizations of the person, by insisting that he is extracting from the liberal tradition a "device of representation." Thus, he need not accede to the gendered characterizations of persons that have marred traditional political philosophy.[5] But I challenge this view. Rawls cannot

---

[3] The person who intervenes may or may not be the same person who provides hands-on care. But the person who provides hands-on care is virtually always in a position in which she has to interpret the needs and desires of their charge. She is not always, however, the person empowered to translate those needs into socially understood interests. See Kittay, *Love's Labor*, especially 33–37.

[4] Rawls, *Political Liberalism*, xxix.

[5] See also his attempts to answer his feminist critics in John Rawls, *Justice as Fairness: A Restatement*, ed. Erin Kelly (Harvard University Press, 2001).

succeed in producing a truly inclusive theory in limiting himself to these "enduring classical problem" because, having drawn mostly from the experiences of men who were not obliged to care for dependents, these classical problems fail to see inevitable human dependency as a question that must be addressed in a theory of justice.

Rawls then will invariably exclude from equal citizenship two classes of persons whom we can charitably suppose he did not intend to exclude: those who are dependent upon others, and those who attend to their needs. The contingent fact that women are, by and large, the dependency workers means that the theoretical formulations of Rawls's theory of justice effectively disadvantage women, as well as those who are inevitably dependent. Thus, the dependency critique argues that inclusion of dependency concerns into a theory of justice is required if we want to have a society in which gender is not a barrier to equality. An addendum is that even if we somehow manage to achieve true gender equality, dependency workers, regardless of gender, would still be disadvantaged if dependency does not inform a theory of justice.

A theory of justice informed by dependency is critical if we want to ensure that each of us, in our times of dependence, will retain our status as equal citizens. Furthermore, we cannot provide for the needs of dependents and dependency workers without a theory that understands that our inevitable dependence results in inextricable interdependencies. Not only do we need to provide for dependents, on the one hand, and dependency workers, on the other, but the relationships of dependency (in which being cared for and needing to care are realized) themselves need to be nurtured. I venture that many of the criticisms applied to Rawls's theory pertain (ceteris paribus) to other theories of liberalism.

The dependency critique is first of all a critique of a certain conception of equality. Equal divisions of the benefits and burdens of social cooperation are a benchmark for "justice as fairness."[6] Thus, equality plays its role at the theory's start and end points: the theory begins with the presumption that persons are moral equals and concludes with principles that ensure that rights and liberties enjoyed equally by all, along with an economic distribution, based on equal opportunity and favoring the least well off.[7]

In my development of the critique of a Rawlsian conception of equality and subsequently, a critique of Rawls's theory of justice, I identify five presuppositions

---

[6] Rawls, *Political Liberalism*, 282.

[7] In *A Theory of Justice*, revised ed. (Harvard University Press, 1999), Rawls says that equality operates on three levels: (1) the administrative and procedural, i.e., the impartial and consistent application of rules, constituted by the precept to treat likes alike; (2) "the substantive structure of institutions" (*A Theory of Justice*, 442) requiring that all persons be assigned equal basic rights; and (3) the situation of the original position addressing the basis of equality, those "features of human beings in virtue of which they are to be treated in accordance with the principles of justice" (*A Theory of Justice*, 441).

standing behind this concept of equality and point to the omission of dependency concerns in each. In calling attention to these omissions, I aim neither to amend Rawls's political theory, nor to say that it cannot be reformed. Rather, I offer the dependency critique to provide a criterion of adequacy, one applicable to any political theory claiming to be egalitarian.

The equality of citizens, Rawls maintains, derives from their equal possession, "to the requisite minimum degree, [of] the two moral powers and other capacities that enable us to be normal and fully cooperating members of society." Insofar as they are equal in this respect, they all, "have the same basic rights, liberties and opportunities and the same protections of the principles of justice."[8] That is, equal citizens of a well-ordered society, which for Rawls is one that is based on fair terms of social cooperation, are so situated and empowered that they equally positioned to partake in the benefits and burdens of social cooperation. In a constructivist account, how is this equality represented? Rawls writes, "The representation for equality is an easy matter: we simply describe all the parties [in the original position] in the same way and situate them equally, that is, symmetrically with respect to one another. Everyone has the same rights and powers in the procedure for reaching agreement."[9]

In *Political Liberalism*, he puts it this way: "To model this equality in the original position we say that the parties, as representatives of those who meet the condition, are symmetrically situated. This requirement is fair because in establishing fair terms of social cooperation (in the case of the basic structure) the only relevant feature of persons is their possessing the moral powers . . . and their having the normal capacities to be a cooperating member of society over the course of a lifetime."[10]

If we begin to unpack these remarks we see that what makes "representing equality" an "easy matter" is that so much has been presumed already. If we examine five central conceptions that lead to a theory of justice for equal citizens, we will see what has been presumed.

First, Rawls, borrowing from Hume, identifies the "circumstances of justice." These are preconditions for justice in a society and include facts that are known and recognized by the free and equal persons who constitute society. The circumstances of justice set the parameters for all subsequent considerations. The circumstances of justice include both objective conditions, such as moderate scarcity of resources, and subjective circumstances, such as the desire of people to pursue their own conception of the good, and the fact that not all people share

---

[8] Rawls, *Political Liberalism*, 79.
[9] John Rawls, "Kantian Constructivism in Moral Theory," in *Collected Papers*, ed. Samuel Freeman (Harvard University Press, 1999), 336.
[10] Rawls, *Political Liberalism*, 79.

a single conception. But nowhere in the account of the circumstances of justice does Rawls (again following Hume) take into account the fact that we do not spring up full grown.[11] Nor does he mention the fact that human beings, even as adults, are vulnerable to disease and disabilities that constrain their full participation in assuming the burdens and deriving the benefits of social cooperation. These do not figure in the idealizations operative in building the liberal theory that can be part of an overlapping consensus. That is, for long periods of our lives—for some throughout their lives and for others for the major portion of their life—we lack the ability to participate as equals, each with our own conception of the good, in political, social, and economic life. These facts of inevitable human dependency, like all objective circumstances of knowledge, are well known in any human society. Without attending to them a society cannot sustain itself beyond a given generation.

While inevitable human dependency may be an objective circumstance of justice that fails to get considered, there is a subjective correlate. Because dependents are in fact cared for, we need to assume that there are subjective features of human psychology and social life that make it possible for some to elide their own immediate concerns to care for another. We need to count on dispositions and conditions that will allow people to care for dependents on a regular basis. The subjective circumstance is then the desire and need to care, as well as the imperative that we are cared for when we need care. The impact of this subjective circumstance is that a just society must not only see to it that all who need care will receive it, but also that those who do the caring are not exploited when their efforts and attention are directed at the needs of another. Nor that those who *need and desire* to care, who regard caring for others (especially familial dependents) as a part of their own conception of the good, fall prey to exploitation and serious disadvantage by virtue of the circumstances leading them to do dependency work. Another way to say this is that the needs and desires to care and be cared for can give rise to a free-rider problem that a well-ordered, just society ought to avoid. Rawls remarked that he wanted his theory of justice, even though it was an idealization, to give us a "realistic utopia." Without considering dependency, this utopia falls far short of reality—and if our society free-rides on

---

[11] Of course, Rawls is not indifferent to the fact that we undergo the period of dependency called childhood, for he devotes a full chapter in A *Theory of Justice* to moral psychological development. He is also importantly concerned with stability and how a society can "sustain itself beyond a given generation." But these concerns do not make it into the fundamental structure of the theory as it is constructed from the original position and takes center stage in *Political Liberalism*. The moral psychology is part of the comprehensive liberalism that Rawls divides off from the liberalism that can be the basis of an overlapping consensus. Moreover, the concern with children is the concern for the future adult rather than for the child qua *dependent being*. This mirrors his eventual adoption of Norman Daniel's idea of healthcare as a matter to be included under fair equality of opportunity. See the discussion that follows.

the desire and sense of obligation that some have to provide care or fails to provide care when needed, the "realistic utopia" is not utopian for those who do the work of dependency care nor for those who need care (which is all of us at some time).[12]

Second, when Rawls provides the sense in which citizens in a well-ordered society are equal moral persons, he starts with an idealization of citizens in a well-ordered society—that "all citizens are fully cooperating members of society *over the course of a complete life*."[13] As we see from the passage cited previously in *Political Liberalism*, Rawls constructs an ideal in which no one has particularly taxing or costly needs to fulfill, such as unusual medical requirements. Rawls provides further clarification:

> The normal range [of functioning] is specified as follows: since the fundamental problem of justice concerns the relations among those who are full and active participants in society, and directly or indirectly associated together over the course of a whole life, it is reasonable to *assume that everyone has physical needs and psychological capacities within some normal range. Thus the problem of special health care and how to treat the mentally defective are set aside.* If we can work out a viable theory for the normal range, we can attempt to handle these other cases later.[14]

We learn here that although he excludes dependency concerns that are outside the "normal range" from the initial articulation of justice, Rawls does not mean to leave people with these conditions without a right to equal justice.[15] Nor does he mean to exclude the dependency concerns of those who have physical needs "within a normal range," needs that often need to be met in dependency relationships. That is to say, although equality is represented as pertaining to "full and active participants in society," a full theory of justice ought to cover relationships between people who are not—at least at a given time in their life— "full and active participants."

---

[12] In chapter 3 of *Love's Labor*, I provide an extensive discussion of how one might read Rawls so that the omission I charge him with is less jarring. Unfortunately, I cannot engage in such a lengthy hermeneutical exercise and defense of my position here.

[13] Rawls, "Kantian Constructivism," 332, emphasis mine.

[14] Rawls, *Political Liberalism*, 272 n. 10, emphasis mine.

[15] Although Rawls writes earlier: "[The idealization] means that everyone has sufficient intellectual powers to play a *normal* part in society, and no one suffers from *unusual* needs that are *especially difficult* to fulfill, for example *unusual and costly medical requirements*" (Rawls, "Kantian Constructivism," 332, emphasis mine). The idealization requires the condition of adulthood as well as health. Since both children and the temporarily disabled merely temporarily and contingently fail to meet the requirements for equal moral worth, they are included in the category of equal citizen. See Rawls, *A Theory of Justice*, 445–446. The appropriate treatment of those who are permanently disabled seems to be another matter.

But how to move from idealization to the more inclusive theory was a vexing problem for Rawls. Norman Daniels attempted to repair Rawls's omission of healthcare by incorporating it into the primary good of equal opportunity. That move is only satisfactory to the extent that we provide healthcare so as to bring everyone back to full functioning. That leaves too much, and too many, out of consideration in a just society even when we confine ourselves to the good of healthcare, much less the broader category of dependency care.

Third, the theory of justice constructed for the "normal case" presumes that everyone is equally capable of understanding and complying with the principles of justice (to a certain minimal degree) and equally capable of honoring them. Furthermore, it presumes that all persons are free in the sense that they are a "self-originating" or "self-authenticating source of valid claims."[16] That is, each views him- or herself as worthy of being represented in a procedure by which the principles of justice are determined. An equality with respect first to a sense of justice and second to freedom (as being a self-authenticating source of valid claims and so one who determines his own good) establishes the grounds for the claim to equal worth. How are we then to understand the equality of those whose capability to act as a self-authenticating source of valid claims is limited by circumstances that are not political? How are we to understand the equality of those who, by virtue of disability, cannot fully express their wants, desires, needs, or interests? If the restriction is a matter of limits on movement or sensation, we can include provisions and accommodations to allow greater freedom and per- haps equal freedom for the expression of those claims. If the disability is mental, the problem is far more grave, for we have, as of now at least, often no, sometimes only attenuated, access to such self-authenticating valid claims. To the extent that the reason or judgment is impaired, we may not be able to confirm that these are self-authenticating[17] or valid claims, or to reason a person out of what may be self-injurious claims. In what sense then can the person be said to have the freedom that issues in equal worth and an equal claim to just treatment?

Another sort of problem arises with respect to the dependency worker. Here we presumably have a person who is of sound judgment and has a mind of her own, but can we really say that her claims are self-originating or even self- authenticating? In some circumstances this is no problem, namely when the de- pendency worker is making claims only on her own behalf. But the claims of the

---

[16] In *Political Liberalism* Rawls drops the term "self-originating source of claims" (Rawls, "Kantian Constructivism," 330) and substitutes the term "self-authenticating source of valid claims" (*Political Liberalism*, 32). See *Political Liberalism*, 96–99, for a discussion of this difference.

[17] Nor are many willing to accede to what may be self-originating claims of mentally impaired individuals, because, they will object, people with significant mental impairments lack the self- reflection needed for self-authentication. I think this is overstated and is more often unfair to people with mental disabilities than we know.

dependency worker are also claims on behalf of her dependent, and sometimes also for the sake of the relationship in which both the dependent and the dependency worker are embedded.

Consider the claims of a parent that affect the well-being of her children, for example, her insistence on an education for them. This demand is to benefit her children, not herself—and it is her duty, given her relationship to the children, to make such claims. These are valid claims on other citizens. These are not self-originating but other-originating, valid claims. Furthermore, as all parents know, although the claims we make on the part of our children are claims we make in conformity with our role as parents, these claims can be at odds with claims we might otherwise make as individuals. To stay with our example, consider that the parent who agitates for better schools is, willy-nilly, committing herself to acquiesce to higher taxes, which in turn leaves her with a reduced income.

A retort might be that it is not only the dependency worker, qua dependency worker, who fails to be a self-originating source of claims (since these claims issue from her as she fills a particular social role). Most work involves bracketing, at some point, one's own claims in favor of the demands of a job. This response fails to recognize a vital difference between dependency work and most other forms of labor. Because of the moral demands of dependency work, dependency workers' moral selves cannot easily be peeled from their social roles. We do not leave our job as a mother at the doorstep when we go to do another job. Even the paid dependency worker, certainly those who work with very vulnerable human beings, cannot just leave their job and the dependents whose care they are charged with, even when compelling needs call them to do so.

The freedom that demands a view of oneself as a self-originator of valid claims is not a freedom applicable to the situation of the dependency worker. Rawls remarked that slaves could not be self-originators of valid claims under slavery. And slavery has no place in a well-ordered society. In contrast, we cannot eliminate dependency work, and justice could never demand that we abolish it. Nor would we want to. If, as Rawls writes, the members of a well-ordered society are to "view their common polity as extending backward and forward in time over generations,"[18] and the course of human development inevitably requires that some persons care for dependents, we cannot tell the dependency worker to abandon her concern for the well-being of her charge, even though this constraint renders her freedom—construed as the self-origination of valid claims— an empty abstraction.

Rawls replaced his early term "a self-originator of valid claims" with the term "a self-*authenticating* source of valid claims." The revision addresses some

---

[18] Rawls, "Kantian Constructivism," 323.

communitarian and feminist objections to a metaphysical conception of a person that is highly individualist—a problem aggravated when we drop the idea of parties as representing generational lines or heads of households. By altering his formulation, Rawls can now state: "Claims that citizens regard as founded on duties and obligations based on their conception of the good and the moral doctrine they affirm in their own life are also, for our purposes here, to be counted as self-authenticating."[19]

This new formulation opens a space for an expanded notion of "self"-interest, compatible with the interests of the dependency worker. The mother who insists on the child's right to an education may not be acting on a self-originating claim, but she surely is acting on a self-authenticating one. The particular claims she makes as a dependency worker may be self-authenticating in this sense. There are two difficulties even with the idea that dependency workers are self-authenticating in ways that others who pursue their own vision of the good are.

The first difficulty is that the turn to self-authentification encounters a free-rider problem. It returns us to the vagaries of the contingent choices individuals make about their work or their conception of the good. We are left with the uncertainty of whether representatives in the original position will choose principles that will take care of dependency needs in a just and equitable fashion, as judged by our considered reflections (see the prior discussion). Without the assurance that dependency concerns will be handled equitably, those who do not choose dependency work will be free-riders, thus effectively obliging those who do such work to do it under relatively compulsory and exploitative conditions.

If dependency work were well paid, had a high status, or received other distinctive social recognition, we could conclude that a sufficient supply of dependency work was chosen freely by self-authenticating agents. A clear-eyed look at the nearly universal twin features of female caregiving and female subordination indicates (1) that a certain class of persons has been subjected to and socialized to develop the character traits and the volitional structure needed for dependency work;[20] (2) that certain sexual behaviors commensurate with forming attachments, being submissive to another's will, and so forth have been made compulsory for women;[21] and (3) that poor women and women of color have

---

[19] Rawls, *Political Liberalism*, 32.

[20] See, for example, Simone de Beauvoir, *The Second Sex*, trans H. M. Parshley (Vintage, 1989); Nancy Chodorow, *The Reproduction of Mothering: Psychoanalysis and the Sociology of Gender* (University of California Press, 1978); Dorothy Dinnerstein, *The Mermaid and the Minotaur: Sexual Arrangements and Human Malaise* (Harper and Row, 1976); Carol Gilligan, *In a Different Voice* (Harvard University Press, 1982); Sandra Lee Bartky, "Feeding Egos and Tending Wounds: Deference and Disaffection in Women's Emotional Labor," in *Femininity and Domination: Studies in the Phenomenology of Oppression* (Routledge, 1990).

[21] See Adrienne Rich, *Of Woman Born: Motherhood as Experience and Institution* (W.W. Norton, 1995).

been forced into paid employment as dependency workers by the scanty financial resources and limited employment opportunities available to them, and that middle-class women have been forced out of paid employment not commensurate with their (largely unpaid) duties as dependency workers. It has not merely "happened" that women have consistently "chosen" to make dependency relations and dependency work central to their vision of the good life, while men have chosen a wider variety of options. Because care of dependents is nonoptional in any society, some societal measures are inescapably taken to meet the inevitable need for care. If the means by which a society distributes responsibility for dependency work is not guided by principles of justice, then coercive measures—often in the guise of tradition and custom, sometimes in the guise of merely apparent voluntary life choices—are the predictable response.

Under these conditions, the dependency worker will be no more a self-authenticating source of valid claims than she is a self-originating source of valid claims. Yet even in more favorable and ideal circumstances, the very nature of dependency work constrains us in ways that most other choices that conform with our conception of the good do not. This leads us to the second problem. This is the problem of exit options. Rawls always characterizes one of the moral powers the ability to form and *revise* one's conception of the good. As we choose not to make the revisions, we are effectively authenticating the initial choices.

Now consider the paradigmatic dependency worker, the mother who chooses as the good, motherhood as traditionally understood. Once you choose (if it was indeed a choice) motherhood, there is no revision, no morally acceptable exit option. One's responsibilities usually diminish with time, but that is not because the mother has revised her conception of the good. A similar situation pertains to the situation of paid dependency workers. They may revise their career choice, but while they are engaged as dependency workers their freedom to exit is both legally and morally prohibited, until and unless they can find others who will take over these responsibilities. The moral repercussions of exiting are scarcely equal to those of other workers. If only those who are equals and free in the Rawlsian sense are eligible to participate in social cooperation, then dependency workers cannot be included among the "free" individuals who have an equal claim to the fruits of social cooperation.

Fourth, the realization of equality assumes a common measure. But insofar as each person forms her or his own conception of the good, Rawls proposes an index comprised of those goods all persons require given the two moral powers of a person: an ability to form and revise one's conception of one's own good and a sense of justice. This index is given by the five primary goods. The possession of the two moral powers is itself a feature of the modeling of the parties as equals, and the just distribution of these primary goods is the benefit of social cooperation in a well-ordered society.[22] The list of primary goods has remained substantially unaltered since *A Theory of Justice*:[23]

   i. The basic liberties (freedom of thought and liberty of conscience) . . .
   ii. Freedom of movement and free choice of occupation against a background of diverse opportunities . . . as well as [the ability] to give effect to a decision to revise and change them . . .
   iii. Powers and prerogatives of offices and positions of responsibility . . .
   iv. Income and wealth . . .
   v. The social bases of self-respect.[24]

Assuming that those in dependency relations count as citizens, assessing the adequacy of the list requires asking whether a list of primary goods tied to Rawls's two moral powers will ensure justice in the giving and receiving of care. As we have already pointed out, we all need care at some point in our lives. Furthermore, when we are neglected at such times of need, we are devalued both as a person and as a citizen—we are not treated as individuals recognized to have equal worth. In addition, those who are responsible for the care of dependents are not treated as equals if the larger society free-rides on their sense of responsibility and when their responsibilities to their dependents inhibit their own ability to compete as equals in a society based on fair terms of social cooperation. The five primary goods do not accommodate the importance of care as something that is essential to recognizing the equal worth of all citizens and as essential to any conception of the good.

The absence of care among the primary goods is tied to the view that the two moral powers essential to a just society are the sense of justice and the ability to form and revise a conception of the good. Yet an ethic reflecting concern for dependents and those who care for them requires that citizens have other moral powers: a sense of attachment to others, an empathetic attention to their needs,[25]

----

[22] Rawls acknowledges that some will have a more developed sense of justice than others. Equality with respect to a sense of justice demands only that persons have a sense of justice "equally sufficient relative to what is asked of them" (Rawls, "Kantian Constructivism," 333) insofar as they are "fully cooperating members of society over a complete life" (Rawls, "Kantian Constructivism," 333).

[23] Rawls later (*Political Liberalism*, 308–309) gives essentially the same list but accompanies it with an explanation of why each is included. Conspicuously absent from the considerations adduced in the explanations are the elements of "nurture," "interdependence," and "phases of life," all of which are mentioned as general facts about human life on the preceding page. Effectively, these elements are still omitted in the hard-core center of the theory.

[24] Rawls, "Kantian Constructivism," 313–314.

[25] See Diana T. Meyers, *Self, Society, and Personal Choice* (Columbia University Press, 1989) and *Subjection and Subjectivity: Psychoanalytic Feminism and Moral Philosophy* (Routledge, 1994), who speaks of the necessity of empathetic thought as a feature of a moral person. What I am considering is such a moral capacity.

and a responsiveness to these needs. The cultivation of these capacities would be required if one's understanding of justice recognized caring for dependents as a requirement of justice. This is to say that, first, equal access to care and justly distributed and compensated giving of care is as essential to any conception of the good as are liberties and equal opportunities; and, second, a distinct moral power, a moral power shaped by the demands of care is necessary if dependents and dependency workers alike are to be accorded equal worth in a just society.

Fifth, the idealization of citizens operative in Rawls's theory of justice is as persons who possess the two moral powers and have the normal capacities that are the requirements for establishing fair terms of social cooperation. This accords with the egalitarian liberal tradition that Rawls exemplifies: justice should provide principles that fairly distribute the benefits and burdens of social cooperation among free and equal persons given the circumstances of justice. The two principles of justice, the equality of rights and liberties, fair equality of opportunity, and the maximin distributive principle provide us with these fair terms for social cooperation among an association of equals.

Dependency concerns, if they are both reasonable and rational, ought to be, but are not now, included within the features of a well-ordered society reflected in the public conception of social cooperation.[26] Unless a human society exists under especially hard conditions, we think it reasonable and right that humans care for those in a weakened or impaired condition. Thus, it is reasonable to expect that a well-ordered society is one that attends to the needs of dependents, and whatever else that necessitates. To be concerned that dependency needs and relationships in which these needs are satisfied are among the fair terms of social cooperation is also rational—that is, to view dependency in this way accords with each individual's self-interest. For, even if we are fully functioning and without dependency responsibilities when we are engaged in social cooperation, we have at one time been dependent and may again find ourselves dependent, or we may find ourselves with dependents. In these circumstances, we would want to know that the means are available by which we can either be properly cared for or have resources and supports available to care for the needs of those dependent upon us.

Given the notion of a well-ordered society as one based on fair terms of social cooperation, we can see that dependency concerns *are* pertinent to political justice: First, they are rational and reasonable considerations in choosing a conception of justice. Second, as I have already argued, a society that does not care

---

[26] In *Political Liberalism* Rawls characterizes social cooperation as more than just efficiently organized social activity. It involves the "fair terms of cooperation," which in turn articulate "an idea of reciprocity and mutuality: all who cooperate must benefit, or share in common burdens, in some appropriate fashion judged by a suitable benchmark of comparison" (*Political Liberalism*, 300).

for its dependents or that cares for them only by unfairly exploiting the labor of those who do the caring cannot be said to be just or well ordered. Third, when we reorient our political insights to see the centrality of human relationships to our happiness and well-being, we recognize dependency needs as basic motivations for creating a social order. That is to say, we need social cooperation in the *first place* because we require a means by which to care for dependents and to provide for those who care for dependents. We cannot limit our understanding of social organization to interactions between independent and fully functioning persons because it obscures or minimizes the social contributions of those who care for dependents and of dependents—who, even in their neediness, contribute to the ongoing nature of human relationships, which are the core of any human society.

One could turn about this formulation. One could say that if we limit our view of a just society to one in which principles that provide the fair terms of social cooperation prevail, and such cooperation is the province of equal and fully functioning citizens, we have missed the most important point of social organization. The just end we ought to seek cannot be limited to fair terms of social cooperation; it needs to provide fair terms for living with one another, given our inevitable dependency and inextricable interdependency. And we cannot get there with the idealization of citizens that is prevalent in liberal theory as a whole, namely that citizens are equal, free, and independent. We may deserve moral parity throughout our lives, but we are not always equally empowered or situated; we may value equal freedom, but such freedom cannot be bought at the expense of free-riding on those who are caring for dependents; and most important of all, no human being can be invulnerable to the demands of human dependency. As human beings we experience periods of inevitable dependency and live our lives enmeshed in inextricable interdependencies. A theory of equality that ignores these cannot be an adequate theory of justice.

12

A Feminist Liberal Response to the Dependency Critique

Amy R. Baehr

Dependency must be faced from the beginning of any project in egalitarian theory that hopes to include *all* persons within its scope.[1]

Justice that is caring begins with an acknowledgment of our dependency and seeks to organize society so that our well-being is not inversely related to our need for care or to care; such justice makes caring itself a mode of just action.[2]

I begin with the intuition that a just society is, among other things, a fair caregiving and care-receiving society. I mean a society in which individuals receive the caregiving they need to survive and thrive; while those with dependents needing caregiving are able to provide or procure it and are able to do so voluntarily and without being disadvantaged; under conditions of equal respect for the caregiving needs of each. In section 2 I argue that the just society envisioned in John Rawls's justice as fairness does not guarantee this justice in caregiving. Nor, I add here without argument, do the just societies envisioned by many of the liberal tradition's most recognized and venerated political philosophers. Unsatisfied with this state of the moral imagination of liberal political philosophy, and inspired by Eva Kittay's challenge, I argue here that a society is just only if it is in compliance with principles of justice in caregiving. In section 3 I present such principles in a Rawlsian way, namely as those that would be chosen in a suitably designed "initial situation,"[3] and constitute part of a "political conception of justice"[4] in Rawls's terms. The view I present—a *feminist political constructivism*—concedes as much to the dependency critique as it defends in Rawls. The view is

---

[1] Eva Feder Kittay, *Love's Labor* (Routledge, 1999), 77.
[2] Eva Feder Kittay, "When Caring Is Just and Justice Is Caring: Justice and Mental Retardation," *Public Culture* 13 (2001), 576.
[3] John Rawls, *A Theory of Justice*, rev. ed. (Harvard University Press, 1999), 11.
[4] John Rawls, *Political Liberalism*, expanded ed. (Columbia University Press, 2005), 11.

Amy R. Baehr, *A Feminist Liberal Response to the Dependency Critique* In: *John Rawls*. Edited by: Jon Mandle and Sarah Roberts-Cady, Oxford University Press (2020). © Oxford University Press.
DOI: 10.1093/oso/9780190859213.003.0019.

also responsive to antiracist criticism of Rawlsian ideal theory,[5] attending to the intersectional nature of the challenge of justice in caregiving.

1. Situating the Fact of Human Dependency

Rawls is charged with failure to appreciate the fact of human dependency. By "the fact of human dependency" I mean that to survive and thrive each of us needs constant and loving caregiving for more than a decade as infants and children; and many of us need intermittent, and some of us constant, caregiving after that. I mean also that those who provide caregiving often become dependent on others because providing caregiving can reduce one's ability to see to one's own basic needs.[6]

A theory of justice properly situates that fact when it (1) proposes principles that recognize dependency-related injustice; (2) conceives of a just society as one in which mechanisms are at work keeping dependency-related injustices at bay; and (3) provides insight into remedies for dependency-related injustices to deploy here and now to move society toward stable, just caregiving arrangements.

When I refer to dependency-related injustice, I have five considered convictions in mind, culled from feminist and antiracist theory and activism. It is unjust when, due to the arrangements of the basic structure of society, (A) one fails to receive the caregiving one needs to survive and thrive; B) providing or procuring the caregiving one's dependents need puts one at a disadvantage vis-à-vis primary social goods; (C) one is unable to provide or procure the caregiving one's dependents need; (D) one is forced to provide caregiving to, or procure caregiving for, particular others; and (E) society's public culture fails to recognize some as worthy of having their dependency needs satisfied, or as worthy of satisfying the needs of their dependents.[7]

Injustices A and C involve failures to reach a threshold due to mismatches between the need for and the provision of caregiving or caregiver support. Mismatches can result from maldistribution—where society's caregiving and support resources are sufficient, but its distribution leaves some with inadequate shares. Mismatches can result also when social arrangements make society's

---

[5] See Charles Mills, *Black Rights, White Wrongs: The Critique of Racial Liberalism* (Oxford University Press, 2017).

[6] Eva Feder Kittay, "Taking Dependency Seriously: The Family and Medical Leave Act Considered in the Light of the Social Organization of Dependency Work and Gender Equality," *Hypatia* 10 (1995), 10.

[7] By "provide caregiving" I mean the hands-on satisfaction of needs. By "procure caregiving" I mean supporting the provision of caregiving, for example, by financially supporting a caregiver. By "thrive" I mean achieve the "species-typical functioning" of which one is capable. See Norman Daniels, *Just Health Care* (Cambridge University Press, 1985), 28.

caregiving resources scarce. Injustice B involves receiving a smaller share of primary social goods than one would receive were one not providing or procuring caregiving for one's dependents. B does not entail that it is unjust when some do more caregiving than others; uneven distribution of caregiving work in society generally, or within families, is not, on its own, an injustice.

Injustice D involves being *forced* to provide caregiving to, or procure caregiving for, *particular* others. "Being forced" includes being compelled by law or by nonstate actors (with the state's permission); being left no other (reasonable) option; or being socialized to the discrete social role of caregiver. D does not entail that being forced to contribute to society's general ability to provide or procure caregiving is unjust. Also, D does not entail that it is unjust to compel those who voluntarily provide caregiving to provide the sort of caregiving needed to survive and thrive; without this standard, injustice A threatens. Injustice E involves a kind of civic disrespect. Receiving less caregiving than someone else, or not managing to provide or procure as much caregiving as someone else, is not always unjust; but when arrangements affording some less ability to provide or procure needed caregiving track group membership, they express an unequal worthiness to receive, or to provide or procure, caregiving.

Perhaps caregiving is scarce or maldistributed because people eschew providing or procuring it in an attempt to avoid its disadvantages. But human beings regularly provide or procure caregiving even when it is to their disadvantage. They do so when they are forced. Another reason is that human beings often don't distinguish neatly between their own interests and the interests of their dependents in receiving caregiving. This not-neat distinction is among the most noble and precious of our species traits.[8]

A just society is compliant with principles of justice in caregiving. We arrive at these principles, as Rawls does his own, through a process of reflective equilibrium: seeking coherence between considered convictions and a set of principles that justify them.[9] This process results in principles of justice in caregiving calling for (1) universal receipt of caregiving needed to survive and thrive; (2) caregiver nondisadvantage (vis-à-vis primary social goods); (3) universal capability to provide or procure needed caregiving for one's dependents when one is willing and otherwise able; (4) freedom from forced caregiving and caregiver support for particular others; (5) and equal civic respect for the caregiving needs of each.[10] Section 3 presents these principles as chosen in a suitably designed initial situation, and as part of a political conception of justice in Rawls's terms.

[8] Compare Kittay, *Love's Labor*, 51–53.
[9] Rawls, *A Theory of Justice*, 18.
[10] Compare Kittay, *Love's Labor*, 113; and Eva Feder Kittay, "A Theory of Justice as Fair Terms of Social Life Given Our Inevitable Dependency and Our Inextricable Interdependency" in *Care Ethics and Political Theory*, ed. Daniel Engster and Maurice Hamington (Oxford University Press, 2015), 62–64.

Recall that properly situating the fact of dependency involves conceiving of a just society as one in which mechanisms are at work keeping dependency-related injustices at bay. Justice as fairness conceives of a just society as one in which we should expect class origins, native endowments, and luck to cause drift away from just arrangements;[11] so a just society includes mechanisms—Rawls sometimes calls them "regulations"[12]—that work continually to re-establish just arrangements in response. Mechanisms respond to specific ways the forces of class, natural endowments, and luck threaten to disturb just arrangements. But we should also expect dependency to cause drift away from just arrangements; people become disabled, adopt or have children, and so on. So we add that a just society includes mechanisms that continually re-establish just arrangements in response to this force as well. We should also expect historically entrenched behavioral and institutional patterns and associated ways of thinking to cause drift from just arrangements.[13] For example, if just arrangements make caregiving nondisadvantaging, gendered institutional patterns may reassert themselves, and gendered ways of thinking may re-emerge, causing drift toward the disadvantaging of caregivers. And if just arrangements secure the equal entitlement to provide or procure caregiving, racist institutional patterns may reassert themselves and racist thinking may re-emerge, causing drift toward arrangements expressing disrespect for caregiving needs of black and brown people. So we add that a just society includes mechanisms that continually re-establish just arrangements in response to the specific ways these forces threaten to disturb just arrangements as well.

When we conceive of a just society in this way, we have in mind a concrete ideal: an idea of a specific society, with a specific history of injustice threatening in specific ways to cause drift away from just arrangements, and mechanisms keeping those injustices at bay.[14] Critics of Rawlsian ideal theory rightly contend that we need a theory of justice to help us understand our own society and recommend measures we might take here and now.[15] That is the function of a concrete ideal. Rawls suggests a concrete ideal when he explains that principles of justice must be expressed in constitutional and legislative rules, and in the application of such rules in the light of "the general facts" about the specific society so that the "most effective" means of realizing them may be found.[16] Reading Rawls in this way makes sense of his claim that his proposal is a realistic utopia.[17] The

[11] Compare John Rawls, *Justice as Fairness: A Restatement*, ed. Erin Kelly (Harvard University Press, 2001), 66.

[12] Rawls, *Justice as Fairness*, 56; *A Theory of Justice*, 401.

[13] Erin Kelly, "The Historical Injustice Problem for Political Liberalism," *Ethics* 128 (2017), 93. See also Mills, *Black Rights*, 158.

[14] Compare Mills, *Black Rights*, 156.

[15] Mills, *Black Rights*, 215.

[16] Rawls, *A Theory of Justice*, 173.

[17] Rawls, *Justice as Fairness*, 4.

problem is not that Rawls proposes an ideal, it's that his ideal fails to recognize the full array of forces that disturb just arrangements.

To develop a concrete ideal, we look at a specific society in its historically contingent specificity to discover how injustices are manifested and sustained in it; then we propose mechanisms that might characterize a just version of that society, and remedies that might move it in the direction of stable, just arrangements. I use the term "mechanism" for how a just society keeps at bay the injustices that threaten; for example, legally secured arrangements and institutions, but also voluntary associations, conventions, identities, attitudes, and an ethos guiding individual and collective conduct. Mechanisms make just arrangements stable, securing them over time. What counts as a mechanism varies from society to society because injustices threaten in diverse and historically contingent ways. Since any set of threats could, presumably, be effectively met in a specific society with more than one set of mechanisms, there probably isn't only one just version of any given not-just society.

I use the term "remedy" for what we may or should do here and now to move toward stable, just arrangements. Remedies can take the same form as mechanisms. Like mechanisms, there are different sets of remedies because there are different unjust societies, and because any given not-just society could presumably be made more just by more than one set of remedies. What works as a mechanism might not work as a remedy; some mechanism might be something to aim for but might not move an unjust society in the direction of stable, just arrangements. Similarly, a remedy might not work as a mechanism—it might be a ladder to throw away.

Wisely proposing mechanisms and remedies for our society requires understanding its injustice. (Our focus is dependency-related injustice.) Lacking space for a comprehensive account, this sketch must suffice. First, many children lack caregiving necessary to become thriving adults—for example, sufficient hands-on, loving caregiving in infancy and childhood, and adequate formative experiences in and outside of classrooms. Many individuals with disabilities, including the frail elderly, lack hands-on, loving caregiving necessary for the dignified completion of everyday activities, for development and maintenance of their capacities and talents, and for access to meaningful work and full participation in the life of their communities. Some lack sufficient caregiving even to survive. Second, many are unable to provide or procure needed caregiving; they are too poor or lack sufficient time away from paid work, are incarcerated or lack associational support, or have had dependents coercively removed from their homes. Third, providing and procuring caregiving puts many at a disadvantage vis-à-vis primary social goods. It frustrates their ability to develop talents and compete for positions that confer social recognition and authority, and to earn income, accumulate wealth, and access time away from paid work necessary for activities definitive of a good life for them. Fourth, much caregiving is insufficiently voluntary—some lack family planning resources, are saddled with overwhelming child-support debt, or are subject to socialization to the discrete social role of caregiver. And fifth, many institutional arrangements express and reinforce an ethos of disrespect for the caregiving needs of some groups. While these injustices are endemic, a disproportionate burden of this injustice is borne by women and their dependents, and especially by women of color and poor women.

Mechanisms and remedies must be tailored to the specific ways injustices threaten. Some proposals reflect a misunderstanding. For example, to address caregiver disadvantage, some recommend that homemaking women receive half of their husbands' paychecks and half of family assets at divorce,[18] that resident men do 50 percent of caregiving and housework,[19] and that women "lean in"[20] at work outside of the home. These proposals are often labeled liberal feminist. But liberal feminism is a capacious family of doctrines[21] that includes the doctrine presented here that finds them to be wholly insufficient.

Paycheck sharing and the equitable division of family assets at divorce tie caregivers' and dependents' fortunes to a wage-earner in their household. This leaves unaddressed disadvantage suffered by those who support caregivers and those without a wage-earning partner; and it leaves unaddressed the myriad ways financial dependence renders caregivers vulnerable. Exhorting men to take up 50 percent of work in the home often merely spreads disadvantage around; and since many lack a resident or associated adult, caregiving often gets offloaded to older children, commonly girls. Affluent and wealthy families avoid much disadvantage by outsourcing caregiving to others for pay, freeing themselves to volunteer and nurture the larger associations on which their dependents' thriving depends. Less affluent families rarely escape the disadvantage and usually pass it on to their communities.[22]

Those who can afford to offload caregiving can lean in at work while also procuring adequate caregiving for their dependents. Many who can't afford to do so find themselves nonetheless required to lean in at work, leaving their dependents bereft. While the wealthy would be able to offload caregiving at nearly any price, many depend on the surfeit of women, often immigrants and women of color, who provide caregiving, working long hours for little pay and few benefits.

---

[18] Susan Moller Okin, *Justice, Gender, and the Family* (Basic Books, 1989), 166.

[19] Okin, *Justice, Gender*, 181.

[20] Sheryl Sandberg, *Women, Work and the Will to Lead* (Knopf, 2013).

[21] Amy R. Baehr, "A Capacious Account of Liberal Feminism," *Feminist Philosophy Quarterly* 3 (2017), 1–23.

[22] Mary Romero, "Who Takes Care of the Maid's Children: Exploring the Costs of Domestic Service," in *Feminism and Families*, ed. Hilde Lindeman (Routledge, 1997), 63–91.

Dependency-related injustice results from a public ethos celebrating independence, recognizing caregiving needs only as the sole responsibility of individuals or families, and delegating caregiving to women and girls. This ethos celebrates families and communities that satisfy their dependency needs privately and recognize their dependents as worthy of caregiving and their women as virtuous for providing it. It also stigmatizes and blames families and communities unable to satisfy their caregiving needs privately, and it conceives of their dependents as unworthy of receiving caregiving and their caregivers as unworthy of providing or procuring it. It is impossible to disentangle classist from racist (and especially antiblack) aspects of this ethos; but it is equally clear that the latter is not reducible to the former. This distinguishing of worthy from unworthy families is also evident in the hesitancy to recognize LGBTQ families' dependency needs.

This ethos is expressed and reinforced by legal arrangements and institutions. Many girls and women lack access to contraception and abortion services; and many men are reduced, by child-support rules, to indentured servitude. Some are legally denied the ability to provide or procure caregiving—by a punitive child-welfare system, immigration policy, and a criminal justice system that promiscuously incarcerates parents. Workplaces and educational institutions pit opportunities for the development of talents and accumulation of wealth against caregiving; for example, the law permits employers to pay much less than what is required to support dependents and to fire employees who take time off to provide caregiving. Policies aimed at alleviating the poverty caused by such employment arrangements are stigmatizing and fall far short of a remedy. Policies aimed at alleviating conflict between caregiving and remunerative work fail dramatically; for example, entitlement to leave from work to care for a newborn or newly adopted child, or a dependent who is ill, covers only a minority of workers and, because unpaid, is of little help to most, who live paycheck to paycheck.

2. Justice as Fairness

Rawls explains that children "are society's future citizens and have claims as such" (*JF*, 165); that children require caregiving to develop a sense of justice necessary for a just and stable regime;[23] and that caregiving plays a role in the development of talents and thus in fair equality of opportunity.[24] The aged who have been fully cooperating members of society also have a claim on caregiving when it is among their basic needs.[25] We may conclude that such individuals' caregiving

---

[23] Rawls, *A Theory of Justice*, chap. 7. Rawls recognizes that caregiving must often be loving caregiving (*A Theory of Justice*, 406).
[24] Rawls, *A Theory of Justice*, 148.
[25] Rawls, *Political Liberalism*, 7.

needs would be satisfied in Rawls's just society.[26] Should needed caregiving not be spontaneously provided by associated others, justice as fairness would underwrite measures to produce caregiving, for example state-funded day-care and caregiver allowances. The liberty principle ensures that caregivers are not overtly forced. This underwrites mechanisms securing personal freedoms, including reproductive rights and free choice of occupation.

The fair equality of opportunity principle rules out discrimination against women and girls in employment and education, removing important obstacles to their having options other than caregiving. Rawls explicitly calls for measures compensating women for shouldering more than their fair share of caregiving; and for equalizing women's share. He writes: "If a basic, if not the main, cause of women's inequality is their greater share in the bearing, nurturing, and caring for children in the traditional division of labor within the family, steps need to be taken either to equalize their share or to compensate them for it" (JF, 167). Equalizing women's share means increasing men's; I lack space to explore permissible measures to accomplish this. As compensation, Rawls mentions paycheck sharing and postdivorce equitable distribution of assets.[27] We've seen that those measures are insufficient, but perhaps more adequate measures could be underwritten in this way.

But note that Rawls's principles apply only to those who are, were, or will be "fully cooperating members of society over a complete life."[28] They do not apply to individuals whose disabilities render them wholly noncooperating; so failing to meet the needs of such individuals for survival and thriving is not, for that reason, unjust according to justice as fairness. To be sure, Rawls writes: "I take it as obvious, and accepted as common sense, that we have a duty towards all human beings however severely handicapped" (JF, 176 n. 59). But, as Cynthia Stark points out, "Rawls does not tell us whether these are duties of justice."[29] And even if they are, Rawls's principles are not their normative foundation.

Also, Rawls fails to object to caregiver disadvantage as such; he objects to it insofar as it is a cause of women's inequality. In a just society, full cooperators receive caregiving, and Rawls explains that caregiving is "socially necessary labor" (JF, 162), but justice as fairness does not ensure that those who provide caregiving are not disadvantaged for it. The fair equality of opportunity principle doesn't rule out caregiver disadvantage any more than it rules out disadvantage to monks. Nor does the difference principle rule it out—if caregivers

---

26 Caregiving, just like material resources, could become scarce. But justice only applies when such resources are only moderately scarce.

27 *Justice as Fairness*, 167, citing Okin, *Justice, Gender and the Family*, chaps. 7–8.

28 Rawls, *Political Liberalism*, 18; see also Kittay, *Love's Labor*, 79.

29 Cynthia Stark, "How to Include the Severely Disabled in a Contractarian Theory of Justice," *Journal of Political Philosophy* 15 (2007), 130 n. 10.

are disproportionately represented among the least well off, that this inequality benefits them suffices to permit it.

Rawls's principles fail to recognize, as unjust in itself, the inability to provide or procure caregiving for one's own dependents. The interest in providing or procuring caregiving is just a preference, not an interest society's basic arrangements must satisfy. And finally, Rawls holds that the liberty of the family rules out measures to ensure that some are not forced via socialization,[30] so socialization does not count as liberty-infringing. This is hard to square with the quotation presented previously in which Rawls calls for equalizing women's share of caregiving—how would that be done if not by measures affecting socialization in families?—but I lack space necessary to explore this further.[31]

3. Feminist Political Constructivism

Principles of justice in caregiving can be presented as chosen in a suitably designed initial situation, and as part of a political conception of justice in Rawls's terms. Following Aaron James, let us say that Rawls identifies basic institutions of constitutional democracy—"the political constitution and the principal economic and social arrangements," which he calls "the basic structure"[32]—as a kind of "social practice";[33] that he then asks whether there might be, implicit in the public political culture, a conception of the "purpose or aim" of this social practice; and finally that he uses original position reasoning to clarify what "requirements . . . must be fulfilled in order for [that] practice to achieve [that] goal or aim."[34]

Rawls explains, as James puts it, that it is implicit in our public political culture that "the aim of the basic structure of a modern constitutional democracy is to create primary social goods, and to do so as a cooperative scheme . . . for mutual or reciprocal advantage."[35] A normative conception of the person as a fully cooperating member accompanies this normative conception of society. But Rawls notes that the "public culture is not unambiguous: it contains a variety of possible organizing ideas that might be used instead."[36] Feminist political

---

[30] John Rawls, "The Ideal of Public Reason Revisited," in *Collected Papers*, ed. Samuel Freeman (Harvard University Press, 1999), 599; see also *Justice as Fairness*, 165.

[31] See Amy R. Baehr, "Feminist Receptions of the Original Position," in *The Original Position*, ed. Timothy Hinton (Cambridge University Press, 2016), 119–138.

[32] Rawls, *A Theory of Justice*, 6.

[33] Aaron James, "Constructing Justice for Existing Practice: Rawls and the Status Quo," *Philosophy and Public Affairs* 33 (2005), 282.

[34] James, "Constructing Justice," 301.

[35] James, "Constructing Justice," 300, citing Rawls, *Political Liberalism*, 16.

[36] Rawls, *Justice as Fairness*, 25; *A Theory of Justice*, 105.

constructivism makes use of this idea: the aim of the basic structure of a constitutional democracy is to create primary social goods—including caregiving—and to do so as a scheme that is to everyone's advantage. Accompanying this normative conception of society is a normative conception of the person that includes needing caregiving to achieve the degree of species-typical functioning of which one is capable, and having dependents whose interest in receiving caregiving can't be neatly distinguished from one's own interests.

These latter normative conceptions are implicit in our public political culture. There is a consensus that arrangements of the basic structure should satisfy the caregiving needs of all persons, and for all to be able to see to the caregiving needs of their dependents. As we have seen, the dominant ethos delegates responsibility for dependency to individuals and families; but disagreement about what arrangements are preferable for the satisfaction of caregiving needs is consistent with agreement that basic arrangements should satisfy them.

Following Rawls, we use initial situation reasoning to work out what the basic structure must do to realize this aim, imagining parties behind a veil of ignorance concerned to maximize the least advantageous outcome. But we add that caregiving is a primary good;[37] that parties know they will not neatly distinguish their own interests from the interest of some particular others in receiving caregiving; and that parties know that gendered and racist institutional patterns may assert themselves and gendered and racist ways of thinking may emerge.[38]

Wanting to avoid not receiving needed caregiving, parties choose the first principle of justice in caregiving calling for universal receipt of caregiving needed to survive and thrive, scaled to the species-typical functioning of which individuals are capable. Wanting to avoid disadvantage due to providing or procuring caregiving, parties choose the second principle disallowing caregiver disadvantage. Wanting to avoid being unable to provide or procure caregiving for their dependents, parties choose the third principle calling for all who are willing and otherwise able to be able to provide or procure caregiving for their dependents. Wanting to avoid being forced to provide or procure caregiving for particular others, parties endorse the fourth principle insisting on voluntariness in caregiving. And wanting to avoid the effects of historically entrenched patterns of disrespect, parties choose the fifth principle calling for equal public recognition of the caregiving needs of each. In a society compliant with these principles, the caregiving needs of the fully and the not fully cooperating are satisfied by caregivers in a robustly voluntary way and without disadvantage; and individuals

[37] Kittay, Love's Labor, 100–102. See also Asha Bhandary, Freedom to Care: Liberalism, Dependency Care, and Culture (Routledge, 2019), 23–52.
[38] Compare Kelly, "Historical Injustice"; and Mills, Black Rights, 213.

with dependents are able to provide or procure caregiving under conditions of equal civic respect for everyone's caregiving needs.

Principles of justice in caregiving are political principles, not dependent on any particular comprehensive doctrine. They are proposed as part of, to use Rawls's words, "a moral conception . . . worked out for a specific subject, namely . . . for the basic structure of a democratic society" (*JF*, 26). They are "formulated . . . solely in terms of fundamental ideas familiar from, or implicit in, the public political culture of a democratic society" (*JF*, 27). Accepting a political conception including them "does not presuppose accepting any particular comprehensive doctrine" (*JF*, 26).

While Rawls's principles underwrite state-funded *day care* or *caregiver allowances* if sufficient caregiving is not otherwise forthcoming, principles of justice in caregiving underwrite these mechanisms as ways to ensure that caregiving is voluntary and nondisadvantaging and to ensure that individuals are able to provide or procure the caregiving their dependents need. While Rawls's principles prohibit educational and workplace discrimination against women and girls, principles of justice in caregiving prohibit discrimination against caregivers regardless of sex or gender and do so as one way among others to ensure that caregivers are not disadvantaged vis-à-vis primary social goods. While Rawls's principles ensure that caregivers are not overtly forced, principles of justice in caregiving secure a more robust voluntariness, protecting individuals from being socialized to the discrete social role of caregiver. Satisfaction of the first four principles could still allow arrangements that afford members of historically disrespected groups less ability to provide or procure needed caregiving and thus express an unequal worthiness for caregiving. The fifth principle of justice underwrites mechanisms that block this tracking, among them, for example, those that aim to rectify past wrongs—note that among the injustices done by slave owners and colonizers, and their accomplices, were significant dependency-related injustices.

I lack space to explore these and other mechanisms underwritten by principles of justice in caregiving. Recall that a theory of justice situates the fact of dependency properly when it provides insight into remedies to deploy here and now. I lack space to explore remedies except to suggest that the measures just described seem appropriate as remedies as well. I also lack space to explore how principles of justice in caregiving may be combined with Rawls's principles to produce one set—which is how I intend them.

4. Conclusion

I have provided some support for the intuition—culled from feminist and antiracist theory and activism—that a just society is a fair caregiving and care-receiving society. I have suggested that such a society would be compliant with principles of justice in caregiving chosen in an initial situation whose design reflects normative ideals implicit in our public political culture. This feminist constructivism is a response to the dependency critique, as well as to antiracist criticisms, of Rawls's justice as fairness. To be sure, I have conceded as much to the criticisms as I have defended in Rawls. But the project remains in outline a Rawlsian and a liberal one, to propose, in a manner appropriate to a democracy, a political conception of justice on which citizens may ground "claims on the main institutions of the basic structure" (*JF*, 27).

Acknowledgments

Many thanks to Eva Kittay and the editors for helpful comments.

PART VII

RAWLS AND FEMINISM

Introduction

In the United States, full-time working women on average earn 82 percent of what full-time working men earn.[1] Globally, women often fare much worse, earning an average of 68 percent of men's earnings.[2] In addition to getting paid less than men to do the same jobs, women often do not have the opportunity to do the jobs men do. Men still occupy most business leadership positions both in the United States and in the world more broadly. In 2019, less than 5 percent of Fortune 500 companies had a female CEO.[3] Women do not fare much better in government leadership positions. In the 116th Congress of the United States, women hold less than 24 percent of the congressional positions (and this has been celebrated as a record high). While these are just a few ways to measure the status of women in contemporary societies, these data make it clear that women are far from equal to men in power and representation, even in an allegedly liberal society like the United States. Any adequate theory of justice must be able to address these issues of gender injustice. Does Rawls's theory offer adequate resources to critique the social structures that create and maintain gender inequality?

On the face of it, it appears that Rawls's theory of justice is rich with possibilities for feminists concerned with the status of women in society. Rawls defends principles of justice that require equal liberty and fair equality of opportunity for all. On the other hand, feminists have cited a number of concerns about Rawls's development of these ideas. Some feminists express concern that Rawls's theory is insufficiently attentive to the role of emotions and relationships in moral theory.[4] For a discussion of these concerns and an overview of how one might defend Rawls against this challenge, see Martha Nussbaum's "Rawls and Feminism."[5] Other feminists are concerned about Rawls's inattention to human

---

[1] "Highlights of Women's Earnings in 2017," United States Bureau of Labor Statistics, August 2018, https://www.bls.gov/opub/reports/womens-earnings/2017/home.html.

[2] "Global Gender Gap Report 2017," World Economic Forum, http://reports.weforum.org/global-gender-gap-report-2017/key-findings/.

[3] "List: Women CEOs of the S&P 500," *Catalyst: Workplaces the Work for Women,* January 24, 2019, https://www.catalyst.org/research/women-ceos-of-the-sp-500/.

[4] Virginia Held, *Feminist Morality: Transforming Culture, Society and Politics* (University of Chicago Press, 1993); Annette Baier, "The Need for More Than Justice," in *Justice and Care: Essential Readings in Feminist Ethics,* ed. Virginia Held (Westview Press, 1995).

[5] Martha Nussbaum, "Rawls and Feminism," in *The Cambridge Companion to Rawls,* ed. Samuel Freeman (Cambridge University Press, 2003).

Introduction In: *John Rawls.* Edited by: Jon Mandle and Sarah Roberts-Cady, Oxford University Press (2020). © Oxford University Press. DOI: 10.1093/oso/9780190859213.003.0020.

dependency and dependent-care work, areas of society in which women are disproportionately represented.[6] For a discussion of this debate, see Part VI in this volume. In this part, we will focus on two other major categories of feminist criticisms of Rawls's theory: the problem of justice in the family and the problem of liberal tolerance.

First, there is a concern among some feminists that in focusing on state power and individual rights, Rawls overlooks the role of informal social structures in maintaining the domination and oppression of women. Perhaps most famously, Susan Moller Okin drew attention to Rawls's neglect of how issues of injustice in the family impact women's rights and opportunities.[7] Although at certain points in *A Theory of Justice* Rawls acknowledges the family as a part of the basic structure of society, he largely ignores it as a possible source of injustice. He presumes the family is a private and nonpolitical association to which the principles of justice do not directly apply. Indeed, the only place in *A Theory of Justice* that he discusses the role of family in any detail is in his discussion of children's moral development. Okin points out that in doing so he does not raise questions about the justice of family structures, but only presumes the family as a rich source of moral development. In failing to ask the question of justice within the family, Rawls fails to acknowledge the role that the gender socialization of children and the sexual division of labor in the family plays in limiting women's rights and opportunities. Okin points out specifically that the gendered division of labor in the family impacts people's liberty regarding choice of occupation. As long as women are primarily responsible for household labor, they will not have equality of opportunity in the workplace. Accordingly, Okin argues that justice in the public realm cannot be addressed apart from justice in the family.

Despite her criticisms of Rawls's own treatment of gender justice, Okin remains optimistic about the potential of Rawls's theory to be developed in ways that address the issue. She argues that if one takes seriously Rawls's commitment to equal liberties and opportunities, one would have to address justice in the family and critique the construction of gender more broadly. Rawls himself seems to have been convinced by her arguments. In "The Idea of Public Reason Revisited," Rawls references Okin's work, acknowledging her point and agreeing that "if a basic, if not the main, cause of women's inequality is their greater share in the bearing, nurturing, and caring for children in the traditional division of labor within the family, steps need to be taken either to equalize their share or to compensate them for it."[8] It remains controversial as to whether or not his brief discussion of Okin's work was sufficient to address the concerns she raised.

---

[6] Eva Kittay, *Love's Labor* (Routledge, 1999).

[7] Susan Moller Okin, *Justice, Gender and the Family* (Basic Books, 1989).

[8] John Rawls, "The Idea of Public Reason Revisited" in *Political Liberalism*, expanded ed. (Columbia University Press, 2005), 472–473.

A second, related theme in the feminist literature on Rawls stems from his commitment to political liberalism. In *Political Liberalism*, Rawls points out that any contemporary democratic society will be made up of people with different but reasonable comprehensive moral, religious, and philosophical doctrines. The task of political liberalism is to identify terms of cooperation that individuals holding these diverse doctrines can all reasonably recognize to be fair. In order to satisfy this requirement, a political conception of justice cannot be exclusively grounded in any particular comprehensive moral theory. The worry raised by feminists is that perhaps political liberalism will be too tolerant of oppressive doctrines.[9] In tolerating different conceptions of the good life, does Rawls also recommend we tolerate the major religious traditions that hold we ought to limit women's roles in society? Does liberal neutrality prevent political liberalism from taking a strong stance against traditions that allow for the subordination of women?

In this volume, first Costa and then Hartley and Watson take up both of these feminist concerns. Costa remains skeptical about the feminist potential of Rawls's theory. She formulates the problem with Rawls's theory as one of indeterminacy; depending on how one interprets the principles of justice, the theory may or may not effectively critique the social structures that maintain the domination of women. She argues that Rawls leaves room for reasonable disagreement about the interpretation of the two principles of justice and consequently disagreement about their policy implications. Do basic rights include reproductive rights? Should pornography be protected as free speech? How might one balance freedom of religion against equality of opportunity for girls? How ought one balance parental rights against equal opportunity of children? Costa argues that Rawls's theory does not provide determinate answers to these questions and therefore is limited in value as a tool for critiquing women's oppression.

Hartley and Watson argue that Rawls's theory can be defended against these challenges. Rawls is not just interested in equal formal rights, but in ensuring the social conditions necessary for people to make effective use of their freedoms. Insofar as gender socialization creates conditions in which women do not make effective use of their freedom, then justice requires that state institutions concern themselves with the construction and reproduction of gender in the family and religious institutions.

---

[9] John Exdell, "Feminism, Fundamentalism, and Liberal Legitimacy," *Canadian Journal of Philosophy* 24 (1994), 441–463; Sharon A. Lloyd, "Family Justice and Social Justice," *Pacific Philosophical Quarterly* 75 (1994), 353–371; Susan Moller Okin, "Political Liberalism, Justice and Gender," *Ethics* 105 (1994), 23–43; Amy Baehr, "Toward a New Feminist Liberalism," *Hypatia* 11 (1996), 49–66; Lisa Schwartzman, *Challenging Liberalism* (Penn State University Press, 2006); Ruth Abbey, ed., *Feminist Interpretations of John Rawls* (Penn State University Press, 2007).

Suggested Reading from Rawls to Accompany These Chapters

A Theory of Justice: Chapter 2
Political Liberalism: Lecture VIII, §§6–14; "The Idea of Public Reason Revisited," §5
Justice as Fairness: A Restatement: §50

For Further Reading

Abbey, Ruth, ed. *Feminist Interpretations of John Rawls* (Penn State University Press, 2013). This anthology includes diverse feminist perspectives on the work of John Rawls, including essays by Amy Baehr, Elizabeth Brake, Anthony Simon Laden, and Lisa H. Schwartzman.

Baehr, Amy. "Liberal Feminism" (revised 2013). *The Stanford Encyclopedia of Philosophy*. https://plato.stanford.edu/archives/fall2018/entries/feminism-liberal/. This entry provides an overview of some of the common tenets of liberal feminism, as well as an explanation of the primary disagreements among liberal feminists.

Laden, Anthony Simon. "Radical Liberals, Reasonable Feminists: Reason, Power and Objectivity in MacKinnon and Rawls." *Journal of Political Philosophy* 11 (2003), 133–152. This article argues that Rawls's *Political Liberalism* provides the resources for a radical liberal feminism.

Lloyd, S. A. "Family Justice and Social Justice." *Pacific Philosophical Quarterly* 75 (1994), 353–371. Lloyd defends *Political Liberalism* against Okin's challenge that it is improperly tolerant of sexist comprehensive doctrines.

Nussbaum, Martha. "Rawls and Feminism." In *The Cambridge Companion to Rawls*, ed. Samuel Freeman (Cambridge University Press, 2003). Nussbaum's overview of a range of feminist criticisms of Rawls's work includes concerns stemming from Rawls's inattention to care and relationships, concern about justice in the family, concerns about religion and public reason, and concerns about dependency.

Okin, Susan Moller. "'Forty Acres and a Mule' for Women: Rawls and Feminism." *Politics, Philosophy and Economics* 4 (2005), 233–248. Okin argues that Rawls's later work fares worse than his earlier work in addressing the feminist concern that one must attend to justice in the family in order to protect women's equal rights and opportunities outside the family.

Okin, Susan Moller. *Justice, Gender, and the Family* (Basic Books, 1989). This highly influential book argues that modern political philosophers' inattention to injustices in the family leads to theories of justice that cannot adequately address injustices women face outside the family in the social, political, and economic realms.

Watson, Lori, and Christie Hartley. *Equal Citizenship and Public Reason: A Feminist Political Liberalism* (Oxford University Press, 2018). This book represents a fuller development of Watson and Hartley's theory of political liberalism as a liberal feminism.

13

The Indeterminacy of Rawls's Principles for Gender Justice

M. Victoria Costa

1. The Feminist Reception of Justice as Fairness

John Rawls's theory of justice as fairness has been the subject of sustained discussion among feminists since its initial appearance. But no consensus has emerged. Rather, feminists have given mixed responses to the question of whether justice as fairness offers valuable conceptual tools for theorizing about social justice, or for justifying various progressive policies.[1] In this chapter I will focus my discussion on Rawls's later work, in order to shed some light on a number of points of disagreement among feminists. One of these points concerns whether the ideal of free and equal citizenship articulated in justice as fairness is a truly inclusive and emancipatory ideal. In order to examine this issue, I will argue that we need to focus on the two principles of justice that are built on this ideal and determine whether they would suffice to dismantle the relationships of domination and subordination that permeate the lives of women and girls. Another point of disagreement that is related specifically to Rawls's later work is whether or not the political method of justification he describes can actually be useful for feminist purposes, since it sets a number of constraints on the justification of policies. To assess the political method, I will argue, we should focus on Rawls's principles of justice, since Rawls considers them to be the most reasonable principles that pass the test of political justification.

According to S. A. Lloyd, Rawls was surprised by the feminist criticisms of his theory.[2] In his later writings on justice and the institution of the family, he briefly addressed some of them.[3] He argued that his liberal theory of justice is

---

[1] Regarding the feminist reception of Rawls's work see Martha Nussbaum, "Rawls and Feminism," in *The Cambridge Companion to Rawls*, ed. Samuel Freeman (Cambridge University Press, 2003), 488–520; and Ruth Abbey, ed., *Feminist Interpretations of John Rawls* (Penn State University Press, 2013).

[2] S. A. Lloyd, "Feminism," in *The Cambridge Rawls Lexicon*, ed. Jon Mandle and David Reidy (Cambridge University Press, 2015), 284.

[3] See John Rawls, *Justice as Fairness: A Restatement*, ed. Erin Kelly (Harvard University Press, 2001), 162–168; and John Rawls, *The Law of Peoples* (Harvard University Press, 2001), 156–164.

M. Victoria Costa, *The Indeterminacy of Rawls's Principles for Gender Justice* In: *John Rawls*. Edited by: Jon Mandle and Sarah Roberts-Cady, Oxford University Press (2020). © Oxford University Press.
DOI: 10.1093/oso/9780190859213.003.0021.

committed to the view that men and women should be treated as equal citizens, and he admitted that it was a mistake not to have been more explicit about this.[4] Rawls endorsed the analysis offered by Susan Moller Okin regarding the systematic vulnerabilities produced by the gendered division of labor in societies like the United States.[5] These vulnerabilities stem from gender norms according to which women have responsibility for a larger share of unpaid care work and housework within their families, and—when they have paid jobs—typically receive lower salaries than men. The result is that many women and their children are in a precarious position in cases of divorce. Rawls explicitly endorses Okin's recommendations to reform family law, so that divorce rulings recognize women's work and their entitlement to a fair share of the family's assets. However, against Okin, Rawls stresses that couples should be free to make decisions about how to distribute paid and unpaid work in their family life. He argues that a traditional division of labor along gender lines could be fully reasonable, as long as it was voluntary and was endorsed on the basis of a reasonable conception of the good. Rawls only condemns a gendered division of labor inside the family when it is the result of coercive circumstances and a lack of options. This suggests that Rawls also would have agreed with feminist proposals to reform the labor market: for example, providing accommodations for workers with young children, ensuring paid pregnancy and parental leave, and subsidizing childcare. Overall, Rawls was confident that the correct implementation of his two principles of justice would suffice to remedy injustices that affect women, and to secure their equality and independence.[6]

2. Political Liberalism, Reasonable Disagreements, and Feminist Goals

A number of feminists have welcomed the strategy of offering a strictly political defense of key normative concepts of justice as fairness.[7] The political method

---

[4] Rawls, *The Law of Peoples*, 156 n. 58.

[5] See Susan Moller Okin, *Justice, Gender, and the Family* (Basic Books, 1989). On the disagreements between Rawls and Okin regarding what kind of family arrangements count as just see M. Victoria Costa, *Rawls, Citizenship and Education* (Routledge, 2011), 38–55.

[6] Rawls, *Justice as Fairness*, 164; Rawls, *The Law of Peoples*, 159.

[7] See S. A. Lloyd, "Situating a Feminist Criticism of John Rawls's *Political Liberalism*," *Loyola of Los Angeles Law Review* 28 (1995), 1319–1344; Amy Baehr, "Perfectionism, Feminism and Public Reason," *Law and Philosophy* 27 (2008), 193–222; Amy Baehr, "Liberal Feminism: Comprehensive and Political," in Abbey, *Feminist Interpretations*, 150–166; Christie Hartley and Lori Watson, "Is a Feminist Political Liberalism Possible?," *Journal of Ethics and Social Philosophy* 5 (2010), 1–21; Christie Hartley and Lori Watson, "Political Liberalism, Marriage and the Family," *Law and Philosophy* 31 (2012), 185–212; Christie Hartley and Lori Watson, "A Feminist Defense of Political Liberalism," this volume.

of justification relies on a number of ideals that Rawls thinks are present in the public culture of liberal democratic societies, and that can be considered as widely shared among their citizens. The attractiveness of such a method is due, in part, to the fact that political liberalism promises to have wide appeal among reasonable people, even if they endorse a variety of incompatible comprehensive doctrines about the good. In fact, feminists disagree among themselves about the particular comprehensive ideals that sustain a good life, but they do share the political project of ending the domination of women.[8] The political approach offers a way to articulate and defend a set of common values shared by the women's movement and other progressive social movements, which can help further their political goals.

There are feminists, however, who are suspicious of Rawls's goal of accommodating such a wide variety of comprehensive doctrines about the good, and even more suspicious of regarding most of them as reasonable.[9] One problem is that Rawls describes reasonable comprehensive doctrines as doctrines that cover the major religious, philosophical, and moral aspects of human life, provide a coherent picture of the world, and structure a set of values in a more or less systematic way.[10] This account of reasonable comprehensive doctrines does not seem to exclude certain religious doctrines that support a traditional division of labor in the family along gender lines, that deny women leadership roles in their religious communities, that deny a number of rights to reproductive freedom, or that are opposed to granting same-sex couples the right to get married and enjoy the protections and benefits associated with that legal status. If political liberalism accepts such doctrines as reasonable, or at least as doctrines that a just society ought to tolerate when freely endorsed by some citizens, this seems to entail that it must refrain from combating them as significant obstacles to social justice. For this reason, some feminist critics argue that, insofar as it is strictly political, justice as fairness provides only modest protections of the freedom and equality of women, which are not enough to end their social, economic, and political subordination.[11]

According to Rawls, justifying fundamental principles of justice by means of political arguments makes it at least possible for an overlapping consensus on these principles to emerge over time, even under conditions of pluralism.

---

[8] See Baehr, "Liberal Feminism."

[9] See Susan Moller Okin, "*Political Liberalism*, Justice and Gender," *Ethics* 105 (1994), 23–43; Susan Moller Okin, "Forty Acres and a Mule for Women: Rawls and Feminism," *Politics, Philosophy and Economics* 4 (2005), 233–248; John Exdell, "Feminism, Fundamentalism, and Liberal Legitimacy," *Canadian Journal of Philosophy* 24 (1994), 441–464.

[10] John Rawls, *Political Liberalism*, expanded ed. (Columbia University Press, 2005), 59. On difficulties interpreting the concept of "reasonable" as applied to doctrines and persons see Leif Wenar, "Political Liberalism: An Internal Critique," *Ethics* 106 (1995), 32–62.

[11] Okin, "Forty Acres," 244.

Although Rawls thinks that the balance of public reasons supports his two principles of justice as the most reasonable, he admits that there might be alternative conceptions of justice that are political, liberal, and reasonable as well. These political liberal conceptions will have to contain the following:

First, a list of certain basic rights, liberties, and opportunities (such as those familiar from constitutional regimes);

Second, an assignment of special priority to those rights, liberties, and opportunities, especially with respect to the claims of the general good and perfectionist values; and

Third, measures ensuring for all citizens adequate all-purpose means to make effective use of their freedoms.[12]

In the following section I will argue that there is significant indeterminacy in Rawls's principles of justice that affects their policy implications. As it turns out, the basic liberties require further specification by the legal and judicial system. And there is a certain amount of indeterminacy regarding the kinds of policies that ought to be implemented to equalize opportunities and redistribute resources to improve the life prospects of the worst off. Rawls's concession that there can be other political liberal conceptions of justice that are reasonable aggravates these application problems. Each liberal political conception will have its own particular set of principles of justice, and each of these can be used to derive slightly different policy recommendations. Although one can expect some significant convergence on the policies supported by political liberal principles of justice, some of these policies will better serve the goal of eradicating the domination of women than others. I will leave these difficulties aside, and assume for the sake of argument there is only one set of reasonable political liberal principles of justice: Rawls's own. As I will now argue, even if that were the case, the political method allows for a variety of reasonable disagreements regarding how to implement the principles at the legislative and policy stages. As a consequence, it does not give a unique answer to the question of whether political principles of justice would eradicate relationships of domination.

3. Do the Principles of Justice Protect Women from Domination?

Rawls's argument for the principles of justice is built on two intuitive ideas, which are seen as implicit in the political institutions and public culture of democratic

---

12 Rawls, *The Law of Peoples*, 141.

societies. These are the idea of society as a fair system of cooperation and the idea of citizens as free and equal.[13] Rawls understands the idea of society as a fair system of cooperation as involving publicly recognized rules and procedures that regulate social life, and that can be reasonably accepted by all citizens. Rawls assumes that reasonable citizens are willing to treat each other according to the demands of reciprocity. This means that they are willing to offer one another terms such that they "think it at least reasonable for others to accept them, as free and equal citizens, and not as dominated or manipulated, or under the pressure of inferior political or social positions."[14] Turning to the second intuitive idea, Rawls explains his general understanding of citizens as free and equal by stating that citizens have certain moral capacities that enable them to be fully cooperating members of society over the course of their lives: the capacity to act justly and the capacity to pursue a conception of the good.[15] This is a very general normative idea that only constrains the public rules and procedures of social institutions by requiring that they treat citizens as responsible for their behavior, as capable of cooperating with others on fair terms, and as having authority to decide how to live their lives.

In order to establish whether Rawls's theory actually protects women from domination, we need to look at the full political conception of justice he offers, and not simply at his commitment to freedom and equality. Theories of justice as different as Robert Nozick's libertarianism, John Stuart Mill's utilitarianism, Phillip Pettit's republicanism, and Rawls's justice as fairness, to name just a few, can all be read as giving an answer to the question of how society ought to be organized to treat its citizens in ways that respect their status as free and equal persons. But it is far from clear whether all such views will be satisfactory from a feminist perspective. For this reason, it is important to see that Rawls's political principles of justice are not separable from the rest of the theory. Rather, they provide, in a sense, his interpretation of what it is for the basic institutions of a society to treat its members in ways that recognize their status as free and equal. These political principles also guide the design of laws and policies a society would have to implement to be just. Here they are, as Rawls presents them.

(a) Each person has an equal claim to a fully adequate scheme of equal basic rights and liberties, which scheme is compatible with the same scheme for all; and in this scheme the equal political liberties, and only those liberties, are to be guaranteed their fair value.

---

[13] See Rawls, *Justice as Fairness*, 5–8, 18–24.
[14] Rawls, *The Law of Peoples*, 136–137.
[15] See Rawls, *Political Liberalism*, 18–20.

(b) Social and economic inequalities are to satisfy two conditions: first, they are to be attached to positions and offices open to all under conditions of fair equality of opportunity; and second, they are to be to the greatest benefit of the least advantaged members of society.[16]

3.1. Equal Rights and Liberties

Let us begin with (a), the principle of equal liberty, and discuss its contribution to the eradication of domination, including the domination of women. Rawls supplements this principle with a quite heterogeneous list of rights and liberties that specify what is included in a "fully adequate scheme." The rights and liberties included are freedom of thought and liberty of conscience; the political liberties; freedom of association; freedoms specified by the liberty and integrity of the person (including freedom from enslavement and physical harm, and freedom to choose one's occupation); and rights and liberties covered by the rule of law.[17] These rights and liberties are inalienable, and are to be guaranteed by law. The scheme of rights and liberties specifies certain "areas" or activities of citizens that ought to be secure against interference by third parties, including the government, individual citizens, associations, or groups. Although the elements of the list are intuitively significant, courts have the role of making more precise the extensions of the areas of protected liberty, and the relative priority of particular liberties when they clash. Unavoidably, there will be some reasonable disagreements concerning the precise implications of these liberties; for example, there will be disagreements about whether pornography is protected as a form of free speech, or how far the protections of religious freedom extend for religious associations that run businesses or schools.

One significant omission from Rawls's list are reproductive rights, particularly rights to contraception and abortion services, which are fundamental if women are to be able to exercise the moral capacity associated with the pursuit of their conception of the good. One could argue that reproductive rights are covered by the liberty and integrity of the person. But since there are significant political controversies regarding these rights, it is not clear whether Rawls would include them among the liberties protected by the first principle of justice, or leave decisions about whether they ought to be protected or not to the legislative stage.[18]

---

[16] Rawls, *Political Liberalism*, 5–6.

[17] Rawls, *Political Liberalism*, 291. Regarding the precise content of these liberties see Samuel Freeman, *Rawls* (Routledge, 2007), 44–59.

[18] See Rawls's very cautious claims about public reason and the right to abortion, *The Law of Peoples*, 169.

Leaving aside the question of whether the list should be further refined to include additional freedoms, it is beyond doubt that adequate enforcement of the rights and liberties in Rawls's official list is necessary to protect individuals from significant forms of domination.[19] At least, this is true on a neorepublican account of domination, which seems to me to be a useful way of specifying what is wrong with a variety of situations that involve the oppression and subordination of individuals and groups. On such an understanding, one agent, A (which can be an individual or a collective), dominates another agent, B, to the extent that A has the capacity for arbitrary interference with B's choices.[20] A's capacity for interference is arbitrary when there are no mechanisms to check A's behavior, and as a consequence A can coerce, intimidate, or manipulate B's actions and choices, and can so do at will and with impunity. Consider societies that do not outlaw slavery, or that do not grant equal civil and political rights to women, or that criminalize sex between consenting adults outside the context of legally sanctioned marriage. In these societies there are women (and men) who are subject to a significant amount of arbitrary interference in their lives, by government and other individuals. That is, these individuals are dominated.

Those who are dominated live at the mercy of the will of their dominators, who can subject them to different forms of physical coercion, threats, and manipulation. When one agent has arbitrary power to interfere with others, even when such power is not being exercised, the structural relationship of domination remains. For example, the law of coverture made it so that all women were dominated by their husbands. Under such a law, husbands had extensive legal rights over their wives, even if some men did not use them against their wives' wishes. Such asymmetrical power is definitive of relationships of domination. Adequate protections of basic rights and liberties is therefore necessary if one is to enjoy nondomination with regard to one's important choices and activities. But such protections are not sufficient to eradicate all types of domination. Adequate protection of the basic liberties is still consistent with the existence of significant asymmetries of power among individuals, which allow powerful parties extensive capacities to interfere with the lives of others. This may be the case, for example, when employees' means of subsistence are dependent on keeping their jobs, so they can be subject to disrespectful and abusive treatment at work.[21] Similar concerns arise when women are financially dependent on their

[19] On the role of the basic liberties in blocking domination see Costa, *Rawls, Citizenship and Education*, 72–90. See also Philip Pettit, *On the People's Terms: A Republican Theory and Model of Democracy* (Cambridge University Press, 2012), 92–107.

[20] See Philip Pettit, *Republicanism: A Theory of Freedom and Government* (Oxford University Press, 1997).

[21] See Elizabeth Anderson, *Private Government: How Employers Rule Our Lives (and Why We Don't Talk about It)* (Princeton University Press, 2017)

partners to support themselves and their young children, and would face economic hardships if they got divorced.[22]

3.2. Fair Equality of Opportunity

The second principle of justice arguably protects individuals from some forms of arbitrary interference not covered by the liberty principle. The second principle is complex, and it is subdivided into two parts. The first of these is (b1): the fair equality of opportunity principle. This principle requires that "those who are at the same level of talent and ability, and have the same willingness to use them, should have the same prospects of success regardless of their initial place in the social system."[23] Every citizen is to have the same legal rights to access to desirable jobs, positions of authority, and the education and training necessary to compete for such jobs and positions. The principle prohibits not only formal legal discrimination against women and members of minority groups, but also informal forms of discrimination and harassment that reduce the effective options available. In my view, discrimination generates arbitrary restrictions on the options and choices available to those who suffer from it. Even when prejudiced parties are not aware of their biases and are not trying to interfere, their aggregated actions and decisions often create significant external obstacles to the options of their victims, and when this happens prejudiced individuals count as agents of domination. A thorough application of Rawls's principle of fair equality of opportunity would therefore have to include policies to prevent or reduce discrimination against women, thus increasing their nondominated options.

Rawls's own discussion of the principle of fair equality of opportunity focuses on lowering the social and class barriers that restrict the options available to members of the least advantaged groups. However, Rawls admits that the principle can only be imperfectly realized, given the existence of a variety of family arrangements and parenting styles associated with different reasonable conceptions of the good.[24] Resulting differences in the functioning of families unavoidably shape the kind of education that children receive at home, which in turn deeply shapes the particular talents and abilities they are encouraged to develop, and the norms and values they accept. Rawls thinks that schools and other social institutions can and should play an important role in compensating for these differences, reducing inequality of opportunity to a certain extent. But

[22] M. Victoria Costa, "Is Neorepublicanism Bad for Women," *Hypatia* 28 (2013), 929.
[23] John Rawls, *A Theory of Justice*, rev. ed. (Harvard University Press, 1999), 63.
[24] See Rawls, *A Theory of Justice*, 64.

the need to balance a commitment to equal opportunity for children against a commitment to parental rights (protected by the first principle) results in significant indeterminacy. Rawls thinks that parents' values and preferences regarding the education of their children should be accommodated, both because of the interests of parents in their children's upbringing, and because of reasonable disagreement about what is in the best interests of children. But given the resulting need to balance the two commitments, there is no clear answer to questions such as whether parents should be allowed to homeschool their children, or to send them to religious schools that share their same world view, even when such arrangements seriously limit children's exposure to alternative conceptions of the good life.

A significant consequence of protecting parental authority to decide—within reasonable limits—how to raise their children is that norms that support a gendered division of labor will tend to be passed on from one generation to another. Gendered norms impact the opportunities of all girls and women: those who endorse those norms and those who do not. The existence of these norms creates expectations about the interests and motivations of women, and these expectations impact the evaluation of women's qualifications to perform different types of jobs. Moreover, when these norms are taught and internalized, they limit the range of options perceived as feasible and attractive.

On one reading of the principle of fair equality of opportunity, the passing on of gendered norms would not be a source of concern because the principle only compares the life prospects of those who are similarly talented and motivated, and one might argue that differences in motivation to pursue certain options acceptably leads to differences in life prospects.[25] But this reading of fair equality of opportunity is too permissive and betrays Rawls's intended purpose of undoing social determinants of life prospects. After all, some women's lack of desire and motivation to go to college, to graduate school, or to pursue well-paid jobs might well be an adaptive response to an environment that seriously limits the options perceived as available to them.

If we dismiss the overly permissive interpretation of the principle of equal opportunity just discussed, it seems reasonable to appeal to the principle to justify policies that not only expand educational opportunities, but that also— more controversially—challenge and undermine the transmission and expectation of a gendered division of labor in society. These policies might include implementing educational strategies for contesting gender stereotypes, setting quotas for women and men in different professions, offering parental leave for men, or providing tax breaks that encourage women's participation in the labor

[25] See Andrew Mason, "Equality, Personal Responsibility, and Gender Socialization," *Proceedings of the Aristotelian Society* 100 (2000), 227–246.

market. Such policies can certainly be defended by appeal to public reasons that avoid relying on controversial comprehensive views. But reasonable persons could still disagree on whether the balance of public reasons actually supports them. So the possibility of a public justification does not settle the outcome of public debates on policy. Such policies favor the considered preferences of citizens who endorse gender-egalitarian norms and a gender-egalitarian division of labor in society. But they also aim at transforming the preferences of others, and their implementation would make the pursuit of some reasonable plans of life more costly in ways that could be perceived as unfair.

3.3. The Difference Principle

The second part of Rawls's second principle of justice is (b2): the difference principle. This principle justifies the existence of social and economic inequalities when these inequalities maximally benefit the least advantaged members of society. According to Rawls, the principle applies primarily to the basic structure of society; in particular, it applies to the legal and economic institutions that regulate the production, exchange, and consumption of goods, by specifying property rights, the terms of contracts, a set of taxes, regulations of inheritance, and so on. This principle requires that the functioning of basic social and economic institutions make the least advantaged members of society better off than they would be under any alternative feasible socioeconomic arrangement. This normative principle has been the subject of an enormous critical literature, which cannot be surveyed here. In what follows, I will concentrate on the problem of indeterminacy regarding who counts as the "least advantaged" members of society, and on Rawls's proposal that income and wealth be used as a proxy for advantage, so as to enable comparisons of relative advantage among social groups.

According to one interpretation of this principle, the "least advantaged" are the class of minimum-wage workers who have the lowest lifetime expectation for enjoying the social primary goods.[26] Rawls assumes a strong correlation between income and wealth and other social primary goods, so that those with expectations of earning the least are also expected to have fewer social primary goods in general. One problem with this reading of the principle is that it cannot directly consider the interests of those—typically women—who do the bulk of the unpaid but socially necessary work of caring for children and family members who are disabled, ill or infirm. In other words, it fails to take into account the independent interests of those who perform care work as fully cooperating members

[26] See Freeman, *Rawls*, 106.

of society. Moreover, it seems to presuppose that maximizing the economic prospects of unskilled workers who participate in the formal labor market will also maximize the economic prospects of their "dependents." But this simplifies matters too much, since those who earn an income typically have more power to decide how it will be used, and the economic prospects of those who rely on their partner's income can radically change if the relationship ends.

A more plausible reading of the difference principle takes "least advantaged" to mean "belonging to the income class with the lowest expectations," regardless of the source of income.[27] This would directly include, among the least advantaged, women (and men) who do not earn any wages. One advantage of this reading is that it allows that divorce, or the death or disability of one's partner, can impact one's life prospects, and that social policies inspired by the principle need to address this. But there is a deeper problem even in this alternative reading: it measures life prospects in terms of income. This ignores the fact that social primary goods are heterogeneous and that there may be reasonable disagreement regarding which bundles of primary goods are better or worse. Focusing on income and wealth without factoring in hours of socially useful work will also yield a misguided assessment of social (dis)advantage. This supports the suggestion that free time should be added to the list of social primary goods.[28] And when we consider the question of who counts as least advantaged, we might also factor in the following consideration: the power to make decisions about important aspects of one's life. This yields a distinctive set of concerns. When one partner is economically dependent on the other to support herself and her children, and knows that they will face significant hardships if the relationship dissolves, this partner often has less power to set and negotiate the terms of the relationship. In this way, economic dependency is often a source of domination when it contributes to the income-earning partner's power to threaten or intimidate his spouse, or even to have a final say in family decisions. This remains true even within relationships between people who are not among the poorest members of society.

I have been pointing out that some aspects of relationships of domination are economic and can be mitigated by policies based on the difference principle. For example, there might be reforms in family law that grant a fair share of family assets to each spouse, and consider the needs of the parent who gets custody of children. But a number of additional policies are necessary to support women in poorer families, where there is not much income or many assets to divide to

---

[27] Rawls, *Justice as Fairness*, 59.

[28] Including free time in the index of social primary goods complicates the question of who are the least advantaged. See Philippe van Parijs, "Difference Principles," in Freeman, *Cambridge Companion to Rawls*, 200–240.

begin with, as well as women who are single parents and are raising children on their own. But, again, policies should avoid replacing one form of domination with another, leaving recipients of benefits at the mercy of the discretionary power of welfare agencies. Universal or unconditional programs that do not require recipients to prove that they qualify for benefits do reduce the problem of bureaucratic domination. But such programs are more expensive than targeted ones, and less likely to be selected under budgetary constraints. What these admittedly sketchy remarks suggest is that there will be some difficulties identifying who the least advantaged are, and what sources of social disadvantage should be the primary concerns of those trying to implement the difference principle.

Concluding Remarks

Rawls's theory of justice certainly has some feminist implications, and I agree with feminists who claim that there are significant advantages to be had by restricting policy arguments to political considerations—at least if one wants them to have wide appeal. Nevertheless, indeterminacy regarding the precise implications of Rawls's principles of justice allows for reasonable disagreements about policies, even when all of them pass the test of political justification. And some of these disagreements will be disappointing from a feminist perspective. The main unsettled question regarding the basic liberties seems to be whether they fully protect sexual and reproductive rights of individuals. When it comes to setting guidelines for economic and redistributive policies in particular, the implications of the second principle remain somewhat open and contestable. Social policies have to secure citizens' access to income and wealth and fair opportunities to pursue their plans of life. An additional concern that has guided this chapter's discussion is that social policies should also prevent some members of society from being exposed to the arbitrary power of others. This adds another layer of complexity to the design of policy, and is also the source of some reasonable disagreements regarding the relative weight of different considerations when selecting policies to implement the principles of justice. Feminists who want to use the tools of political liberalism to support policies that combat forms of domination and oppression can take Rawls's account of free and equal citizenship as a starting point. But if they want to contest many forms of domination, they will inevitably need to go beyond Rawls, and appeal to considerations such as concern with the existence of arbitrary power in many areas of social life.

14

A Feminist Defense of Political Liberalism

Christie Hartley and Lori Watson

Introduction

Feminist critics of liberal theories of justice often claim liberalism lacks the resources necessary for diagnosing and, so, remedying inequalities characterized by relationships of domination and subordination grounded in group membership. They emphasize that social norms and scripted roles function in the background of liberal institutions to perpetuate and maintain group-based subordination. Liberalism's commitment to "neutral" principles and institutions in contexts of such inequality further maintains or produces injustices.

For example, liberal theories of justice have failed to adequately address the way gender norms, expectations, and roles produce gender inequality in the distribution of care work, domestic labor, and labor market participation. Women disproportionately care for dependents and perform household work, and the best jobs in the labor market assume that workers do not have responsibility for caring for dependents.[1] As a result, women are disadvantaged in the labor market and in the political sphere and are often dependent on others for income, access to healthcare, and retirement savings as well as subjected to abusive treatment.

One way of characterizing the inadequacy of liberal theories is to charge that they rely on a simplistic notion of power. Liberal theorizing about power centrally focuses on the state as the locus of political power and, so, concerns the legitimate and illegitimate uses of such power and the protection of individual rights. Certainly, some exercises of nonstate power related to the social subordination of women and other socially marginalized groups takes the form of violations of individual rights (for example, murder, rape, and discrimination in education, employment, and housing). Yet feminists, critical race theorists, and others stress that social equality, including equality among persons as free and

[1] See, for example, Joan Williams, *Unbending Gender: Why Family and Work Conflict and What to Do about It* (Oxford University Press, 2000).

Christie Hartley and Lori Watson, *A Feminist Defense of Political Liberalism* In: *John Rawls*. Edited by: Jon Mandle and Sarah Roberts-Cady, Oxford University Press (2020). © Oxford University Press.
DOI: 10.1093/oso/9780190859213.003.0022.

equal citizens, is not simply thwarted or frustrated by the state's illegitimate use of power or by violations or denials of liberal rights.

Whether liberals can respond to such critiques depends upon, first, whether liberal theory can recognize that state power is not the only form of power that is important when thinking about justice; and, second, whether liberal theories can recognize the way that nonstate systems of power construct persons. Indeed, key to feminist critiques of liberalism is that the social processes that make people into men and women are also a form of power. By failing to adequately theorize a broader notion of power that creates and sustains social hierarchy, liberalism maintains and perpetuates inequality in conditions under which persons are socially subordinated on the basis of group membership.[2] Liberals must recognize that the particular laws and policies needed to secure what justice requires depends on how various forms of social power operate in the background culture, how norms and practices shape persons and behavior in society, and how law and policy functions in a particular social context.

We argue that a Rawlsian-inspired form of political liberalism has the resources to address these concerns. First, we argue the aforementioned feminist critiques raise a deep challenge for political liberals. Next, we argue that political liberalism, properly understood, entails a commitment to substantive equality such that it has the internal resources to address the kinds of inequality produced by unjust forms of social power. Finally, we consider an objection that any view that remains committed to the claim that the basic structure is the subject of justice will fail to secure substantive gender justice. We reply to this concern by clarifying that the principles of justice function as "rules for rules" for the design of particular laws in the relevant institutional domains. However, we emphasize that this doesn't mean there are particular areas of social life in which citizens' basic status—as free and equal persons—is suspended. This basic social position—as a free and equal citizen—secures for each citizen equal standing across all social domains.

The Feminist Critique: Power and Domination

Catharine A. MacKinnon argues that the social division of persons into the groups "men" and "women" is not simply a division based on "differences," but that division itself is hierarchical, grouping persons along power lines.

---

[2] Catharine A. MacKinnon and Clare Chambers have each of stressed these concerns. See MacKinnon's *Toward a Feminist Theory of the State* (Harvard University Press, 1989); and Chambers's *Sex, Culture, and Justice: The Limits of Choice* (Penn State University Press, 2008).

Membership in the social category "man" confers systematic authority, standing, and superiority over those in the social category "woman." Gender is an unequal power division because it is a category through which social power is conferred, exercised, and realized.[3] A central focus of MacKinnon's critique is the way the liberal state is implicated in both ignoring and perpetuating the forms of gender inequality that sustain women's subordinate—second-class—status. This critique emphasizes that the core commitments of liberal theory and jurisprudence prevent liberals from properly understanding and diagnosing sex-based inequalities. Our specific interest here is in her claim that feminists "need a theory of the substance of law, its relation to society, and the relationship between the two."[4] She says: "Such a theory would comprehend how law works as a form of state power in a social context in which power is gendered. It would answer the questions: What is state power? Where, socially, does it come from? How do women encounter it? What is the law for women? How does law work to legitimate the state, male power, itself? Can law do anything for women? Can it do anything about women's status? Does how the law is used matter?"[5]

In MacKinnon's view, answering these questions requires a specific feminist theory of the state, including a substantive theory of equality. As she demonstrates, failure to theorize gender as a hierarchical form of power in the context of designing laws and policies that aim at securing the rights and equality of women reproduces gendered forms of inequality. For example, in the law of rape, consent is meant to provide legal grounds for distinguishing between sex and rape. However, the assumption that consent, independent of background factors including inequalities between men and women, is the only relevant determinate of whether some act was "just sex" or "rape" results in a lot of rape being adjudicated as "just sex."[6] In the standard liberal approach to pornography, such materials are deemed a form of freedom of expression, and granted protection on those grounds (provided they are nonobscene).[7] Absent an analysis of the way gender functions as a system of power, this approach appears to guard individual rights to freedom of expression. However, as MacKinnon argues, such an approach, absent recognition of the way gender power operates independent of the law, secures the rights of the powerful (men) at the expense of the powerless

---

[3] MacKinnon, *Toward a Feminist Theory.* Central to MacKinnon's view is that sexuality is the linchpin of gender. By contrast, Susan Okin claims that the family is the linchpin of gender. *Justice, Gender and the Family* (Basic Books, 1989).

[4] Mackinnon, *Toward a Feminist Theory,* 159.

[5] Mackinnon, *Toward a Feminist Theory,* 159.

[6] See MacKinnon, "Rape: On Coercion and Consent," in *Toward a Feminist Theory,* 171–183.

[7] Here the practice of liberal jurisprudence and liberal theory need sharp distinction, as the obscenity based approach to pornography found in US law is foundationally inconsistent with genuine liberal principles, whereas liberal theorists emphasize freedom of expression as the central value that warrants protection for pornography.

(women). Similar analyses reveal the ways in which liberal legal approaches to family law, sex discrimination, prostitution, and reproduction typically fail to address the substance of gender inequality; in part, as liberal jurisprudence seeks "neutral principles" or formal equality, it abstracts away from the substantive facts that give rise to the particular inequalities at stake.[8]

Clare Chambers develops a similar critique of liberalism's limitations. Unlike MacKinnon, she aims to defend a comprehensive liberalism as capable of securing gender equality. Chambers's critique is aimed at the role that choice plays in liberal theory. Liberals tend to view choice as a normative transformer in the sense that choice "transforms an unjust situation into a just one."[9] Liberals, she stresses, do not appropriately scrutinize the social conditions in which choices are made and so fail to notice the way in which options, preferences, and subjects are socially constructed in ways that subordinate some persons as members of groups to others.[10] Chambers argues that our culture is imbued with gender norms and in our diverse and varied social interactions we are judged and benefited in accordance with our compliance with such norms. Compliance with such norms is often the result of habituation and internalization. Gender identities are created, and individuals get pleasure (but sometimes frustration, too) from realizing gender ideals. Gender norms shape our preferences, desires, opportunities, and even our bodies. Compliance with these norms results in the subordination of women to men. This creative power is not considered to be a threat to liberal freedom or equality, within dominant modes of liberal thinking, but it can be the source of unjust domination and unfreedom.

Given these critiques, one may conclude that liberals inadequately theorize social power, especially in its gendered forms. In particular, liberals fail to see the way in which individuals are socially constructed through forms of social power that create and sustain social hierarchies in which some persons are socially subordinated on the basis of group membership. Further, if liberals fail to attend to such exercises of social power as bearing on the realization of a democratic society of "free and equal citizens," then liberalism provides an inadequate account of justice.

---

[8] MacKinnon's own legal interventions specifically address the concrete forms of gender inequality that serve to deny women substantive equality in the particular context of concern. Thus, in developing the legal theory that sexual harassment is a form of sex discrimination, she gave voice, and provided legal remedy, to the sex-based harms women routinely experience in employment and education. This substantive approach to equality rests on the view that social equality is a precondition of legal equality. For a systematic analysis of all these issues from a substantive sex equality perspective, see MacKinnon, *Sex Equality*, 3rd ed. (Foundation Press, 2017).

[9] Chambers, *Sex, Culture, and Justice*, 21.

[10] Chambers, *Sex, Culture, and Justice*, especially chap. 1 and chap. 2.

Political Liberalism

In response to these criticisms, some feminists reject *political* liberalism in favor of a (partially) *comprehensive* liberalism;[11] in particular, some claim that political liberals do not properly secure autonomy (or important senses of autonomy) and, therefore, cannot secure gender justice. We reject this strategy for "saving liberalism." Instead, we argue a Rawlsian-inspired political liberalism can address forms of social domination and hierarchy when they threaten or frustrate the status of persons as free and equal citizens.[12]

Like Rawls, we think that in a well-ordered liberal democratic society reasonable people will accept a plurality of diverse and contrary but reasonable comprehensive doctrines.[13] This "fact of reasonable pluralism" creates a challenge for the justification of a conception of justice. If reasonable people accept different reasonable comprehensive doctrines and if a conception of justice is publicly justified in accordance with a particular comprehensive doctrine, then there will be reasonable persons to whom the view of justice is not justified, as they reject the comprehensive doctrine upon which it rests. Were the state to use its coercive power in accordance with a conception of justice not reasonably justified to all reasonable persons, then the use of such power would be illegitimate.

Given the fact of reasonable pluralism, Rawls develops political liberalism to address how a just and stable liberal democratic society is possible.[14] He claims the possibility of such a society depends on finding a reasonable conception of *political* justice[15] that can be given a free-standing justification solely on the basis

---

[11] See, e.g., Ruth Abbey, "Back toward a Comprehensive Liberalism? Justice as Fairness, Gender and Families," *Political Theory* 35 (2007), 5–28; Chambers, *Sex, Culture, and Justice*; Susan Moller Okin, "*Political Liberalism*, Justice and Gender," *Ethics* 105 (1994), 23–43, and *Is Multiculturalism Bad for Women* (Princeton University Press, 1999), 129–130.

[12] We develop a full defense of political liberalism as a feminist liberalism in our *Equal Citizenship and Public Reason: A Feminist Political Liberalism* (Oxford University Press, 2018). Anthony Laden defends political liberalism against one important thread of MacKinnon's feminist criticism of liberalism, the norm of objectivity. We don't address objectivity here. See Anthony Simon Laden, "Radical Liberals, Reasonable Feminists: Reason, Power, and Objectivity in MacKinnon and Rawls," in *Feminist Interpretations of John Rawls*, ed. Ruth Abbey (Penn State University Press, 2013).

[13] John Rawls, *Political Liberalism*, expanded ed. (Columbia University Press, 2005), 36–37.

[14] Rawls, *Political Liberalism*.

[15] The matter is a bit more complicated, although not important for our argument here. As Rawls originally states his view, he is concerned with an overlapping consensus on one reasonable political conception of justice for a well-ordered society. This view must be revised to recognize that there will be multiple reasonable political conceptions of justice, and citizens will not all endorse one such conception. We think that this issue can be resolved with this revision: "1. All citizens (as reasonable persons) endorse *a* reasonable political conception of justice (one member of the family of reasonable political conceptions of justice). 2. The basic structure is organized in compliance with (at least) one member of the family of reasonable political conceptions of justice. 3. All citizens (reasonable persons) know (1) and (2) (that is, the 'publicity condition' is satisfied). 4. A public political culture obtains as characterized by a reasonable overlapping consensus and a shared commitment (among reasonable citizens) to public reason." See Blain Neufeld and Lori Watson, "The Tyranny—or the Democracy—of the Ideal?," *Cosmos + Taxis* 5 (2018), 47–61.

of political values and be the object of an overlapping consensus of reasonable comprehensive doctrines.[16] Political conceptions of justice are free-standing in the sense that the values upon which they are based do not require that individuals accept any particular reasonable comprehensive doctrine. Rather, such conceptions rest on political values, which concern the interests of persons as free and equal citizens. For such a political conception of justice to be the object of an overlapping consensus of reasonable comprehensive doctrines, though, it must be the case that reasonable persons embed the political conception of justice within their reasonable comprehensive doctrine in some way and, so, provide full justification.[17]

Some think that insofar as political liberals claim that the possibility of a just and stable liberal democratic state depends on a *political* conception of justice, political liberals will lack the resources to address certain forms of injustice.[18] As a political conception of justice is based on the shared values of persons as free and equal citizens, some feminists argue these are not sufficient to secure full gender justice. Chambers, for example, thinks the kind of autonomy that political liberals recognize is not enough to protect women from unjust disadvantage. However, as Rawls makes clear, the political values from which political conceptions of justice are constructed are moral values,[19] and these values, we argue, together with the central features of political liberalism, such as the criterion of reciprocity, protect women and other socially marginalized groups from subordination in the spheres of life central to liberal democratic citizenship. This is the starting point for our defense of political liberalism as a view with the resources to address relationships of domination and subordination that serve as social bases for sustained patterns of inequality. That is, despite its being a political, and not comprehensive, view, political liberalism is, nonetheless, a substantive account of political morality. It is often misunderstood just how substantive a doctrine it is.

Political Liberalism, Equal Citizenship, and Domination

At the normative core of political liberalism is the claim that the justification of political power is always addressed to others and such justifications must satisfy the criterion of reciprocity. This criterion requires that when proposing terms of cooperation "those proposing them must also think it at least reasonable

---

[16] Rawls, *Political Liberalism*, 10.

[17] See Rawls, "Reply to Habermas," in *Political Liberalism*, 386.

[18] See, for example, Susan Moller Okin, "*Political Liberalism*, Justice and Gender" and "Justice and Gender: An Unfinished Debate," *Fordham Law Review* 72 (2004), 1537–1567.

[19] Rawls, *Political Liberalism*, 13–14.

for others to accept them, as free and equal citizens, and not as dominated or manipulated, or under the pressure of an inferior political or social position."[20] A commitment to reciprocity constrains all reasonable political conceptions of justice, as it imposes substantive content on them. Rawls says that it constrains reasonable political conceptions of justice such that they must all (1) secure "a list of basic rights, liberties, and opportunities (such as those familiar from constitutional regimes," (2) provide "an assignment of a special priority to those rights, liberties and opportunities, especially with respect to the claims of the general good and perfectionist values," and (3) provide "measures ensuring all citizens adequate all-purpose means to make effective use of their freedoms."[21] Rawls also emphasizes that the liberal principle of legitimacy itself is "based" on this criterion. Political legitimacy requires that the "exercise of political power is proper only when we sincerely believe that the reasons we would offer for our political actions—were we to state them as government officials—are sufficient, and we also reasonably think that other citizens might also reasonably accept those reasons."[22]

Elsewhere we argue that the criterion of reciprocity is more demanding than Rawls imagined and that it is the key to understanding the resources within political liberalism for theorizing relationships of domination and subordination grounded in group membership as unjust. As we develop this view, we argue it grounds the feminist content of political liberalism. In particular, we argue that (1) the reasoning that Rawls uses to generate the list of features that will be characteristic of any reasonable political conception of justice can be employed to justify access to other social goods, including social goods that have been of particular concern to feminists, and (2) the criterion of reciprocity itself has negative and positive aims that require securing substantive equality for all. Concerning the latter, the criterion of reciprocity requires (1) the eradication of social conditions of domination and subordination relevant to democratic deliberation and participation among equal citizens and (2) the provision of the social conditions of recognition respect.[23] Here we turn our attention to the claim that criterion of reciprocity includes a principle of nondomination, which demands the elimination of social conditions of domination and subordination relevant to democratic deliberation and participation among free and equal citizens. In short, we hold that social equality in the domains relevant to free and equal citizenship is required for equal citizenship and legitimate democratic deliberation.

[20] John Rawls, "The Idea of Public Reason Revisited," in *Collected Papers*, ed. Samuel Freeman (Harvard University Press, 1999), 578.
[21] Rawls, "Idea of Public Reason," 582.
[22] Rawls, "Idea of Public Reason," 578.
[23] See our *Equal Citizenship* and "Is a Feminist Political Liberalism Possible?," *Journal of Ethics and Social Philosophy* 5 (2010), 1–21.

The criterion of reciprocity is a principle for democratic deliberation. It is within the domain of public reason that the particular content of citizens' relationships to each other and the state take shape. Proposals for law and policy related to matters of basic justice and constitutional essentials must rest on others' standing and authority as free and equal citizens. Where such standing is lacking, substantive policies are required to secure it. Thus, we defend political liberalism as premised on the guarantee of relational equality among persons as free and equal citizens. Social hierarchies that frustrate or threaten persons' standing as free and equal citizens must be addressed and eliminated. Accordingly, political liberalism is committed to securing conditions of nondomination insofar as such relations undermine substantive equality for citizens.

To illuminate what the principle of nondomination requires, recall that Rawls claimed that any reasonable political conception of justice includes certain basic rights, liberties, and opportunities, priority for these, and access for persons to have "adequate all-purpose means to make effective use of their freedoms." These basic protections alone do not guarantee that women will not be subordinated. For example, in a society in which gender norms, roles, and expectations disproportionately socialize women for caregiving, in which the best jobs in the labor market assume that workers do not have responsibility for caring for dependents, and in which caring for dependents is not recognized and compensated for as socially necessary work, women will be unjustly disadvantaged. In his later work, Rawls briefly acknowledged that caring for children is socially necessary work and stated that "if the cause of women's inequality is their greater share in the bearing, nurturing and caring for children in the traditional division of labor in the family, steps need to be taken either to equalize their share, or compensate them for it."[24] However, Rawls's brief remarks do not show how it is that his theory can address the problem.

The criterion of reciprocity, though, requires the elimination of social conditions of domination and subordination relevant to democratic citizenship. Political liberals should recognize that caring for dependents is socially necessary work, and those who perform this work should not be disadvantaged relative to others citizens with respect to their ability to participate in the various spheres of social life central to citizenship.[25] That is, if some persons are effectively marginalized from participation in any of the spheres of life central to citizenship because of society's gendered structure, or if the ability to participate in all spheres of life is effectively precluded due to the way that social norms

[24] Rawls, "Idea of Public Reason," 600.
[25] See Nancy Fraser's antimarginalization principle in her "After the Family Wage: A Postindustrial Thought Experiment," in *Justice Interruptus: Critical Reflections on the "Postsocialist" Condition* (Routledge, 1997), 41–66, esp. 48.

constrain choice and shape institutions, then free and equal citizenship is not guaranteed to those so frustrated. The principle of nondomination demands such inequality be addressed. Feminists have proposed a number of policies to do so, including state-supported day care and aftercare, paid family leave, shortened workweeks, and state incentives for families who coparent. Political liberals can and must recognize those policies required to address the needs of caregivers and those for whom they care.[26]

A further illustration of political liberalism's feminist potential and so its resources for supporting substantive polices that aim to eliminate relationships of domination and subordination is shown through considering how it can support the Nordic model for regulating prostitution.[27] In short, the Nordic model criminalizes the buying of sex while decriminalizing the selling. It is often defined as a "sex equality" approach to prostitution because it rests on the claim that prostitution is a system of gender inequality. "Liberal" approaches to prostitution frequently endorse full decriminalization or legalization of prostitution, as many liberals claim that any continued criminalization of any aspects of "markets in sex" must rest upon controversial and partial views about the value of sex or sexuality that amount to comprehensive claims about the role of sex or sexuality.[28]

However, despite liberal defenses to the contrary, the claim that "sex work" is a job like any other is indefensible.[29] Common liberal values concerning worker health and safety, worker autonomy, and rights to bodily integrity cannot be secured when sex is the "work." In support of these claims, consider that current worker health and safety standards for occupations other than selling sex cannot be met in the context of selling sex. Such standards require elimination of "known risks" in the course of performing the work. Given that condoms are insufficient protection and often not used even where mandated, and that violence, including rape, is an intrinsic risk to prostitution, elimination of known risks is simply not compatible with "the work." Additionally, the structure of legalized or decriminalized prostitution fails to secure worker autonomy, with respect to brothel owners, pimps, and johns. Finally, the incidences of violence and trauma, even in decriminalized and legalized states, are such that prostitutes' basic citizenship rights are denied.[30] Moreover, given that women are overwhelmingly

---

[26] See our full defense in *Equal Citizenship*.

[27] For a full defense of this claim, see our *Equal Citizenship*, chap. 7, "Prostitution and Public Reason."

[28] See, for example, Martha Nussbaum, "'Whether from Reason or Prejudice': Taking Money for Bodily Services," in *Prostitution and Pornography: Philosophical Debate about the Sex Industry*, ed. Jessica Spector (Stanford University Press, 2006), 175–208.

[29] For further defense of this claim, see "Why Sex Work Isn't Work," *Logos* 16 (2017), http://logosjournal.com/2014/watson/; and Lori Watson and Jessica Flannigan, *Debating Sex Work* (Oxford University Press, forthcoming).

[30] See Watson's contribution to *Debating Sex Work*.

the sellers and men the buyers (a fact that is the product of sex inequality), state support of decriminalized or legalized prostitution constitutes state support for sex inequality. Because prostitution is an institution through which women are subordinated and denied substantive equality, the politically liberal state can and must adopt legal measures to end such inequality.

The Basic Structure

Feminist critics of political liberalism may claim a principle of nondomination as we've defended it is insufficient for full gender justice insofar as the basic structure restriction may leave unaddressed some important aspects of gender. One way to develop this concern is to stress that gender norms, roles, and expectations that are part of the background culture of society and outside the basic structure are central to constructing gender and seem to be outside the purview of justice.

Further complicating matters is the fact that giving precise meaning to the claim that the basic structure is the fundamental subject of justice is in no way straightforward. For example, Gerald Cohen argues that there is no principled line between the institutions that Rawls identifies within the basic structure and those he excludes.[31] Clare Chambers adds that Rawls's "position on justice within the family is at odds with his claim that the basic structure is uniquely the subject of justice."[32] She concludes that Rawls's "basic-structure distinction is doomed," for there is no principled way to reconcile the claim that the family is part of the basic structure with the claim that principles of justice do not apply directly to the family.[33]

Providing a full explanation and defense of how to understand the basic structure and its relation to the principles of justice is beyond the scope of this chapter.[34] However, there are some initial reasons for thinking the criticism of the basic structure requirement is misguided. Our main concern is with the point that political liberalism's commitment to the basic structure as the subject of justice entails that certain aspects of social life in which women are unjustly disadvantaged are outside the scope of justice.

---

[31] G. A. Cohen, *Rescuing Justice and Equality* (Harvard University Press, 2008).

[32] Clare Chambers, "The Family as a Basic Institution: A Feminist Analysis of the Basic Structure as Subject," in Abbey, *Feminist Interpretations*, 76.

[33] Chambers, "Family as Basic Institution," 93.

[34] For such a defense as it pertains to the way in which the principles of justice do constrain institutions within the basic structure, such as the family, see Blain Neufeld, "Coercion, the Basic Structure, and the Family," *Journal of Social Philosophy* 40 (2009), 37–54.

The principles of justice direct and constrain the way in which the basic structure is arranged such that persons' needs as free and equal citizens are met. The principles are the rules for framing the particular rules, policies, and practices of the institutions that are part of the basic structure and their relationship to one another. Chambers recognizes this: "an institution to which the principles of justice apply thereby becomes a candidate for legal coercion," and so, "If some aspect of the family, for example, is part of the basic structure, then it follows that it might appropriately be the site of laws that ensure that it is structured in such a way as to instantiate the principles and ensure justice."[35] Economic institutions, markets, and the system of property are clearly within the basic structure. It does not follow from this that businesses themselves are to be directly governed by the principles of justice. Individual businesses will operate as self-interested economic actors, but their actions will be constrained by the legal rules that govern and structure markets. The rules for firms are *designed* so as to realize the principles of justice when they operate together with the rules for the other institutions that constitute the basic structure.

The family, too, as a political institution is part of the basic structure, but, again, the principles of justice do not apply directly to its internal operations. The difference principle does not and could not regulate the distribution of birthday gifts or dishwashing duties, for example. However, we reject Rawls's view that the principles of justice merely provide external constraints on the family.[36] Rather, we start from the recognition that material caretaking is among the needs of all persons as citizens and, as such, socially necessary work. We hold that those who perform this work should not be disadvantaged relative to other members of society. Furthermore, emotional care is fundamental to children's cognitive, emotional, and moral development and, as Elizabeth Brake argues, among the needs of adults in exercising the two moral powers.[37] Political liberals should view certain socially necessary caring relationships as defining the family as a political institution for legal purposes; particular laws and policies, in accordance with the principles of justice, will specify persons' rights and obligations within the family, specify how the state is to protect and support those relationships, and address how third parties or other institutions must recognize or support the relationships.[38] Given their comprehensive doctrines, persons may view the

---

[35] Chambers, "Family as Basic Institution," 92.

[36] Rawls, "Idea of Public Reason," 597.

[37] Elizabeth Brake, *Minimizing Marriage* (Oxford University PRESS, 2012).

[38] Just as Brake thinks that the state must recognize and support (nondependent) adult caring relations in this way, we are claiming that there are other caring relationships that should be part of the family and recognized and supported by the state. We think that, even though different types of relationships fall within the domain of the political family, frameworks for specifying rights, obligations, and support for those in different types of relationships should be kept separate (e.g., laws concerning adult-caring frameworks should be distinct from laws concerning the parent-child relationship). Compare with Brake's *Minimizing Marriage*, 156–188.

relationships recognized as part of the political family as having a purpose or character beyond their political function; persons are free to live in accordance with these views so long as they are consistent with the laws and policies that define and support the political family.[39]

This argument suggests that the principles of justice must secure the goods of citizenship on a basis of equality within the institutions of the basic structure. But it further suggests that if the internal dynamics of those institutions sustain unjust hierarchies that undermine equal citizenship, then the state must act. Rawls expresses a similar point that some have puzzled over: "The principles defining the equal basic liberties and opportunities of citizens always hold in and through all so-called domains. The equal rights of women and the basic rights of their children as future citizens are inalienable and protect them wherever they are. . . . If the so-called private sphere is alleged to be a space exempt from justice, then there is no such thing."[40] Some think this claim implies that the basic structure distinction is doing no work in the view, since the principles of justice appear to apply everywhere. This is mistaken. Through the basic structure, persons are to have their needs as citizens secured, but, certainly, the institutions that are part of the basic structure will constrain other institutions in society. There is no space exempt from justice in this sense. For example, the constitution will guarantee rights for persons as citizens to freedom of movement and bodily integrity, and no institution or individual can deny that to a citizen, including, for example various associations that are not part of the basic structure. The criminal law will protect the bodily integrity of persons, and this will constrain behavior anywhere in society. If women or minorities are targeted for assault because of their sex or race, then such assault is a civil rights violation and it can be recognized as such wherever it occurs. The rights and privileges of citizenship must be protected on an equal basis, in all domains of social life.

Thus far we have only provided an initial sketch of how to respond to the concerns about the basic structure distinction as raised in regard to securing gender justice. This sketch only aims to establish that the standard way that concern is raised is misguided. Nonetheless, a deeper concern remains. The scope of the basic structure still suggests that there are areas of social life in which the state will not directly intervene to change gendered patterns of behavior.

Consider gendered beauty norms and practices. They operate in all spheres of social life, and, as feminists have argued for decades, they disparately impact women and girls and serve as a site of social subordination. The impact of these norms and practices are psychological and material. Women and girls are the

---

[39] We develop our view in *Equal Citizenship* and Hartley's "Political Liberalism and Children," *Philosophical Studies* 175 (2018), 1095–1112.

[40] Rawls, "Idea of Public Reason," 599.

majority of persons with eating disorders. They wear high heels that damage their feet and restrict their movement. They undergo costly and risky cosmetic surgeries and procedures to try to meet beauty standards. They use expensive injectables to smooth out their skin and resist the look of aging. And they invest in other costly and time-consuming grooming and dressing rituals. To make matters worse, beauty norms present a double bind for women. The more women conform to "traditional" concepts of beauty, often the less seriously they are taken in the labor market; while the further they are from them, the more marginalized and dismissed they are.

Certainly, political liberals can address some gender inequalities that stem from gendered beauty norms and practices. For example, when and where gender norms operate to deprive women of fair equality of opportunity, such as in employment contexts, the politically liberal state can recognize this and address it through civil rights law. Where and when women's health and safety are at stake—whether psychological or physical—the politically liberal state can also take action. Cosmetic surgeries and procedures, for example, can be regulated. Chambers, however, argues that such procedures should be banned. She claims that if certain practices are significantly harmful or pose significant risk of harm and if compliance with the practice is required to comply with a social norm (that is unjust or maintains/perpetuates social inequality) and to receive a benefit, then the state should ban the practice.[41] While we would not claim that there are no circumstances under which political liberals could support a ban on cosmetic procedures (as one reasonable option among others) or even that there are no circumstances under which a ban would be demanded given the demands of justice (because no reasonable alternative exists), we think that such conditions would be quite unusual. In most conditions, we think that the state should regulate cosmetic procedures for health and safety reasons and that as part of person's basic education the state must make sure that all children have information about good health, including diet, exercise, and variations among human beings. Feminists should lead campaigns in the background culture to bring attention to the health and safety risks of these procedures and to promote healthy body images for women and girls.

What determines whether state action is warranted, though, and when? Norms and practices that serve to undermine the status of persons as free and equal citizens in the relevant domains must be addressed. Insofar as norms and practices affect life outside of the basic structure but affect the fundamental interests of citizens, such as health, then the state can or must address these norms and practices on the grounds that the principles of justice constrain all

---

[41] Chambers, *Sex, Culture, and Justice*, 195–196.

institutions as discussed previously. Sometimes, though, state action is not the best way to address certain norms that underwrite social inequalities. Makeup and grooming practices as well as gendered practices for the division of house-work affect who we are and what we think of others. But direct state intervention on such matters is not only impractical but exceeds the limits of appropriate state authority. The role of the state is to secure conditions of freedom and equality such that individuals can pursue their reasonable conceptions of the good on a basis of equality. Aiming to direct, via state policy, the intimate details of persons' lives can itself be an unjust form of domination and deny the basic respect owed to persons to determine their own conception of the good, including the role that gender plays in it.

The crucial point here is that feminist interventions aimed at addressing gender-inegalitarian norms and practices require justification, as do all similar interventions. But political liberals are fundamentally committed to securing the conditions of free and equal citizenships for all members of society. Whether feminist interventions can be justified depends on whether they are important to securing the conditions of free and equal citizenship for women and whether they are the most reasonable course of action given other political values and other mechanisms for affecting change.

PART VIII
RAWLS AND NONHUMAN ANIMALS

Introduction

Almost everyone agrees that the treatment of nonhuman animals matters morally to some extent. People are outraged by cases of animals abused by their owners—starving horses or battered dogs. On the other hand, many people regularly and openly sacrifice central animal interests for the sake of relatively trivial interests of their own. For example, people wear leather and eat meat, when alternative nonanimal products are readily available. There is vast disagreement about whether and when it is acceptable to sacrifice nonhuman interests for the sake of human interests. Thus, it is not surprising that there is considerable debate about the extent to which nonhuman animals should be protected through our political systems. Many countries have laws that protect some pets from abuse by owners or laws that set limits on the treatment of animals raised for food. There are environmental regulations that protect wild animals from territorial encroachment or extinction. Are legal protections for nonhuman animals requirements of justice? Does justice require even more legal protections for animals?

These questions are more complicated than they first appear. What does it mean to ask if the legal protection of animals is a requirement of justice? On the one hand, one might be asking whether there are moral obligations regarding nonhuman animals that ought to be enforced through our laws. This opens up other questions: one might wonder whether the legal protection of nonhuman animals is based on moral obligations directly to the animals, or whether the protection of nonhumans matters only if it is necessary to fulfill moral obligations to humans. On the other hand, John Rawls might pose the question of justice for nonhumans differently. He was interested in social justice, which, for him, concerned the question of fairness in the basic structure of society. He was interested in identifying principles for determining a fair way of distributing the benefits and burdens of social cooperation. Thus, he might take the question to be whether fairness requires that society consider the benefits and burdens of social cooperation on nonhuman animals as well as humans.

In the next two chapters, we will explore the debate about the place of nonhuman animals in John Rawls's theory of justice. Rawls himself wrote very little on nonhuman animals, but what he did write expressed skepticism about the inclusion of nonhumans in his theory. After all, Rawls frames the main task of his theoretical work as identifying the fair terms of cooperation between free

Introduction In: *John Rawls*. Edited by: Jon Mandle and Sarah Roberts-Cady, Oxford University Press (2020). © Oxford University Press. DOI: 10.1093/oso/9780190859213.003.0023.

and equal persons. He assumes that fair principles governing social cooperation would be principles that could be reasonably justified to those on whom
they were imposed. Accordingly, the focus of his theory was on individuals with
the cognitive and moral capacities to consider, accept, and abide by such principles.[1] He was clear that those moral persons with the capacity to be regulated by
principles of justice are also those to whom justice is owed.[2] This doesn't mean
that only the needs and interests of fully morally responsible adults were taken
into consideration in his theory of justice. Rawls writes that the good of infants
and children are included in his theory of justice because they have a capacity to
develop the requisite cognitive traits needed to participate in full citizenship.[3]
Rawls struggled a little more with explaining how individuals with permanent
severe cognitive disabilities could be owed justice on his theory, though he stated
that he believed they ought to be included.[4] With regard to nonhumans, Rawls
indicates that his intuition is that they should be excluded from considerations of
justice. In *A Theory of Justice*, he writes,

> Last of all, we should recall here the limits of a theory of justice. Not only are
> many aspects of morality left aside, but no account is given of the right conduct
> in regard to animals and the rest of nature. A conception of justice is but one
> part of a moral view. While I have not maintained that the capacity for a sense of
> justice is necessary in order to be owed the duties of justice, it does seem that we
> are not required to give strict justice anyway to creatures lacking this capacity.
> But it does not follow that there are no requirements at all in regard to them,
> nor in our relations with the natural order. Certainly it is wrong to be cruel to
> animals and the destruction of a whole species can be a great evil. The capacity
> for feelings of pleasure and pain and for the forms of life of which animals are
> capable clearly imposes duties of compassion and humanity in their case.[5]

Rawls's considered intuition seems to be that nonhumans are not owed justice.
Nevertheless, Rawls concludes that even if animals are not owed justice, they are
owed something morally. However, he did not develop this idea or make an explicit argument for this. In his later work, he became even more noncommittal,
declining to take a position on justice for animals at all.[6] Accordingly, it is worth

---

[1] John Rawls, *A Theory of Justice*, rev. edition. (Harvard University Press, 1999), 442.
[2] Rawls, *A Theory of Justice*, 446.
[3] Rawls, *A Theory of Justice*, 446.
[4] John Rawls, *Justice as Fairness: A Restatement*, ed. Erin Kelly (Harvard University Press, 2001),
176 n. 59.
[5] Rawls, *A Theory of Justice*, 448.
[6] John Rawls, *Political Liberalism*, expanded ed. (Columbia University Press, 1993), 21.

noting that most of what has been written about the relation between Rawls's work and nonhuman animals has been written by other philosophers.

Many thinkers, such as Michael Pritchard and Wade Robeson, Peter Carruthers, Robert Garner, and Martha Nussbaum, argue that Rawls's political theory cannot without distortion include duties of justice to nonhuman animals.[7] For example, Pritchard and Robeson note that for Rawls, the principles of justice are those that rational people would select when in a position of equality. Rawls asks readers to imagine a situation in which free, equal people are behind a veil of ignorance about their own, unique traits. They do not know their own race, ethnicity, sex, gender, class, or even their own conception of the good life. He thinks that whatever principles are chosen under these conditions (which he calls the original position) are fair and just, since one cannot choose principles that favor oneself over others. Pritchard and Robeson emphasize Rawls's claim that the persons behind the veil of ignorance are choosing self-interestedly. The veil of ignorance serves as a check on self-interested motivation only in that it prevents them from favoring themselves over other persons, but the self-interest still serves to limit the choice to only the interests of persons. In their view, this leaves no reason to extend concern for nonhumans. In fact, they write,

> Since those who can take part are presumed to be exclusively self-interested, they cannot consider the interests of nonparticipants except insofar as it is in their self-interest to do so. But they are choosing under conditions of moderate scarcity and cannot therefore treat animals, for example, in any other way than as resources. Self-interest requires that, for if "it is rational for (them) to suppose they. . . want a larger share of social goods," it is certainly not rational for them to accede to a lesser amount by, say, granting a right to life to nonparticipant sentient beings who have no right to have their interest in such a right taken into account. Like other natural resources, animals are simply there to be used.[8]

In short, Pritchard and Robeson think that the framework of the social contract adopted by Rawls would rule out the possibility of including nonhuman animals.

---

[7] Michael Pritchard and Wade Robeson, "Justice and the Treatment of Animals: A Critique of Rawls," *Environmental Ethic* 3 (1981), 55–61; Peter Carruthers, *The Animals Issue* (Cambridge University Press, 1992); Robert Garner, "Rawls, Animals, and Justice: New Literature, Same Response," *Res Publica* 18 (2012), 159–172; Roberts Garner, *A Theory of Justice for Animals: Animal Rights in a Nonideal World* (Oxford University Press, 2013); Martha Nussbaum, *Frontiers of Justice: Disability, Nationality, and Species Membership* (Harvard University Press, 2006).

[8] Pritchard and Robeson, "Justice," 57.

One might argue in response that Pritchard and Robeson misinterpret what Rawls means by self-interest. They confuse the *interests of a self* with *interests in a self*. The parties in the original position are self-interested in the sense that they are trying to advance their own conception of the good. But there is no assumption that this conception of the good is selfish. A conception of the good may very well include valuing animals in various ways for their own sake, or it may involve treating them as resources. Nevertheless, one could still argue that it would be difficult to get agreement on obligations of justice to nonhuman animals in the original position, given that the parties in the original position don't know whether they hold a conception of the good that includes the good of nonhuman animals or not.

Other philosophers have argued that there are ways to extend Rawls's theory to include justice for nonhuman animals. One way to try to include nonhuman animals is to thicken the veil of ignorance so that it includes ignorance of one's species. For example, Mark Rowlands takes this approach. Rowlands begins with an argument about the moral irrelevance of properties over which one has no control. Rowland writes,

> Properties like gender, race, innate intellectual and physical endowments, are all excluded behind a veil of ignorance precisely because they are properties over which we have no control. They are, that is, features we have in no way earned or merited. In the impartial position, knowledge of which of these features we have is excluded because they are morally irrelevant features. And they are morally irrelevant because we have no control over whether or not we have them.[9]

On this basis, Rowlands argues that Rawls holds the *intuitive equality principle* (IEP), which is this: "If a property is undeserved in the sense that its possessor is not responsible for, or has done nothing to merit, its possession, then its possessor is not morally entitled to whatever benefits accrue from that possession. Possession of the property is a morally arbitrary matter and, therefore, cannot be used to determine the moral entitlements of its possessor."[10] Rowlands goes on to argue that species membership is also a property over which we have no control and have done nothing to merit. For that reason, he argues for thickening the veil of ignorance to include ignorance of species. This, of course, results in a social contract that takes into account the interests of many different species.

Rowland's argument is clearly a kind of luck egalitarian argument. Reading Rawls as a luck egalitarian is controversial, and a more thorough discussion can

[9] Mark Rowlands, *Animals Like Us* (Verso, 2002), 60–61.
[10] Mark Rowlands, *Animals Rights: Moral Theory and Practice* (Palgrave MacMillan, 2009), 134.

be found in Part IV of this text. Regarding Rowland's argument for nonhuman animals in particular, several philosophers have raised concerns, including Robert Garner and David Svolba.[11] For example, Svolba argues against Rowland's approach for a number of reasons. One reason is that he does not think Rawls is or should be committed to the intuitive-equality principle as Rowlands articulates it. Svolba argues that Rawls is only committed to *the intuitive equality of persons principle* (IEPP), which focuses on not arbitrarily favoring one *person* over another. Svolba argues that Rawls holds that moral personhood—the capacity for a sense of the good and a sense of justice—is the basis of one's political status. "Since the properties constitutive of personhood in Kant, or moral personality in Rawls, are undeserved properties, the IEP seems to imply that these properties are morally irrelevant."[12] Svolba goes on to write,

> What Rowlands overlooks, I think, is that Rawls's objection to undeserved inequalities is grounded in his affirmation of the moral equality of persons. Rawls should not be understood as objecting to undeserved inequalities per se, but rather to undeserved inequalities among persons who are moral equals and hence have equal moral claims to the necessary means for living a decent life.[13]

In addition to arguing that the IEP is inconsistent with Rawls's own view, Svolba also argues that there are good reasons for rejecting the IEP, whether or not it is Rawlsian. The IEP seems to rule out of consideration all kinds of traits that most philosophers (even animal rights activists like Regan and Singer) think are morally relevant. Under the IEP, not only is rationality not grounds for mattering morally, neither is sentience or being subjects-of-a-life since they are not traits one has any control over having. Even Rowlands's own criterion (being the kind of thing "which one could rationally worry about being") is a property that one didn't earn. So either some properties one didn't earn matter, or even that property doesn't matter.

A different way philosophers have argued for why it is reasonable to include nonrational beings in the scope of justice is to argue for expanding the concept of community.[14] For example, Mark Coeckelbergh proposes that Rawls's theory of justice be extended to include animals by reconceiving the contractualist concept of a cooperative community. Rather than having an ontological requirement

---

[11] Garner, "Rawls, Animals, and Justice"; David Svolba, "Is There a Rawlsian Argument for Animal Rights?," *Ethical Theory and Moral Practice* 19 (2016), 973–984.
[12] Svolba, "Rawlsian Argument," 978.
[13] Svolba, "Rawlsian Argument," 979.
[14] Carlo Filice, "Rawls and Non-rational Beneficiaries," *Between the Species* 13 (2006), 1–27; Mark Coeckelbergh, "Distributive Justice and Co-operation in a World of Humans and Non-humans: A Contractarian Argument for Drawing Non-humans into the Sphere of Justice," *Res Publica* 15 (2009), 67–84.

for who is included in the social contract (e.g., having certain cognitive capacities), Coeckelbergh argues that the necessary condition for being a party to the social contract is a purely relational one: one must engage in cooperation.[15] Coeckelbergh observes that humans and nonhumans are interdependent. Thus, as a matter of fact, nonhumans are part of our cooperative community. He concludes from this that they ought to be included in a scheme of justice.

It is instructive to explore how Coeckelbergh's view of cooperative communities is different from Rawls's. Rawls doesn't actually use the term "cooperative communities." Instead, he refers to "social cooperation."[16] Specifically, Rawls argues that what defines a just society is that it is a fair system of social cooperation. In *Justice as Fairness*, he states that he is referring to cooperation that "is guided by publicly recognized rules and procedures which those cooperating accept as appropriate to regulate their conduct."[17] Rawls is referring to cooperation among responsible citizens because, as a contract theorist, he is interested in the question of what principles these individuals could reasonably accept as appropriate to guide their cooperation. The component of this argument that is central to the social contract tradition is that the individuals' own agreement to the rules, or more precisely the fact that the individuals have good reasons to agree to the rules, is the source of the justification of applying the rules (and thereby establishing both rights and obligations). Thus, the fact that the cooperating individual is rational and capable of contractual agreement is crucial to the argument.

Coeckelbergh proposes broadening the concept of cooperative communities by including any being with which we are interdependent and cooperate. But Coeckelbergh cannot simply plug this kind of cooperative community into the old contractualist argument and have a valid argument for including nonhuman animals in the sphere of justice. In other words, the reasons for including non-rational beings cannot involve their reasonable agreement to the contract, since that is beyond their abilities. Establishing that we have duties of justice to non-rational beings under a contract theory will require more than merely noting that these beings are interacting with us; it will require giving us rational citizens reasons for limiting how we respond to all those who interact with us. That is, it requires arguing that it is reasonable for people to consent to a contract with duties to members of their larger community who are not part of the community of moral persons. This premise is the crucial one that establishes justification for the claim that we owe nonhuman animals anything. This is the one that is not clearly provided.

---

15 Coeckelbergh, "Distributive Justice."
16 Rawls, *Justice as Fairness*, 5–8; *Political Liberalism*, 299–304.
17 Rawls, *Justice as Fairness*, 6.

So is it reasonable for citizens to consent to a political and social system that creates duties to nonhuman animals? In this volume, Patrick Taylor Smith and Sarah Roberts-Cady answer this question differently. Roberts-Cady argues that there are reasons that can be given for extending justice to nonhuman animals that are compatible with Rawls's core commitments in political liberalism. In contrast, Smith argues that Rawls's theory of justice cannot be extended to include direct obligations of justice to nonhuman animals without significant theoretical costs. However, he argues that Rawls's theory can support indirect obligations of justice to animals (obligations derivative of our obligations to other humans) that may suffice to accommodate important considered judgments at the heart of the animal rights challenge.

Suggested Reading from Rawls to Accompany These Chapters

A Theory of Justice: §77
Political Liberalism: Lecture I, §3; "The Idea of Public Reason Revisited," §1
Justice as Fairness: A Restatement: §§7, 51

For Further Reading

Abbey, Ruth. "Rawlsian Resources for Animal Ethics." *Ethics and the Environment* 12 (2007), 1–22. In this article, Abbey defends and develops Rawls's suggestion in *A Theory of Justice* that there are moral duties to animals that fall outside the realm of justice.

Cochrane, Alasdair. *An Introduction to Animals and Political Theory* (Palgrave Macmillan, 2010). This is a short, clear book explaining how different political theories address the relation between political communities and nonhuman animals.

Berkey, Brian. "Prospects for an Inclusive Theory of Justice: The Case of Non-human Animals." *Journal of Applied Philosophy* 34 (2017), 679–695. Berkey argues that three widely accepted premises of liberalism preclude the idea of justice for nonhuman animals.

Donaldson, Sue, and Will Kymlicka. *Zoopolis: A Political Theory of Animal Rights* (Oxford University Press, 2011). This is an original theory regarding how liberal political communities can and should integrate animal rights.

Garner, Robert. "Rawls, Animals, and Justice: New Literature, Same Response." *Res Publica* 18 (2012), 159–172. In this article, Garner explores a variety of attempts to extend Rawls's theory of justice to include nonhuman animals and argues that none of them succeed.

Nussbaum, Martha. *Frontiers of Justice: Disability, Nationality, and Species Membership* (Harvard University Press, 2006). Nussbaum's book explores issues of justice for persons with disabilities, justice across political borders, and justice across species, and argues that there is no room for justice for nonhuman animals in Rawls's theory of justice.

Rowlands, Mark. "Contractarianism and Animal Rights." *Journal of Applied Philosophy* 14 (1997), 235–247. In this article, Rowlands argues that a Rawlsian-type contractarianism can and should be extended to include nonhuman animals.

15

Extending Rawlsian Justice
to Nonhuman Animals

Sarah Roberts-Cady

What is the proper role of government in protecting nonhuman animals? This interesting question is rather new in political philosophy. Some of the most influential political theories in history never addressed it. John Rawls barely mentioned it. Yet increasingly people are recognizing that the question of how humans interact with other living beings is a matter of deep concern, both morally and politically. It is a question political philosophers should examine more rigorously. In this chapter, I will argue that the Rawlsian theoretical framework can be used to argue for justice for nonhuman animals.

Clarification of Terms and Questions

I will begin by clarifying certain terms I am using and questions I am asking. Because the primary argument against extending Rawls's theory to include non-human animals (hereafter "animals") is related to their lack of rationality, it is important to specify how the term "rationality" will be used in this chapter. I will use the term "rational beings" broadly to designate all those beings who have whatever intellectual powers are required for a person to be able to understand and follow moral norms. Thus, my category of rational beings is roughly equivalent to Rawls's category of moral persons. Moral persons are defined by Rawls as individuals who possess the two moral powers—a capacity for a sense of the good and a capacity for a sense of justice.[1] The capacity for a sense of the good is the capacity to identify, revise, and pursue one's own conception of a good life. The capacity for a sense of justice is the ability to engage in social cooperation with others, honoring fair terms of cooperation with others. Note my use of the phrase "rational beings" is different from the way Rawls sometimes uses

---

[1] John Rawls, *A Theory of Justice*, rev. ed. (Harvard University Press, 1999), 442; John Rawls, *Political Liberalism*, expanded ed. (Columbia University Press, 2005), 30–31; John Rawls *Justice as Fairness: A Restatement*, ed. Erin Kelly (Harvard University Press, 2001), 18–19.

Sarah Roberts-Cady, *Extending Rawlsian Justice to Nonhuman Animals* In: *John Rawls*. Edited by: Jon Mandle and Sarah Roberts-Cady, Oxford University Press (2020). © Oxford University Press.
DOI: 10.1093/oso/9780190859213.003.0024.

the term "rationality" to refer to the instrumental thinking people do in identifying, revising, ordering, and calculating how to achieve their own ends.[2] Rawls distinguishes this from the reasonable, which involves the capacities and inclinations required to honor the fair terms of cooperation. When identifying rational beings in this chapter, I am using the term "rational" in a broader way to capture whatever intellectual powers are necessary for understanding and following moral norms.

It is possible that some higher mammals have a capacity for a sense of the good and a sense of justice such that they would be properly characterized as rational beings. I will not attempt to argue for or against that claim here. If it turns out some animals are rational beings, it would certainly follow from Rawls's theory that they are owed justice. However, I take it as obvious that the vast majority of animals do not have this rational capacity. One important question this chapter will address is whether or not the lack of rationality excludes these animals from Rawls's theory of justice.

In examining the question of justice for animals, I will be focusing specifically on the question of social justice. That is, following Rawls, I am asking about fair principles to guide "the way in which the major social institutions distribute fundamental rights and duties and determine the division of advantages from social cooperation."[3] In other words, the question is whether or not protections for animals ought to be built into the basic structure of society (our political, social, and economic institutions).

In exploring the place of animals in Rawls's conception of justice, it will also be useful to make a distinction between the subjects and objects of duties of justice. In the sentence, "x has a duty of justice to y," x is the subject of the duty of justice (the one who has a duty to discharge) and y is the object of the duty of justice (the one to whom the duty is owed). The object of a duty of justice would be any individuals with established rights or protections under a just institution, to whom one owes respect for those rights or protections. Thus, one might frame the questions at hand in these ways: Are animals the objects of justice? Is rationality a necessary condition for being an *object* of duties of justice?

Before we explore these questions about the *objects* of duties of justice, it is worth briefly discussing the relevance of rationality to the *subjects* of duties of justice. John Rawls is interested in identifying fair principles for guiding political, social, and economic institutions. In his view, the fair principles are those that people would reasonably consent to follow. The subjects of duties of justice are those individuals who are capable of endorsing the principles of justice. Rawls holds that the subjects of justice must possess the two moral powers. In short, in

---

[2] Rawls, *Political Liberalism*, 48–54.
[3] Rawls, *A Theory of Justice*, 6.

order to be a *subject* of justice one must have capabilities, including the intellectual capabilities, sufficient to be a morally and politically responsible agent. Although one might dispute Rawls's way of carving up the relevant intellectual components necessary for moral agency, it would be absurd to dispute some sort of intellectual requirement for being the subject of duties of justice. In order to have duties that one ought to follow, one must be able to understand and voluntarily fulfill those duties. No one seriously holds that sheep and grasshoppers should be held morally responsible. They lack the intellectual capacities to understand, endorse, and follow moral rules. It is clear that rationality is a necessary condition for being a subject of duties of justice.

The more interesting question concerns the criteria for the *objects* of duties of justice. That is, by what criteria does one determine to whom justice is owed? Here the relevance of rationality is less obvious. According to Rawls, do we only have duties of justice to rational beings or do we have duties of justice to some nonrational beings as well? In particular, do we have duties of justice to nonrational animals?

John Rawls on Animals

Rawls clearly states that having the capacity for full "moral powers" is *sufficient* for being owed justice (being an object of a duty of justice). Are full moral powers also *necessary* for being owed justice? Rawls is inconsistent on this point, but his most considered view leaves open the question of necessity. In *A Theory of Justice*, Rawls admits that he is inclined to think that only moral persons are entitled to justice, but he isn't certain of it.[4] In asking what sort of beings are owed justice, Rawls writes,

> We see, then, that the capacity for moral personality is a *sufficient* condition for being entitled to equal justice. Nothing beyond the essential minimum is required. Whether moral personality is also a *necessary* condition I shall leave aside.[5]

Rawls recognizes the danger of holding the capacity for rationality to be necessary for being owed justice: doing so would exclude permanently nonrational humans, such as the severely cognitively disabled. Thus, he doesn't commit himself to holding that rationality is a necessary condition for being entitled to equal

---

[4] Rawls, *A Theory of Justice*, 441–442.
[5] Rawls, *A Theory of Justice*, 442–443, my italics.

justice. However, he has a strong, undefended intuition that justice isn't owed to animals. Rawls writes,

> Last of all, we should recall here the limits of a theory of justice. Not only are many aspects of morality left aside, but no account is given of the right conduct in regard to animals and the rest of nature. A conception of justice is but one part of a moral view. While I have not maintained that the capacity for a sense of justice is necessary in order to be owed the duties of justice, it does seem that we are not required to give strict justice anyway to creatures lacking this capacity.[6]

So in *A Theory of Justice*, Rawls didn't conclude with certainty that animals are excluded from justice, but merely said it "seems" they are. In his later work, he became even more tentative about this conclusion. In *Political Liberalism* and *Justice as Fairness*, Rawls declined to address this issue at all, writing that he will "discuss later" "problems of extension" such as duties to animals.[7] That later discussion never took place.

In short, Rawls never really developed his view about duties of justice to animals, but many other thinkers have offered different suggestions about what position is consistent with his other philosophical commitments.

The Naysayers

One position many scholars take is to argue that Rawls's theoretical framework simply *cannot* accommodate obligations to animals under his theory of justice.[8] Philosophers argue for this in various ways, but it often comes down to one central claim: as a theorist in the social contract tradition, Rawls can only generate duties from and to those rational beings capable of consenting to a social contact. For example, Peter Carruthers writes,

> Morality is here [in contract theory] pictured as a system of rules to govern the interaction of rational agents within society. It therefore seems inevitable, on the face of it, that only rational agents will be assigned direct rights on this

---

[6] Rawls, *A Theory of Justice*, 448.

[7] Rawls, *Political Liberalism*, 21; *Justice as Fairness*, 176 n. 59.

[8] Michael S. Pritchard and Wade L. Robeson, "Justice and the Treatment of Animals: A Critique of Rawls," *Environmental Ethics* 3 (1981), 55–61; Peter Carruthers, *The Animals Issue: Moral Theory in Practice* (Cambridge University Press, 1992); Robert Garner, "Animals, Politics and Justice: Rawlsian Liberalism and the Plight of Non-humans," *Environmental Politics* 12 (2003), 3–22; Robert Garner, "Rawls, Animals and Justice: New Literature, Same Response," *Res Publica* 19 (2012), 159–172; Martha Nussbaum, *Frontiers of Justice: Disability, Nationality, Species Membership* (Harvard University Press, 2007).

approach. Since it is rational agents who are to choose the system of rules, and choose self-interestedly, it is only rational agents who will have their position protected under the rules.[9]

Of course, claiming that there are no duties of justice to nonrational beings is not the same as claiming that there are no moral duties to nonrational beings altogether. In fact, Rawls himself suggested that there are. Continuing the passage from Rawls quoted previously:

> While I have not maintained that the capacity for a sense of justice is necessary in order to be owed the duties of justice, it does seem that we are not required to give strict justice anyway to creatures lacking this capacity. But it does not follow that there are not requirements at all in regard to them, nor in our relations with the natural order. Certainly it is wrong to be cruel to animals and the destruction of a whole species can be a great evil. The capacity for feelings of pleasure and pain and for the forms of life of which animals are capable clearly imposes duties of compassion and humanity in their case.[10]

Taking this passage as her guide, Ruth Abbey developed an argument that Rawls's *A Theory of Justice* has the resources for supporting obligations to animals—but obligations that fall outside the duties of justice.[11]

Many people are dissatisfied with this approach, however. They want to argue that how we treat animals is a matter of justice, rather than charity or some other category of moral thinking. Why? What's at stake in calling something a matter of justice? Social justice concerns those aspects of morality that ought to be protected and enforced through the basic institutions of society. So the question at stake is this: are there moral rights and/or interests of animals that ought to be protected by our basic social and political structures?

A Framework for Expanding Rawls's Theory to Include Animals

To understand why or how Rawls's theory of justice might be extended to include animals, one must first explore more deeply why some people think they might be excluded. Perhaps the reason some people think that a Rawlsian contract

[9] Carruthers, *The Animals Issue*, 98–99.
[10] Rawls, *A Theory of Justice*, 448.
[11] Ruth Abbey, "Rawlsian Resources for Animal Ethics," *Ethics and the Environment* 12 (2007), 1–22.

theory requires rationality as a precondition for being an object of justice is because they identify Rawls's theory with the Hobbesian contractarian view, which holds that parties would accept a contract only if it is mutually advantageous.[12] The idea is that it wouldn't be rational for an individual to accept the burden of duties to others unless it will result in advantages to that individual. To get from this premise to the conclusion that only subjects of duties of justice are objects of duties of justice, one must add the premise that it is not mutually advantageous for people to establish duties to noncontracting parties. There is reason to doubt this latter assumption is true. Anyone with an introductory understanding of ecology recognizes that the well-being of humans depends on the well-being of other living things. However, I won't develop that obvious point here since there is also reason to doubt that Rawls is a Hobbesian contractarian.

T. M. Scanlon contrasts the Hobbesian contractarian view with a contractualist view. The roots of the contractualist view are identified with Immanuel Kant's kingdom-of-ends formulation of the categorical imperative. In this formulation, Kant asks readers to envision a society in which all the members are both the authors and the subjects of the law. He argues one should only act on those principles that could also be endorsed and acted upon by all other reasonable persons in one's community.[13] In a slightly different approach, Scanlon adopts a negative standard of reasonableness: "An act is wrong if its performance under the circumstances would be disallowed by any set of principles for the general regulation of behaviour that no one could reasonably reject as a basis for informed, unforced, general agreement."[14] In either form of contractualism, the requirement for mutual advantage is no longer central. Instead, it is simply a requirement of reasonableness: what principles could all reasonably accept or no one reasonably reject? On contractualist views, establishing duties of justice to animals seems easier to do. All one must establish is that it is reasonable for people to consent to a contract that includes duties to animals.

A close reading of Rawls's work reveals he is a contractualist, not a Hobbesian contractarian. The question that Rawls is trying to answer is about a fair system of cooperation for citizens with diverse conceptions of the good. He asks this contractualist question: what are the terms of cooperation that rational and reasonable persons would accept as fair? He was convinced that a fair system would

---

[12] On this issue, I need to credit Christie Hartley, "Justice for the Disabled: A Contractualist Approach," *Journal of Social Philosophy* 4 (2009), 17–36. Hartley argues persuasively that one can extend Rawls's theory of justice to include cognitively disabled persons if Rawls is read as a contractualist, rather than a contractarian. Although Hartley's contractualist argument is very different from mine, my own approach was inspired by her pointing out that this distinction offers a pathway for understanding and solving the problem.

[13] Immanuel Kant, *Grounding for the Metaphysics of Morals*, trans. James W. Ellington (Hackett, 1981), 38.

[14] T. M. Scanlon, *What We Owe to Each Other* (Harvard University Press, 1998), 153.

be grounded in reciprocity. In a *Theory of Justice*, Rawls writes that there are two things involved in reciprocity between free and equal persons: (1) a principle of *mutual benefit*, that is, adopting policies that serve each person's own good, harmonizing our social interests so one doesn't gain at the expense of another.[15] This is certainly where people (rightly) note an assumption of some self-interest. However, reciprocity also involves (2) a principle of *mutual respect*.[16] People publicly express respect for one another by offering up reasons for political positions that they believe others will understand and find reasonable. In *Political Liberalism*, Rawls describes it this way,

> The criterion of reciprocity requires that when those terms are proposed as the most reasonable terms of fair cooperation, those proposing them must also think it at least reasonable for others to accept them, as free and equal citizens, and not as dominated or manipulated, or under the pressure of an inferior political or social position.[17]

It is worth noting that the goal of mutual benefit is subordinated to this goal of mutual respect. The idea is that reasonable people may be willing to sacrifice their self-interest in some cases, if it is necessary for a system of mutual respect. In fact, in *Political Liberalism*, Rawls goes further, explicitly stating that the "idea of reciprocity is not the idea of mutual advantage."[18] He writes that "reciprocity lies between the idea of impartiality, which is altruistic (being moved by the general good), and the idea of mutual advantage understood as everyone's being advantaged with respect to each person's present or expected future situation as things are."[19] Rawls thought that reasonable people would accept that a fair system might be one in which *not* everyone is better off than they are in their current situation. Rawls notes that in our current, imperfect, and unjust system, some people are quite wealthy as a matter of luck or because they are benefiting from previous injustices. He points out that these wealthy people might be worse off in a system governed by the principles of justice. Thus, it is not solely the commitment to self-interest, but also a commitment to mutual respect that would lead reasonable people to adopt Rawls's principles of justice. Rawls writes,

> Citizens are reasonable when, viewing one another as free and equal in a system of social cooperation over generations, they are prepared to offer one another fair terms of cooperation according to what they consider the most reasonable

[15] Rawls, *A Theory of Justice*, 88.
[16] Rawls, *A Theory of Justice*, 154–155.
[17] Rawls, *Political Liberalism*, 446.
[18] Rawls, *Political Liberalism*, 17.
[19] Rawls, *Political Liberalism*, 16–17.

conception of political justice; and when they agree to act on those terms, *even at the cost of their own interests in particular situations*, provided that other citizens also accept those terms.[20]

So, in Rawls's view, it is reasonable to agree to a system of cooperation in which one has to sacrifice some benefits to oneself for the sake of a more just system overall. Thus, what is reasonable cannot be reduced to what is mutually advantageous. Accordingly, Rawls is clearly a contractualist, not a contractarian. Given this, the question of the status of animals in Rawls's theory hinges on the answer to this question: would it be reasonable for moral agents to agree to terms of social cooperation that include legal protections for animals?

Answering this question will require sorting out more clearly what counts as a reasonable argument in Rawls's view. The criteria for what counts as reasonable in the context of political arguments are different from the criteria for what counts as reasonable in other realms, such as scientific arguments or epistemic arguments.[21] So what is a reasonable argument in the context of political arguments? The foundation of Rawls's answer to the question has already been established: Rawls argues that, in the political realm, people are reasonable when they have the capacity and willingness to propose and accept fair terms of cooperation among moral subjects. This requires more clarification, though. In *Political Liberalism*, Rawls frames the problem of justice as a problem of finding fair terms of cooperation among people who have conflicting but reasonable comprehensive doctrines of the good. Rawls assumes that reasonable people will disagree about comprehensive religious or philosophical views about what the good of life is. Respecting others as free and equal requires offering them terms of cooperation that one believes they would find acceptable, despite their different comprehensive theories of the good life. This is what Rawls calls the idea of public reason. By using public reason, one shows respect for others as free and equal. A reasonable argument, then, is one that is grounded in public reasons.

One can think of Rawls's famous thought experiment, "the original position," as a model of public reasoning. Rawls asked his readers to imagine a situation in which people have unlimited access to general knowledge about the world, but are behind a "veil of ignorance" about their own unique traits—their race, ethnicity, gender, talents, and even their own conception of the good. Further imagine that these people are then asked to select principles of justice to guide social cooperation. Rawls argued that whatever principles would be chosen by persons in this position would be fair principles.[22] Notice that this thought

---

[20] Rawls, *Political Liberalism* 446, my italics.
[21] Rawls, *Justice as Fairness*, 93.
[22] Rawls, *A Theory of Justice*, 11.

experiment models both equal respect for persons generally and public reasoning specifically. Although we are to imagine that the people in the original position are choosing self-interestedly, when the self-interest is combined with the ignorance of self, it results in modeling equal respect for persons.[23] Because one does not know one's own position in society, one cannot design principles that favor one's own position. Instead, one chooses principles that show equal respect for everyone. Further, the original position models acceptable restrictions on reasons; it models public reason. Because the people in the original position do not know their own conception of the good, they will choose principles based on arguments that can be found reasonable by all parties, regardless of their conception of the good. So when one asks if political obligations to animals would be chosen from behind Rawls's veil of ignorance, one is asking this: are there reasons that could be offered for including legal obligations to animals that are consistent with equal respect for all persons and can be grounded in public reason?

Arguments for Extending Some Basic Rights to Animals Using Public Reason

I will argue that there are arguments for extending at least some basic legal rights to animals that are grounded in public reasons, and therefore that are consistent with respect for persons as free and equal. While it certainly is the case that some arguments for animal rights are grounded in specific comprehensive philosophical theories, some of the most persuasive and widely used arguments are not. These arguments are grounded in public reasons. I will describe two of these arguments: an argument from consistency and an argument for nonarbitrary starting points. Neither of these arguments is uniquely my own; I cite them here as examples of other widely offered arguments using public reason.

Before I explain these arguments, it is worth noting that no philosopher argues that animals should have all the same rights as human citizens. Even the most radical of animal rights theorists would agree that not all basic rights should be extended to animals. It is reasonable that only those individuals with a certain level of intellectual capacity ought to have those rights that require some intellectual capacity to be exercised. For example, political liberties such as the right to vote or run for office require an intellectual capacity to be exercised. Since a human infant cannot exercise the right to vote, it is reasonable not to assign them these rights. One could argue the same about a horse or a pigeon.

[23] Rawls, *A Theory of Justice*, 148.

On the other hand, it doesn't seem reasonable to limit other rights to rational beings alone. Consider rights against physical aggression. To whom ought institutions grant the right against battery? Recall that for Rawls, the answer to this question hinges on what reasonable people would accept—what criterion would be found reasonable by people with diverse conceptions of the good? It is not reasonable to have an intellectual requirement for a right against battery. Indeed, despite differences in religion and philosophical theory, almost everyone thinks that physical abuse of infants and severely cognitively disabled persons is not only wrong, but a wrong that ought to be prevented and prosecuted by the government. A lack of some intellectual capacity is not considered a reason to exclude a human individual from this right against battery. This reasonable overlapping consensus among diverse views is enough for a Rawlsian to argue for legal protections of these individuals as a matter of justice.

The tougher argument to make is for including animals. People are deeply divided on the issue of the legal rights of animals. However, the standards of justice do not depend on existing consensus. They depend on reasonable consensus. More specifically, they depend on the possibility of offering up public reasons for including animals—arguments that could be persuasive to any reasonable person. Many philosophers do this by making an argument from consistency from the premise established earlier. Out of consistency, if a lack of rational capacity does not rule out humans having legal rights against battery, then a lack of rational capacity is not a reason for ruling out animals from having legal rights against battery. Therefore, the lack of rationality is not a reason why animals should be excluded from protection from assault and battery. This is often called "the argument from marginal cases," though I think the "argument from consistency" is a better label.[24]

Some form of this argument has been offered up by thinkers with a wide range of philosophical commitments—from utilitarians like Peter Singer to deontologists like Tom Regan to liberal political philosophers like Will Kymlicka.[25] The argument does not depend on any particular philosophical or religious theory about why every human deserves certain protections; it begins with the reasonable overlapping consensus that all humans deserve these protections and makes an argument from consistency about what this entails. Accordingly, this is an example of an argument that shows respect for persons as free and equal by appealing to public reasons.

[24] As many others have pointed out before me, the lack of rationality is not a state of a few marginal cases of human beings, but in fact a state that all humans experience for at least part of their lives, certainly for the first years. For that reason, I call this the argument from consistency rather than the argument from marginal cases.

[25] Peter Singer, *Animal Liberation* (HarperCollins, 2002); Tom Regan, *The Case for Animal Rights* (Routledge, 1984); Will Kymlicka and Sue Donaldson, *Zoopolis: A Political Theory of Animal Rights* (Oxford University Press, 2011).

Of course, it's not enough to rule out rationality as a criterion for a right against battery. One also needs an argument for a positive criterion for determining who has this right. One starting point about which diverse people could agree is that the criteria for whom is given rights should be nonarbitrary. With humans, most of us recognize that the color of one's skin or the results of one's IQ test is irrelevant to whether or not one ought to have a right against physical aggression. To exclude some people from protection for these reasons would be arbitrary and unjustified. In the same way, philosophers like Peter Singer have famously argued that including only the human species is also arbitrary. There is no relevant trait that all humans have that no other animal has that could justify drawing the line at the species boundary. For any trait that one identifies (e.g., intellectual capacity, language capacity, relational status) there will be humans who lack this trait and/or animals who have it. So what would be a nonarbitrary criterion for determining who has a right against battery? Peter Singer argued that a nonarbitrary answer to who should have some protection from physical harm is to include anyone who could be physically harmed. That is, a nonarbitrary standard is to include any being with the capacity to feel pain.[26] Notice this doesn't arbitrarily exclude any individual who can be battered from a right against battery; all and only those who feel pain can be battered. Therefore, the standard of including anyone who can feel pain is a nonarbitrary starting point. This criterion most certainly would entail that infants, cognitively disabled humans, and animals have a right against battery.

This argument does not depend on any particular comprehensive philosophical theory of the good. Indeed, one can imagine arguments for extending the right against battery to all sentient beings grounded in a wide variety of comprehensive doctrines. Utilitarians like Singer clearly focus on the capacity to feel pleasure and pain because of their focus on the value of promoting happiness. Yet one need not be a utilitarian to think sentience matters morally. A Kantian could argue for laws against assault of all sentient beings as a result of the indirect duty not to be cruel to animals. Kant argued that, given the similarities in the capacity to suffer between humans and animals, one who is insensitive to the pain of animals may be more likely to be insensitive to the pain of humans. Therefore, out of respect for humans he argued for some protections for animals. Although each comprehensive doctrine may come to the conclusion for different foundational reasons, one can see the possibility of a reasonable overlapping consensus among them about the fact that the capacity to feel pain is a nonarbitrary standard for who should be protected from battery. Because this argument is grounded in public reasons, rather than any specific doctrine of

---

[26] Singer, *Animal Liberation*, 7.

the good, it shows respect for the diverse views of citizens in pluralistic society. Respecting other citizens doesn't just require serving their interests; it requires respecting their conceptions of the good more broadly. This is how the interests of nonhumans can find their way into a contractualist conception of justice.

Of course, not everyone will be convinced by these brief arguments. One may be able to come up with counterarguments based on public reason alone. Further, others might offer better public reasons for extending justice to animals. The point is this: the conversation can be held (and often is held) using public reason alone. Accordingly, there is room in Rawls's theory for a cooperative agreement between free and equal persons that includes duties of justice to nonrational beings.

Admittedly, a fully worked out theory of justice for animals would require more than protection from battery. There are other negative rights that must be examined: for example, what is the criterion for determining who has a right against being killed? Further, arguments would need to be considered for positive rights as well. Presumably there are arguments to be made for the positive obligations to care for domestic animals and protect endangered species. This is only one part of what must be a longer discussion. What I hope to have done is to provide an example of an argument for extending at least one right to animals using public reason. The point is to map out a route by which a Rawlsian can argue for including animals in a theory of justice: all one must do is make the case that it is reasonable for people to consent to a system of justice that includes legal protections for animals.

Conclusion

What I have argued is that Rawls's theory does not, as many philosophers assume, rule out the possibility of justice for animals. A careful reading of Rawls shows that the issue hinges on the answer to this question: would it be reasonable for moral agents to agree to terms of social cooperation that include protections for animals? To establish that it is reasonable, one must make an argument for these legal protections that is grounded in public reason alone. I have argued that such arguments exist and, indeed, dominate discussions of the status of animals. Thus, a Rawlsian framework can be used to argue for justice for animals.

Acknowledgments

Thanks to Dugald Owen, Justin McBrayer, Peter McCormick, Patrick Taylor Smith, and Jon Mandle for their helpful comments on earlier drafts of this chapter.

16

Rawls and Animals

A Defense

Patrick Taylor Smith

Introduction

The central, paradigm case of John Rawls's political philosophy is that of working adults engaging in common deliberation about the distribution of rights, privileges, benefits, and opportunities created by their reciprocal social cooperation. Rawls then went on to argue that the insights of this central case can be used to describe our obligations to future people and to members of other states.[1] However, these extensions have dealt with how we should treat adults who are members of cooperative systems that are not our own. In both cases, our fundamental obligation is to ensure that these other cooperative structures can operate sustainably and legitimately, whether through the just savings principle or the duty of assistance to burdened societies.[2] Yet Rawls himself suggested that there were other scenarios—those that did not obviously involve adult, rational humans engaged in social cooperation—that needed to be developed and that a failure to provide plausible responses to these noncooperative scenarios could potentially undermine justice as fairness.[3] Our obligations toward nonhuman animals seem to be a particularly difficult fit with his contract-oriented justice as fairness, and some have argued we should reject Rawls's view because it

---

[1] Rawls's extension to future peoples can be found in the "present time of entry" interpretation of the original position. See John Rawls, *Justice as Fairness: A Restatement*, ed. Erin Kelly (Harvard University Press, 2001), 86–87, 160. This justifies the just savings principle. His extension of the duty of assistance to burdened peoples can be found in his *The Law of Peoples* (Harvard University Press, 1999).

[2] The just savings principle is that we are required to pass sufficient resources onto future generations such that they can sustain their well-ordered institutions (*Justice as Fairness*, 160) and the duty of assistance is an obligation to ensure that other contemporaneous states have sufficient human and material resources to maintain well-ordered institutions (Rawls, *The Law of Peoples*, 105–111).

[3] Rawls argues that it cannot be determined in advance whether other extensions require revisions and whether those revisions decisively undermine his views. Rawls himself is skeptical that justice as fairness cannot accommodate direct status for animals. See John Rawls, *A Theory of Justice*, rev. ed. (Harvard University Press, 1993), 15; John Rawls *Political Liberalism*, expanded ed. (Columbia University Press, 2005), 21, 244–235.

Patrick Taylor Smith, *Rawls and Animals* In: *John Rawls*. Edited by: Jon Mandle and Sarah Roberts-Cady, Oxford University Press (2020). © Oxford University Press. DOI: 10.1093/oso/9780190859213.003.0025.

cannot incorporate direct obligations of justice toward nonhuman animals.[4] In response, others have adopted what could be called a *conciliatory* approach that aims to fit a fundamental, justice-based concern for animal welfare into a revised Rawlsian system.[5]

This chapter, on the other hand, will adopt a more *confrontational* tack, arguing that it would be a mistake to water down or abandon core commitments of the Rawlsian view in order to incorporate direct obligations of justice to non-human animals. The argument proceeds in three steps. First, I draw a distinction between direct and indirect obligations of justice[6] and between different ways an objection can undermine a theory. Second, I argue that incorporating a direct obligation of justice toward nonhuman animals will require substantial revisions of Rawlsian commitments that are independently plausible and attractive. Third, I argue that the net theoretical improvement we might gain by including a direct obligation of justice for nonhuman animals is—given the extent to which our considered judgments can be captured by indirect obligations—outweighed by its costs. To put it another way, once we adopt a more sophisticated and self-conscious understanding of theory and model construction, then we can see that our political theories would not be improved by including direct claims to animal rights.

Two Kinds of Obligations and Two Kinds of Objection

We could imagine someone developing an objection that, on the Rawlsian view, a just state would be required or permitted to legalize bullfighting and that this was a normatively unacceptable result. Yet essentially all challengers to Rawls either fail to provide any such counterexample or provide counterexamples that manifestly fail to take the entire Rawlsian view into account.[7] Instead, the "animal rights challenge," as I shall call it, is that any acceptable theory of justice must

[4] Robert Garner, "Rawls, Animals and Justice: New Literature, Same Response," *Res Publica* 19 (2012), 159–172; Michael S. Pritchard and Wade L. Robeson, "Justice and the Treatment of Animals: A Critique of Rawls," *Environmental Ethics* 3 (1981), 55–61; Martha Nussbaum, *Frontiers of Justice: Disability, Nationality, Species Membership* (Harvard University Press, 2007); Brian Berkey, "Prospects for an Inclusive Theory of Justice: The Case of Non-human Animals," *Journal of Applied Philosophy* 34 (2015), 679–695.

[5] Mark Rowlands, "Contractarianism and Animal Rights," *Journal of Applied Philosophy* 14 (1997), 235–247; Ruth Abbey, "Rawlsian Resources for Animal Ethics," *Ethics and the Environment* 12 (2007), 1–22; Mark Coeckelbergh, "Distributive Justice and Co-operation in a World of Humans and Non-humans: A Contractarian Argument for Drawing Non-humans into the Sphere of Justice," *Res Publica* 15 (2009), 67–84; Tom Regan, *The Case for Animal Rights* (Routledge, 1984); and Roberts-Cady in this volume.

[6] Immanuel Kant originates this distinction in his *Lectures on Ethics*, ed. Peter Heath and J. B. Schneewind (Cambridge University Press, 1997), 27:459–461.

[7] Or they simply assume that a lack of direct status leads to an acceptance of abuse and exploitation.

incorporate a justice-based obligation to create basic structural protections for animals, and the justification for these protections must be a direct, noninstrumental concern for animal interests.[8] The conceptual worry, as presented by animal rights advocates, is that indirect obligations—namely, those that rely upon human interests to justify concern and protection for animals—rely upon the wrong kinds of reasons to protect animals and that a theory that did not centrally locate animal interests would be inadequate. It is not an objection based on upon the policy outputs of Rawls's political philosophy because the political, legal, and social consequences of direct and indirect moral obligations to animals might be equivalent in our world. So the animal rights challenge is generated through two claims. First, animals or their interests have intrinsic moral status,[9] and, second, any adequate theory of justice must justify its animal protection regime on the basis of that status. So, we have a foundational moral claim about intrinsic status and a theoretical claim about how that intrinsic status ought to relate to a complex set of legal, political, social, and economic entitlements.

Understanding these two elements of the animal rights challenge suggests another distinction between *counterexamples* and *theoretical desiderata*. Let's define a counterexample as a considered judgment[10] about a reasonably well-specified particular case that is meant to be directly disqualifying against a philosophical theory. Kant's view is false because you cannot lie to the murderer at the door,[11] Gettier cases demonstrate that justified, true belief is not knowledge, and so on. But "centrality" arguments purport to show that it is *theoretically desirable* to adopt a particular commitment or concern as being central or paradigmatic a theory. "Centrality objections" to Rawls are quite common: Stephen Gardiner argues for climate change centrality in global justice,[12] Charles Mills for the centrality of racial oppression,[13] and Martha Nussbaum for the centrality of disability.[14] In each case, the idea is that core commitments of the Rawlsian

---

[8] An admirably clear example of this is Berkey ("Prospects"), who is straightforward in assuming that the issue is that Rawls cannot generate *direct* obligations of justice for nonhuman animals. Indirect duties are insufficient on his view. I show later that my interlocutor, Professor Cady-Roberts, is an example of this strategy.

[9] Of course, some pro-animal views, such as those that are based on utilitarianism, might not be committed to animals or humans having intrinsic moral status at all. Perhaps only pain or pleasure has moral status, but this is not a challenge from the perspective of animal *rights*. What's more, utilitarians must accept that animal *interests* have intrinsic moral status.

[10] For the features of considered judgments—carefully considered opinions that persist over time in the face of contrary arguments, see T. M. Scanlon, "Rawls on Justification," in *The Cambridge Companion to Rawls*, ed. Samuel Freeman (Cambridge University Press, 2003), 143.

[11] This objection was famously presented against Kant's view by Benjamin Constant in his essay "On Political Reactions."

[12] Stephen Gardiner, "Rawls and Climate Change: Does Rawlsian Political Philosophy Pass the Global Test?," *Critical Review of Social and Political Philosophy* 14 (2011), 125–151.

[13] Charles Mills, *The Racial Contract* (Cornell University Press, 1997).

[14] Nussbaum, *Frontiers of Justice*.

conception need to be revised in order to fully incorporate the true importance of some set of normative commitments. Perhaps these objectors have
some specific counterexample in mind when making these arguments, but the
key point is that developing counterexamples is not necessary because indirect
justifications for the relevant political protections are inherently flawed. The
argumentative advantage of centrality arguments is they are robust; they apply
even if the target theory gets the "correct" answer for the wrong reasons. The disadvantage is that they make evaluation less obvious. How can we decide when a
centrality objection succeeds if the view suggests the same, or at least very similar, policy prescriptions in our actual world? I want to submit that centrality
objections need to be evaluated *holistically*, where we look at the consequences
of the various revisions and determine whether those revisions are worth their
theoretical costs.

Rawlsian Core Commitments and Animal Rights

So in order to respond to the animal rights challenge, Rawlsians must do two
things. First, they need to show that there are negative theoretical consequences
to incorporating the animal rights concerns. Second, they need to show that the
theoretical benefits of that incorporation are minor.[15] In this section, I do the
former. However, it is important to distinguish between two aspects of Rawls
that may give rise to the animal rights challenge. First, the challenge might be
an objection to the underlying reasoning of justice as fairness, demanding that
we revise the elements of the view that leads to Rawls's two principles of justice.
Second, the animal rights challenge could be aimed at Rawls's commitment to
political liberalism and public reason, where the liberal principle of legitimacy
requires that core entitlements be justified by reasons that are purely "political"
and do not depend upon comprehensive ethical or moral worldviews. In the
former case, the animal rights challenge would imply that the "concept" of justice
that involved the fair distribution of the benefits of social cooperation and our
corresponding understanding of our fundamental interests would be revised. In
the second case, the animal rights challenge would require a revision of what
constituted a properly political consideration, the democratic basis of political
liberalism, or a rejection of the burdens of judgment in lieu of an intuitionistic
balancing of human and animal interests.

---

[15] Strictly speaking, we should accept the Rawlsian view over the animal rights advocates' if the
former generates greater net benefits than the latter. Yet I am skeptical of our ability to make such
fine-grained judgments about theories. Thus, I accept a higher burden: I need to present reasons to
think that the Rawlsian view is *distinctly* superior to the alternative.

Let's begin with justice as fairness. The concept of justice, as Rawls characterizes it, is a set of general principles for the fair distribution of the benefits of social cooperation under conditions of moderate scarcity.[16] This concept focuses our attention on the two moral powers, neither of which is possessed by most nonhuman animals: the power to act upon *and revise* one's understanding of what makes life worthwhile (i.e., the power to form conceptions of the good) and to offer and act upon fair terms of social cooperation (i.e., the sense of justice). While this concept and the corresponding powers presume we are dealing with rational agents, it is important to acknowledge the theoretical benefits of adopting this view of distributive justice *beyond* the mere powers themselves.[17] These two moral powers are the basis for primary goods[18]—which are the benefits of social cooperation that need to be distributed fairly—and are also necessary for establishing the priority of the basic liberties,[19] which is a key commitment of liberal egalitarian and social democratic views. That is, Rawls argues that certain liberties—those associated with freedom of religion, conscience, and association—are, under most conditions, fundamental and cannot be traded off for greater wealth and income. He founds this claim in the idea that these liberties are essential for individuals to form, act on, and revise their own understanding of a good and meaningful life, an interest and a capacity that most animals lack. Fair equality of opportunity, which requires that the valuable offices and positions and society be distributed according to desire and natural ability only, makes sense only for humans since they can take advantage of an opportunity to inhabit a particular office, job, or role. The difference principle assumes that agents will be responsive to incentives such that inequalities in income benefit the least well off, which will not be true of nonhuman animals. What the animal rights challenger needs to show is that revising these principles—and, for example, losing the lexical priority of the basic liberties and their specification—will generate a *net* improvement in the theory. We should understand that the theoretical costs to the proposed revision will be high: even if the arguments for the principles themselves can be reconstructed, the arguments for understanding

---

[16] Rawls, *A Theory of Justice*, 4, 110.

[17] This is a serious failing of conciliatory views, such as Rowlands's or Coeckelbergh's, that purport to show that small revisions of Rawls's view can be used to incorporate animals. They fail to consider the knock-on theoretical effects of those revisions.

[18] Rawls (*Justice as Fairness*, 58–60) clarified the relationship of primary goods to the two moral powers and the priority of basic liberties in response to the criticisms of Herbert Hart, "Rawls on Liberty and its Priority," in *Reading Rawls*, ed. Norman Daniels (Stanford University Press, 1989). Primary goods are only justified by reference to the political conception of the person as having the two moral powers. See Rawls, *Political Liberalism*, 75–78; Samuel Freeman, *Rawls* (Routledge, 2007), 297.

[19] Freeman, *Rawls*, 68; Rawls, *Political Liberalism*, 310–324.

the objects of distribution and the relationship between the distributive princi-ples will become unmoored.[20]

A more promising idea is that justice as fairness should be treated as a module within a broader concept of justice and this broader concept ought to incorpo-rate animal interests as well as the bridge principles needed to weigh distributive justice against the other values. Yet Rawls's commitments to political liber-alism and public reason seem to block this move. Political liberalism and public reason set limits on the kinds of reasons one can deploy when justifying political institutions and entitlements.[21] The structure of political justification operates in the following way: the democratic culture of a society combines with fully po-litical conceptions—that is, conceptions that do not rely on controversial meta-physical or religious views of the person but derive their content from the public political culture of democratic societies—of free and equal persons as citizens in order to specify a free-standing conception of justice. This free-standing con-ception of justice is, according to Rawls, best understood as a family of liberal egalitarian views with the following features: a set of basic liberties, a guaranteed social minimum in income and wealth, and a balancing relation that prioritizes on the former over the latter.[22] The free-standing conception of justice is dif-ferent from comprehensive doctrines, which represent coherent views, secular or religious, about the good life, human nature, and the ultimate value. People are reasonable when they accept the burdens of judgment—which describe why judgments about divisive moral matters are complicated and difficult[23]—and are willing to endorse the free-standing conception of justice as a way of offering fair terms of cooperation on the basis of freedom and equality. These conceptions of justice are *not* therefore the mere overlap of the comprehensive doctrines of society but have independently justified content concerning the appropriately political interpretation of freedom and equality;[24] we do *not* simply survey rea-sonable comprehensive views and determine the range of agreement. Rather, comprehensive views are reasonable, in part, because they are held by reasonable

---

[20] This knock-on effect will also be apparent in Rawlsian responses to other objections. For ex-ample, some (Meckled-Garcia, Valentini) argue that the best Rawlsian response to Cohen's egali-tarian ethos is to make reference to the basic liberties implicated in one's choice of occupation. This makes little sense if the basic liberties and their priority lose their place in the Rawlsian view. See Laura Valentini, "On the Messy 'Utopophobia vs Factophobia' Controversy: A Systematization and Assessment," in *Political Utopias*, ed. Michael Weber and Kevin Vallier (Oxford University Press, 2017); Saladin Meckled-Garcia, "Why Work Harder? Equality, Social Duty and the Market," *Political Studies* 50 (2002), 779–793; G. A. Cohen, "Where the Action Is: On the Site of Distributive Justice," *Philosophy and Public Affairs* 26 (1997), 3–30.

[21] Rawls, *Political Liberalism*, 217.

[22] Rawls, *Political Liberalism*, xlviii.

[23] Rawls, *Political Liberalism*, 54–58.

[24] Scanlon ("Rawls on Justification," 164–165) is best on the relationship between reasonable per-sons and reasonable comprehensive doctrines.

people who are willing to offer fair terms of cooperation between free and equal citizens.

Political liberalism is made necessary by what Rawls calls the "fact of reasonable pluralism."[25] That is, any society characterized by the free exercise of human reason will inevitably lead to reasonable variation and disagreement in fundamental moral and religious matters. So when we are deliberating upon and justifying coercive government policy, it is inappropriate to rely on comprehensive ethical doctrines that others can reasonably reject.[26] This means that when engaging in public reason—voting on legislation, campaigning, writing judicial opinions, and so on—one should only deploy considerations that make reference to the public, political values of the free-standing conception or those that can eventually be translated into those values. For example, a fundamentalist Mormon politician would be acting inappropriately if they argued for polygamy on the basis of divine revelation, but so would a utilitarian who argued against polygamy on the basis that it would maximize welfare; both justifications are blocked by political liberalism. The arguments in favor or against polygamy need to be understood in terms of the values identified in the free-standing political conception of justice: perhaps we might need to weigh freedom of association against the need to protect women's autonomy. Mormons and utilitarians are reasonable insofar as they accept the burdens of judgment, are committed to the political equality and freedom of their fellow citizens, and accept interpretations of Mormonism and utilitarianism that allow them to endorse the free-standing conception and to reason from that conception within the relevant political contexts.

The problem for the animal rights challenge is that it appears to be a comprehensive ethical view like utilitarianism or Mormonism.[27] Remember, the centrality objection is *not* predicated on the idea that the Rawlsian state, complying with public reason and political liberalism, will fail to justify the correct political and legal entitlements for animals. It is, rather, that these entitlements ought to be justified on the appropriate moral grounds that track the fundamental, intrinsic value of nonhuman animals. Those fundamental values, however, are not part of the free-standing political conception of justice as it relies upon the values of freedom and equality—understood politically—that do not meaningfully apply to most nonhuman animals. What's more, the dialectic of the animal rights challenge is different from those of, for example, abolitionists or women's rights advocates. Those groups argued that these concepts of freedom and equality should be applied to classes that had been marginalized. While

---

[25] Rawls, *Political Liberalism*, xix.
[26] Rawls, *Political Liberalism*, 136–137.
[27] Berkey, "Prospects," §2.2.

these advocates understood that the concepts of freedom and equality would change as new groups were included, they were still offering interpretations of the political values within the free-standing conception.[28] Ultimately, the goal was to convince recalcitrant individuals that these marginalized agents were, in fact, able to be full citizens. The animal rights challenge, on the other hand, is an attempt to argue that the relevant capacities and powers that constitute the political conception of the citizen with its claim to freedom and equality is not the relevant normative perspective for being the recipient of direct political entitlements. This is a far more radical revision, and the Rawlsian standard for inclusion of a new value must be quite high, as these values will be used to justify state coercion. The values would need to be sufficiently well justified and accepted via wide reflective equilibrium that we should consider their inclusion constitutive of a democratic culture or sufficiently obvious that its inclusion would not fall afoul of the burdens of judgment.

Sarah Roberts-Cady, my interlocutor in this volume, develops a sophisticated attempt to sidestep these problems by arguing that reasonable people ought to accept some animal interests as directly generating political entitlements. Her argument goes something like this: reasonable people accept certain human interests as being directly politically relevant, reasonable people hold themselves to a standard of consistency, some animal interests are *no different* than at least some politically relevant human interests, and therefore reasonable people will accept those animal interests as directly justifying political entitlements for animals. Similarly, she argues that infants and the disabled ought to be protected by political rights and that these agents are no different in their rational capacities from nonhuman animals. This looks pretty compelling as the argument depends on two strong premises: reasonable people are consistent and animals have interests against, for example, suffering that are the same as humans.

Unfortunately, I do not think Roberts-Cady's argument succeeds without importing controversial and substantive ethical claims excluded by political liberalism. It is not obvious that rights against battery are justified by appeal to their role in preventing suffering. After all, rights to physical security can be easily justified as necessary for the ability to exercise the two moral powers, which can be understood as the political capabilities of citizens. In other words, one need not, on the force of being inconsistent, conclude from "rights against battery prevent suffering" that "all suffering generates a direct political right." We can still maintain that only suffering that can be translated into a properly political concern via the political conception of justice generates direct political rights.

---

[28] Or, at least, their concerns could be readily translated into public reasons. Rawls, *Political Liberalism*, 249–250.

It is true that we think (rightly!) that infants[29] deserve significant political protection. Yet if—as Rawls suggests we must do for a fair evaluation of one's distributive share—we evaluate citizens' position in society *over the course of their entire life*, then we can see that infant protections can be justified because they will develop into citizens with the two moral powers. In other words, we can view childhood as akin to something like a coma or being under general anesthesia: a temporary condition of incapacity to be eventually made good.[30] This has two significant advantages. First, this holistic analysis is not an ad hoc addition; we need to look at a person's entire life because one's income, wealth, and social position are not steady but vary over the course of a lifetime. Second, this allows us to retain the same set of political values that motivate political liberalism: the democratic understanding of the citizen as being free and equal in terms of the two moral powers. Roberts-Cady, on the other hand, will need to include *new* political values, those that are not based on the two moral powers, in order to undergird the new status of animals. And those values will have to be consistent with the addition of agents into the polity that are, even according to Roberts-Cady, neither free nor equal citizens. Roberts-Cady is arguing for a significant *revision* of reasonableness: it is now acceptable to offer reasons—and, importantly, to coerce other citizens—for direct political entitlements on the basis of values that are unrelated to the idea of a political conception of the citizen as a free and equal based upon the two moral powers. It seems that such a revision must be made on the basis that it would be unreasonable to reject it. I am skeptical that such consistency arguments can overcome the demand set by the burdens of judgment, but I cannot deny that Roberts-Cady has offered an intriguing new path forward for the animal rights challenge. Yet, as of now, it does not succeed.

The animal rights challenge to political liberalism cannot be that the political morality of a well-ordered society does not accurately capture all values that meaningfully affect our lives. After all, the point of political liberalism is that the

---

[29] I will discuss the severely disabled in a later section after I have described the resources for indirect protection of animals.

[30] The state also has an interest in the proper development of children as maintaining just institutions over time lies within its purview. However, this might give rise to a question about women's reproductive freedom. If protecting and developing people's two moral powers over the course of their entire lifetime is a legitimate state objective, does this require the prohibition of abortion or a more limited set of rights for infants? After all, a gestating fetus that has sufficiently developed has a similar capacity to develop the two moral powers as a newborn. I would argue, following Mary Ann Warren, "On the Moral and Legal Status of Abortion," *Monist* 57 (1973), 43–61, and *Roe v. Wade* (1973), that while the state does have a legitimate interest in protecting natal life at a certain level of development, there is a substantial difference between a gestating fetus and an infant. Namely, women have a substantial political interest in the bodily autonomy, personal liberty, and economic opportunity that abortion makes possible when they are pregnant. Once the fetus is born, those considerations no longer constrain the state and the interests of the infant are decisive. This might be inadequate as an account of the *ethics* of abortion, but it is acceptable as an account of reproductive justice.

comprehensive moral, ethical, and religious values that inhabit the background culture are not directly relevant when it comes to political justification. The animal rights challenge must be, in order to be understandable in the context of political liberalism (and not a complete rejection of it), that the fundamental values that ground the claim to direct duties of justice to animals are sufficiently self-evident that they can justifiably be coercively imposed upon individuals despite the burdens of judgment and the distance of those values from democratic culture. Rawlsians are not political liberals, if they are political liberals, for no reason. Rather, they think it illegitimate to coercively impose policies upon fellow citizens when they can only be justified by reference to controversial ethical and religious views that are, at worst, inaccessible to others and, at best, can be reasonably rejected. Thus, the animal rights challenge needs to be understood within the proper context: the Rawlsian need not argue that the underlying view about the moral status of animals is false, merely that it is grounded by an inappropriate set of values for the justification of exercises of state power.

Intuitionism and Indirect Justifications of Animal Protection

Yet, this can only be half of the story; I have shown that there are large costs to incorporating animals into the Rawlsian framework. However, we might still think that including direct concern for animal interests would be justified if it was necessary to capture true fixed points in our moral judgments. For example, if it was true that political liberalism or justice as fairness permitted routine, unnecessary, and egregious harm to nonhuman animals in a political context meaningfully close to our own, then that would be a serious problem. And if the only way to prevent that theoretical outcome would be to revise the broader set of values that were properly political such that they included a direct commitment to animal welfare, then perhaps the gains would outweigh the costs of distancing properly political values from the political conception of the citizen and democratic culture. The purpose of this section, then, is to show that the Rawlsian need not adopt this particular trade-off. Rather, the Rawlsian should argue that, while rejecting the animal rights challenge, the protection of animals can be justified indirectly. I will readily concede that relying upon indirect duties to animals could be problematic as an account of animal *ethics* or as a full theory of how we should relate to animals. However, the successful Rawlsian defense against the animal rights challenge does not need to be a full-fledged ethical theory of our relationship with animals or nature. Rather, the Rawlsian response need only be that indirect justifications are *good enough* to make the costs of revision too great in the context of theorizing about justice. This indirect strategy has three elements. First, reasons that are clearly acceptable within public reason can justify extensive entitlements for animals in many contexts. Second, there are good public policy reasons to refrain from trying to carefully gerrymander those entitlements to the specific reasons that apply in the specific case; that is, we have good public policy reasons to be overinclusive in animal entitlements. Third, there seem to be borderline or penumbral cases where animal interests should be sacrificed in a way that would be unacceptable for human beings. In these cases, the animal rights advocate will need to rely upon intuitionistic balancing that is opaque in its operation and not especially plausible.[31]

Some animal protections can be justified by appeal to reasons that are obviously acceptable to the political liberal. If the balance of public reasons is in favor of a policy, it is irrelevant whether that policy will make some conceptions of the good or comprehensive doctrines less attractive over the long run; neutrality in terms of *justification* is not neutrality in terms of *effects*. For example, Rawls argues that women must be protected by equitable divorce policies even if some traditional religious doctrines might be disadvantaged.[32] With that in mind, I want to suggest that there are at least four kinds of public reasons that justify animal protections even if they burden traditional practices or the interests of hunters. First, there are human-based environmental interests. Many of the most egregiously harmful practices for animal interests, such as factory farming, generate pollution. They also involve unsustainable environmental practices, including excessive greenhouse gas emissions, soil erosion, and groundwater consumption.[33] These environmentally degrading practices likely fall afoul of our political obligations to contemporary citizens and to future people. What's more, we would likely to want to sustain certain environmental areas such that human agents will be able, both now and in the future, to pursue conceptions of the good involving nature that they find valuable. Second, humans have interests—based on pet ownership and agents' direct relationship with animals—in the proper and sustainable treatment of animals. So policies ensuring that feral animals are well cared for as well as not unsustainably reproducing could likely be justified. What's more, insofar as better pet ownership and breeding standards make those relationships more sustainable and resilient, we have good reasons to pursue

---

[31] I take this worry about balancing to be a key feature of recent defenses of centering only human interests in political contexts. See Nicole Hassoun, "The Anthropocentric Advantage: Environmental Ethics and Climate Change Policy," *Critical Review of International Social and Political Philosophy* 14 (2011), 235–257.

[32] Rawls, *The Law of Peoples*, 162–163. For a more extensive argument that Rawls rejects policy neutrality, see Emily McGill, "Gender and Liberal Neutrality," *Social Philosophy Today* 33 (2017), 91–111.

[33] For example, extensive livestock husbandry and meat consumption contribute significantly to climate change, and factory farming generates large quantities of animal waste that pollute groundwater and even explode.

them because doing so enables the *general possibility* of pursuing relationships with animals. The idea is that if individuals are pursuing these conceptions of the good, political liberals have an interest in ensuring that they can do so in ways that avoid coordination problems or negative externalities that either contemporary or future people might suffer, assuming that doing so does not conflict with some other public considerations. Third, we might think that there are good educative, expressive, and psychological reasons to restrict or control the abuse of animals. That is, it is possible that observing the routine abuse of animals undermines the inculcation of virtues necessary for free and equal citizenship or contributes to psychological tendencies that we have good public reasons to want to see minimized.[34] Further, it might be the case that animal protections are importantly correlated with the more just treatment of humans. The idea is that making substantial commitments to protect individuals that are always in a vulnerable position encourages agents to remain vigilant in contexts where we deal with humans who are only occasionally vulnerable. Finally, there is evidence that at least some practices that are detrimental to animal interests are associated with inegalitarian political relations. So, in the process of repairing those inegalitarian relations in other spheres, the state will likely undermine those problematic practices. And if those practices impose involuntary restrictions on marginalized or oppressed classes, state action could be correspondingly more direct. For example, work on the sexual politics of meat purports to show—with some plausibility—strong connections between the oppression of women and minorities and the poor treatment of animals. Since the prevention of gender and racial oppression is a properly political value, this would make animal mistreatment relevant on the grounds of public reason.[35]

So there are good public reasons for creating a regime where animals are granted significant protections in a relatively wide range of contexts. Yet we might worry that there will be "gaps" in those protections. One potential response to this worry is that animal entitlements should be "amplified" or made more robust in order to ensure the *efficacy* of those protections in light of foreseeable limitations in implementation and enforcement. Since animals themselves cannot play a role in their own protection and will need to rely on the actions of regulators who are held accountable by other human agents, protections should err on the side of caution and offer animals greater protection. This argument

---

[34] This is, for example, Kant's argument. See note 6.

[35] The locus classicus of arguments connecting these injustices is Carol Adams, *The Sexual Politics of Meat: A Feminist-Vegetarian Critical Theory* (Bloomsbury Academic, 1990). One need not agree with Adams's full theoretical views to take seriously the idea that poor treatment of animals correlates—for a variety of reasons—with inegalitarian gender and racial attitudes. Since gender and racial equality are properly political values, this is one reason for a Rawlsian to be concerned with the treatment of animals.

is, however, bootstrapped from the prior human interests that require a particular set of animal protections. These protections, typically legal and political entitlements, are merely tools for furthering the relevant public reasons. Broad, overinclusive regulations are more likely be effective than narrow regulations that depend upon the judgments of specific regulators. In particular, certain features of animals and human cognition concerning animals make it likely that a narrow legal regime will be biased toward granting insufficient protection, administrative instability, and regulatory capture. If this is true, then we would have public reasons to ensure that citizens had their interests protected indirectly by providing more robust, direct protection of animal interests. Facts about animal vulnerability can play a role, albeit indirectly, in a politically liberal account of animal protections.

Finally, most of us believe that animal interests are not as weighty as humans' even if we grant that they should have some weight. We might think of tribal hunting practices, medical research, or humane livestock harvesting. Yet animal rights challengers tend to be too complacent about the difficulties weighing animal interests against humans presents to their view. Roberts-Cady and others are faced with a dilemma: accept an absolutist understanding of animal rights and be subjected to serious counterexamples that—given the Rawlsian indirect protections previously described—are worse than those facing Rawls or develop a weighing principle where human interests are more important than animal interests. But such a principle, especially one that can be usefully action-guiding, has not been forthcoming—it is often not even attempted—and it is an advantage of Rawls's view that we can have animal protections with a single set of underlying values that avoid the trade-off problem.

While I have already discussed children, it is worth pausing to discuss whether my view generates adequate protections for the severely disabled. Three points are important. First, the moral powers are flexible and minimal; the cognitive capacities to develop a view of the good life and to follow what you take to be fair principles of cooperation are not very demanding.[36] So, only very severe cognitive disabilities—and essentially no physical disabilities—would exclude a human being from direct political consideration. Second, many people become disabled over the course of their lives and so spend much of their life as citizens with rights over their body. We ought to respect those claims even if they are no longer in a position to press them. So disabled humans often have an additional reason for protection that animals lack based upon their past rights to their body. Finally, the indirect reasons, as described previously, we have to protect

---

[36] This is one reason that I find it plausible that at least some higher-order nonhuman animals could be said to have the two moral powers. In these cases, Rawlsians should straightforwardly accept that such animals are rights-bearers.

animals in order to ensure our virtuous development apply even more strongly to disabled humans. Thus, we have good reasons, both direct and indirect, for protecting the interests of severely disabled humans that are stronger than our reasons for protecting animals. So the standard Rawlsian view can accommodate the idea that we have good reasons to protect the disabled and that those reasons are stronger than we have to protect the interests of most nonhuman animals. This is no guarantee that some clear counterexample will not be forthcoming or that other theoretical benefits have been overlooked, but the "centrality" argument for the direct relevance of sentience is not yet persuasive.

Conclusion

It is a testament to the power of the animal rights challenge that the Rawlsian response is both complicated and provisional. Here is where we are: the animal rights challenge is that animal interests ought to be "central" to any theory of justice and that indirect responses to counterexamples—even if successful—are inadequate because they offer the wrong kind of reason for protecting animals. However, this challenge amounts to the claim that it is a *theoretical desideratum* to make animal interests central. If so, then any claim that a theory should include that desideratum should be evaluated holistically, which must include a full accounting of its theoretical costs and benefits. Making animal interests central to the Rawlsian account, either in terms of justice as fairness or political liberalism, would involve abandoning core commitments that are independently plausible. So the theoretical costs of the revision are high. Those costs might be worth paying if Rawlsian political philosophy had no way of justifying political and legal entitlements for animal interests. Yet this is not true. First, there are many political liberal reasons that *indirectly* justify significant protections for animal interests. Second, there are good public reasons for adopting a precautionary approach on animal interests even when the public reasons run out. That is, we have reasons—which, again, are indirect—to adopt wider and more robust protections of animal interests given that there are likely to be biases in how the indirectly justified protections will be administered. Finally, most plausible understandings of animal ethics allow for balancing of human interests of less comparative importance—religious observation, nonfatal health, cultural practice—against more basic animal interests. If one adopts a pro tanto balancing view where animal interests are direct and "central" to the view, then one must sacrifice publicity. Given that the Rawlsian view can capture important considered judgments about particular cases, it does not seem like the theoretical benefits of making animal interests central to our political theorizing are worth the costs.

However, it is important to see the limitations of this result. First, this argument relies on a fairly strong distinction between the kinds of reasons and arguments that are appropriate for first-order normative theorizing and those that are appropriately deployed via public reason. Nothing I have said here should be understood as an attempt to show that animals do not have moral rights or that we should not, as a moral matter, grant them fundamental status in our moral theorizing. Rather, it is an argument that—within the context of political theorizing—an appropriate deference to the public nature of political judgments restricts the kind of dialectical moves available to the animal rights advocate. Yet, it is entirely possible that a direct counterexample to the Rawlsian view is available. However, in order for that objection to succeed, it would need to meet certain requirements. First, it would need to be a case where an animal was maltreated in ways that a wide set of considered judgments by reasonable persons would view as obviously unacceptable. Second, it would need to be the case where a careful consideration of the full gamut of public reasons a Rawlsian could deploy to justify an animal protection regime would fail to protect the animal in a well-ordered society. And finally, it would have to be the case that revising the view to incorporate cases of this kind would not lead to new principles that would justify other, more serious injustices or suffer from serious theoretical problems. This is a tall order but not necessarily an insurmountable one. The purpose of this chapter, then, is not to show that the animal rights challenge cannot succeed. Rather, it is to argue that *current* understandings of the animal rights challenge do not take the Rawlsian view, or the issues of theory selection and justification, sufficiently seriously in order for them to succeed. But in the name of wide reflective equilibrium, I welcome attempts to make good on that lack and offer truly strong challenges to the Rawlsian view.

PART IX
INTERNATIONAL ECONOMIC JUSTICE

Introduction

In 2015, an estimated 736 million people (about 10 percent of the world's population) lived below the level that the World Bank identifies as "extreme poverty," with many more living precariously just above it.[1] This extreme poverty was partially responsible for 815 million people being undernourished in 2016,[2] and the life expectancy in low-income countries remaining at sixty-three years compared to eighty years in high-income countries.[3] This severe deprivation exists in conjunction with a stunning inequality in global wealth: "While the bottom half of adults collectively owns less than 1% of total wealth, the richest decile (top 10% of adults) owns 85% of global wealth, and the top percentile alone accounts for almost half of all household wealth (47%)."[4] The economist Branko Milanovic observes that in 2013, globally there were 1,426 billionaires. This group—"one-hundredth of one-hundredth of the global 1%"—collectively had total assets estimated at $5.4 trillion, or "twice as much wealth as exists in all of Africa."[5] If this combination of absolute deprivation and inequality existed within a single country, most theories of justice would hold that it would constitute a very serious injustice. But how, if at all, should a theory of justice address global poverty and inequality? In particular, should the same principles of distributive justice developed for a society also be used to evaluate the global distribution of wealth?

In *A Theory of Justice*, Rawls did not address questions of global distributive justice. In developing his theory of domestic justice, he makes a number of simplifying assumptions that he believes will help him to identify and defend his principles of justice. One assumption is that the basic structure, to which the

---

[1] *Poverty and Shared Prosperity 2018: Piecing Together the Poverty Puzzle* (International Bank for Reconstruction and Development / The World Bank, 2018), 19, https://openknowledge.worldbank.org/bitstream/handle/10986/30418/9781464813306.pdf (accessed April 7, 2019). This represents a significant decrease since 1990. However, the progress has been very uneven, with a massive reduction of extreme poverty occurring in China, while the rate in sub-Saharan African remains over 40 percent (14). Further, "The pace of poverty reduction has slowed in recent years" (15).

[2] "United Nations Sustainable Development Goals Report 2018," https://unstats.un.org/sdgs/files/report/2018/TheSustainableDevelopmentGoalsReport2018-EN.pdf (accessed October 14, 2019), 4.

[3] https://data.worldbank.org/indicator/SP.DYN.LE00.IN (accessed April 7, 2019).

[4] Anthony Shorrocks, James Davies, and Rodrigo Lluberas, Global Wealth Report 2018, https://www.credit-suisse.com/corporate/en/research/research-institute/global-wealth-report.html (accessed April 7, 2019), 9.

[5] Branko Milanovic, *Global Inequality: A New Approach for the Age of Globalization* (Harvard University Press, 2016), 41–42.

Introduction In: *John Rawls*. Edited by: Jon Mandle and Sarah Roberts-Cady, Oxford University Press (2020). © Oxford University Press. DOI: 10.1093/oso/9780190859213.003.0026.

principles are to be applied, is conceived of as "a closed system isolated from other societies."[6] His "conjecture" is that "once we have a sound theory for this case, the remaining problems of justice will prove more tractable in the light of it."[7] Since no actual society is closed in this way, one of the "remaining problems" concerns distributive justice among societies, or global distributive justice. It took more than two decades before Rawls addressed this issue directly in his 1993 article "The Law of Peoples."[8] But before he did so, a number of other authors developed a cosmopolitan extension of his principles.

In a 1973 article, T. M. Scanlon followed Rawls in applying the principles of justice to social institutions, rather than directly to individual actions. He noted, therefore, that "it may make a great deal of difference on Rawls' theory where the boundary of society is drawn."[9] And he argued: "The only satisfactory solution to this problem seems to me to be to hold that considerations of justice apply at least wherever there is systematic economic interaction. . . . Thus the Difference Principle would apply to the world economic system taken as a whole as well as . . . to particular societies within it."[10] This direct extension of Rawls's principles of domestic justice to the "world economic system" was the template for many forms of cosmopolitanism in the decades to come. But while suggestive, Scanlon's argument for this extension was underdeveloped.[11]

Scanlon's student Charles Beitz elaborated the argument, first in his 1975 article, "Justice and International Relations,"[12] and then in his book *Political Theory and International Relations*.[13] Beitz thought it obvious that citizens of relatively affluent countries have humanitarian obligations to those in need throughout the world. But, he argued, "Obligations of justice might be thought to be more demanding than this, to require greater sacrifices on the part of the relatively well-off, and perhaps sacrifices of a different kind as well. Obligations of justice, unlike those of humanitarian aid, might also require efforts at large-scale institutional reform."[14] Beitz developed two arguments in support of the conclusion that obligations of egalitarian distributive justice do, in fact, apply at the global

---

[6] John Rawls, *A Theory of Justice*, rev. ed. (Harvard University Press, 1999), 7.

[7] Rawls, *A Theory of Justice*, 7.

[8] Rawls did not take up the issue of distributive justice when he briefly mentioned the "law of nations" in section 58 of *A Theory of Justice*.

[9] T. M. Scanlon, "Rawls' Theory of Justice," in *Reading Rawls*, ed. Norman Daniels (Basic Books, 1975), 202.

[10] Scanlon, "Rawls' Theory of Justice," 202.

[11] See also Brian Barry, *The Liberal Theory of Justice* (Oxford University Press, 1973), 128–133; and Peter Danielson, "Theories, Institutions and the Problem of World-Wide Distributive Justice," *Philosophy of the Social Sciences* 3 (1973), 331–340.

[12] Charles Beitz, "Justice and International Relations," *Philosophy and Public Affairs* 4 (1975), 360–389.

[13] Charles Beitz, *Political Theory and International Relations* (Princeton University Press, 1979; reprinted with a new afterword, 1999).

[14] Beitz, "Justice and International Relations," 360.

level. First, following Scanlon, he pointed to the "world economic system"[15] that "produce[s] benefits for some while imposing burdens on others."[16] Since Rawls holds that justice is concerned with the fair distribution of institutional benefits and burdens, it ought to apply here as well as to domestic institutions. But Beitz introduced an additional argument. Observing that "natural resources are distributed unevenly over the earth's surface," he argued that societies established on resource-rich areas "can be expected to exploit their natural riches and to prosper," while societies in resource-poor areas "despite the best efforts of their members . . . may attain only a meager level of well-being due to resource scarcities."[17] Since the distribution of natural resources is an even "purer case of something's being 'arbitrary from a moral point of view' than the distribution of talents,"[18] he held that this makes it a concern of justice, as well. This argument does not depend on there being a shared global institutional structure. Considerations of distributive justice, he argued, do not apply only "to those with whom we share membership in a cooperative scheme."[19] Therefore, Beitz concludes: "Assuming that the arguments for the two principles are successful as set out in Rawls' book, there is no reason to think that the content of the principles would change as a result of enlarging the scope of the original position so that the principles would apply to the world as a whole."[20]

In his initial 1993 article,[21] and then in *The Law of Peoples* (1999),[22] Rawls rejects this cosmopolitan extension of his domestic principles: "There is no reason to think that the principles that apply to domestic justice are also appropriate for regulating inequalities in a society of peoples."[23] While in the domestic case, Rawls argues for limiting structural inequalities to those that benefit the least advantaged, in the global case he rejects any such egalitarian distributive principle. Instead, he holds that well-ordered and wealthier societies have a "duty of assistance" to help all societies secure human rights and basic human needs in order to become "a full and self-standing member of the society of peoples, . . . capable of taking charge of their political life and maintaining decent political and social institutions."[24] In the ideal, once all societies are well ordered, justice does not require the further elimination of inequalities in wealth. Unlike the domestic case, in which the difference principle would continue to apply even in the ideal, the

---

[15] Beitz, "Justice and International Relations," 360.
[16] Beitz, "Justice and International Relations," 360, 374.
[17] Beitz, "Justice and International Relations," 376.
[18] Beitz, "Justice and International Relations," 369.
[19] Beitz, "Justice and International Relations," 370.
[20] Beitz, "Justice and International Relations," 376.
[21] John Rawls, "The Law of Peoples," in *Collected Papers*, ed. Samuel Freeman (Harvard University Press, 1999).
[22] John Rawls, *The Law of Peoples* (Harvard University Press, 1999).
[23] Rawls, "The Law of Peoples," 558.
[24] Rawls, "The Law of Peoples," 558–559. Compare Rawls, *The Law of Peoples*, 111.

duty of assistance applies only in the nonideal case. Rawls holds that a "burdened society," suffering severe economic deprivation, cannot be well ordered because (among other reasons) it is unable to secure human rights.[25] Still, he emphasizes that "great wealth is not necessary to establish just (or decent) institutions,"[26] and he "conjecture[s] there is no society anywhere in the world—except for marginal cases—with resources so scarce that it could not, were it reasonably and rationally organized and governed, become well-ordered."[27] From the point of view of global justice, once societies become well ordered, "The arbitrariness of the distribution of natural resources causes no difficulty."[28] Because the duty of assistance has a cut-off point beyond which it need no longer be invoked, it is, strictly speaking, not a principle of *distributive* justice.[29]

Unfortunately, beyond two controversial but perhaps suggestive examples, Rawls's rejection of an egalitarian principle of global distributive justice is underexplained. The examples involve imagining two well-ordered societies at the same level of wealth with the same size population. While one "decides to industrialize and to increase its rate of (real) savings," the second prefers and chooses "a more pastoral and leisurely society." Over time, this results in a large inequality in wealth between the two. Since both societies are well ordered "and their peoples free and responsible, and able to make their own decisions" it "seems unacceptable" to tax the wealthier society for the benefit of the poorer.[30] The second example parallels the first, except that instead of a decision to industrialize and save, it chooses a population policy (stressing equal rights for women) that results in greater aggregate wealth.

What Rawls fails adequately to explain is which features are present in the domestic case and underwrite egalitarian principles of distributive justice but are absent (he believes) in the global case. The grounds for egalitarian principles, and whether these grounds are actually absent in the global case, have become central points of contention in the contemporary debate, and a variety of answers have been defended.

Since Rawls holds that his egalitarian principles of domestic justice apply to the basic structure of society, some theorists have defended a cosmopolitan extension of the principles by arguing that there is a "global basic structure."[31] Allen

[25] Rawls, *The Law of Peoples*, 65.

[26] Rawls, *The Law of Peoples*, 107.

[27] Rawls, *The Law of Peoples*, 108. In a footnote to "marginal cases" he comments: "Arctic Eskimos, for example, are rare enough, and need not affect our general approach. I assume their problems could be handled in an ad hoc way" (*The Law of Peoples*, 108 n. 34).

[28] Rawls, *The Law of Peoples*, 117.

[29] Rawls, *The Law of Peoples*, 106.

[30] Rawls, *The Law of Peoples*, 117.

[31] See the discussion in Andreas Follesdal, "The Distributive Justice of a Global Basic Structure: A Category Mistake?," *Politics, Philosophy and Economics* (2011), 46–65; and Miriam Ronzoni, "Two Concepts of the Basic Structure, and Their Relevance to Global Justice," *Global Justice* 1 (2008), 68–85.

Buchanan argues, for example, that "there is a global basic structure. Its existence and major features are documented in a vast and growing interdisciplinary literature that goes under various headings: globalization, structural dependency, and theory of underdevelopment."[32] He then cites various international institutions and agreements and argues that they have "profound enduring effects on the distribution of burdens and benefits among peoples and individuals around the world." Therefore, "Principles of justice for it will be required, just as principles of justice are required for domestic basic structures."[33]

In contrast, Samuel Freeman argues that "nothing comparable to the basic structure of society exists on the global level."[34] Freeman points out that there are global institutions, of course, and that Rawls refers to "the basic structure of the Society of Peoples," but, he argues, "These global institutions are very different—qualitatively different—from the basic structure of a society that makes social cooperation possible."[35] Specifically, "The Society of Peoples is not a political society, and thus has no original political jurisdiction or effective basic political power. . . . The effective political power and jurisdiction that global institutions exercise are possessed by these institutions only to the degree that they have been granted such power and jurisdiction by independent peoples."[36] Granting that global institutions have profound effects on many lives, it does not follow that the same principles apply globally as domestically. Freeman points out that as part of Rawls's "political constructivism," he holds that "the principles that appropriately regulate social and political relations depend on the kinds of institutions or practices to be regulated."[37]

In an influential 2001 article, Michael Blake makes a version of this argument.[38] Blake emphasizes the coercive nature of legal systems (both criminal and private law) and asks what is required for such coercion, which involves a denial of autonomy, to be justifiable. He answers that a necessary, although not sufficient, condition for such justification is a commitment to egalitarian distributive principles: "A liberal theory that begins with a concern for autonomy may properly develop a concern for relative deprivation as a way of justifying state coercion."[39] In contrast, "No matter how substantive the links of trade, diplomacy, or international agreement, the institutions present at the international

---

[32] Allen Buchanan, "Rawls's Law of Peoples: Rules for a Vanished Westphalian World," *Ethics* 110 (2000), 705.

[33] Buchanan, "Rawls's Law of Peoples," 705–706.

[34] Samuel Freeman, *Justice and the Social Contract* (Oxford University Press, 2007), 268.

[35] Freeman, *Justice*, 268.

[36] Freeman, *Justice*, 269.

[37] Freeman, *Justice*, 270.

[38] Michael Blake, "Distributive Justice, State Coercion, and Autonomy," *Philosophy and Public Affairs* 30 (2001), 257–296. See also his *Justice and Foreign Policy* (Oxford University Press, 2013).

[39] Blake, "Distributive Justice," 283.

level do not engage in the same sort of coercive practices against individual moral agents [that the state exercises domestically]."[40] Although coercion exists internationally, "Only the relationship of common citizenship is a relationship potentially justifiable through a concern for equality in distributive shares."[41] Therefore, a theory of justice grounded in autonomy requires the application of egalitarian principles to domestic political social orders, while internationally it only requires a concern with absolute deprivation.[42]

Most cosmopolitans, in contrast, hold that there are egalitarian demands of justice even in the absence of shared coercive *political* institutions. Darrel Moellendorf, for example, concedes that "duties of egalitarian distributive justice do not exist between persons merely in virtue of their personhood. Such duties are special moral duties."[43] What is required is that they participate in a shared institution that affects their "highest order moral interests"[44] or has a "substantial impact" on their interests.[45] Since, he argues, the global economic order has profound effects on the lives of almost all individuals, egalitarian principles of justice apply even in the absence of globally coercive legal structures. Shared *political* institutions are not required to ground egalitarian principles. Others have argued in a similar vein that coercion is not necessary to underwrite egalitarian principles.[46]

But some cosmopolitans defend egalitarian principles regardless of any particular shared global institutions or relationships. Simon Caney defends the claim that "the very logic that underpins most domestic theories of justice actually implies that these theories of justice should be enacted at the global, and not (or not simply) the domestic, level."[47] This implication holds regardless of shared (global) institutions or relationships since "it is hard to see why economic interaction has any moral relevance from the point of view of distributive justice."[48] In fact, "Institutional schemes do not track any properties that would generate entitlements and as such they treat people unfairly, denying some their entitlements."[49]

Finally, we can note that Beitz's original contrast between humanitarian obligations and duties of justice seems to parallel a common distinction between

40 Blake, "Distributive Justice," 265.
41 Blake, "Distributive Justice," 265.
42 Blake, "Distributive Justice," 294.
43 Darrel Moellendorf, "Equal Respect and Global Egalitarianism," *Social Theory and Practice* 32 (2006), 608.
44 Moellendorf, "Equal Respect," 611.
45 Darrel Moellendorf, *Cosmopolitan Justice* (Westview Press, 2002), 37.
46 Andrea Sangiovanni, "The Irrelevance of Coercion, Imposition, and Framing to Distributive Justice," *Philosophy and Public Affairs* 40 (2012), 79–110.
47 Simon Caney, *Justice beyond Borders* (Oxford University Press, 2005), 107.
48 Caney, *Justice beyond Borders*, 111.
49 Caney, *Justice beyond Borders*, 111.

positive and negative duties. If, as is commonly assumed, positive duties are less demanding or strict than their corresponding negative duties, we can understand why Beitz would suggest that a humanitarian duty seems to be less demanding than a duty of justice. And this, in turn, would explain some of the urgency in determining whether principles of distributive justice are global in scope. Thomas Pogge, in some of his earlier work, defends a cosmopolitan approach to this question.[50] But elsewhere, he attempts to bypass this debate. In his influential book *World Poverty and Human Rights* he "deliberately set aside [his] commitments to positive duties and to global egalitarianism . . . and rests [his] case entirely on negative duties: duties not to harm."[51] Summarizing the structure of the argument, he writes:

> If the global economic order plays a major role in the persistence of severe poverty worldwide and if our governments, acting in our name, are prominently involved in shaping and upholding this order, then the deprivation of the distant needy may well engage not merely positive duties to assist but also more stringent negative duties not to harm.[52]

He then argues that aspects of the global order are, in fact, partially responsible for severe deprivation and other human rights violations, and therefore wealthy societies and their citizens are violating their *negative* duties not to impose such deprivations on others.[53] Crucially, on Pogge's account, these international causes of severe deprivation do not compete with other domestic explanations. Rather, the international mechanisms typically work through domestic causes, for example, by providing support and comfort to illegitimate local tyrants.[54] To make his case, Pogge need not establish that international forces are the only, or even the primary, cause of these deprivations. If he can establish that they contribute significantly, then even without engaging egalitarian distributive principles, we can say that strong demands of justice are at stake since there is an ongoing violation of our negative duties not to

[50] Thomas Pogge, *Realizing Rawls* (Cornell University Press, 1989) and "An Egalitarian Law of Peoples," *Philosophy and Public Affairs* 23 (1994), 195–224.

[51] Thomas Pogge, "Responses to the Critics," in *Thomas Pogge and His Critics*, ed. Alison Jagger (Polity Press, 2010), 195. He continues: "However, by forswearing appeal to certain premises, [*World Poverty and Human Rights*] is not thereby denying these premises." Compare Thomas Pogge, *World Poverty and Human Rights*, 2nd ed. (Polity Press, 2008), 13.

[52] Thomas Pogge, "'Assisting' the Global Poor," in *The Ethics of Assistance*, ed. Deen Chatterjee (Cambridge University Press, 2004), 265.

[53] See, for example, his discussion of the "international resource privilege" and the "international borrowing privilege" in *World Poverty*, 22–23, 113–115. See also Mathias Risse, "How Does the Global Order Harm the Poor?," *Philosophy and Public Affairs* 33 (2005), 349–376; and Thomas Pogge, "Severe Poverty as a Violation of Negative Duties," *Ethics and International Affairs* 19 (2005), 55–83.

[54] Pogge, *World Poverty*, 21–22.

harm (unnecessarily). If this is right, then it is misleading to describe the duty of wealthy societies toward those in severe poverty as a matter of "assistance." Rather, the morally urgent task is to *stop harming*. Virtually all philosophers who have been influenced by Rawls's work—and, indeed, many who endorse rival perspectives[55]—agree that the current extent of severe poverty globally is a moral catastrophe. The disagreements are not over whether wealthy individuals and societies generally should do more to address this urgent issue. Rather, the issues concern how these requirements should be conceptualized and understood. One fundamental issue concerns whether the moral failure is a matter of justice or humanitarian principles (or both). If principles of justice are being violated, a second question is whether the same (or similar) egalitarian principles apply both domestically and globally, or whether a less-demanding threshold conception applies globally. The resolution of this question forces us to confront directly the grounds for egalitarian obligations of distributive justice. Rawls himself was surprisingly unclear about this, and it has become a focus of vigorous philosophical debate. For some cosmopolitans, we are entitled to an egalitarian distribution of goods simply in virtue of our humanity. More common answers are that such principles hold only when: our prospects are significantly affected by shared institutions, or a shared basic structure; or are affected by shared institutions of certain types, such as political; or when we are subjected to coercive institutions. The appropriate principles of global justice will depend on how this question is answered, together with the kind of relationship that holds among individuals or societies globally. In 1971, Rawls initiated an abundance of scholarly interest in principles of domestic justice. Although perhaps fewer philosophers endorse his approach to global justice, his work remains at the center of fundamental debates concerning global justice as well. In this volume, Rekha Nath surveys some of the literature regarding Rawls's approach to global economic justice and finds that the three most common defenses of Rawls are unsuccessful. Unless and until defenders of Rawls can adequately explain why egalitarian principles of distributive justice should be restricted to the domestic domain, the cosmopolitan extension will remain powerful. In contrast, Gillian Brock, in her chapter, finds that Rawls's "often maligned views about the duties of assistance actually offer a much more tolerant, open-minded set of ideas than critics have appreciated." In particular, his focus on self-government helps us "to appreciate when global inequalities are problematic and when they are not."

---

[55] See, for example, Peter Singer, who, writing from a utilitarian perspective, called attention to the issue in 1972, in "Famine, Affluence, and Morality," *Philosophy and Public Affairs* 1 (1972), 229–243.

Suggested Reading from Rawls to Accompany These Chapters

A Theory of Justice: §§1–4, 11
The Law of Peoples: §§4, 15, 16

For Further Reading

Beitz, Charles. *Political Theory and International Relations* (Princeton University Press, 1979; reprinted with new afterword, 1999). Beitz's book is an early and influential cosmopolitan extension of Rawls's theory of justice.

Blake, Michael. "Distributive Justice, State Coercion, and Autonomy." *Philosophy and Public Affairs* 30 (2001), 257–296. Blake's article is an influential defense of the use of different standards of distributive justice in different domains (domestic and international).

Brock, Gillian. "Recent Work on Rawls's Law of Peoples: Critics versus Defenders." *American Philosophical Quarterly* 47 (2010), 85–101. In this article, Brock surveys the secondary literature in response to *The Law of Peoples*.

Buchanan, Allan. "Rawls's *Law of Peoples*: Rules for a Vanished Westphalian World." *Ethics* 110 (2000), 697–721. Buchanan critiques *The Law of Peoples* by arguing that it neglects the fact of globalization and the extent of international institutions and practices.

Cohen, Joshua, and Charles Sabel. "Extra Rempublicam Nulla Justitia?" *Philosophy and Public Affairs* 34 (2006), 147–175. This article aims to refute Nagel's argument (in "The Problem of Global Justice") that principles of global justice do not apply in the absence of a global state, but it also holds that the global order requires principles of evaluation distinct from those appropriate for a domestic state.

Freeman, Samuel. "The Law of Peoples, Social Cooperation, Human Rights, and Distributive Justice." In *Justice and the Social Contract* (Oxford University Press, 2007). Freeman argues that while social cooperation among liberal and decent societies is possible, the principles of distributive justice appropriate domestically (including the difference principle) are inappropriate globally in the absence of a globally shared political structure.

Moellendorf, Darrel. *Cosmopolitan Justice* (Westview Press, 2002). This book develops a clear and powerful cosmopolitan extension of justice as fairness.

Nagel, Thomas. "The Problem of Global Justice." *Philosophy and Public Affairs*, 33 (2005), 113–147. This article presents an influential argument that while there may be global humanitarian duties, in the absence of a global political order, principles of justice do not apply globally.

Pogge, Thomas. "An Egalitarian Law of Peoples." *Philosophy and Public Affairs* 23 (1994), 195–224. This is an early and influential cosmopolitan extension of Rawls's principles of domestic justice.

Pogge, Thomas. *World Poverty and Human Rights* (Polity Press, 2002; 2nd ed., 2008). Pogge argues not only that severe poverty is a human rights violation, but also that wealthy countries are actively violating negative duties by enforcing a global order that predictably and avoidably leads to severe poverty.

Sangiovanni, Andrea. "Global Justice, Reciprocity, and the State." *Philosophy and Public Affairs* 35 (2007), 3–39. This article grounds egalitarian principles of distributive justice in an understanding of reciprocity (making a positive contribution to certain collective goods) that holds domestically but not globally.

17

Rawls on Global Economic Justice

A Critical Examination

Rekha Nath

1. Introduction

Compared to the domestic account of justice that Rawls defends in *A Theory of Justice*, in *The Law of Peoples* the demands of justice that he takes to arise beyond state borders are very modest.[1] On his international theory, states are mostly free to leave one another alone. Only in certain specific cases does Rawls think that justice might call for a departure from this default position of noninterference between states. These are cases that involve international aggression, serious human rights violations, and states that cannot achieve minimally just governments without external assistance.[2] In addition, Rawls suggests that states may incur obligations to one another by voluntarily joining international organizations or by forming international agreements.[3]

In this chapter, I will focus on one specific part of Rawls's international theory that many of his cosmopolitan critics have taken issue with: his claim that demands of egalitarian distributive justice do not arise beyond the state. Indeed, as we shall see, Rawls does not think that cross-border inequalities as such or the material well-being of badly off individuals worldwide are matters that warrant any direct concern from the standpoint of justice. Are there good reasons for Rawls's rejection of egalitarian demands of justice arising globally? We will consider several defenses of this position. Although, at first glance, some of these defenses might seem compelling, I will argue that upon more careful examination they do not succeed. The chapter proceeds as follows. In section 2, I set out an overview of Rawls's account of the distributive demands that arise between states. In sections 3–5, I discuss different arguments that have been advanced in defense of Rawls's claim that demands of egalitarian distributive justice do not

---

[1] John Rawls, *A Theory of Justice*, rev. ed. (Harvard University Press, 1999) and John Rawls, *The Law of Peoples* (Harvard University Press, 1999).
[2] Rawls, *The Law of Peoples*, 36–38, 41.
[3] Rawls, *The Law of Peoples*, 42–43, 115.

Rekha Nath, *Rawls on Global Economic Justice* In: *John Rawls*. Edited by: Jon Mandle and Sarah Roberts-Cady, Oxford University Press (2020). © Oxford University Press. DOI: 10.1093/oso/9780190859213.003.0027.

arise at the global level as well as replies to those arguments made by his cosmopolitan critics.

2. The Duty of Assistance

Let us turn to what Rawls says about distributive demands that arise in the global
domain. Of the eight principles of justice regulating the terms of cross-society
interaction that he defends, only one has clear implications for distributive
obligations arising between states. The relevant principle states that "Peoples
have a duty to assist other peoples living under unfavorable conditions that prevent their having a just or decent political and social regime."[4] Rawls refers to the
recipients of this duty of assistance as *burdened societies*—societies that, owing
to unfavorable conditions, are unable to become well ordered on their own. And
those charged with carrying out this duty are all well-ordered peoples in the
world. While the primary aim of this duty is to help burdened societies establish
self-sustaining, just domestic institutions, the establishment of such institutions
is important for a different reason besides that of securing justice internally for
the sake of a society's own populace: doing so is a necessary condition for a state
to become a part of the international society of peoples, whose members engage
with one another on reasonable, cooperative terms. As Rawls puts it, "The crucial
point is that the role of the duty of assistance is to assist burdened societies to become full members of the Society of Peoples and to be able to determine the path
of their own future for themselves."[5]

Practically speaking, what does the fulfillment of this duty require? As Rawls
sees it, there are different factors that stand in the way of burdened societies becoming well ordered. He explains that such societies "lack the political and cultural traditions, the human capital and know-how, and, often the material and
technological resources needed to be well-ordered."[6] Consequently, he thinks
that fulfilling the duty of assistance will call for different approaches in different
cases.[7] Rawls does note that a society's culture and its population policy are
often crucial factors that stand in need of change.[8] He further emphasizes that
changing these things does not tend to be an easy matter: there's no quick fix to
helping burdened societies, and although material assistance will usually (but

---

[4] Rawls, *The Law of Peoples*, 37.
[5] Rawls, *The Law of Peoples*, 118, cf. 111.
[6] Rawls, *The Law of Peoples*, 106.
[7] For further discussion of this issue, see Gillian Brock, "Rawls's Reasoning about International
Economic Justice: A Defense," in this volume, chapter 18.
[8] Rawls, *The Law of Peoples*, 108, 117.

not always) be in order, it certainly will not suffice to achieve the stated goal of the duty.[9]

It will be helpful to offer a few clarifications about this duty—in particular, clarifications that aim to provide a clearer sense of that which the duty of assistance does *not* require. To begin with, this duty arises only in cases of burdened societies, who, by definition, suffer from institutional deficits; it does not, more broadly, call for assistance to societies that are very poor but that still manage to maintain liberal or decent institutions.[10] Thus, Rawls maintains that in a world in which all societies had liberal or decent institutions, there would be no need for any cross-society distributive transfers, even if some of those societies were very rich and others very poor. He emphasizes that the object of the duty of assistance is not to address economic inequalities between states, nor is its object to improve the lives of individuals who are very badly off in burdened societies, at least not directly.[11]

Some commentators on Rawls's international theory refer to the duty of assistance as a *humanitarian* duty.[12] As we will see subsequently, there is a sense in which this label proves helpful to our understanding of the nature of this duty. But there are two other ways in which applying this label to the duty of assistance could be misleading. First, doing so might give the mistaken impression that the duty of assistance is fundamentally grounded in a direct humanitarian concern for the deprivation of basic needs suffered by poor individuals globally. It is not. For one thing, the duty does not directly aim to make poor persons in burdened societies better off. In emphasizing the "cutoff point" of this duty, Rawls is unequivocal about this: he takes the duty to be satisfied once formerly burdened societies have established decent or liberal institutions that they can sustain on their own.[13] It is true that fulfillment of this duty might help poor citizens in burdened societies.[14] But it will only do so indirectly, by helping recipient societies establish domestic institutions that would, in turn, enable them to address the suffering of their own needy populations.[15] What is more, Rawls does not think that any material assistance is owed to poor individuals who belong to societies that neither are well ordered nor stand to become well ordered through assistance provided by other societies.[16]

---

[9] Rawls, *The Law of Peoples*, 108, 110.

[10] Rawls, *The Law of Peoples*, 106.

[11] Rawls, *The Law of Peoples*, 106, 114, 118–120.

[12] See, e.g., Kok-Chor Tan, *Justice without Borders* (Cambridge University Press, 2004), 21–29, 65–70; Samuel Freeman, "Distributive Justice and *The Law of Peoples*," in *Rawls's Law of Peoples: A Realistic Utopia?*, ed. Rex Martin and David Reidy (Blackwell, 2006), 245.

[13] Rawls, *The Law of Peoples*, 111, 118–120.

[14] Rawls himself suggests that the goal of "meeting basic needs," which he takes to be important, would be "covered by the duty of assistance" (*The Law of Peoples*, 116).

[15] Thomas Pogge, "Do Rawls's Two Theories of Justice Fit Together?," in Martin and Reidy, *Rawls's Law of Peoples*, 211–212.

[16] Pogge, "Rawls's Two Theories," 212.

Second, compared to duties of justice, humanitarian duties are sometimes thought to place less stringent demands on agents. On this view, demands of humanitarianism are seen as akin to charity: while their fulfillment would be morally commendable, a failure to fulfill them would not be morally wrong. Duties of justice, in contrast, are not generally thought to admit of such discretion. In this respect too, the duty of assistance does not qualify as a humanitarian duty. Indeed, Rawls is clear that the duty of assistance is a duty of justice, one that places a strict moral requirement upon well-ordered societies to assist burdened societies.[17]

There is, however, a sense in which the label *humanitarian* is usefully applied to Rawls's duty of assistance. Here the relevant distinction to be drawn is between duties of humanitarian assistance and duties of *distributive* justice. Principles of distributive justice, as Rawls understands them, provide a standard for assessing the background rules and norms that, among other things, determine the distributive shares to which parties are entitled in the first instance. Principles of humanitarian assistance address a different, narrower matter than this: how we should respond to the plight of those who are badly off.[18] It is in this sense that the distributive issues Rawls addresses at the global level are ones of humanitarian assistance and not of distributive justice. By focusing his attention only on a matter of humanitarian assistance—that is, what is owed to burdened societies—his account is silent on broader issues of distributive justice concerning the justification of background institutions that shape the global economic distribution. Indeed, Rawls's account would seem to carry the implication that as long as the duty to assist burdened societies is fulfilled, wealthier societies would be entitled to the greater material advantages they command. As Kok-Chor Tan puts this point,

> If we accept that rich countries have *only* a duty of humanity to poorer countries, we are also accepting that the *existing* baseline resource and wealth distribution is a just one.... Duties to assist each other ... are duties that take place within a just institutional framework.... [And] while duties of humanity aim to *re*distribute wealth, duties of justice aim to identify what counts as a *just distribution* in the first place.[19]

A clarification is in order. It does not follow from the foregoing that if the duty of assistance were to be satisfied, then Rawls would take the current global

---

[17] Freeman, "Distributive Justice," 248–249.

[18] On this distinction, see Brian Barry, "Humanity and Justice in Global Perspective," in *Ethics, Economics and the Law (Nomos XXIV)*, ed. J. Roland Pennock and John W. Chapman (New York University Press, 1982), esp. 244–250; Tan, *Justice without Borders*, 20–29, 66–69.

[19] Tan, *Justice without Borders*, 66–67.

economic distribution (with that one alteration) to be justified. This is because he intends his international theory to apply only under certain idealized conditions.[20] Chief among these conditions is that the principles he defends serve to regulate international relations only between well-ordered peoples who, he presumes, will strive to genuinely cooperate with one another. In the actual world, which departs sharply from the ideal case, Rawls might well support a distributive principle intended to rectify serious historical injustices, such as colonialism, that have contributed to the gross disparities in income and wealth that obtain globally.[21]

Nevertheless, in the ideal case involving only well-ordered societies, Rawls is clear that concerns of international distributive justice do not arise. Consequently, even significant material inequalities at the global level would not be a matter of injustice on his view. Rawls does think that states, in the ideal case, would establish cooperative international organizations and would agree to standards of fair trade.[22] This call for states to regulate their interaction according to some normative standards might have cross-border distributive implications. However, these demands do not amount to requirements of distributive justice insofar as they do not address the fundamental matter of what a justified system of distributive entitlements at the global level would look like.[23] Examining that matter might, in turn, require consideration of such pressing issues as whether states should enjoy exclusive ownership and control of the land and natural resources found in their respective territories. These are simply not issues that Rawls addresses.

3. The Political Autonomy Argument and the Rejection of Explanatory Nationalism

Cosmopolitan critics of Rawls argue that he ought to have supported more demanding distributive principles at the global level. These critics find his account of cross-border distributive demands wanting in two key respects. First, outside of the state, Rawls argues that justice does not have an egalitarian component: on his account, neither *global* inequalities—that is, inequalities between individuals worldwide—nor *international* inequalities—that is, inequalities between different societies—pose an injustice. Second, at the global level, Rawls rejects

---

[20] Rawls, *The Law of Peoples*, §§2, 3, 5.

[21] Rawls, *The Law of Peoples*, 89–90, 117; Freeman, "Distributive Justice," 244, 250–252.

[22] Rawls, *The Law of Peoples*, 42–43, 115.

[23] To be fair, it is hard to assess these demands since Rawls says very little about them. On the face of it, though, it would be surprising if this underdeveloped part of his account were to call for anything so radical as evaluating the global institutional rules and norms that determine cross-border economic shares, as a principle of distributive justice would do. See Pogge, "Rawls's Two Theories," 216–217.

concerns of *distributive justice* entirely. As we have just seen, he does not address such issues as what would be a just design of global background rules and norms regulating the ownership of resources and wealth. Rather, his main international distributive concern is with a quite limited form of redistribution.[24]

Let's turn, then, to Rawls's reasoning against the adoption of more demanding distributive principles at the global level, in particular, principles of *egalitarian* distributive justice. A principle intended to curb cross-society inequalities on an ongoing basis would, as Rawls sees it, lead to "unacceptable results."[25] To illustrate what he finds objectionable about such a principle, he offers the following example. Suppose that two societies start out equally wealthy. Over time, one society becomes much richer because it chooses to industrialize and to increase its savings, while the other society remains at the same level as before because it doesn't make parallel efforts to improve its material position, preferring instead to prioritize its leisure.[26] According to Rawls, it would be wrong to mandate a redistribution from the now wealthier society to the now poorer society. Doing so, he suggests, would violate the political autonomy of each society: it would be unfair to take from the richer society gains it earned through its adoption of economically prudent policies reflecting its industrious values, while transferring funds to the poorer society would fail to appropriately hold it responsible for the material consequences of the values it has chosen to embrace. Call this argument against the adoption of a cross-society egalitarian principle *the political autonomy argument*.

The political autonomy argument faces an important challenge that has been forcefully raised by Thomas Pogge. Pogge points out that this argument relies, at least tacitly, on a doctrine he calls *explanatory nationalism*.[27] According to explanatory nationalism, it is domestic factors—factors internal to a society that lie in its control, such as its public policies or cultural traditions—that serve to explain why some societies fare badly while others prosper. Rawls's reliance on explanatory nationalism is suggested both by the hypothetical example set out

---

[24] To be clear: Rawls's cosmopolitan critics do not deny that adoption of the duty of assistance would mark a not-insignificant moral improvement upon the status quo. Nevertheless, the gist of their criticism is that from the standpoint of justice—which concerns that which we should *ideally* strive for—Rawls's global theory is far too undemanding in its requirements. There have been some authors, however, who argue that, on reflection, the requirements of Rawls's duty of assistance might be much more robust than is usually thought to be the case. See, e.g., Rex Martin, "Rawls on International Distributive Economic Justice: Taking a Closer Look," in Martin and Reidy, *Rawls's Law of Peoples*, 237–238.

[25] Rawls, *The Law of Peoples*, 117.

[26] Rawls, *The Law of Peoples*, 117. Rawls offers a second example that's intended to support the same general point as this one. Instead of differing in terms of their industriousness, in the second example, an inequality emerges between two societies on the basis of their respective social values, which, in turn, affect their respective population rates (117–118).

[27] Pogge, "Rawls's Two Theories," 217.

in the previous paragraph and, more generally, by the reflections he offers on the causes of wealth and poverty in his discussion of burdened societies.[28] Should we accept this doctrine, which if true might provide a compelling basis for holding states responsible for their level of material prosperity and, consequently, for opposing an international egalitarian principle that would interfere with an apparently justified inequality?[29]

Pogge argues that explanatory nationalism should be rejected. He acknowledges a body of academic literature pointing to different domestic factors that appear to play a role in accounting for why some societies fare worse than others, which would seem to support explanatory nationalism. But, he explains, to dispute explanatory nationalism, one need not deny that domestic factors matter in this way. Rather, what must be shown is that factors external to a society also significantly influence how different societies fare. And Pogge thinks this can be shown. To make this case, he begins by observing the breadth of issues subject to global regulation, pointing out that "conventions and treaties are negotiated about trade, investments, loans, patents, copyrights, trademarks, double taxation, labor standards, environmental protection, use of seabed resources, and much else."[30] It would be astonishing, he suggests, if it turned out "that *no* feasible modifications of *any or all* of these elements of the global institutional order would appreciably affect" the well-being of poorer societies.[31] Indeed, he notes that it is widely acknowledged that poorer societies would benefit from more favorable terms of trade than those they are granted under the status quo arrangement that disproportionately benefits wealthier societies.[32]

A different, related line of reasoning Pogge raises against explanatory nationalism begins by inviting us to consider the possibility that domestic factors that affect a society's prosperity (the sort of factors that Rawls focuses on) might themselves be influenced by external factors. He offers a detailed analysis of two ways in which this does, in fact, occur, discussing the role the "international resource privilege" and the "international borrowing privilege" play in fueling domestic corruption and violence that greatly threatens an afflicted country's prospects for economic success (in addition to a host of other serious damages these privileges produce).[33] So, it seems plausible that at least some domestic factors that impede

---

[28] Rawls, *The Law of Peoples*, 108–111, 114, 117–118.

[29] Here I say "*might* provide a compelling basis" because putting aside the veracity of the doctrine of explanatory nationalism, we need not accept the principle that those who become badly off through their own free choices should be made to bear the full consequences of those choices. For further discussion of this point, see Pogge, "Rawls's Two Theories," 214–216.

[30] Pogge, "Rawls's Two Theories," 217–218.

[31] Pogge, "Rawls's Two Theories," 218.

[32] Pogge, "Rawls's Two Theories," 219.

[33] Thomas Pogge, *World Poverty and Human Rights* (Polity Press, 2002).

a society's prosperity do not lie entirely in its own hands but rather are influenced by global institutional factors.

What is the upshot of showing that explanatory nationalism is false? For the political autonomy argument to plausibly support Rawls's rejection of a cross-society egalitarian principle, he would need to establish that the variance in wealth between different societies is attributable only to domestic factors and not also to global ones. Since that empirical claim is false, the political autonomy argument is not compelling. And, Rawls's cosmopolitan critics press, if global institutional factors do matter in this way, then he is wrong to reject principles of distributive justice at the global level. In particular, many authors who argue along these lines question the coherence of Rawls's views: as they see it, his views about the demands of justice that arise domestically do not square up with those he takes to arise (and, more importantly, to *not* arise) globally.

To understand the basis of this criticism, let us review the basics of Rawls's familiar reasoning about why demands of justice arise in the context of the state and what form those demands take. According to Rawls, demands of distributive justice arise in the state because fellow citizens are engaged in social cooperation that produces important benefits and burdens.[34] The *basic structure* of society—that is, the background institutional rules regulating interaction between citizens—can be designed in different ways, each of which would give rise to different ways of dividing up those benefits and burdens. And so the central concern of distributive justice arises: how should the terms of this cooperative enterprise be structured with respect to the distribution of benefits and burdens that they produce? Principles of distributive justice, for Rawls, apply to the basic structure of society, and they are egalitarian insofar as they serve to constrain social and economic inequalities. With this admittedly brief sketch of Rawls's domestic theory in hand, the cosmopolitan critique that follows is straightforward. Given the existence of extensive global cooperation that has significant material effects on how different individuals worldwide fare, by the logic of Rawls's own reasoning in the state context, he ought to support global principles of distributive justice—principles at the global level that would both apply to background structural rules and serve to regulate inequalities.

4. Feasibility Concerns about Global Distributive Justice

It might be thought that Rawls's opposition to global egalitarian principles can be explained by a well-grounded skepticism about the prospects of such principles

---

[34] Rawls, *A Theory of Justice*, 6.

being practically realized in our world. One form of this worry concerns whether we can realistically expect individuals who belong to different political societies to have sufficient mutual affinity to support a principle aimed at reducing cross-border inequality. If individuals in richer nations cannot be expected to care enough about those in poorer nations to support making the requisite economic contributions called for by such a principle, then it would appear that such a principle could not be satisfied. Rawls considers a parallel concern, of whether we can reasonably expect sufficient affinity among peoples to support even the less-demanding duty of assistance.[35] On reflection, however, he does not take this worry to threaten the duty of assistance. This is because he thinks that over time the bounds of caring between peoples can expand in scope; in particular, we can expect this to occur as relations of cooperation between the relevant parties grow. Based on his reasoning about that case, it would be difficult for Rawls to argue that we could not expect great enough affinity to develop to support a cross-society egalitarian principle as well—specifically in the face of ever-growing relations of global cooperation.[36]

A different objection holds that satisfying the demands of a global egalitarian principle would require a world government, and because the establishment of a world government would be objectionable, such a principle should be rejected. However, this is not a view Rawls endorses. Although he does express familiar reservations about the desirability and stability of a world government, he does not suppose that egalitarian principles at the global level would require a world government.[37] Indeed, he discusses the prospects of realizing demands of justice at the international level via institutions that fall short of anything as extreme as world government.

Another concern about feasibility is prompted by Gillian Brock's discussion of the efficacy of different strategies of addressing global poverty. In particular, she assesses the comparative merits of an approach aimed at improving the domestic institutions of poorer societies (as the duty of assistance aims to do) versus a resource transfer from wealthier societies to poorer ones. In her estimation, the former approach is superior to the latter. On the one hand, as she sees it, a focus on improving the quality of a state's institutions tends to be crucial to "lifting people out of poverty," while, on the other hand, she suggests that Rawls is right to emphasize that "resource transfers are not necessarily an effective way

---

[35] Rawls, *The Law of Peoples*, 112–113. See also Brock's discussion of this matter in this volume.

[36] This point is made by Leif Wenar, "Why Rawls Is Not a Cosmopolitan Egalitarian," in Martin and Reidy, *Rawls's Law of Peoples*, 99.

[37] Rawls, *The Law of Peoples*, 36. See also Wenar, "Rawls Not Cosmopolitan Egalitarian," 99–100; Tan, *Justice without Borders*, 80–81.

to assist developing countries, and they are certainly not sufficient."[38] These empirical claims concerning what works in addressing poverty might be thought to support an argument along the following lines that would tell in favor of the duty of assistance and against a global principle of distributive justice aimed at improving the position of badly off individuals worldwide:[39]

1. A principle of global distributive justice requires transferring resources from richer to poorer nations as a means of assisting the world's worst-off individuals.
2. A cross-society resource transfer will not help the world's poor (unless it is accompanied by domestic institutional change).[40]
3. The duty of assistance, with its focus on improving domestic institutions, is likely to help the world's worst-off individuals.
4. So we have a clear reason for favoring the duty of assistance over a principle of global distributive justice.

A few lines of reply to this argument are in order. To begin with, it is important to clarify the fundamental respect in which the duty of assistance differs from a duty of global distributive justice. This difference concerns the *object* of the respective duties, which is the ideal that each strives to realize or at least to make progress toward realizing, and not the best *means*, practically speaking, of working toward realizing the given ideal.[41] While the object of a duty of global distributive justice is to improve the position of the world's poorest individuals, that is not the object of the duty of assistance.[42] Indeed, Rawls is clear on this point: his disagreement with his cosmopolitan critics about whether principles of distributive justice arise at the global level ultimately centers on a disagreement about values rather than about practical application. Even if a global redistributive principle that would improve the position of poorer individuals worldwide could

---

[38] Brock, "Rawls's Reasoning," in this volume, 333–334. Her use of "people" here should be read as referring to "persons" rather than to "societies." That her primary focus here is on how we might best address the suffering of poor persons is made clear in her surrounding discussion of this matter.

[39] This argument as I formulate it here is neither explicitly made by Rawls in *The Law of Peoples* nor advanced by Brock on his behalf. It does, however, seem that Brock's remarks that have just been set out are at least suggestive of such an argument.

[40] There is a stronger and a weaker version of this premise. The stronger version omits the parenthetical qualification and thus suggests that resource transfers won't help alleviate poverty at all; the weaker version suggests that resource transfers might help alleviate poverty but only if they are accompanied by changes to domestic institutions.

[41] For further discussion of this point, see Tan, *Justice without Borders*, 74.

[42] Thus, while Brock focuses on the promise Rawls's duty of assistance holds in helping the global poor in virtue of its institutional focus (i.e., the idea encapsulated in premise 3 in my formulation of the argument), this is not a part of Rawls's reasoning in favor of that duty.

be feasibly implemented, he doesn't think such a principle would be preferable to his favored duty of assistance.[43]

This brings us to a related point, which is that there is no reason to suppose that a principle of global distributive justice would *necessarily* require a resource transfer between societies. That is to say, we should reject the first premise of the argument. If focusing on improving domestic institutions is what turns out to most effectively help the world's worst-off members, then the proponent of global distributive justice would advocate doing just that. In some cases, especially those involving poor societies with corrupt governments, it is plausible to expect that a resource transfer would not do any good, and might even do harm, in the absence of significant institutional changes being made in the recipient society. Still, it is hard to imagine that there aren't any cases at all of poorer societies that wouldn't stand to benefit from cross-society resource transfers, even in the absence of institutional changes. The upshot is that although a principle of global distributive justice would not necessarily mandate resource transfers, it may well call for such transfers and would likely do so in tandem with calling for the adoption of other measures. The proponent of global distributive justice simply advocates for measures that, practically speaking, can be expected to improve the lives of worse-off individuals globally, whatever those measures happen to be.

So we see that Rawls's rejection of demands of distributive justice obtaining globally is not ultimately explained by a skepticism of there being any feasible means by which to satisfy, or at least make progress toward satisfying, such demands.

5. Rawls's Methodology and the Limits of Toleration

Let us consider one final explanation for why Rawls does not think that demands of distributive justice similar to those that arise in the state arise in the global domain. This explanation concerns the methodology he employs for arriving at the principles of justice that he takes to be appropriate for a particular context. For Rawls, the terms regulating institutional interaction in a given domain must be guided by principles that could be endorsed by, and thus prove acceptable to, all reasonable parties who are subject to those terms.[44] Finding principles that can be justified in this way poses a challenge in any institutional context in which there is considerable variance in the worldviews held by different reasonable

---

[43] Rawls, *The Law of Peoples*, 41, 119–120.
[44] John Rawls, *Political Liberalism*, expanded ed. (Columbia University Press, 2005), 136–137, 446–447; Rawls, *The Law of Peoples*, 57.

parties. Rawls refers to the existence of such diversity of viewpoints as "the fact of reasonable pluralism."[45] And in the face of reasonable pluralism, he thinks that for terms to be generally acceptable to those they are imposed on, they cannot be based on ideas that reflect worldviews held by only some segments of the population.[46] That would be unfair.

For reasonable parties to move past a clash in their basic values and perspectives and arrive at principles that could be acceptable to all of them, those principles must be grounded in ideas sourced from what Rawls refers to as the *public political culture* of a given domain.[47] The public political culture contains such ideas as those reflected in the design of political institutions, in public traditions, and in well-known historic texts, and these ideas will be widely embraced by parties in a shared social context. According to Rawls, reasonable parties will recognize these ideas as providing a justified basis for informing principles that regulate the character of the terms upon which they cooperatively interact.[48]

Appreciation of Rawls's methodology in devising principles of justice enables us to see how he might consistently maintain that certain values central to his domestic theory ought not play any role in his global theory: on his favored methodology, we cannot assume that the same values would be suitable for different domains. In particular, Rawls thinks that while members of a liberal society can be reasonably expected to accept principles grounded in certain liberal egalitarian values, such values may not find adequate support in the more diverse global context.[49] Indeed, given the greater diversity found at the global level, he favors extending the bounds of toleration—that is, the range of viewpoints we regard as reasonable—to allow for at least some nonliberal viewpoints qualifying as reasonable in that scope.[50]

As Rawls sees it, two specific liberal values that might ground principles regulating cross-border interaction could be reasonably rejected by nonliberal (but decent) societies, whom he wishes to accommodate in his international theory. The first of these values is *normative individualism*, the notion that individuals are the basic units of moral concern.[51] A number of Rawls's cosmopolitan critics who embrace normative individualism at the global level have, on that basis, defended the use of a *global* original position populated by representatives

[45] Rawls, *Political Liberalism*, 36.
[46] Rawls, *Political Liberalism*, 9–10; Rawls, *The Law of Peoples*, 54–55.
[47] Rawls, *Political Liberalism*, 8–15, 100–101.
[48] Rawls, *The Law of Peoples*, 30–32.
[49] Rawls, *The Law of Peoples*, 18–19.
[50] John Rawls, "The Law of Peoples" (1993) in *Collected Papers*, ed. Samuel Freeman (Harvard University Press, 1999), 530, 537, 561–563. See also Rawls, *The Law of Peoples*, 59–60, 63, 82–84, 122–125. For further discussion of Rawls's views on the toleration of nonliberal (but decent) societies, see Jon Mandle, "Tolerating Decent Societies," in this volume, chapter 20.
[51] I borrow the term *normative individualism* from Tan, *Justice without Borders*, 75.

of *individuals* worldwide rather than employing Rawls's favored approach of an *international* original position populated by representatives of *peoples*.[52] Which construction of the original position is used has significant bearing on the substantive principles of justice that follow. Advocates of a global original position explain how that starting point would lead to global distributive principles that are concerned with individual well-being, whereas, as we have seen, the international distributive principle that Rawls defends shows no direct concern for how individuals worldwide fare, in either absolute or relative terms.[53]

Rawls, however, opposes the use of a global original position on the grounds that it problematically relies on such "liberal ideas" as "treating all persons, regardless of their society and culture, as individuals who are free and equal," and in doing so it "makes the basis of the law of peoples too narrow."[54] So he objects to an approach to devising global principles that is firmly rooted in normative individualism because nonliberal peoples could reasonably protest that they do not endorse that ideal. But even if nonliberal peoples do not endorse normative individualism, might we find support for that doctrine in our global public political culture (which is the source of ideas that Rawls thinks we must consult to ground acceptable principles)? Leif Wenar bolsters Rawls's contention that normative individualism should not inform the character of principles adopted at the global level by arguing that

> the global public political culture is primarily *international*, not interpersonal. The ideas that regulate the institutions of global society are concerned primarily with the nature of nations and their proper relations—not with the nature of persons and their proper relations.... There simply is no robust global public political culture which emphasizes that citizens of different countries ought to relate fairly to one another as free and equal within a single scheme of social cooperation.[55]

Rawls appeals to parallel reasoning to explain why a second key liberal value— that of egalitarianism—also has no place in his international theory.[56] Others have argued that egalitarian principles similar to those that Rawls defends in the

---

[52] See, e.g., Charles Beitz, *Political Theory and International Relations* (Princeton University Press, 1979), part 3.

[53] Beitz, *Political Theory*, part 3.

[54] Rawls, "The Law of Peoples," 549–550. See also Rawls, *The Law of Peoples*, 82–83.

[55] Wenar, "Rawls Not Cosmopolitan Egalitarian," 103.

[56] Rawls's remarks in the 1993 article, "The Law of Peoples," on this line of reasoning against the adoption of a global egalitarian principle (as set out in this paragraph) are extremely brief, and he makes no appeal to this reasoning at all in the later book *The Law of Peoples*. For critical discussion of Rawls's rejection of global egalitarianism on this basis, see Thomas Pogge, "An Egalitarian Law of Peoples," *Philosophy and Public Affairs* 23 (1994), 215–219; Tan, *Justice without Borders*, 77–80.

domestic context, such as the difference principle, ought to apply globally.[57] But Rawls resists this proposal, in part, because he supposes that by not including an egalitarian component, an international theory of justice would prove more acceptable to nonliberal peoples. He writes that "not all" of the "various kinds of societies in the society of peoples . . . can reasonably be expected to accept any particular liberal principle of distributive justice."[58] Specifically, he emphasizes that the nonliberal peoples whom he wants to include in the society of peoples "reject all liberal principles of domestic justice," and, consequently, he thinks that "[w]e cannot suppose that they will find such principles acceptable in dealing with other peoples."[59] Although Rawls does not explicitly state that strong egalitarian ideals do not find expression in our global public political culture, that claim could be advanced to further strengthen his case.

Do the foregoing reflections provide a compelling basis for Rawls's rejection of normative individualism and egalitarianism at the global level? Let's turn to a few reasons to doubt that they do. To begin with, one might question the empirical claim that the relevant liberal values fail to find expression outside the confines of liberal societies. On this count, let us first take up the suggestion that our global public political culture is mostly unconcerned with the moral status of individuals. No doubt, states dominate the global landscape in our times. Still, the idea that individuals are owed moral consideration as members of a single global community also, arguably, finds expression in our shared global culture. This is, perhaps, most clearly demonstrated by the widespread endorsement of human rights that we find enshrined in numerous international institutions and norms. Furthermore, increasingly, we witness individuals advancing moral claims concerning the terms of global interaction that shape their lives—doing so through social movements that focus on environmental justice, migration, and labor conditions, to name just a few illustrations—and such claims are not dismissed wholesale by the global community on the grounds that individuals lack moral standing.

We might also question the claim that nonliberal societies would oppose an international egalitarian principle on the grounds that such a principle would reflect foreign, liberal values that they do not accept. As some of Rawls's cosmopolitans critics have observed, in the actual world, nonliberal societies tend to be poorer than liberal societies and thus would stand to benefit from greater international equality; consequently, it seems plausible that these poorer, nonliberal societies would not, in fact, find such principles unacceptable by the

---

[57] Beitz, *Political Theory*, part 3; Pogge, *Realizing Rawls* (Cornell University Press, 1989), part 3; Darrel Moellendorf, *Cosmopolitan Justice* (Westview Press, 2002).

[58] Rawls, "The Law of Peoples," 558.

[59] Rawls, "The Law of Peoples," 558.

lights of their own values and preferences.[60] For Rawls to maintain otherwise, then, seems disingenuous: effectively, doing so would be tantamount to telling those societies that we do not want to impose principles on them that are antithetical to their own values even when they themselves favor the very principles at issue, and it turns out to be wealthier, liberal societies who are reluctant to adopt them.[61]

For the sake of argument, however, let us suppose that the liberal values at issue would be strongly opposed by nonliberal peoples, and, moreover, that those values wouldn't find expression in our shared global culture. In that case, should we favor global principles that do not uphold these liberal values so as to accommodate the preferences of nonliberals? It is far from obvious that we should. Surely, Rawls is right to emphasize that toleration of diverse viewpoints is a crucial part of liberalism. But granting that, we must consider how far the bounds of toleration on a liberal theory can stretch for that theory to still qualify as liberal. Rawls's cosmopolitan critics contend that he has gone too far in the case of his international theory: in rejecting such core commitments as normative individualism and egalitarianism, he ends up with a liberalism so watered down it is not clear whether it is even worthy of that label.[62]

6. Conclusion

In this chapter, we have considered whether Rawls's claim that principles of egalitarian distributive justice do not arise globally is plausible. I have argued that it is not. In particular, we have examined three ways one might argue otherwise. First, we assessed the merits of the political autonomy argument. The problem with that argument is that it depends on explanatory nationalism, an empirical doctrine that should be rejected. Second, we took up the suggestion that perhaps Rawls's opposition to global principles of distributive justice is grounded in a concern about their feasibility. But, in fact, such a concern does not ultimately seem to tell against those principles. Third, we considered how Rawls's methodological approach might help us make sense of why principles of distributive justice such as the ones that he takes to apply in the state are not well suited for the global domain. That defense was shown to be wanting—both for relying on questionable empirical claims and, more problematically, for its implication that Rawls's international theory may end up sacrificing core liberal values that are very much worth preserving in theorizing about the demands of global justice.

---

[60] Pogge, "Egalitarian Law of Peoples," 218–219; Tan, *Justice without Borders*, 77–78.
[61] Pogge, "Egalitarian Law of Peoples," 218–219.
[62] Pogge, "Egalitarian Law of Peoples," 215–218; Tan, *Justice without Borders*, 78–80, 82.

To be sure, there are other defenses of Rawls's position on this issue that I have not been able to discuss here. There are also further cosmopolitan challenges to that position that we have not been able to examine. And so this chapter has not provided a comprehensive overview of the (voluminous) debate on global distributive justice between Rawls and his cosmopolitan critics. That being said, my intention has been to offer a representative survey of key points of disagreement between Rawls and those critics. On the basis of that survey, Rawls's position against global principles of distributive justice appears to face formidable challenges.

18

Rawls's Reasoning about International Economic Justice

A Defense

Gillian Brock

1. Introduction

What responsibilities, if any, do high-income countries have to low-income ones? Should international income inequality levels trigger moral concern? If affluent countries try to help disadvantaged ones, what form should any assistance take? What kinds of principles should guide liberal peoples in their international affairs concerning economic policy? These are important questions worthy of considerable reflection, and these are just some of the issues that Rawls aims to address in his highly influential work *The Law of Peoples*.

In this chapter I discuss Rawls's reasoning concerning how to navigate issues of international economic justice. Rawls offers a sophisticated account that presents many significant insights. This chapter aims to highlight some of these. In the next section I outline Rawls's argument which aims to provide substantial guidance in international affairs. Section 3 covers some frequently voiced key criticisms of Rawls's views in this domain. Section 4 offers an extended discussion of some ways in which Rawls, or rather those who would defend him, might address these challenges. In the process we come to appreciate the important insights that Rawls provides. So in this chapter I argue that Rawls's position on duties to address global poverty and his views concerning how to assist burdened societies to make the improvements they seek contain considerable wisdom that is not adequately acknowledged.

2. International Economic Justice: The Basic Framework

In *A Theory of Justice* Rawls aims to derive the principles of justice that should govern liberal societies. Rawls invites us to consider which principles of justice governing the basic structure of society we might choose if we do not know

Gillian Brock, *Rawls's Reasoning about International Economic Justice* In: *John Rawls*. Edited by: Jon Mandle and Sarah Roberts-Cady, Oxford University Press (2020). © Oxford University Press.
DOI: 10.1093/oso/9780190859213.003.0028.

what position we will occupy in that society. Rawls famously argues for two principles: namely, one protecting equal basic liberties and a second permitting social and economic inequalities when (and only when) they are both to the greatest benefit of the least advantaged (the difference principle) and attached to positions that are open to all under conditions of fair equality of opportunity (the fair equality of opportunity principle).

In *Law of Peoples* Rawls explicitly rejects these ideas as generally applicable in the international sphere. Rather, in this area, Rawls argues that eight completely different principles would be chosen. These are principles acknowledging peoples' independence, their equality, their right to self-defense, their duties of nonintervention, their need to observe treaties, to honor a limited set of human rights, to conduct themselves appropriately in war, and to assist other peoples living in unfavorable conditions. Importantly, Rawls also adds that three international organizations would be chosen: one aimed at securing fair trade among peoples, one that enables peoples to borrow from a cooperative banking institution, and one that plays a role similar to that of the United Nations.[1]

Critics and defenders have much to say about whether these two apparently radically different positions are justified.[2] In considering the merits or otherwise of the two views, we should consider Rawls's own thoughts about how the two projects differ. Unlike his earlier work in which he was concerned with ideal notions of what justice requires, in *Law of Peoples* he is ambitiously aiming to arrive at principles that could legitimately lay claim to being a realistic utopia. Rawls believes that he appropriately takes account of salient facts about diversity in our world, such as that many peoples of the world do not and cannot reasonably be made to endorse liberal principles as their orienting world view. The ideas he offers are more realistic also in being "workable and applicable to ongoing political and social arrangements."[3]

Even if Rawls has been realistic, has he offered us a sufficiently compelling normative picture of the principles that ought to govern our world, one that can lay claim to being utopian? Critics believe not. For our purposes in this chapter, the key principle around which much of the debate centers is principle 8:

> Peoples have a duty to assist other peoples living under unfavorable conditions that prevent their having a just or decent political and social regime.[4]

---

[1] John Rawls, *The Law of Peoples* (Harvard University Press, 1999), 37–42.
[2] For a summary of much of this criticism see Gillian Brock, "Recent Work on Rawls's Law of Peoples: Critics versus Defenders," *American Philosophical Quarterly* 47 (2010), 85–101.
[3] Rawls, *The Law of Peoples*, 13.
[4] Rawls, *The Law of Peoples*, 37.

Those who are critical of Rawls's account of international justice often take issue with this principle, interpreting it as a weak requirement and arguing that Rawls has been inconsistent in failing to endorse a global difference principle. But if we understand this principle properly, it is far from a weak requirement. As will become apparent in later sections, Rawls's views contain some important insights that are underappreciated and, if properly acknowledged, yield robust duties to others in the international sphere.

Continuing with the exposition of central points for now, Rawls says that some societies "lack the political and cultural traditions, the human capital and know-how, and, often, the material and technological resources needed to be well-ordered" (by which he means appropriately self-governing).[5] In such cases, well-ordered peoples have a duty to assist those societies. Assistance should aim at helping "burdened societies to be able to manage their own affairs reasonably and rationally and eventually to become members of the society of well-ordered peoples. This defines the target of assistance. After it is achieved, further assistance is not required, even though the now well-ordered society may still be relatively poor."[6] The idea is to preserve, or bring into being, just (or decent) institutions that are self-sustaining.

Rawls considers the position, often associated with cosmopolitans, that a global difference principle should operate at the global level. Rawls has several reasons for rejecting this view. First, he believes that wealth owes its origin and maintenance to important domestic factors such as the quality of the political and social institutions of particular societies. So these are the right foci for attention. Second, and arguably even more importantly stressed in his argument, is that any global principle of distributive justice we endorse must have a target and a cut-off point. For Rawls, these are secured when just or legitimate institutions are in place that can ensure political autonomy. By contrast, a global difference principle provides no target or cut-off point. Rawls believes that since cosmopolitans are concerned with the well-being of *individuals*, there is no obvious cut-off point at which redistribution ceases in the global arena, and this result is problematic for several reasons, for instance, in undermining proper incentives for a people to take responsibility for its well-being. So a third reason for rejecting the global difference principle is that endorsing it would undermine government's taking appropriate responsibility for the well-being of its people. This third reason connects well with the first reason Rawls offered about factors that sustain prosperity.

[5] Rawls, *The Law of Peoples*, 106.
[6] Rawls, *The Law of Peoples*, 111.

3. Some Key Criticisms of Rawls's *Law of Peoples*

Critics challenge many of these key claims, including some of the assumptions Rawls makes about the empirical base on which his account seems to rely. Critics question, for instance, whether states are sufficiently independent of one another, so that each society can take responsibility for the well-being of its citizens. Rather, in our globalized world, there is a high level of interconnection between what states do. Actions and policies taken in one part of our world can have dramatic consequences for others in an entirely different region. The global recession which began in 2008 and climate change are prominent examples of this phenomenon.

Critics also challenge Rawls's view that differences in levels of prosperity are largely attributable to differences in domestic factors such as political culture and the virtuous nature of its citizens. By contrast, they maintain that Rawls ignores two important issues: the extent to which unfavorable conditions within one society can arise from factors external to the society; and the morally relevant connections between states, for instance, that the global economic order perpetuates the interests of wealthy states with insufficient attention to the interests of poor ones.

To give some specific examples of how this plays out, consider two frequently discussed international institutions that are viewed as particularly worrisome: the international borrowing privilege and the international resource privilege.[7] Oppressive governments may borrow freely on behalf of the country (the international borrowing privilege) or dispose of its natural resources (the international resource privilege), and these actions are legally recognized internationally. This has huge implications for the prosperity of poor countries because these privileges often influence what sorts of people are motivated to seek power, provide incentives for coup attempts, help maintain oppressive governments, and generally significantly drain the country of resources. Foreigners benefit significantly from the two privileges, often at the expense of local citizens. For instance, foreigners can frequently buy resources more cheaply than they would otherwise be able to. They can also profit substantially from lending to dictators who may take out large loans to buy weapons and loyal soldiers to consolidate their power (of greater value to many authoritarians compared with investing in healthcare, education, or other projects likely to benefit disadvantaged citizens). Because the current

---

[7] Much of this is discussed in chapter 17 in this volume. One prominent advocate of such a view is Thomas Pogge. See, for instance, Thomas Pogge, *World Poverty and Human Rights*, 2nd ed. (Polity Press, 2008).

world order is to the advantage of wealthy and powerful states, there is little incentive to reform it.

Critics take issue with Rawls's claim that he has offered us a realistic utopia. It is insufficiently realistic because it fails to appreciate interdependence, coercion, and domination in the global arena. And it cannot lay claim to the description of a utopia, they argue, because the ideals are too tame and seem to endorse the unjust status quo.

4. Defending Rawls's Model

There are several strategies available to those who would defend Rawls. One strategy is to focus again on Rawls's project and what he himself thought he was doing. So, for instance, we might note that Rawls was particularly concerned with giving liberal states guidance in their foreign policy, and of particular concern in this chapter is his advice in relation to matters of duties to assist those states struggling to become self-governing nations. What kinds of principles should guide liberal peoples in their international affairs concerning duties of assistance and economic policy? What is the target of assistance? What can and should we reasonably hope for?

I believe that the framework Rawls offers contains considerable wisdom worth defending as we develop an account of a realistic set of guidelines applicable to international affairs. We explore these insights in more detail in this section. This will help us appreciate why the duties of assistance he endorses offer rich guidance.

4.1. The Effectiveness of Assistance

Let us begin by considering an important set of questions central to our duties of assistance: How can we help promote prosperity in countries struggling with widescale poverty? What are some of the drivers of desirable pro-poor prosperity? There is a huge literature on these topics.[8] It has emerged that the quality of institutions in a particular state is especially important, no matter what other factors are also found to play a role.[9] For instance, those institutions that promote respect for the rule of law and accountability make for an environment conducive to innovation and investment in education, health, and infrastructure, all

---

[8] For an introduction to these debates see Gillian Brock, *Global Justice: A Cosmopolitan Account* (Oxford University Press, 2009), chap. 5.

[9] For more on this topic see Brock, *Global Justice*, chap. 5.

key ingredients for lifting people out of poverty. Rawls is a firm believer in the view that institutions play a key role. And so he draws attention to the fact that resource transfers are not necessarily an effective way to assist developing countries, and they are certainly not sufficient. Rather, what burdened societies need is reformed domestic institutions *so that members can make effective use of resources and opportunities.* Targeting domestic institutional reform is therefore likely to be a more effective focus for our assistance. So, for instance, transparent and accountable institutions of government are more likely to assist citizens in their efforts to use public funds in ways that convert resources into genuine pro-poor development gains for citizens. Institutions of government that lack these features may present far too many opportunities for corrupt officials to siphon off resources for their personal use or other corrupt purposes. Assisting in ways that strengthen and support strong institutional capacity is an especially good target for our efforts. This view, often called "the institutional view," orients much of Rawls's thinking and explains many features that might otherwise seem puzzling.

4.2. The Duty of Assistance: Three Key Guidelines on Content, Target, Cut-Off Point, and Relevance of Aiming at Equality

In discussing the duty of assistance in more detail, Rawls offers a number of astute points worth reviewing, including three particularly important guidelines and reflections on the relevance of aiming at equality, when it matters, and when it does not. We review these key passages in more detail in the following subsections.

4.2.1. Reasons for Differences in Levels of Wealth among Societies
The first guideline on the duty of assistance considers the factors that are relevant to pro-poor prosperity and whether we should aim to equalize wealth among peoples. I have just introduced and given an overview of the importance of these topics in the previous section, 4.1. In discussing what might assist burdened societies, Rawls advocates for the view that political traditions, institutions of law and property, class structure, sustaining religious and moral beliefs, and underlying culture "shape society's political will."[10] In considering the form the duty of assistance should take, he says: "It does not follow . . . that the only way, or the best way, to carry out this duty of assistance is by following a principle of distributive justice to regulate economic and social inequalities among societies. Most

---

[10] Rawls, *The Law of Peoples*, 106.

such principles do not have a defined goal, aim, or cut-off point, beyond which aid may cease."[11]

Furthermore, he continues, "The levels of wealth and welfare among societies may vary, . . . but adjusting those levels is not the object of the duty of assistance. . . . A society with few natural resources and little wealth can be well-ordered if its political traditions, law, and property and class structure with their underlying religious and moral beliefs and culture are such as to sustain a liberal or decent society."[12] And so he gets to the view that "great wealth is not necessary to establish just (or decent) institutions. How much is needed will depend on a society's particular history as well as on its conception of justice. Thus the levels of wealth among well-ordered peoples will not, in general, be the same."[13] Having identified the factors that do matter to establishing and maintaining well-ordered societies, we can now appreciate why we should not be surprised if well-ordered peoples have different wealth levels. Further discussion of these points continues below (especially in section 4.6).

4.2.2. A General Focus, but No Single Recipe
The second guideline for the duty of assistance emphasizes that even though there is a general area of focus that is likely to pay especially good dividends for assisting peoples, there is no single recipe. He says:

> The political culture of a burdened society is all-important; and . . . , at the same time, there is no recipe, certainly no easy recipe, for well-ordered peoples to help a burdened society to change its political and social culture. . . . I would further conjecture that there is no society anywhere in the world—except for marginal cases—with resources so scarce that it could not, were it reasonably and rationally organized and governed, become well-ordered. Historical examples seem to indicate that resource-poor countries may do very well (e.g. Japan), while resource-rich countries may have serious difficulties (e.g. Argentina). The crucial elements that make the difference are the political culture, the political virtues and civic society of the country, its members' probity and industriousness, their capacity for innovation, and much else. Crucial also is the country's population policy: it must take care that it does not overburden its lands and economy with a larger population than it can sustain. But one way or the other, the duty of assistance is in no way diminished. What must be realized is that merely dispensing funds will not suffice to rectify basic political and

---

[11] Rawls, *The Law of Peoples*, 106.
[12] Rawls, *The Law of Peoples*, 106.
[13] Rawls, *The Law of Peoples*, 107.

social injustices (though money is often essential). But an emphasis on human rights may work to change ineffective regimes and the conduct of the rulers who have been callous about the well-being of their own people.[14]

Here Rawls offers some important reflections on the mechanisms that often reliably bring about positive change, isolating some factors that are especially important. Along with noting the importance of character, of both politicians and members of civil society, he draws attention to population policy and environmental sustainability issues as also highly relevant. Figuring out what mechanisms for positive change exist in particular societies is a complex business, but note that just because assistance must be rendered in more careful ways that are attuned to the circumstances, this does not reduce the strength of the duty to assist. (More discussion of these issues follows in section 4.6).

4.2.3. Self-Determination That Promotes the Freedom and Equality of Peoples

The third guideline emphasizes that the aim is to assist with self-determination, but in ways that adequately reflect commitments to peoples' freedom and equality. He says: "Thus the well-ordered societies giving assistance must not act paternalistically, but in measured ways that do not conflict with the final aim of assistance: *freedom and equality for the formerly burdened societies*."[15]

He notes that there is surely space for people to rightfully feel attached to their culture and for a sense of belonging to ground an important part of their well-being in life, so long as they respect the freedom and equality of other peoples to do this as well. He defends these views as follows:

It is surely a good for individuals and associations to be attached to their particular culture and to take part in its common public and civic life. In this way belonging to a particular political society, and being at home in its civic and social world, gains expression and fulfillment. This is no small thing. It argues for preserving significant room for the idea of a people's self-determination and for some kind of loose or confederative form of a Society of Peoples, provided the divisive hostilities of different cultures can be tamed, as it seems they can be, by a society of well-ordered regimes. We seek a world in which ethnic hatreds leading to nationalistic wars will have ceased. A proper patriotism . . . is an attachment to one's people and country, and a willingness to defend its legitimate claims while fully respecting the

---

[14] Rawls, *The Law of Peoples*, 109.
[15] Rawls, *The Law of Peoples*, 111.

legitimate claims of other peoples. Well-ordered people should try to encourage such regimes.[16]

There is no question that examining the world we live in today, a sense of attachment to a particular nation plays a prominent role in the psychology of vast numbers of people. Such attachments can change, as they have done in the past. Indeed,
Rawls himself is hopeful they will change in the future (as discussed in section 4.5).
However, any proposed set of realistic guidelines for here and now must take them
into account. (Further discussion of these points continues in sections 4.4. and 4.5.)

4.3. Rawls: The Relational Egalitarian

In section 16.1 of *Law of Peoples*, titled "Equality among Peoples," Rawls says that
"inequalities are not always unjust, and . . . when they are, it is because of their
unjust effects on the basic structure of the Society of Peoples, and *on the relations
among peoples and among their members*."[17] The discussion following this passage also underscores relational issues. Reasons to find inequality problematic in
the domestic case include that they prevent persons from making "intelligent and
effective use of their freedoms," stigmatization, and unequal treatment. When
people are treated as inferiors, that is certainly unjust. Inequalities of wealth that
yield inequalities in political or other fair opportunities are again grounds for
normative concern, and would demand remedy, such as through "fair education"
and elimination of unjust discrimination.[18]
    Parallel concerns have a role to play in the international arena. Representatives
in the second original position wish to maintain relations of equality among peoples, along with their independence. The international cooperative organizations
in which they participate, such as those governing fair trade, borrowing, and
other common affairs, need to ensure their activities do respect peoples freedom
and equality. Should any policies or organizational decisions have unjustified
distributive effects, such as when policies or decisions undermine the freedom
and equality of peoples, "These would have to be corrected in the basic structure
of the Society of Peoples."[19] These passages and thoughts help us to see that Rawls
is indeed rather more concerned with equality (or rather unjust inequality)
than is frequently assumed. Though he stops short of giving us details on how
corrections to the basic structure might proceed, he has certainly made space for

16 Rawls, *The Law of Peoples*, 111–112.
17 Rawls, *The Law of Peoples*, 115.
18 Rawls, *The Law of Peoples*, 114–115.
19 Rawls, *The Law of Peoples*, 115.

these in his account. At any rate, viewing Rawls as a relational egalitarian, we see his level of concern with equality is greater than is often acknowledged.

4.4. Political Leadership, the Role of the Statesman, and Encouraging Constructive Change

Rawls reflects on how difficult it is to change destructive patterns that may be found in political culture. Simple resource transfers won't change political culture. But, he says, an "emphasis on human rights may work to change ineffective regimes and the conduct of rulers who have been callous about the well-being of their own people."[20] After a very interesting discussion on prospects and challenges with discharging the duty of assistance, he concludes: "There is no easy recipe for helping a burdened society to change its political culture. Throwing funds at it is usually undesirable. . . . But certain kinds of advice may be helpful, and burdened societies would do well to pay particular attention to the fundamental interests of women."[21] He also emphasizes again the important role discourse about human rights can play in improving the political culture and its institutions.

So here, once again, Rawls is acknowledging the important role human rights can play in changing political culture and reforming unjust societies, contra his critics. And, as he goes on, in emphasizing that particular attention should be paid to the fundamental interests of women, Rawls indicates that he thinks there is a role for criticism albeit that it might be embedded in carefully worded, diplomatic, and strategic conversations.[22] The impression that critics have that Rawls is overly tolerant of nonliberal societies is, I think, mistaken. Rather, as I have been suggesting, we might interpret Rawls's position as one in which he is sensitive to a range of important considerations that must be balanced in international affairs. We should be particularly attentive to when and how we offer advice, if we are concerned about which courses of action are likely to be effective and which are likely to prove counterproductive in trying to assist constructively in any reform process. Rawls identifies an important role for political leaders, particularly "the statesman" to play in this process. The statesman must make judgments assessing when opportunities are ripe for offering advice that might prove to be constructive and when it would be more appropriate to refrain from doing so.

[20] Rawls, *The Law of Peoples*, 109.
[21] Rawls, *The Law of Peoples*, 110.
[22] Rawls, *The Law of Peoples*, 110.

4.5. Duty of Assistance, Affinity among Peoples, and the Task of Political Leadership

Mindful of the levels of conflict and tension around the world, we may despair that the model Rawls presents really can be realistically achieved in our world in the foreseeable future. While we may be some way from the model that Rawls presents, he is hopeful that over time we may well come to have more affinity for other peoples. He says:

> It is the task of the stateman to struggle against the potential lack of affinity among different peoples and try to heal its causes insofar as they derive from past domestic institutional injustices, and for the hostility among social classes inherited through their common history and antagonisms. Since the affinity among peoples is naturally weaker (as a matter of human psychology) as society-wide institutions include a large area and cultural distances increase, the statesman must continually combat these shortsighted tendencies.[23]

While there may be current psychological limitations to how much members of one nation can empathize or identify with members of another, he adds that these relations of affinity can develop and "grow stronger over time as peoples come to work together in cooperative institutions they have developed."[24] People may well come to care about each other more as the ties among them develop. As cooperation proceeds, "They may come to care about each other, and affinity between them becomes stronger."[25]

4.6. More Power to the Peoples

Rawls's approach is more open to individual countries being given space to set their own path for beneficial development, one that is more compatible with their preferred conception of a good society. To be sure, Rawls states that there are limits on that toleration; requirements to respect minimal human rights and to refrain from aggression play an important role in setting those limits (and more of these limits are discussed in the next chapter). But the focus on assisting burdened societies to become self-governing allows scope for a more open-ended articulation of just what the duties to others in the global sphere are.

---

[23] Rawls, *The Law of Peoples*, 112. In footnote 44 he says: "In a realistic utopia this psychological principle sets limits to what can sensibly be proposed as the content of the Law of Peoples" (112 n. 44).

[24] Rawls, *The Law of Peoples*, 112.

[25] Rawls, *The Law of Peoples*, 113.

Respecting the equality of all peoples means we must carve out substantial space for them to lead their lives along orienting principles that may well not be the ones dominating conversation among Western, affluent, developed nations. What might be an example of this? Within the liberal democratic capitalist economic framework, there is much focus on economic growth. Growth figures play an extraordinary role in orienting economic strategy and evaluating countries' success. More growth, it is presumed, is good for the well-being of citizens and a key marker of prosperity. This focus leaves out the detrimental consequences (for human beings and the environment) of high levels of industrialization, patterns of increasing consumption, and ever-increasing material affluence. And such consequences can be in considerable tension with aspects of living a good life that other peoples may value highly. Indeed, for those who value a certain kind of simplicity and living in balance with nature, or a life oriented around harmony with fellow humans, a focus on growth, industrialization or increased consumption can act as a barrier to living in ways they consider valuable. What might appear to be a life that seems to lack many of the goods that overstock Western households may well be one that gives genuine satisfaction. So long as those communities are capable of robust self-government so they can make relevant genuine and effective choices about how to shape their lives, we should not interfere with those choices to steer them toward lifestyles that are more similar to our own.

A Rawlsian duty of assistance requires us to offer assistance to those burdened societies suffering crippling poverty that prevents them enjoying the ability to enjoy self-government. But the content of that assistance needs to be highly respectful of those different peoples' visions of a good life. We should not try to impose some one-size-fits-all economic prescription on them. Indeed that is inconsistent with treating other peoples respectfully as equals. Rather, we should aim to assist them through the political, social, economic, and other arrangements that accord with their own interests and conceptions of the good. Particular indigenous world views may require us to assist in ways more congenial to their orienting world views. And those looking to industrialize might prefer help in other ways. And there is plenty of scope for dialogue so we can get things right in ways that reflect proper understanding, show due respect and equal regard, and assist with empowerment, along with many other desirable features of genuinely empathetic dialogue aimed at constructive assistance.

5. Concluding Thoughts (and How Rawlsians Can Respond in Defending His Views against Critics)

Rawls's often-maligned views about the duties of assistance actually offer a much more tolerant, open-minded set of ideas than critics have appreciated. We should look to the communities we are aiming to assist for ideas about how best to assist them, along with presenting our thoughts concerning what has worked well for us in the past that might be relevant if adapted to local contexts. Rawls offers more reflective ideas on how to help effectively than the discussion about transfer of resources or a difference principle has tended to do.

By putting in view the self-determination of peoples, and aiming for a world in which all self-determining peoples are truly free and equal, he is able to offer us a more nuanced picture on how to achieve an international order that both takes seriously our starting point and offers us a vision of something that could— under the right leadership—be implemented in the decades ahead.

The target of self-government is an excellent focus. It can also help us to appreciate when global inequalities are problematic and when they are not. So we should be concerned with global inequalities when they have effects on peoples' abilities to be self-governing. And when they do, we should work out how to mitigate the inequalities, block the undesirable effects, and so forth. There is certainly scope for concern about how global inequality undermines self-government and for important duties to reduce inequalities when they do so. We also want states to be able to have meaningful control over their own basic structures, for instance to make decisions, such as those around tax policy, that best reflect their values. So we need to be sensitive to their own orienting normative views.

We have seen that there are plenty of areas in which misinterpretations and uncharitable readings of Rawls's work abound. The scope for concern about equality is one such issue, as is the common view that Rawls's duty of assistance is quite minimal. Critics have a mistaken view about what is included within the scope of concern. In fact Rawls can accommodate all of their concerns within his duty of assistance. Consider again central criticisms from section 3. There we saw that critics claim Rawls has failed to appreciate the high level of interconnection between states in our globalized world, ignores the extent to which unfavorable conditions in one society can arise from factors external to society, and overlooks a global economic order that perpetuates the interests of the wealthy states at the expense of poorer ones. Rawls's sophisticated position appreciates the substance of all these concerns. In fact his duty of assistance aims to take account of them in an appropriately nuanced way. As we have seen, we must appreciate that there is a connection between the current global order (including the borrowing and resource privileges) and domestic institutions, and make sure that the global order is better aligned with assisting peoples in achieving meaningful self-determination, equality, and well-being. The duty of assistance requires such alignment and requires us to assist in the many ways we can bringing this about. Importantly, the duty of assistance also requires us to refrain from preventing societies developing legitimate domestic institutions through (for instance) our interference and support for illegitimate regimes.

What I particularly admire about the Rawlsian framework is that he asks some of the fundamental questions about what are the mechanisms for change in the direction of promoting prosperity and well-being in burdened societies. That seems to me a crucial area that will inevitably shape the form our assistance should take. He gets that right. Having a proper appreciation of the role institutional quality and human rights should play, he is then able to orient much further advice about how mechanisms for change might proceed effectively. Once we understand Rawls's views better, we can also see that there is more continuity with his previous projects, since he is concerned with the basic institutional structure of societies and the core role the basic structure can and ought to play in promoting justice. A charitable interpretation of Rawls's project might also emphasize several other important elements, such as his concern with the effectiveness of assistance and a proper sense of humility about knowledge concerning how we ought to live to promote good lives. All in all, Rawls has rich advice to offer in how we ought to approach international economic justice. Contra his critics, Rawls's project of offering a realistic utopia is quite successful.

PART X
INTERNATIONAL JUSTICE AND TOLERATION

Introduction

In the aftermath of the Holocaust, traditional notions of absolute state sovereignty seemed no longer defensible. States could no longer claim that the worst atrocities must be tolerated as long as they remained confined within their own borders. Sometimes, at least, an injustice can be so severe that states lose their claim to legitimacy and sovereign immunity, and they become subject to coercive intervention of one kind or another. But whether all injustices properly subject a country to potential intervention is far less clear. Are there principled grounds, for example, to tolerate certain nonliberal societies? Rawls holds that there are. Such societies are unjust according to the principles that Rawls himself endorses. Yet he holds that in some cases, there are principled—not only pragmatic—grounds for toleration. One of his main goals, first in "The Law of Peoples" (the 1993 article)[1] and then in *The Law of Peoples* (the 1999 book)[2], is to defend this position:

> Surely tyrannical and dictatorial regimes cannot be accepted in good standing in a reasonable society of peoples. But equally not all regimes can reasonably be required to be liberal, otherwise the law of peoples itself would not express liberalism's own principle of toleration for other reasonable ways of ordering society.

And he draws the following analogy:

> Just as a citizen in a liberal society must respect other persons' comprehensive religious, philosophical, and moral doctrines, provided they are pursued in accordance with a reasonable political conception of justice, so a liberal society must respect other societies organized by comprehensive doctrines, provided their political and social institutions meet certain conditions that lead the society to adhere to a reasonable law of peoples.[3]

[1] John Rawls, "The Law of Peoples," in *Collected Papers*, ed. Samuel Freeman (Harvard University Press, 1999).
[2] John Rawls, *The Law of Peoples* (Harvard University Press, 1999).
[3] Rawls, "The Law of Peoples," 530.

Introduction In: *John Rawls*. Edited by: Jon Mandle and Sarah Roberts-Cady, Oxford University Press (2020). © Oxford University Press. DOI: 10.1093/oso/9780190859213.003.0029.

The grounds and limits of (principled) toleration of nonliberal societies, and the appropriateness of the analogy between toleration of diverse comprehensive doctrines within a society and toleration of nonliberal social orders among societies, have been major areas of controversy and research ever since.

In *Political Liberalism*, Rawls defends a distinctive notion of political toleration. In the face of what he believes to be the persistent, ineliminable diversity of conflicting but reasonable comprehensive doctrines, he defends a *political* conception of justice, which, while "of course, a moral conception,"[4] is "presented as a freestanding view"[5] not derived from any particular comprehensive doctrine. The hope, then, is to "gain the support of an overlapping consensus of reasonable religious, philosophical, and moral doctrines in a society regulated by [the political conception of justice]."[6] However, an overlapping consensus is not pursued directly by "look[ing] to the comprehensive doctrines that in fact exist and then draw[ing] up a political conception that strikes some kind of balance between them." To proceed in this way would "make it political in the wrong way."[7] Part of the problem with attempting such a compromise is that it would be likely to include—that is, aim to accommodate—*unreasonable* comprehensive doctrines. And Rawls sees no principled reason to hold hostage a conception of justice to unreasonable doctrines. On the contrary, as he puts it, "Of course, a society may also contain unreasonable and irrational, and even mad, comprehensive doctrines. In their case the problem is to contain them so that they do not undermine the unity and justice of society."[8]

Rawls treats the international case as analogous to the domestic, and he distinguishes conceptually between those societies that can be expected to endorse the law of peoples and those that cannot—those that he calls "outlaw regimes."[9] As in the domestic case with respect to those espousing unreasonable doctrines, members of the society of peoples "can at best establish a modus vivendi with the outlaw expansionist regimes and defend the integrity of their societies as the law of peoples allows."[10] In the 1993 article, Rawls writes that a society is well ordered, and therefore to be tolerated, even if it is not liberal, as long as it is "peaceful and not expansionist" and "its legal system satisfies certain requisite conditions of legitimacy in the eyes of its own people; and, as a consequence of this, it honors basic human rights."[11] Rawls supposes that it is possible, at least in principle, that nonliberal societies—for example, a hierarchical,

---

4   John Rawls, *Political Liberalism*, expanded ed. (Columbia University Press, 2005), 11.
5   Rawls, *Political Liberalism*, 12.
6   Rawls, *Political Liberalism*, 10.
7   Rawls, *Political Liberalism*, 39–40.
8   Rawls, *Political Liberalism*, xvi–xvii.
9   Rawls, "The Law of Peoples," 555.
10   Rawls, "The Law of Peoples," 556.
11   Rawls, "The Law of Peoples," 530.

nondemocratic one—could adequately protect human rights and satisfy the other requirements of legitimate law. Being intolerant of such a society "would not express liberalism's own principle of toleration for other *reasonable* ways of ordering society" (our emphasis).[12] Near the end of "The Law of Peoples," he comments: "This illustrates what happens whenever the scope of toleration is extended: The criteria of reasonableness are relaxed."[13] But Rawls shows some ambivalence about this extension of the category of the "reasonable." When he gives an example of a nonliberal society that should be fully tolerated, he balks at saying that such a society is reasonable. Instead, in a footnote, he comments that, rather than claiming such a society to be reasonable, it is "not unreasonable. One should allow, I think, a space between the reasonable or the fully reasonable, which requires full and equal liberty of conscience, and the unreasonable, which denies it entirely."[14] To be sure, societies may be more or less reasonable. But such a judgment depends on some fixed criteria of reasonableness. It becomes very unclear why and to what degree the conception should be "relaxed."

Critics saw no answer to these questions. Kok-Chor Tan argued that Rawls failed to "prove a satisfactory answer" for justifying the relaxed criteria of reasonableness and that his position seemed "blatantly inconsistent."[15] Despite Rawls's denials, Tan argued, his "international project is beneath it all a project of modus vivendi, of seeking a compromise between liberal and nonliberal regimes, rather than that of achieving stability with respect to liberal justice."[16] In other words, there were no principled grounds for tolerating nonliberal societies. Two years later—after Rawls made a change in presentation that we will note later—Charles Beitz echoed the criticism, charging that Rawls was "excessively deferential to societies with discriminatory or undemocratic institutions."[17] Darrel Moellendorf agreed, arguing that the nonliberal, hierarchical societies that Rawls would tolerate,

are internally unreasonable, intolerant, and oppressive by the standards of *Political Liberalism*. To be "tolerant" of such regimes is akin to being "tolerant" of unjust actions or oppressive cultural practices. In short, there are no good reasons for being so. In fact, just as institutionalizing an arrangement that permitted individuals to be unjust could be seen as being complicit in the injustice,

---

[12] Rawls, "The Law of Peoples," 530.
[13] Rawls, "The Law of Peoples," 561.
[14] Rawls, "The Law of Peoples," 347 n. 28.
[15] Kok-Chor Tan, "Liberal Toleration in Rawls's Law of Peoples," *Ethics* 108 (1998), 283. See also Kok-Chor Tan, *Toleration, Diversity, and Global Justice* (Penn State University Press, 2000).
[16] Tan, "Liberal Toleration," 285.
[17] Charles Beitz, "Rawls's Law of Peoples," *Ethics* 110 (2000), 687.

so institutionalizing principles of international conduct that licensed oppression could be seen as being complicit in the oppression.[18]

In short, the objection is that justice as fairness already identified the doctrines that are to be tolerated in its domestic account: the *reasonable* ones. There is no need to relax this standard internationally, although of course there may be practical differences in how one ought to deal with doctrines that fall short of this ideal. In effect, these critics charged, Rawls is "political in the wrong way."

Between his 1993 article and 1999 book, Rawls introduced new terminology to describe his account of toleration, although his insistence on toleration of some nonliberal societies remained unchanged. Specifically, he introduced the category of "decent peoples" or "decent hierarchical societies" to describe those nonliberal societies that are to be tolerated in the society of peoples.[19] A decent society meets several criteria, the first of which concerns its foreign policy and conduct: it "does not have aggressive aims, and it recognizes that it must gain its legitimate ends through diplomacy and trade and other ways of peace."[20] There are three further criteria concerning its domestic arrangements. First, it must affirm a "common good idea of justice" and must secure human rights for all. Rawls lists some human rights that must be recognized, discussed later. Second, the system of law "must be such as to impose *bona fide* moral duties and obligations (distinct from human rights) on all persons within the people's territory." And third, "There must be a sincere and not unreasonable belief on the part of the judges and other officials who administer the legal system that the law is indeed guided by a common good idea of justice."[21] Substantively, this is not a significant change from the 1993 article. But Rawls no longer claims that these societies represent "other reasonable ways of ordering society." On the contrary, he states: "I am not saying that a decent hierarchical society is as reasonable and just as a liberal society. . . . A decent hierarchical society honors a reasonable and just Law of Peoples even though it does not treat its own members reasonably or justly as free and equal citizens, since it lacks the liberal idea of citizenship."[22] Rather than relaxing the criteria of reasonableness, Rawls now introduced a new concept to cover this type of society: "I think of decency as a normative idea of the same kind as reasonableness, though weaker (that is, it covers less than reasonableness does)."[23]

[18] Darrel Moellendorf, *Cosmopolitan Justice* (Westview, 2002), 28.
[19] As quoted previously, in the 1993 paper he had described respect for human rights as "a necessary condition of a regime's legitimacy and of the *decency* of its legal order" (554, our emphasis), although this term was apparently not used in a technical sense.
[20] Rawls, *The Law of Peoples*, 64.
[21] Rawls, *The Law of Peoples*, 65–66.
[22] Rawls, *The Law of Peoples*, 83.
[23] Rawls, *The Law of Peoples*, 67.

But the change in terminology didn't resolve the controversy concerning toleration. In his 2013 book, *Justice and Foreign Policy*, for example, Michael Blake lists various reasons "to restrict our coercive actions to those cases in which we can safely predict the consequences of our intervention will be more respect for individual autonomy." Epistemic modesty should make intervention "comparatively rare."[24] Yet such restraint is importantly different from principled toleration. By "extending the idea of toleration to illiberal states," Blake argues, Rawls's position "represents an abandonment of the moral universalism at the heart of liberalism's appeal."[25] In his contribution to this volume, Blake expands his defense of what he calls a "Democratic Law of Peoples" according to which principled toleration—again, as opposed to pragmatic—extends only to liberal democracies. Such a conception can better deal with threats to justice that have only recently become apparent, including the "democratic decay" that has occurred in many countries over the last decade and the effort of some nonliberal societies to destabilize the political order of liberal democracies, as happened with the Russian troll farm during the 2016 US presidential election.

But some authors, perhaps still a minority, have offered reconstructions and defenses of Rawls's toleration of decent societies. For example, in 2004, David Reidy argued that "decent peoples are legitimate to a degree sufficient to place them within the class of bodies politic constituted as corporate moral agents and thereby entitled to justice in their mutual relations."[26] If subjected to external coercion, even in the name of justice, "They would lose a morally significant measure of self-determination."[27] In other work, Reidy aims to deflect the criticism that *The Law of Peoples* represents an unprincipled compromise ("political in the wrong way") by noting that Rawls believes that the law of peoples "is the conception that would be morally appropriate (at the level of first principles enforceable against peoples regardless of consent or voluntary undertaking) even in a world of only liberal democratic peoples."[28] Jon Mandle emphasizes a similar point, noting that Rawls's inclusion of decent peoples comes only after identifying the principles that govern the relations among liberal democracies.[29] He offers an account of why, at this first stage, liberal democracies would not agree

---

[24] Michael Blake, *Justice and Foreign Policy* (Oxford University Press, 2013), 58.

[25] Blake, *Justice and Foreign Policy*, 61. See also his claim: "Where actual people will resent and resist external agitation in favor of democracy—which is to say in very nearly all actual cases—then we have a solid moral reason to avoid such agitation." However: "Why, *if we could make it work*, should we avoid attempting to make an undemocratic society more democratic?" Michael Blake, "*Justice and Foreign Policy*: A Reply to My Critics," *Ethics and International Affairs* 29 (2015), 311.

[26] David Reidy, "Rawls on International Justice: A Defense," *Political Theory* 32 (2004), 298.

[27] Reidy, "Rawls on International Justice," 304.

[28] David Reidy, "Political Authority and Human Rights," in *Rawls's Law of Peoples: A Realistic Utopia?*, ed. Rex Martin and David Reidy (Blackwell, 2006), 178.

[29] Jon Mandle, "Tolerating Injustice," in *The Political Philosophy of Cosmopolitanism*, ed. Harry Brighouse and Gillian Brock (Cambridge University Press, 2005).

to enforce full principles of liberal justice on one another, despite the fact that they all endorse some such conception. In his chapter in this volume, Mandle explores the analogy that Rawls draws between toleration in the domestic case and in the international case. The difference between the objects to be tolerated—individuals in the domestic case and peoples in the international case—accounts for the different standards they have to meet in order properly to be tolerated.

A related issue concerns Rawls's characterization of human rights. Since Rawls claims that decent, nonliberal societies are able to respect human rights (at least in principle), he must hold that human rights are a limited subset of full liberal rights. And, indeed, he distinguishes his position from those who "think of human rights as roughly the same rights that citizens have in a reasonable democratic regime."[30] Human rights, Rawls says, are "a special class of urgent rights."[31] He does not give an authoritative list of human rights, but notes that they include: "the right to life (to the means of subsistence and security); to liberty (to freedom from slavery, serfdom, and forced occupation, and to a sufficient measure of liberty of conscience to ensure freedom of religion and thought); to property (personal property); and to formal equality as expressed by the rules of natural justice (that is, that similar cases be treated similarly)."[32] Conspicuously absent are rights to democratic participation (according to the ideal of one person, one vote) and to a broad freedom from discrimination. And among the rights listed in the Universal Declaration of Human Rights, Rawls distinguishes what he calls "human rights proper" (listed in Articles 3 to 18) from those that "seem more aptly described as stating liberal aspirations."[33]

While some may applaud Rawls's resistance to "rights inflation," the more frequent reaction is to claim that Rawls's account of human rights is insufficiently robust, and the common suspicion is that the list is limited in order to accommodate (some) nonliberal societies, once again making it "political in the wrong sense." Allen Buchanan expresses this criticism when he writes: "It is at least in part because he takes the problem of parochialism so seriously that in order to avoid it he is willing to reduce the list of human rights found in the six major human rights conventions by more than 50%."[34] And James Nickel characterizes Rawls's position not only as minimal but as "ultraminimal."[35] David Reidy argues convincingly in reply that Rawls's "list of basic human rights is less minimalist

[30] Rawls, *The Law of Peoples*, 78. He continues: "Human rights are distinct from constitutional rights, or from the rights of liberal democratic citizenship" (79).

[31] Rawls, *The Law of Peoples*, 79.

[32] Rawls, *The Law of Peoples*, 65. In three footnotes contained in the passage, he elaborates these points.

[33] Rawls, *The Law of Peoples*, 80 n. 23.

[34] Allen Buchanan, "Taking the Human out of Human Rights," in Martin and Reidy, *Rawls's Law of Peoples*, 150.

[35] James Nickel, *Making Sense of Human Rights*, 2nd ed. (Blackwell, 2007), 98.

than many critics have allowed."[36] Part of the confusion on this point, no doubt, is due to the fact that Rawls never gives a definitive list. Nonetheless, it is clear that Rawls's theory relies on what he calls "human rights proper" rather than the more expansive set that can be found in international human rights documents and law.

Rawls's class of human rights is restricted due to the "special role" that they play in his theory:

> They restrict the justifying reasons for war and its conduct, and they specify limits to a regime's internal autonomy. In this way they reflect the two basic and historically profound changes in how the powers of sovereignty have been conceived since World War II. First, war is no longer an admissible means of government policy and is justified only in self-defense, or in grave cases of intervention to protect human rights. And second, a government's internal autonomy is now limited.[37]

In other words, there are no principled grounds for tolerating states that violate Rawls's basic human rights, although, of course, there may be practical grounds. Conversely: "Their fulfillment is sufficient to exclude justified and forceful intervention by other peoples, for example, by diplomatic and economic sanctions, or in grave cases by military force."[38] Rawls's critics accurately point out that Rawls is choosing to focus on one limited, albeit important way in which the concept of "human rights" is used today. As Nickel observes, "As human rights function today within international organizations it is simply untrue to say that they are mainly about intervention using coercion and force."[39] Buchanan agrees: "Appeals to human rights perform many functions, and providing premises in arguments about the justification for intervention is only one of them and, currently, not the most important."[40] But Rawls need not deny the wide range of functions that human rights play in the contemporary world. He is not interested in a "stipulative redefinition,"[41] as Buchanan charges. Rather, as he says from the beginning, he is interested in working out "the ideals and principles of the *foreign policy* of a reasonably just *liberal* people."[42] As part of that project, a liberal society needs to determine the extent of its (principled) toleration of other societies and when it may properly attempt to exert force (in the form of diplomatic

---

[36] Reidy, "Political Authority," 170.
[37] Rawls, *The Law of Peoples*, 79.
[38] Rawls, *The Law of Peoples*, 80.
[39] Nickel, *Making Sense*, 101.
[40] Buchanan, "Taking the Human," 165.
[41] Buchanan, "Taking the Humans," 166.
[42] Rawls, *The Law of Peoples*, 10.

or economic sanctions or military force) in an effort to correct an injustice in another country. Without disparaging the importance of other projects, Rawls claims that we must distinguish "a special class of urgent rights"[43] from the broader conception of human rights that may be appropriate for other projects. A decent society that honored these core human rights would not be fully just. But Rawls conjectures that a "realistic utopia" in which all societies were liberal or decent would be one in which "the great evils of human history—unjust war, oppression, religious persecution, slavery, and the rest"—would be eliminated.[44]

Suggested Reading from Rawls to Accompany These Chapters

A Theory of Justice: §58
The Law of Peoples: §§2, 3, 7–12

For Further Reading

Beitz, Charles. *Political Theory and International Relations* (Princeton University Press, 1979; reprinted with new afterword, 1999). This is an early and influential cosmopolitan extension of Rawls's theory of justice.

Blake, Michael. *Justice and Foreign Policy* (Oxford University Press, 2013). Blake distinguishes between demands of justice to citizens and to foreigners, while arguing that there are good pragmatic reasons—but not principled reasons—for toleration of nonliberal (decent) societies.

Cohen, Joshua. "Is There a Human Right to Democracy?" In *The Egalitarian Conscience: Essays in Honour of G. A. Cohen*, ed. Christine Sypnowich (Oxford University Press, 2006). Cohen argues that although justice requires democracy, this involves a demanding conception of equality that goes beyond what a global public reason can support, and therefore there is not a human right to democracy.

Mandle, Jon. "Tolerating Injustice." In *The Political Philosophy of Cosmopolitanism*, ed. Harry Brighouse and Gillian Brock (Cambridge University Press, 2005). This chapter argues that justice requires toleration of societies with a legitimate system of law and that this requirement is satisfied by decent societies despite their injustices.

Martin, Rex, and David Reidy, eds. *Rawls's Law of Peoples: A Realistic Utopia?* (Blackwell, 2006). This essential collection contains numerous valuable discussions of *The Law of Peoples* from a variety of perspectives.

Neufeld, Blain. "Civic Respect, Political Liberalism, and Non-liberal Societies." *Politics, Philosophy, and Economics* 4 (2005), 275–299. This article argues that Rawls's

---

43 Rawls, *The Law of Peoples*, 10.
44 Rawls, *The Law of Peoples*, 126.

fundamental principle of equal civic respect for citizens is violated by decent hierarchical societies, undermining the principled toleration of such societies.

Pogge, Thomas. "The Incoherence between Rawls's Theories of Justice." *Fordham Law Review* 72 (2004), 1739–1759. This article, part of a special issue titled "Rawls and the Law," argues that Rawls's toleration of decent hierarchical societies is inconsistent with his domestic theory.

Reidy, David. "Moral Psychology, Stability and *The Law of Peoples.*" *Canadian Journal of Law and Jurisprudence* 30 (2017), 363–397. This article is a provocative and original contribution proposing an analogy between Rawls's account of moral psychological development in *A Theory of Justice* and various forms of social organization in *The Law of Peoples.*

Reidy, David. "Rawls on International Justice: A Defense." *Political Theory* 32 (2004), 291–319. Reidy defends important elements of *The Law of Peoples* by emphasizing the need to ground principles of justice in an appropriate conception of shared human reason.

Tan, Kok-Chor. "Liberal Toleration in Rawls's Law of Peoples." *Ethics* 108 (1998), 276–295. This article is an especially clear, early cosmopolitan critique of Rawls's defense of toleration of decent societies.

19

Right-Wing Populism
and Noncoercive Injustice

On the Limits of the Law of Peoples

Michael Blake

Political philosophers are often marked by what we most love; we are theorists of rights, or of utility, or of virtue, according to what we most prize. We ought also, I think, save some thought for what we most *fear*. Every political philosopher has, in the back of his or her mind, some particular vision of the evil whose elimination justifies the effort of writing and reading philosophy. We rarely focus directly on the evils against which we take our work to stand.[1] Doing so explicitly, however, can serve an important function. When we understand the worlds a philosophical theory most wants us to avoid, we can better evaluate whether that theory is positioned to guide us in the world we now share.

John Rawls's *The Law of Peoples* emerges from a lifetime spent in the shadow of a particular sort of evil. We might call this sort of evil *coercive intolerance*. Domestically, it takes the shape of state coercion, where that coercion serves the interests and convictions of only the powerful within society; we can think, here, of the inequalities of a racialized society, in which both voice and money are distributed unequally on the basis of racial identification. Internationally, this evil also involves state coercion—the coercion, here, of one state by a more powerful state, in the name of a particular vision of right or justice; think, here, of the genocidal ambitions of the Nazi regime, or the imperial wars of the nineteenth century. These acts of evil could only be constrained—when they could—by a shared commitment to a particular vision of political ethics, on which coercion requires justification to the coerced; it was Rawls's life work to build this vision, and those of us who do political philosophy owe him an immeasurable debt for his work in having built it.

---

[1] It is instructive to note, however, that John Rawls takes his political liberalism to stand with Judith Shklar's "liberalism of fear" as a response to the particular cruelties of the European wars of religion. See John Rawls, *Political Liberalism*, expanded ed. (Columbia University Press, 2005), xxiv n. 10.

Michael Blake, *Right-Wing Populism and Noncoercive Injustice* In: *John Rawls*. Edited by: Jon Mandle and Sarah Roberts-Cady, Oxford University Press (2020). © Oxford University Press.
DOI: 10.1093/oso/9780190859213.003.0030.

What I want to discuss in this chapter, however, is the fact that the world has changed in the two decades since Rawls wrote his book, and that novel forms of evil may now exist within that world—forms against which Rawls's methods might have comparatively little to say. In particular, I want to argue that the past two decades have seen a rise in respect for authoritarian and right-wing populist governments in states previously committed (sometimes weakly) to constitutional and democratic norms. I cannot, in the present context, give a full account of right-wing populism; I will instead rely upon the ideas of Hans-George Betz, who notes three aspects of the right-wing populist agenda. First, the right-wing populist party mobilizes the anxiety of those whose economic and social status has been put under strain by globalization. Then, the right-wing populist identifies the global elite as the cause of that economic and social dislocation; the elites, whether in the academy or in business, are identified as abandoning their own, in favor of a cosmopolitan and elitist vision of justice. Finally, the right-wing populist identifies the outsider—the migrant, or the racialized other—as the instrument of this cosmopolitan redistribution. Wealth, status, and security—all are identified as the goods unjustly taken by the elite and redistributed to the undeserving outsider.[2]

The right-wing populist vision is not new—but the past two decades have seen a significant increase in that vision's prevalence. I believe this increase puts some pressure on the viability of Rawls's Law of Peoples as a framework through which international justice might be understood.[3] There are, in particular, two related evils associated with right-wing populism that Rawls's vision can only imperfectly address. The first of these is what Larry Diamond calls the *democratic recession*: the fact that, over the past two decades, respect for the distinctive combination of liberal and democratic norms—what I will call the *constitutional ideal*—has been in retreat throughout the world.[4] The number of states that combine a robust rule of law with fair and open electoral democracy is small and is getting smaller. If this is a problem—and I believe it is—it is not one for which Rawls's Law of Peoples is well positioned to offer a solution. The second evil relates to the increasing prevalence of international acts that are only imperfectly analogized to international coercion. States have, in recent years, developed a sophisticated and complex set of covert international policy tools, ranging from electoral hacking to sophisticated and well-funded troll farms; these tools can,

---

[2] Hans-Georg Betz, "The New Politics of Resentment: Radical Right-Wing Populist Parties in Western Europe," *Comparative Politics* 25 (1993), 413–427.

[3] Rawls takes his task as that of guiding the foreign policy of a liberal society; since he guides this policy with reference to political principles that might be reciprocally acceptable to both liberal and decent peoples, though, it is fair to regard him as providing a theory of international (if not global) justice.

[4] Larry Diamond, "Facing Up to the Democratic Recession," *Journal of Democracy* 26 (2015), 144–151.

under some circumstances, effectively make the adherence to the constitutional ideal more difficult—and yet they do not always easily fall within the ambit of co-ercive intervention, and so may fall outside that set of acts against which Rawls's Law of Peoples stands in opposition.

I believe, in sum, that the world now contains evils whose analysis requires us to significantly reinterpret or supplement Rawls's methodology. The states of the world have new tools at their disposal; our moral analyses must change in re-sponse. I will try to make this case in four sections. In the first, I will (briefly) dis-cuss Rawls's methodology, and outline how that methodology led him to identify coercive intolerance as the chief form of international wrongdoing. In the second, I will discuss the ways in which right-wing populism has increased in the decades since Rawls wrote his book. In the third, I will discuss the ways in which right-wing populism puts pressure on Rawls's methodology and on his concep-tion of international right. In the final section, I will identify an alternative way forward: I argue that Rawls might have used materials available to him to offer a more full-throated defense of liberalism, on which liberal states might have sought to enshrine the constitutional ideal within international human rights as a regulative ideal. I have elsewhere argued that such an enshrining would have made liberalism more attractive and coherent.[5] I here add the thought that such an ideal might serve as a partial roadblock against the continued rise of authori-tarian and right-wing populist politics. International law might not simply pres-sure illiberal states to become liberal; it might also pressure liberal states to *stay* liberal—a form of pressure sorely needed in our present political climate.

1. Rawls's *The Law of Peoples:* The Dangers of Analogic Reasoning

It is not essential, in this context, to rehearse a great deal of Rawls's argument; I expect that anyone interested in reading this chapter has already read Rawls himself. Nonetheless, a few notes seem important, if only to show the ways in which Rawls's arguments in the international realm are to some degree deter-mined by the argumentative structure he uses in the domestic realm.

The Law of Peoples emerges from the ideas Rawls discusses under the heading of public reason. The evil in domestic politics against which public reason presses is a particular form of coercive intolerance. Under conditions of freedom, citi-zens will not come to agreement on matters of morality or metaphysics; they will instead display a diversity of comprehensive doctrines. The temptation of the

---

[5] Michael Blake, *Justice and Foreign Policy* (Oxford University Press, 2013).

most powerful, of course, is to deploy state coercion based upon the commands of their own particular comprehensive doctrines. Against this, public reason argues that political agents have some obligation to abide by the duty of civility, on which they are obliged to seek justifications that do not depend upon their own comprehensive views. Thus, public reason requires the creation of a distinctively political conception of justice, derived from the political ideas present in the public political culture of a democratic society. This political conception of justice is the frame against which our shared discussions of politics must proceed.

Rawls's develops his view of international justice along similar lines. The agent in question is an individual state—a liberal state to begin with, although Rawls will identify the public and political conception of justice as one that both liberal and decent illiberal states can endorse.[6] The evil in international politics against which public reason presses is a particular form of coercive intolerance. Under conditions of freedom, states will not come to agreement on matters of morality or metaphysics; they will instead display a variety of political doctrines. The temptation of powerful states, of course, is to use coercion based upon the commands of their own particular political doctrines. Against this, public reason argues that political agents have some obligation to abide by the duty of civility, on which they are obliged to seek justifications that do not depend upon their own political doctrines. Thus, public reason requires the creation of a distinctively political conception of justice, derived from the political ideas present in the public culture of international society. This political conception of justice is the frame against which our shared discussions of politics must proceed.

Much more can be said than this, of course; I have flattened a great many complexities in the Rawlsian vision of political liberalism. This should be enough, however, to start our inquiry. I want to note, already, what the similarity in structure between the two visions of political justice might tend to hide. Persons have comprehensive doctrines about the good; they live their lives in accordance with particular plans. Political communities, however, are not persons; their doctrines deal with the distinct question of how to balance and evaluate the claims of persons. Thus, tolerating an illiberal political conception is not easily or simply analogized to tolerating a dissenting view about religion. We tolerate the latter, on liberalism, because we believe it is right that we do so; liberalism entails, we tend to think, the right to freedom of conscience and belief. To tolerate the

---

[6] I refer to these entities as states, rather than peoples; my thinking is that, while Rawls identifies these entities as lacking some of the strong rights of sovereignty given to states in traditional international law, this is not enough of a difference to justify the elimination of the concept of a "state" from discussions of international justice. I would also note that the traditional conception of sovereignty has been under threat since at the very least 1948, even as we have continued to use the concept of the state; the traditional conception of sovereignty is therefore not best understood as an essential part of the state as a legal entity.

former, in contrast, is to tolerate the rights of some people to be *intolerant*—and coercively so—of the rights of others. An illiberal state that refuses to recognize rights of conscience or belief might nonetheless be worthy of being tolerated; the argument, though, cannot be simply derived from the argument from individual toleration. Rawls's analogy between a comprehensive doctrine and a political doctrine obscures a deep disanalogy between the functional roles those two doctrines play.

I have discussed this elsewhere; in the present context, I want to note something else that is obscured by the analogy between the domestic and the international case. In the domestic case, it is rarely a matter of moral concern when an individual's conception of the good changes. If a natural person changes from Kantian to utilitarian—or Catholic to Buddhist—it is a matter of no immediate moral concern except to that person herself. A change in *political* doctrine, in contrast, may be more salient to a wider variety of people, each of whom has moral rights that might be affected by that change. If a state changes from liberal to illiberal, for instance, we might think that this is a to be regretted—as Rawls, indeed, argues it should be, when he acknowledges that he takes liberal states to be simply more accurate in their moral views than illiberal ones. Rawls insists, however, that a liberal state should not *act* upon this conviction that liberalism is superior, lest international relations lapse into "contempt for the other, on one side, and bitterness and resentment, on the other."[7] I am not sure, I should note, that all forms of acting in favor of the constitutional ideal will actually have this effect; resentment might be as much a product of *how* we promote that ideal as it is of the fact *that* we are promoting it. For the moment, I want to note only two related facts. The first is that the transition from liberal to illiberal states may have concrete effects upon the ability of citizens to act upon their comprehensive doctrines; democratic recession is not a matter of mere academic concern, but involves real people losing access to real rights. When a state that was committed to the constitutional ideal loses that commitment, it is always particular people whose rights and goods are made vulnerable under the new regime. If we are worried about the concrete effects of resentment and contempt, we have reason to weight them against the concrete effects of a retreat away from liberalism's guarantees. The second fact follows from this: it should not be a matter of moral indifference, for anyone who calls himself a liberal, when a liberal state begins to backslide. Even if illiberal states will feel resentment when coercively forced to liberalize, it should not follow that the transition from liberal constitutionalism to something less than that should not trouble us—nor, I think, should we be confident that international institutions should not seek to halt the process of retreat. The next section will defend this thought, by briefly

---

[7] John Rawls, *The Law of Peoples* (Harvard University Press, 1999), 123.

describing some of the ways in which global politics has changed since *The Law of Peoples* was written.

2. Democracy in Decline

When the Soviet Union fell, many political commentators felt that liberal democratic norms had won a decisive victory over alternative forms of political organization. Francis Fukuyama's *The End of History and the Last Man* argued that those who witnessed the collapse of the Soviet Union had witnessed the end of the ideological development of human political life and that no significant deviation from the constitutional ideal could now be expected.[8] This prediction was challenged within the decade. Less than six years after the collapse, Fareed Zakaria noted disturbing tendencies within democratic states; while many countries had nominally democratic forms of government, many of those states had not supplemented their democratic norms with constitutional norms of civil rights and the rule of law—creating the phenomenon he dubbed "illiberal democracy."[9] These countries were democratic, but failed to create the background norms necessary for free and fair political discourse; their leaders displayed open hostility to press freedom, were willing to imprison political adversaries, gave political jobs and patronage to their friends and allies, and so on. Over the next two decades, this process of decay took hold even more strongly. Writing in 2016, Larry Diamond noted that between 2000 and 2015, democracy itself broke down in more than twenty-seven countries, including such significant powers as Turkey and Russia.[10] Freedom House's annual survey has now highlighted a decline in democratic governance every year for more than a decade—a decline affecting all regions of the globe.[11]

The causes of this democratic recession are difficult to pin down with any degree of certainty. One factor appears to be the increasing economic vulnerability of many laborers in the developed world. As globalization moves production chains closer to cheaper labor in the developing world, many laborers in the developed world have seen significant reductions in both wealth and in social status.[12] The globalization of production has led to much greater economic

---

[8] Francis Fukuyama, *The End of History and the Last Man* (Free Press, 1992).

[9] Fareed Zakaria, "The Rise of Illiberal Democracy," *Foreign Affairs* 76 (1997), 22–43.

[10] Larry Diamond, "Democracy in Decline: How Washington Can Reverse the Tide," *Foreign Affairs* 95 (2016), 151–159; Diamond, "The Democratic Rollback: The Resurgence of the Predatory State," *Foreign Affairs* 87 (2008), 36–48.

[11] See generally. Larry Diamond and Marc F. Plattner, eds., *Democracy in Decline?* (Johns Hopkins University Press, 2015).

[12] Joseph Nye, "Will the Liberal Order Survive? The History of an Idea," *Foreign Affairs* 96 (2017), 10–16.

inequality in those developed countries; the advantages of international trade have been concentrated in the hands of the global elite, leading to increased stratification of both economic and political power within that elite's hand.[13] This vulnerability and anxiety has been exacerbated by rapid demographic change, as immigration alters both the ethnic makeup of society and the distribution of power within that society.[14] Right-wing populism finds an easy home under these circumstances. Political parties and agents have been able to use the anxiety of the displaced and vulnerable and identify the migrant and the foreigner—together with the global economic elite—as the sources of their pain. Hence, the rise throughout Western Europe and North America of right-wing populist parties. In Hungary, Jobbik (the Movement for a Better Hungary) identified the Roma as the primary outsiders causing disruption; their platform promised a crackdown on both the Roma and on global processes of "cowboy capitalism."[15] In Germany, the right-wing Alternativ für Deutschland has positioned itself as the party of resistance to refugees from Syria; its strongest appeal is found in regions with few refugees—but in which unemployment and economic insecurity are highest.[16] In the United States, finally, Donald Trump introduced his successful candidacy for president by referring to Mexican migrants as users of drugs, criminals, and rapists.[17]

All this should be familiar to those of us who have lived through the past few years. What I want to note, here, is that there are two related political trends that emerge from these ideas, both of which should give us reason for concern. The first is the rise of authoritarianism as a viable option in political life. Right-wing populists have been so successful in portraying democracy as corrupt that there is an increased willingness to consider abandoning the democratic project. Robert Stefan Foa and Yascha Mounk have noted a radical difference in how different age cohorts in the United States view the necessity of democratic governance. Those people born before the end of World War II placed a high value on the preservation of democracy; 72 percent of them rated the importance of living in a democracy as a 10—the highest value available. For those born since 1980, in contrast, only 30 percent rated democracy this highly.[18]

[13] Thomas Piketty, *Capital in the Twenty-First Century* (Harvard University Press, 2013).

[14] David Coleman, "Immigration and Ethnic Change in Low-Fertility Countries: A Third Demographic Transition," *Population and Development Review* 32 (2006), 401–446.

[15] Paul Hockenos, "Inside Hungary's Anti-Semitic Right-Wing," *PRI*, June 1, 2010. Available at https://www.pri.org/stories/2010-06-01/inside-hungarys-anti-semitic-right-wing.

[16] Jefferson Chase, "AfD Populists Milk Anti-refugee Anger in German Region with Few Asylum Seekers," *Deutsche Welt*, August 16, 2017. Available at http://www.dw.com/en/afd-populists-milk-anti-refugee-anger-in-german-region-with-few-asylum-seekers/a-39876990.

[17] A transcript of his speech is available at http://time.com/3923128/donald-trump-announcement-speech/.

[18] Robert Stefan Foa and Yascha Mounk, "The Danger of Deconsolidation," *Journal of Democracy* 27 (2016), 5–17.

Support for antidemocratic and authoritarian ideals, in contrast, has begun to rise among all age ranges. In 1995, just one in sixteen American believed that a military takeover of the United States would be a good thing; that has now risen to one in six.[19]

The second trend that should give us pause is the increased possibility—given this willingness to consider radical challenges to democratic governance—of some significant degree of civil warfare or insurrection. If democracy depends upon the voluntary compliance of a great many people—and evidence suggests it does[20]—then the decreased importance placed upon democratic self-government might tend to lay the groundwork for more violent sorts of challenge to current political institutions. In March 2016, *Foreign Policy* magazine asked a set of experts to evaluate the chances of a new American civil war. The consensus was 35 percent.[21]

3. John Rawls and the Russian Troll Farm

These facts above are undoubtedly worrying; one might, though, about why they're relevant to our analysis of Rawls's Law of Peoples. There are, I think, two reasons to think there might be some connection. The first is that they indicate that there might be something wrong with Rawls's assumptions about the stability of a well-ordered liberal society. Rawls assumes that a society whose institutions are reasonable and just stands no serious risk of devolution into falling into tyranny:

> I shall also assume that, if we grow up under a framework of reasonable and just political and social institutions, we shall affirm those institutions when we in turn come of age, and they will endure over time. In this context, to say that human nature is good is to say that citizens who grow up under reasonable and just institutions—institutions that satisfy any of a family of reasonable liberal political conceptions of justice—will affirm those institutions and act to make sure their social world endures.[22]

The preceding facts might indicate that this assumption is, at the very least, questionable; and this, in turn, opens up the possibility that a plausible Law of

[19] Foa and Mounk, "The Danger of Deconsolidation," 12.

[20] I have in mind here the work of Gene Sharp. See Gene Sharp, *How Nonviolent Struggle Works* (Albert Einstein Institution, 2013).

[21] This result is discussed in Robin Wright, "Is America Headed for a New Kind of Civil War?," *New Yorker*, August 14, 2017.

[22] Rawls, *The Law of Peoples*, 7.

Peoples might want to keep an eye out for the possibility of democracy failing from within.

The second reason we might connect current facts to Rawls's analysis has to do with the multiplicity of ways in which states might affect the internal politics of other states. On Rawls's account, international wrongdoing takes coercive intolerance as the central image of how states might wrong one another. Recent political events, however, have shown that states can do things to one another that are only poorly understood with reference to this image.

We can begin with this second reason. Rawls assumes that the hallmark of a reasonable society is its lack of aggressive aims. It refuses to use violence in the pursuit of state interests.[23] The centrality of violence recurs throughout Rawls's analysis of the foreign policy of a liberal state. Even when Rawls explicitly discusses the giving of incentives for democratization, he does so through the lens of coercion; liberal states must avoid providing incentives that "take on the appearance of being coercive."[24] Recent political interaction between Russia and the United States, however, has tended to involve political tools that are only imperfectly described as coercive. To take one central example: Russian troll farms—including the notorious Internet Research Agency—have sought to inflame divisions between Americans.[25] They have published inflammatory images and narratives through social media, which were subsequently republished by American political agents. The same agency spent up to $150,000 on Facebook ads intended to demonize such left-leaning groups as Black Lives Matter in the eyes of Republican voters.[26] What is more interesting, though, is that the same agency appears to have provided the *same services* to the protestors those Republicans were demonizing.[27] The point of these interventions appears to be nothing more than the simple creation of division and distrust among the American populace—with, presumably, benefits accruing to a geopolitical adversary of the United States. These interventions are hard to understood as coercive acts; they are, after all, acts of *speech*, even if the motives for that speech are hardly admirable. (Publishing an inflammatory meme still seems speech-like, even if barely so.) In order to adequately judge the moral permissibility of such acts, we would have to have a broader inquiry of the ways in which states are and are not permitted to act upon their own principles or interests abroad—and that is precisely what Rawls has not provided us.

[23] Rawls, *The Law of Peoples*, 64.

[24] Rawls, *The Law of Peoples*, 85.

[25] Adrian Chen, "The Agency," *New York Times*, June 2, 2015.

[26] Noor Al-Sibai, "Pro-Trump Russian Twitter Bots Promoted 'Divisive' Anti-BLM Narrative: Report," *Raw Story*, September 13, 2017. Available at https://www.rawstory.com/2017/09/pro-trump-russian-twitter-bots-promoted-divisive-anti-blm-narrative-report/.

[27] Shaun Walker, "Russian Troll Factory Paid US Activists to Help Fund Protests during Election," *The Guardian*, October 17, 2017.

Ideas similar to these have already been noticed by James Nickel.[28] Nickel argues that human rights norms are primarily defended not through coercive intervention, but through more subtle forms of social normativity and shame—through, as Nickel puts it, *jawboning* about human rights. Rawls's Law of Peoples, however, gives us very little insight into what forms of jawboning are morally permissible. What I want to add to this conversation is that we might worry, too, about forms of speech—if the Russian trolls can be understood in this way—that are not intended to promote human rights, but mere social division. I believe we stand in need of this sort of inquiry; the tools deployed by Russian agents during the last American election are likely to be used elsewhere, in future elections, and they are likely to become more sophisticated and complex. I further believe that not *all* forms of speech about the politics of other societies are morally prohibited. Take, for instance, the National Endowment for Democracy, which is funded by the US government with the express purpose of fostering democracy abroad. It amplifies the voices of democratic agents abroad by providing them with training, forums in which to publish, and publicizing their work.[29] While doubtless an organization like the NED *could* perform actions that violate the political rights of other countries— as countries like Venezuela have claimed it is doing[30]—I want to say that there is nothing in principle wrong with *this* sort of intervention. I also want to say that there is something morally wrong with the Russian use of troll farms to weaken what remains of American political solidarity. The problem, of course, is that we have no particularly good theory of how these two conclusions might be grounded, or why they are compatible. The more specific problem, further, is that there seem to be very few resources in Rawls's Law of Peoples with which to even begin an analysis of this sort of intervention.

With that, we can return to the first, and more central, problem: Rawls's unwarranted assumption about stability. The Law of Peoples assumes that a liberal state will stay liberal. The central problem for international justice is preventing those liberal states from coercively insisting that other states join them in liberalism. A people, says Rawls, is taken to have common sympathies and a particular moral character; these facts are simply presented as part of the concept of a people.[31] The facts presented in this chapter, however, show us that these things are fragile. A people can, under pressure, begin to loosen its grip both on its sympathies and on its moral principles. After the election of Donald Trump,

---

[28] James W. Nickel, "Are Human Rights Mainly Implemented by Intervention?," in *Rawls's Law of Peoples: A Realistic Utopia?*, ed. Rex Martin and David A. Reidy (Blackwell, 2006).
[29] See the NED's website at www.ned.org.
[30] Eva Golinder, "The Dirty Hand of the National Endowment for Democracy in Venezuela," *Counterpunch*, April 25, 2014.
[31] Rawls, *The Law of Peoples*, 24–25.

the words of Richard Rorty began to be widely circulated on social media; they are worth re-examining in this context:

> Members of labor unions, and unorganized unskilled workers, will sooner or later realize that government is not even trying to prevent wages from sinking or to prevent jobs from being exported. Around the same time, they will realize that suburban white-collar workers—themselves desperately afraid of being downsized—are not going to let themselves be taxed to provide social benefits for anyone else. At that point, something will crack. The nonsuburban electorate will decide that the system has failed and start looking around for a strongman to vote for—someone willing to assure them that, once he is elected, the smug bureaucrats, tricky lawyers, overpaid bond salesmen, and postmodernist professors will no longer be calling the shots. . . . All the resentment which badly educated Americans feel about having their manners dictated to them by college graduates will find an outlet.[32]

These words are shockingly prescient. What Rorty shows is that—to use Rawls's terms—the United States has begun to loosen its grip both on its common sympathies and on its moral nature. What I want to note, though, is that this sort of democratic decay is not inevitable. While there is no single policy or legal tool that might have by itself prevented this retreat into right-wing populism, the decay of the constitutional ideal might have been *slowed* by a set of international norms more willing to insist upon that ideal as a value worth pressing for. Rawls assumed that the liberal state was stable, simply in virtue of its liberalism. This assumption, however, has made it more difficult for us acknowledge, and to counteract, the very real risk of democratic decay. Every theory must make simplifying assumptions; a theory cannot avoid being less complex than the phenomenon it models. Where the theory assumes away a morally significant part of that phenomenon, though, it fails to provide morally rightful advice, and that, I think, is what has happened to Rawls's Law of Peoples.

One response to these worries, of course, is to insist that Rawls's own Law of Peoples can deal with them. Rawls does, after all, assert that we have a duty to help other countries in becoming well ordered; if countries fall into disarray, the other countries in the world must seek to help them return to the path of order. Why could we not use these ideas, to show that actions such as those of the Russian trolls are already contrary to the Law of Peoples?[33]

---

[32] Richard Rorty, *Achieving Our Country: Leftist Thought in Twentieth-Century America* (Harvard University Press, 1998), 89–90.
[33] I am grateful to Jon Mandle and to Sarah Roberts-Cady for urging me to be more explicit in my response to these worries.

There are, I think, two obstacles that stand in the way of this rejoinder. The first is that Rawls nowhere makes it impermissible for a liberal people to speak in favor of liberalism. They cannot coerce a decent hierarchical society into becoming liberal; but they are not forbidden from using words that speak in favor of liberalism. The same, though, seems true of the decent hierarchical society. If a country uses speech *against* liberal democracy, it does not thereby violate the Law of Peoples any more than it would by speaking in *favor* of liberal democracy. To the extent that the speech acts of the Russian trolls are intended simply as discursive contributions to the question of how a state ought to order itself, it is hard to think that they are forbidden by the Law of Peoples itself. If the Russian trolls were to describe themselves as conceptual artists, whose online arguments were intended to demonstrate the futility of democratic deliberation, we might see how difficult it would be to regard their acts as simply a sort of coercive violence done against the just state. The acts are, for better or for worse, *arguments*, even if done for cynical and base motives, and arguments are imperfectly analogized to bombs and guns.

It is tempting, of course, to say that some words might be very much like bombs in their effects. This leads to the second obstacle to the Rawlsian response. There is no sharp line between speech designed to simply destroy a political community and speech designed to make that political community less unified and effective in its foreign policy. Even if we were able to say that some forms of speech are the moral equivalent of coercive violence—if we were to say that the intention of that speech was to transform a well-ordered society into an authoritarian one—we would still have to face up to the fact that much of what we're worried about in regard to the Russian trolls isn't that sort of speech at all. Instead, it's speech that makes it more difficult for the people of the United States to work together, in a spirit of mutual trust and respect. If that is what the Russian trolls are doing, then it's hard to think that they're doing something that's rightly condemned by the Law of Peoples as it stands. The mere fact that my speech makes politics more difficult, after all, is not enough for us to think that my speech is rightly controlled by law. If a political philosopher publishes a book whose net effect is to reduce the extent to which people in her society trust one another, I do not think we must rightly regard that political philosopher as having violated the duty to promote just institutions. She has made an argument, and if the effects of that argument are bad, she nonetheless has not made herself a traitor by publishing that argument. The same, though, seems true of foreign agents as much as domestic ones. Even if some words are bombs, we cannot regard all words with malign effects as bomb-like simply in virtue of those effects.

What, then, might Rawls have done instead? I believe a more satisfying Law of Peoples might have acknowledged both of these worries. Rawls might have built a Law of Peoples that did so—or so I will claim, in the next section. For the moment, I will simply note that we might have wanted a political theory of international relations that enabled us to avoid these problems. It might have begun by acknowledging the moral significance of liberalism—taken here not as a shorthand for Western styles of democratic government, but as a moral theory of political right. It might have acknowledged a human right not simply to those minimal rights guaranteed by Rawls's own Law of Peoples, but to democratic governance broadly construed. (It is worth noting that, in this, the Democratic Law of Peoples would not be radical in its ambitions; an international human right to democratic governance has been taken to exist under international law since before Rawls's book was published.)[34] This vision might have taken both democracy and constitutionalism to be essential aspects of members in good standing of the society of peoples, as Rawls would have it. It might therefore expect sullenness and resentment to be a part of politics, but it would weigh these facts against the benefits for those lives lived against a backdrop of human freedom. Besides which, we might note, this sullenness and resentment is accepted within Rawls's system when expressed by the benevolent absolutisms of the world. We accept their sullenness, seek to mollify it as best we can, but nonetheless exclude the absolutist from membership in the society of peoples. It is hard to see why we couldn't do the same for the *merely* illiberal, as well.

This extension of the Law of Peoples, finally, would also have to give us guidance about what sorts of things states can and cannot do to one another in the name of pursuing justice (and, for that matter, self-interest). I cannot, in this context, give any great detail about what that would entail. I believe it might have to make a distinction between speech acts designed to serve as contributions to an internal debate about politics, and speech acts designed to make that debate difficult or impossible. A state that sought to add particular voices or ideas to a foreign democratic discussion might thereby be right to do so. If a state sought to *exclude* voices, or to use deception in order to ensure a particular policy outcome, or—as in the case of the Russian troll farm—simply to make the debate more vicious, we would likely judge it more harshly. I cannot provide much more than these rather unsatisfying conclusions. I only want to note that what we need here is not something that Rawls's own writing can help us achieve.

4. A Democratic Law of Peoples

In what remains of this chapter, I want to note the existence of a path not taken. I believe that Rawls has within his overall theory the tools with which to defend a

---

[34] Thomas M. Franck, "The Emerging Right to Democratic Governance," *American Journal of International Law* 86 (1992), 46–91.

more robust Law of Peoples—one in which liberal democratic norms, including both democratic procedures and constitutional rights sufficient to stand against undemocratic pressures—are taken as universally appropriate standards for international pressure and agency. For want of a better term, I will refer to this as the Democratic Law of Peoples, although the word "democracy" here should be understood to include both democratic procedures and constitutional norms. Rawls, of course, did not believe that he could extend his own domestic liberal commitments to the international realm. Doing so, he felt, would be intolerant—it would insist upon liberalism's validity, in the face of reasonable diversity of political views. I think he could have applied political liberalism to the international realm in a different way, through the insistence upon liberal ideas as a common standard for mutual criticism and judgment.

Why, though, might we think this? To see why, note that there are two aspects of political liberalism in the domestic context. It is *political*, in that it relies upon ideas present in the public political culture, rather than grounding those ideas in a comprehensive doctrine; and it is a *liberalism*, in that the ideas taken to fit within the public political conception of justice are recognizably liberal, including such central liberal values as the equality of citizens before the state. Domestically, we get both of these as a package deal. The values present within the public political culture are liberal, so that we can achieve both stability and (liberal) justice through the use of those values. Internationally, however, we face a rather difficult choice. We can insist upon liberal values at the cost of refusing to extend membership in the Society of Peoples to a great many political societies. Instead, we could search for principles that could be shared by a wider variety of states and rely upon those to adjudicate our interactions—rather than upon our own idiosyncratic, liberal values. Rawls chose the latter. I think he might have done better to choose the former. Remember, after all, that Rawls is not proposing a world in which all, or even most, states will belong to the Society of Peoples. The benevolent absolutisms will still be subjected to pressures to become well ordered, and there is no standing demand to justify policy toward them with reference to reciprocally acceptable principles of justice. I think Rawls might have included the merely illiberal states within this category as well.

I have, elsewhere, tried to defend these conclusions.[35] I have argued, in particular, that we can restrain policy toward the benevolent and merely illiberal states with reference to epistemic and pragmatic limits on what we can expect foreign policy to achieve. Insisting upon liberalism as a universally appropriate standard for evaluation, in short, does not entail being deeply stupid in one's actions in defense of liberalism. I have noted, further, that Rawls accepted within his domestic

[35] Blake, *Justice and Foreign Policy*.

theory that actions might be rightly taken in an unjust society to *build* respect for the norms of liberal justice. The abolitionists, notably, worked in a fundamentally illiberal society, in which the ideals of equality were as weakly supported as they are in most modern tyrannies, and the work of these abolitionists, to build liberal societies out of illiberal ones, are lauded by Rawls.[36] I see no reason why we could not similarly laud work to build liberal societies abroad, today, through our foreign policy.

When I wrote *Justice and Foreign Policy*, though, I was primarily worried about the coherence of a liberal society's foreign policy. In contrast to Rawls, I was convinced that a liberal society could work for the constitutional ideal abroad without running into self-contradiction. It could, of course, get into trouble by working for that ideal in clumsy and violent ways, but that is an indictment of the means chosen, not the end to which those means were devoted. The past few years, though, have shown us what I take to be another reason to think that a Democratic Law of Peoples would have been an improvement over Rawls's own. We ought to be concerned not simply with liberal states violently imposing liberalism on others. We ought to be worried about liberal states persisting in their liberalism. A Democratic Law of Peoples might, in this context, have two distinct advantages. It might, in the first instance, provide us with resources to ground our moral reactions to the Russian troll farm discussed previously. An international ethical framework grounded in respect for the constitutional ideal might provide us with some ways of criticizing efforts to make foreign democracies less able to engage in the shared process of self-government. I am not confident of this conclusion. It remains to be seen exactly how the much purchase the Democratic Law of Peoples would provide us in judging particular sorts of international political speech. But it would, if nothing else, provide a start to the discussion, and it might help us differentiate between the Russian trolls and at least *some* of the actions undertaken by the National Endowment for Democracy.

The second advantage provided by the Democratic Law of Peoples, though, is perhaps more central. International law has a variety of functions, but one of the most important is to provide standards by which countries might call upon each other to account for their actions. Were these liberal ideas used to ground a robust institutional structure, in which deviations from democratic constitutionalism were taken as standing in need of justification or rectification, then we might be able to build some structures capable of halting the slide from democratic self-government to right-wing authoritarianism. The work of Jamie Mayerfeld is particularly salient on this point. Mayerfeld notes that obedience to human rights norms is achieved not simply through pious invocation of their importance but

---

[36] Rawls, *Political Liberalism*, 250–251.

through institutions that enable public accountability to those norms—thus the different degrees to which the United States and Europe deviated from norms against torture during the early twenty-first century.[37] European states had built a variety of institutional structures designed to insist upon compliance with human rights norms and to publicize and criticize violations of those norms; the United States did not. The United States, therefore, slid gradually into practices of torture, while the states of Europe resisted this slide much more effectively.

What I would argue, on a related note, is that a Democratic Law of Peoples would enable us to build international legal structures that could publicize deviations from democratic justice, criticize those who perpetrate injustice, and offer assistance in the process of building democratic accountability. We have traditionally thought of this sort of assistance as involving the Western democracies pressuring other states into compliance with liberal norms. It is increasingly important that the Western democracies need the pressure, too. Rawls's own Law of Peoples provides us with no framework from within which to build these structures. A Democratic Law of Peoples, though, would give us the normative basis to do just that. Respect for the constitutional ideal is, as we have seen, *fragile*. International law and international ethics cannot hope to halt the slide into authoritarianism by themselves. But they can do *something*; and a view of international justice on which they are precluded from trying is a view we have reason to reject.

The Democratic Law of Peoples would have required us to rethink how the Law of Peoples would deal with illiberal states. It would have required us to hold out the constitutional ideal as a framework from which criticism of those states might be made. It would express the hope that liberal states would remain liberal—and that the other states would eventually join them. Done well, it would not entail an expression of disrespect or humiliation toward the illiberal states, any more than Rawls's own Law of Peoples expresses that toward the benevolent absolutisms. It would, however, offer us some tools with which to speak back toward a process I take to be both widespread and deeply dangerous: the transition from the constitutional ideal to a right-wing populism antithetical to liberalism. Those of us who value the constitutional ideal have reason to insist upon it, both at home and abroad—and, in the end, for our own sakes as much as for those of foreign citizens.

I, like most political philosophers writing in the United States, grew up—philosophically speaking—with the thoughts and methods of John Rawls. I write, and think, in a terminology built largely by Rawls himself. I will likely continue to do philosophy within his shadow. The world, however, has become

---

[37] Jamie Mayerfeld, *The Promise of Human Rights* (University of Pennsylvania Press, 2016).

a new and dangerous place, in ways that I think require us to supplement or revise his own philosophical conclusions. We may be Rawlsians—I continue to so identify—but we should not rest easy with Rawls's own Law of Peoples. The world will continue to throw us new horrors and dangers, and we, in turn, must bring fresh new methods and concepts to our philosophical discussions about global justice.

20

Tolerating Decent Societies

A Defense of the Law of Peoples

Jon Mandle

One of the deepest and most distinctive aspects of Rawls's theory of justice is his rejection of teleological conceptions of justice, which he identifies as those in which "the good is defined independently from the right, and then the right is defined as that which maximizes the good."[1] Since he holds that the justice of an object or institution cannot be defined in terms of the instrumental contribution that it makes toward maximizing or achieving some independent and external goal, the criterion of justice instead must be understood as depending on the nature of the object or institution itself. More generally, Rawls holds, "The correct regulative principle for anything depends on the nature of that thing."[2] So it should come as no surprise that Rawls holds that different standards of justice are appropriate for different objects of evaluation. In *A Theory of Justice*, his primary aim is to develop principles for one particular object, the basic structure of society, and he warns: "There is no reason to suppose ahead of time that the principles satisfactory for the basic structure hold for all cases.... The conditions for the law of nations may require different principles arrived at in a somewhat different way."[3] He also suggests a way to identify these "different principles": by "extend[ing] the interpretation of the original position and think[ing] of the parties as representatives of different nations who must choose together the fundamental principles to adjudicate conflicting claims among states."[4]

In the vast secondary literature on *A Theory of Justice*, this brief comment was largely ignored, and when Rawls eventually addressed the issue in more depth, there was widespread disappointment that his principles of international relations did not match his principles of domestic justice. Although Rawls claims that "the Law of Peoples is developed within political liberalism and is an extension of a liberal conception of justice for a domestic regime to a Society of

---

[1] John Rawls, *A Theory of Justice*, rev. ed. (Harvard University Press, 1999), 21–22.
[2] Rawls, *A Theory of Justice*, 25, cf. 352.
[3] Rawls, *A Theory of Justice*, 7.
[4] Rawls, *A Theory of Justice*, 331.

Jon Mandle, *Tolerating Decent Societies* In: *John Rawls*. Edited by: Jon Mandle and Sarah Roberts-Cady, Oxford University Press (2020). © Oxford University Press. DOI: 10.1093/oso/9780190859213.003.0031.

Peoples,"[5] this extension involves, among other things, a broadened conception of toleration. Rawls advocates principled toleration not only of imperfect liberal democracies, but also of nonliberal societies that he calls "decent," or more specifically "decent hierarchical peoples."[6] There are principled limits to this toleration, however, as it is not to be extended to those that he calls "outlaw states." But cosmopolitan critics, who generally hold that the same principles of justice that apply domestically ought also to be applied globally, objected that, in the words of Charles Beitz, Rawls was "excessively deferential to societies with discriminatory or undemocratic institutions."[7] Darrel Moellendorf stated the point plainly: "To be 'tolerant' of such regimes is akin to being 'tolerant' of unjust actions or oppressive cultural practices. In short, there are no good reasons for being so."[8] To many critics, it simply appeared inconsistent to affirm one set of principles for the basic structure of a society and different principles for relations among societies globally. Kok-Chor Tan, for example, argued that Rawls was "blatantly inconsistent,"[9] and Thomas Pogge held that the two parts of Rawls's theory were "incoherent."[10]

We will discuss subsequently how Rawls draws the line between decent hierarchical peoples and outlaw states, and why he thinks the former but not the latter should be tolerated. First, however, let us focus on what this toleration amounts to. Rawls uses the term "Society of Peoples" to describe "all those peoples who follow the ideals and principles of the Law of Peoples in their mutual relations."[11] The "Law of Peoples," in turn, consists in the "particular principles for regulating the mutual political relations between peoples."[12] These are principles designed to regulate such things as conduct in (just) war and the duty of assistance, as well as the "forming and regulating federations (associations) of peoples, and standards of fairness for trade and other cooperative institutions."[13] In addition to affirming these principles, the Society of Peoples has its own public reason, which is the framework within which members of the Society of Peoples debate and work out the terms of their political relationships.[14] This public reason is distinct from the public reason of particular liberal peoples. The overarching principle of the Law of Peoples that will guide its public reason is that "Peoples are

---

5 John Rawls, *The Law of Peoples* (Harvard University Press, 1999), 9.
6 Rawls uses "peoples" to distinguish sharply from "states" as they have figured in traditional international relations (*The Law of Peoples*, 25–26). Like states, however, peoples "have their own internal governments" (*The Law of Peoples*, 3).
7 Charles Beitz, "Rawls's Law of Peoples," *Ethics* 110 (2000), 687.
8 Darrel Moellendorf, *Cosmopolitan Justice* (Westview, 2002), 28.
9 Kok-Chor Tan, "Liberal Toleration in Rawls's Law of Peoples," *Ethics* 108 (1998), 283.
10 Thomas Pogge, "The Incoherence between Rawls's Theories of Justice," *Fordham Law Review* 72 (2004), 1754.
11 Rawls, *The Law of Peoples*, 3.
12 Rawls, *The Law of Peoples*, 3 n. 1.
13 Rawls, *The Law of Peoples*, 38.
14 Rawls, *The Law of Peoples*, 55.

free and independent, and their freedom and independence are to be respected by other peoples."[15] Because of their commitment to this principle, it is "inevitable that, if member peoples employ public reason in their dealings with one another, toleration must follow."[16]

The public reason of the Society of Peoples is predicated on equal respect for all member societies as "free and independent" peoples. This means that the public reason of the Society of Peoples must not assume the superiority of any one member society over another. To repeat, for reasons that we will see, Rawls holds that nonliberal but decent hierarchical peoples (but not outlaw states) are to be admitted into the Society of Peoples when they accept the Law of Peoples. So for purposes of public deliberation within the Society of Peoples concerning the political relations among members, liberal societies cannot assume the superiority of liberal principles of justice. On the other hand, Rawls defends liberal principles of justice for domestic application to the basic structure of society, and this is where some critics see an inconsistency. If liberal principles are correct, why are they excluded from the public reason of the Society of Peoples?

To resolve this apparent conflict, it will be helpful to consider the similarities and differences between toleration in the Society of Peoples and toleration within a liberal democracy. Rawls makes this analogy,[17] but it is important to remember that this is only an analogy and that the *content* of toleration will not be the same. Briefly consider, then, his account of public reason in the domestic case. Rawls holds that in a just society, individuals will hold a variety of reasonable comprehensive doctrines. Despite their religious, philosophical, and moral disagreements, citizens overlap with one another in their reliance on public reason as the framework for deliberation over the basic terms of their political relations and how they will collectively "exercise final political and coercive power over one another in enacting laws and in amending their constitution."[18] And they recognize the "duty of civility": the moral requirement that citizens be "able to explain to one another on those fundamental questions how the principles and policies they advocate and vote for can be supported by the political values of public reason."[19] Because reasonable citizens do not share the same comprehensive doctrine, the duty of civility requires that when the design of the basic structure and the basic political relationship among citizens is at stake, they do not rely on arguments that can only be based on their own particular comprehensive doctrine.[20] It is crucial to recognize that this does not require any skepticism or

---

[15] Rawls, *The Law of Peoples*, 37.
[16] Rawls, *The Law of Peoples*, 19.
[17] Rawls, *The Law of Peoples*, 55.
[18] John Rawls, *Political Liberalism*, expanded ed. (Columbia University Press, 2005), 214.
[19] Rawls, *Political Liberalism*, 217.
[20] According to Rawls's "wide view of public reason," reasonable comprehensive doctrines "may be introduced in public reason at any time, provided that in due course public reasons, given by

lack of commitment on the part of citizens regarding the truth or correctness of their own particular comprehensive doctrine. In contexts where the basic political relationship among citizens is not at stake, citizens are free to guide their conduct according to their comprehensive doctrine, to argue from within its framework, and to advocate on its behalf. What reasonable citizens recognize, however, is that "in discussions of coercive norms to be enacted in the form of legitimate law for a democratic people"[21] they have a moral duty to be able to offer justifications in terms that all reasonable citizens could accept despite their different comprehensive doctrines. Thus, Rawls holds that reasonable citizens can both affirm the truth or correctness of their particular comprehensive doctrine and also that it would be inappropriate to resolve matters of basic political justice based on arguments that can be drawn only from some single comprehensive doctrine—even a true one.

Now consider the structure of toleration in the Society of Peoples. First, note that even in the context of discussing the Law of Peoples, Rawls holds that liberal principles of justice are the most reasonable for assessing the institutions of the basic structure of society. He could not be more explicit that he believes that "a liberal constitutional democracy is, in fact, superior to other forms of society."[22] So why shouldn't liberal principles of justice be included in the public reason of the Society of Peoples? Why not argue as follows: "Nonliberal societies fail to treat persons who possess all the powers of reason, intellect, and moral feeling as truly free and equal, and *therefore* . . . nonliberal societies are always properly subject to some form of sanction—political, economic, or even military—depending on the case."[23] Rawls *accepts* the premise (or antecedent) of this argument. Nonliberal societies are guided by principles that are less just than those that liberal democratic societies accept. Yet he holds that this fact alone does not justify—does not even defeasibly justify—coercive action against them or the imposition of international institutions that they could not accept given their common good conception of justice. The public reason of the Society of Peoples is concerned with determining the political relations and shared institutions among member societies, just as the public reason of a particular society is concerned with justifying the institutions of the basic structure of society that mediate the political relations among citizens within a society. So on the assumption that decent hierarchical peoples can be fully equal members of the Society of

a reasonable political conception, are presented sufficient to support whatever the comprehensive doctrines are introduced to support" (*Political Liberalism*, xlix-l). The details of this "proviso" do not affect the point that I am making.

21 Rawls, *Political Liberalism*, 442.
22 Rawls, *The Law of Peoples*, 62.
23 Rawls, *The Law of Peoples*, 60.

Peoples, the superiority of liberal principles of (domestic) justice is irrelevant to, and indeed must be excluded from, the deliberations within the Society of Peoples. On the other hand, when the coercive norms that guide the political relation among societies are not at stake—that is, outside of the deliberations of the Society of Peoples—Rawls holds that "critical objections, based either on political liberalism, or on comprehensive doctrines, both religious and nonreligious, will continue concerning this and all other matters. Raising these objections is the right of liberal peoples and is fully consistent with the liberties and integrity of decent hierarchical societies."[24]

So the analogy is as follows. In the domestic case, each individual can fully affirm a particular comprehensive doctrine; hold that others who reject it are mistaken; and believe that a proper justification of political power among citizens should not be dependent on one's own particular doctrine, but only on what is shared by other reasonable, although perhaps mistaken, citizens. In the Society of Peoples, each society can fully affirm a particular conception of justice; hold that others that reject it are mistaken; and believe that a proper justification of political power among peoples should not depend on the society's own particular conception, but only on what is shared by other liberal or decent, although perhaps mistaken, peoples. In both cases, we can make a negative moral judgment concerning another individual or society. In both cases, there is freedom (limited only by pragmatic considerations of efficacy) to criticize and attempt to convince the other of the error of their ways. Yet, in both cases, there are principled reasons to tolerate those who are (taken to be) mistaken. Here, toleration means not only not coercing, but also not arguing for shared political decisions on the basis of doctrines that others do not accept (even if they are taken to be mistaken in not doing so). In both cases, there is a morally significant line drawn between the kinds of moral errors for which persuasion is the appropriate and permissible response and those for which the use of force is justified. But the line is drawn at different places. In the domestic case, toleration within the operation of public reason extends to all *reasonable* citizens (all of whom are committed to liberal democratic political principles, even if not comprehensive liberalism), but the Society of Peoples extends the line to the more inclusive standard of *decent* peoples. As Rawls puts it: "I think of decency as a normative idea of the same kind as reasonableness, though weaker (that is, it covers less than reasonableness does)."[25]

Why is the line drawn differently? Some critics allege that Rawls expands the limit of toleration in an effort to accommodate the greater diversity globally compared to the more limited domestic diversity. But the structure of *The Law of Peoples* tells against this interpretation. Rawls first considers which principles would be chosen for a Society of Peoples consisting only of liberal democracies. He then argues that decent hierarchical peoples would be able to accept those same principles. There is no change in the principles to accommodate decent societies.[26] There is a similar problem with what many people take to be the "official" argument for including decent societies in the Society of Peoples. Rawls claims that excluding decent societies ("if there are such") "may wound the self-respect of decent nonliberal peoples as peoples . . . and may lead to great bitterness and resentment."[27] The suggestion, perhaps, is that any attempt to force decent societies to accept liberal principles, or even to insist on the use of liberal principles in the Society of Peoples, would be likely to backfire and nonliberal societies would become even less just. This argument cannot be lightly dismissed, and history certainly suggests countless examples of wars triggered by perceived disrespect (real or imagined) and wounded self-respect, but this cannot be sufficient to determine the principled limits of inclusion in the Society of Peoples. The most this argument could give liberal societies is a pragmatic reason to accommodate those societies where they judge their efforts unlikely to be effective. It invites us to judge whether any particular effort to pressure a decent society to become more liberal is likely to be successful. No wonder Pogge asks, "Is Rawls's insistence, that the rules of good conduct for peoples must be hospitable to decent societies, a matter of principle or is this insistence contingent on historical facts, such as the existence and numerical strength of decent societies?"[28]

To identify a principled basis for toleration, we need to identify an important value that decent societies exemplify and that can ground toleration. Fortunately, Rawls tells us exactly what value that is: "Self-determination, duly constrained by appropriate conditions, is an important good for a people. . . . Decent societies should have the opportunity to decide their future for themselves."[29] There is a sense in which self-determination is the basis for all toleration. In the domestic case, we tolerate (what we take to be) mistaken comprehensive doctrines because we value the autonomy of citizens. But it is exactly here that the analogy between the two cases breaks down because the nature of the two objects—an individual citizen and a society—differ. Unlike an individual, a society requires political institutions in order to exercise deliberate, explicit, collective self-determination. But not all political structures can properly be described as exemplifying a society's self-determination. A tyrannical ruler may be able to impose his will on his population, but it would mendacious to say that such a society is engaged

---

[26] On analogy with the domestic case, this would make the theory "political in the wrong way" (*Political Liberalism*, 39–40).

[27] Rawls, *The Law of Peoples*, 61.

[28] Pogge, "Incoherence between Rawls's Theories," 1757.

[29] Rawls, *The Law of Peoples*, 85.

in collective self-determination. Its actions are the result of a single individual's imposition on all. This is true of a benevolent absolutism, as well, so Rawls holds that such societies are also not well ordered. But collective decisions need not be unanimous, either. Between the extremes of absolutism and a requirement of complete unanimity we can identify a threshold for political procedures that are properly described as forms of collective self-determination. A political procedure that meets this threshold is *legitimate*.[30] The claim, then, is that there is a strong presumption that a society that has a legitimate political structure is entitled to engage in self-determination, free from external coercion.

Our key question, therefore, is whether decent societies meet this requirement of legitimacy, or are only liberal democracies properly described as politically self-determining? Rawls's criteria for decent hierarchical peoples are designed precisely to answer this question. There are three requirements that a society's domestic political institutions must meet in order to count as decent. First, its "system of law . . . secures for all members of the people what have come to be called human rights."[31] A society that fails to secure (or worse, actively violates) the human rights of its members cannot properly be described as legitimate, nor can its political mechanism properly be described as one that makes collective decisions of all. It is no more than a tyranny of the powerful over the weak. Second, the "system of law must be such as to impose *bona fide* moral duties and obligations (distinct from human rights) on all persons within the people's territory."[32] This does not imply a particularly strong political obligation to obey the law, but a political system that was unable to generate *any* additional moral demands would, once again, simply be an exercise of power of some over others. As Rawls states, "Laws supported merely by force are grounds for rebellion and resistance."[33] Third, "There must be a sincere and not unreasonable belief on the part of judges and other officials who administer the legal system that the law is indeed guided by a common good idea of justice."[34] Part of securing the reasonable belief that officials are guided by their stated conception of justice is that they show "their good faith and willingness to defend publicly society's injunctions as justified by law."[35] As part of this requirement, in turn, "Representatives can raise

---

[30] This is my terminology, not Rawls's, and departs from his "liberal principle of legitimacy" in ways that I believe are justified, but that I cannot discuss here. See Rawls, *Political Liberalism*, 136–137. On the other hand, in his original 1993 article, "The Law of Peoples," he held that a nonliberal society was to be tolerated as long as it was "peaceful and not expansionist" and "its legal system satisfies certain requisite conditions of *legitimacy* in the eyes of its own people; and, as a consequence of this, it honors basic human rights" (my emphasis). This was the precursor to the idea of a "decent" society. (John Rawls, "The Law of Peoples" (1993), in *Collected Papers*, ed. Samuel Freeman (Harvard University Press, 1999), 530)

[31] Rawls, *The Law of Peoples*, 65.

[32] Rawls, *The Law of Peoples*, 65–66.

[33] Rawls, *The Law of Peoples*, 66.

[34] Rawls, *The Law of Peoples*, 66.

[35] Rawls, *The Law of Peoples*, 67.

their objections to government policies, and members of the government can express their replies, which the government is required to do. Dissent is respected in the sense that a reply is due that spells out how the government thinks it can both reasonably interpret its policies in line with its common good idea of justice and impose duties and obligations on all members of the society."[36] Without an opportunity for at least some kind of good-faith public deliberation, there is no collective self-determination.

Although meeting these criteria certainly seems necessary to properly describe a political structure as legitimate and the society as self-determining, many critics have argued that they are not sufficient and that a democratic form of government (or the protection of other distinctively liberal rights) is also necessary. "Democracy" can mean many things, but we will follow Rawls's use of the term in *A Theory of Justice* and understand it to refer to the principle that political justice requires honoring "the precept one elector one vote . . . as far as possible."[37] In a decent hierarchical society, individuals do not have "equal representation (according to the maxim: one citizen, one vote),"[38] so it is not a democracy. And yet "Each person belongs to a group represented by a body in the consultation hierarchy."[39] Furthermore, "Persons as members of associations, corporations, and estates have the right at some point in the procedure of consultation (often at the stage of selecting a group's representatives) to express political dissent, and the government has an obligation to take a group's dissent seriously and to give a conscientious reply."[40]

Thomas Christiano argues that "a decent consultation hierarchy is not impossible; it is just very unlikely. The normal operation of a consultation hierarchy is incompatible with the protection of the basic human rights involved with decency."[41] Rawls strikingly does not argue against this instrumental claim:

> It should be noted here that some writers maintain that full democratic and liberal rights are necessary to prevent violations of human rights. This is stated as an empirical fact supported by historical experience. I do not argue against this contention, and indeed it may be true. But my remarks about a decent hierarchical society are conceptual. I ask, that is, whether we can imagine such a society; and, should it exist, whether we would judge that it should be tolerated politically.[42]

[36] Rawls, *The Law of Peoples*, 78.
[37] Rawls, *A Theory of Justice*, 195; cf. Rawls, *Political Liberalism*, 361.
[38] Rawls, *The Law of Peoples*, 71.
[39] Rawls, *The Law of Peoples*, 71–72.
[40] Rawls, *The Law of Peoples*, 72.
[41] Thomas Christiano, "An Instrumental Argument for a Human Right to Democracy," *Philosophy and Public Affairs* 39 (2011), 157.
[42] Rawls, *The Law of Peoples*, 75 n. 16.

What Rawls here calls a "conceptual" question corresponds to how, in *A Theory of Justice*, he suggests we think about institutions. There, he writes that we may think about institutions either "first, as an abstract object, that is, as a possible form of conduct expressed by a system of rules; [or] second, as the realization in the thought and conduct of certain persons at a certain time and place of the actions specified by these rules."[43] In developing principles of justice in ideal theory, Rawls relies on the former model. When we ask whether a society is a liberal democracy or a decent hierarchical society, in the first instance, we are asking something about the ideals that it affirms as found in, for example, its basic laws or constitution and in the terms with which it debates and makes political decisions. But when we ask about the legitimacy (or justice) of a particular society, we are primarily asking a question about that society's actual practice, not about the ideal of its type. Of course, if a society departs in practice too far from its professed ideals we would question its commitment to them. Still, there must be some room to be able to say that a society is an imperfect realization of its ideal type.

The question we must consider is whether an actual decent hierarchical society would be rendered illegitimate simply because of the (nonliberal) ideals that it affirms. To make the comparison vivid, consider an example of an actual, imperfect liberal democracy: the United States.[44] To a large degree, it affirms liberal democratic ideals. Its Constitution requires that all citizens receive "equal protection of the laws" and guarantees a variety of basic rights such as freedom of speech and religion. Political leaders are elected at regular intervals and public deliberation is (at least formally) conducted on the assumption of equal citizenship. But it achieves these ideals imperfectly: it diverges significantly from the ideal of one person, one vote;[45] there is at best only an extremely weak commitment to even a minimal share of resources;[46] the physical integrity of the majority of citizens is not adequately protected;[47] racial discrimination and inequality are widespread;[48] there is virtually no effort to insulate the political process from the

---

[43] Rawls, *A Theory of Justice*, 48.

[44] Nothing hangs on the details of this particular choice.

[45] The Senate, in particular, diverges dramatically from this ideal, and reliance on the Electoral College resulted in the presidential elections of 2000 and 2016 being won by candidates who received fewer popular votes than an opponent. See https://www.theatlantic.com/national/archive/2013/04/senate-filibusters-vs-represented-population/316110/.

[46] See Kathryn J. Edin and H. Luke Shaefer, *$2.00 a Day: Living on Almost Nothing in America* (Houghton Mifflin Harcourt, 2015); and Christopher Jencks, "Why the Very Poor Have Become Poorer," *New York Review of Books*, June 9, 2016, http://www.nybooks.com/articles/2016/06/09/why-the-very-poor-have-become-poorer/.

[47] In 2011, "An exhaustive government survey of rape and domestic violence" found that "nearly one in five women surveyed said they had been raped or had experienced an attempted rape at some point, and one in four reported having been beaten by an intimate partner." http://www.nytimes.com/2011/12/15/health/nearly-1-in-5-women-in-us-survey-report-sexual-assault.html.

[48] In *The Imperative of Integration* (Princeton University Press, 2010), Elizabeth Anderson documents extensive racial inequality in the United States and argues that segregation is the

"curse of money;"[49] and the list could go on. And yet I believe that despite these significant injustices, the United States still maintains a legitimate political structure. This is not uncontroversial, of course, and may change in the future, but because of this, I believe it would be unjust, and not simply counterproductive, for other societies to attempt to force the United States to address these significant domestic injustices, although criticism is always permissible.[50]

Now compare a society that in practice comes close to the ideal that Rawls specifies for a decent hierarchical society. It respects human rights and it guarantees basic needs—food and water, education, and physical security, for example. Again, assume these are not merely formal commitments but are actually achieved to a large degree. When it comes to making political decisions, the interests of all individuals are sincerely considered, and individuals are free to challenge decisions and are owed a good-faith reply in terms of the society's common good conception of justice. On the other hand, individuals do not directly elect their representatives on the basis of the one person, one vote ideal. Rather, they are represented through the group to which they belong. To repeat one final time, Rawls holds that this arrangement, even in the ideal, would not be just. Nonetheless, I submit that such a society would be at least as self-determining and legitimate as the United States currently is. Respecting the value of self-determination means tolerating decent hierarchical peoples (if any exist) that do not depart too far from their own, nonliberal ideal.

I have argued that decent hierarchical peoples have a structure that allows them to realize the value of self-determination despite their injustices. This, I have claimed, grounds liberal democracies' toleration of them and their possible inclusion in the Society of Peoples. But I have not explicitly addressed why self-determination is a weighty enough value to override the duty to correct injustices. Instead, I have pointed to the interplay between ideal and actual institutions to suggest that toleration of highly imperfect liberal democracies ought to carry with it toleration of (at least) less-imperfect decent societies.

"lynchpin" of this inequality. A brief sampling: "One quarter of blacks are poor compared to 8% of non-Hispanic whites, a 3:1 poverty ratio that has persisted since the 1960s. . . . The median black household income is two-thirds that of the median white household, a ratio that has widened since 1967 . . . the median net worth of blacks was less than 10% of that of whites. . . . Black youth are almost twice as likely as white youth to have dropped out of school. . . . Black men are 10.9 times as likely as white men to die of homicide" (23–24, citations omitted).

[49] In *A Theory of Justice*, Rawls argued that justice requires that "political parties are to be made independent from private economic interests by allotting them sufficient tax revenues to play their part in the constitutional scheme. . . . Historically one of the main defects of constitutional government has been the failure to insure the fair values of political liberty. The necessary corrective steps have not been taken, indeed, they never seem to have been seriously entertained" (198); cf. Rawls, *Political Liberalism*, 361, 363.

[50] I leave aside cases of human rights violations (such as the torture of prisoners) and aggressive wars.

I conclude with two observations. First, not all liberal democracies share the same conception of justice. This means that even if a liberal democratic society fully lives up to its own conception of justice, other liberal democracies will likely hold that it has some degree of injustice. If they value self-determination at all, therefore, liberal democracies will need to identify some threshold of injustice that they would be willing to tolerate among other liberal democracies. Put the other way around, they must decide when an injustice is severe enough to authorize the use of coercive force in their relations, even among societies that claim to affirm liberal principles. Rawls's answer is that this threshold is set precisely by the conjunction of respect for human rights and a legitimate political mechanism of self-determination. Second, although a decent hierarchical society is not fully just (according to a liberal conception of justice), it is not "fully unreasonable" either.[51] That is, despite their disagreements, liberal principles of justice and the common-good conception of justice of a decent society are not completely opposed and, in fact, overlap to a considerable extent. In particular, they agree in their opposition to the worst forms of injustice—tyranny and the violation of human rights. Rawls's conjecture—his hope—is that "once the gravest forms of political injustice are eliminated by following just (or at least decent) social policies and establishing just (or at least decent) basic institutions, these great evils [of human history] will eventually disappear."[52] Without diminishing the significant injustices of decent hierarchical societies, or, for that matter the injustices of imperfect liberal democracies, when a society secures human rights and has a legitimate political mechanism that involves genuine self-determination, it is "worthy of toleration"[53] and full inclusion as an equal in the Society of Peoples.

Acknowledgments

Thanks to Sarah Roberts-Cady, Matt Lister, and David Reidy.

---

[51] Rawls, *The Law of Peoples*, 74.
[52] Rawls, *The Law of Peoples*, 6–7.
[53] Rawls, *The Law of Peoples*, 68.

Index

For the benefit of digital users, indexed terms that span two pages (e.g., 52–53) may, on occasion, appear on only one of those pages.

Abbey, Ruth, 236, 271
abortion, 27–31, 43, 225, 242, 242n18, 293n30
 See also public reason; women, status of
Adams, Matthew, 73
affirmative action, 39, 41, 42, 57–58, 84
 See also race / racism
allocative justice, 64, 130, 154–56, 158, 159–60
 See also basic structure of society; difference principle; distributive justice; patterned principles (of distributive justice); primary goods; pure procedural justice
Anderson, Elizabeth, 81–82, 127–28, 129–30, 131, 144, 146, 152, 153–54, 379–80n48
animals, 30–32, 43, 166, 263
 See also citizen; environment; moral powers; political liberalism
Arneson, Richard, 69–70, 131
Arrell, Robbie, 20
autonomy, 47, 91–92, 152, 158, 253, 254, 257–58, 291, 293n30, 304–5, 349, 376
 See also basic rights and liberties; freedom; dependency; moral powers; political autonomy; property

Baehr, Amy, 219, 236
basic rights and liberties, 1–2, 26, 47–48, 85, 89–92, 95, 113, 114, 115, 118, 135, 164–65, 170–74, 176, 177, 178–79, 185, 208–9, 217, 225–26, 234, 239, 240, 242–45, 242n17, 243n19, 248, 249–50, 251–52, 256, 257–58, 260, 274, 276–77, 281–84, 289–91, 289n18, 289n19, 292, 378–80
 See also economic justice; freedom; freedom of speech / expression; human rights; political rights and liberties; priority rules; principles of justice; religion / religious liberty
basic structure of society, 1–2, 4–5, 28, 54, 91, 125–26, 135, 136n13, 137, 140n29, 154–56, 158, 159, 188, 227–30, 234, 246, 250, 258–62, 258n34, 265–66, 286–87, 289–90, 303–5, 320, 329–30, 337–38, 341, 342, 371–75

See also distributive justice, law / rule of law; political liberalism; principles of justice
Beitz, Charles, 71n27, 304–5, 311, 347, 352, 371–72
benevolent absolutism, 365–66, 367, 369, 376–77
 See also decent societies; Law of Peoples; outlaw regimes / states
Berkey, Brian, 271
Betz, Hans-George, 355
Bhandary, Asha, 205
Blake, Michael, 304–5, 311, 349, 349n25, 352, 354
Blythe, Mark, 188, 190, 191
Boettcher, James, 20, 35
Bonotti, Matteo, 18
Brake, Elizabeth, 259–60, 259n38
Brighouse, Harry and Ingrid Robeyns, 168
British Labour Party, 117
Brock, Gillian, 311, 329
Brooks, Thom and Martha Nussbaum, 11
Buchanan, Allen, 311, 350–52
burdened societies / peoples. *See* duty of assistance; humanitarian assistance; Law of Peoples
burdens of judgment, 44–45, 118–20, 288–94
 See also comprehensive doctrine; political liberalism; reasonable pluralism

Caney, Simon, 304–5
capabilities, 65, 161, 207, 212, 274–75, 293
 See also disability; distributive justice; functionings; primary goods
capitalism, 92, 101–2, 106–8, 107n38, 110–13, 114, 118, 160, 189, 193, 199, 340, 359–60
 See also basic rights and liberties; economic justice; property; socialism
care, 201, 237–38, 246–47, 249, 256–57, 259–60, 259n38, 284, 295–96, 320–21, 339
 See also dependency; disability; family; health / healthcare
Carruthers, Peter, 267, 276–77

Chambers, Clare, 250n2, 252, 254, 258, 259, 261
children, 4, 29, 41–42, 125, 203–4, 206, 210n11,
    211n15, 213, 214, 220, 222, 223–24, 225–
    26, 234, 237–38, 244–45, 247–48, 256,
    259–60, 259n38, 261, 265–66, 293, 293n30
    See also care; dependence; equal
    opportunity; family
Christiano, Thomas, 378
circumstances of justice, 64–65, 115–16, 209–11, 217
citizen / citizenship, 22–23, 24–25, 27–34, 95,
    96–97, 104–5, 107–8, 164–66, 173, 203–4,
    208–9, 211, 216–17, 240–41, 248, 254–58,
    259–60, 265–66, 291–92, 304–5, 320,
    348, 374–75
    See also capabilities; duty of civility;
    democracy; moral powers
civil disobedience, 34, 66–67
civility. *See* duty of civility
Claassen, Rutger, 168
climate change, 72, 196, 287–88, 295n33, 332
    See also environment; just savings principle
cloning, 39, 41–42
Cochrane, Alasdair, 271
Coeckelbergh, Mark, 269–70, 289n17
Cohen, G.A., 127–29, 131, 148, 155n40, 155n41,
    258, 290n20
Cohen, Joshua, 311, 352
Cohen, Joshua and Charles Sabel, 311
colonialism, 65, 67, 71, 229, 321
compliance theory, strict / partial. *See* ideal and
    nonideal theory
comprehensive doctrine, 5–7, 16–19, 21, 35, 39,
    40, 47, 49, 163, 168n33, 173, 184–85, 192,
    209–10, 210n11, 229, 235, 238–39, 245–
    46, 252, 253–54, 257, 259–60, 280, 281,
    283–84, 288–92, 293–94, 295–96, 345–46,
    356–59, 367, 373–77
    See also conception of the good; duty
    of civility; overlapping consensus;
    perfectionism; political liberalism; public
    reason; reasonable doctrines / persons;
    reasonable pluralism; religion; toleration
conception of the good, 2–3, 4–5, 18–19, 29, 96,
    101, 102–3, 104–6, 163, 172–73, 209–11,
    212–16, 221, 227–28, 237–38, 242, 261–62,
    268, 358–59
    See also comprehensive doctrine; moral powers;
    original position; primary goods; sense of
    justice
congruence, 4–6, 5n13, 113n14
    See also overlapping consensus; stability
constitutional essentials and matters of basic
    justice. *See* duty of civility; political
    liberalism; public reason

cooperation, 1–2, 27–28, 30–31, 79, 95–97, 99,
    100, 103–5, 109, 149, 150, 154–55, 159–60,
    167–68, 170, 173, 203, 208–10, 215–16,
    217–18, 217n26, 226, 227–28, 235, 240–41,
    254–55, 265–66, 269–70, 273–74, 278–81,
    284, 285–86, 288–91, 304–5, 316–17,
    320–21, 325
    See also basic structure of society; citizen;
    moral powers; reciprocity; respect; sense
    of justice
cosmopolitanism, 301, 355, 371–72
    See also basic structure of society; difference
    principle; duty of assistance; human rights;
    humanitarian assistance; Law of Peoples
Costa, M. Victoria, 237
criminal law, 30, 54–55, 74, 79, 225, 243, 257–
    58, 260, 304–5
    See also ideal and nonideal theory; law / rule
    of law; prostitution
Cross, Ben, 18

Daniels, Norman, 71–72, 167–68, 176–78, 187–
    88, 190, 191, 195–96, 210n11, 212
death, legal definition of, 27–31
decent societies, 76n17, 123, 324–25, 324n50,
    348–50, 351–52, 355n3, 357, 365, 371
    See also benevolent absolutism; democracy;
    human rights; Law of Peoples; liberalism
    / liberal society; outlaw regimes / states;
    toleration
democracy, 6–7, 15–16, 21, 22–25, 35, 41, 45,
    45n26, 53–55, 81, 91–92, 97, 99, 106,
    112–13, 114, 118–19, 192–98, 199, 227–28,
    238–39, 240–41, 252, 255–57, 346–47, 350,
    354, 371
    See also decent societies; citizen; liberalism /
    liberal society; political rights and liberties;
    political autonomy; political rights and
    liberties; property owning democracy;
    public reason; reasonable pluralism
democratic equality, 129–30, 144, 154–55
    See also liberalism / liberal society; principles
    of justice; reciprocity; relational equality
deontology, 155–158, 157n46, 282, 371
    See also Kant / Kantian; teleology;
    utilitarianism
dependency, 47, 50, 91–92, 111, 201, 233–
    34, 237–38, 243–44, 246–47, 249,
    256–57, 269–70
    See also autonomy; capabilities; disability;
    family; moral powers; women, status of
desert / deservingness, 125, 127–29, 138, 139,
    140n29, 141, 149, 150–51, 153–55, 218,
    268–69, 282, 293, 355

See also luck / luck egalitarianism; redress, principle of

Diamond, Larry, 355–56, 359

difference principle, 90–91, 91n16, 107, 115, 117, 126–28, 128n15, 128n16, 130, 135–38, 140–41, 150, 154–55, 160, 172–73, 181, 184, 186, 203–4, 226–27, 246–48, 259–60, 289–90, 304–5, 325–26, 331

See also basic structure of society; cosmopolitanism; distributive justice; economic justice; luck / luck egalitarianism; property; principles of justice; pure procedural justice

dignity, 40–41, 185, 189, 223–24

DiQuattro, Arthur, 112

disability, 29, 31–33, 65, 71–72, 105, 134–35, 150, 150n13, 153–54, 165–66, 170, 176–82, 183, 189, 191, 203–4, 206–7, 209–10, 209n9, 211n15, 212, 222, 223–24, 226, 246–47, 265–66, 275–76, 278n12, 282, 283, 287–88, 292, 297–98

See also capabilities; dependency; functionings; health / healthcare; luck / luck egalitarianism; moral powers

distributive justice, 2, 61, 64, 65, 71–72, 78–79, 83, 87, 123, 167–68, 189–90, 190n33, 195–96, 199, 220–21, 289–90, 293, 301, 357

See also allocative justice; basic structure of society; capabilities; difference principle; economic justice; just savings principle; luck / luck egalitarianism; patterned principles (of distributive justice); primary goods; principles of justice; property; pure procedural justice; relational equality; utilitarianism

Dolovich, Sharon, 74

domination, 113–18, 119, 120, 120n37, 153–54, 157–158, 231, 279

See also democratic equality; reciprocity; republicanism; women, status of

Donaldson, Sue and Will Kymlicka, 271

duty of assistance, 285–86, 304–5, 313, 314–17, 315n14, 318n24, 320–23, 322n42, 329, 372–73

See also cosmopolitanism; humanitarian assistance; Law of Peoples; political autonomy

duty of civility, 6–7, 15, 16, 184, 356–57, 373–74

See also citizen; comprehensive doctrine; political liberalism; public reason

Dworkin, Ronald, 128–29, 138, 146n48, 148, 151

economic justice, 40–41, 79n27, 87, 153, 156, 184, 246–48, 259, 301, 359–60

See also capitalism; difference principle; distributive justice; libertarianism; property; property-owning democracy; socialism

Edmundson, William, 94, 109

Ellerman, David, 112–13n13

environment, 43, 72, 196, 265, 287–88, 295–96, 295n33, 319, 326, 332, 335–36, 340

See also animals; climate change

equal opportunity, 4, 69–70, 71–72, 75, 79n27, 89–90, 92, 98–99, 100, 107, 112, 115, 126–27, 135, 136–37, 139n27, 146, 151n18, 167–68, 171–72, 176–78, 187, 203–4, 208, 210n11, 212, 225–27, 233–34, 244–46, 261, 289–90, 293n30

See also health / health care; luck / luck egalitarianism; principles of justice; women, status of

equality. *See* basic rights and liberties; democratic equality; difference principle; distributive justice; equal opportunity; luck / luck egalitarianism; reciprocity; relational egalitarianism

Estlund, David, 59, 75n11

expensive tastes / preferences, 128–29, 137n22, 152, 164–65

See also autonomy; luck / luck egalitarianism; moral powers; primary goods

family, 27–28, 40–41, 66, 71, 139, 139n27, 151–52, 210–11, 220–21, 224–25, 226, 227, 233–34, 237–38, 239, 244–45, 246–48, 251–52, 251n3, 253n15, 256, 258–60, 258n34, 259n38

See also basic structure of society; care; dependency; feminism; women, status of

Farrelly, Colin, 59, 61

feminism, 207n5, 213–14, 219, 231, 291–92

See also equal opportunity; family; women, status of

Fitzpatrick, Tony, 183

Foa, Robert Stefan and Yascha Mounk, 360–61

Forst, Rainer, 131, 148

Fraser, Nancy, 256n25

freedom, 15–16, 89, 91–92, 95, 115, 119–20, 128–29, 157n48, 170, 184–85, 186, 188, 191, 212–13, 215, 218, 225–26, 239, 243, 251–52, 261–62, 290–92, 293n30, 336–38, 356–57, 364–66, 372–73

See also autonomy; basic rights and liberties; capabilities; economic justice; freedom of speech / expression; moral powers; political autonomy; principles of justice; property

Freedom House, 359
freedom of speech / expression, 16, 67–68, 96,
    184–85, 242, 251–52, 251n7, 362–63, 365–
    66, 374–75, 379–80
    See also basic rights and liberties; political
        rights and liberties; principles of justice
Freeman, Samuel, 11, 94, 304–5, 311
Friedman, Barbara, 94
Fukuyama, Francis, 359
functionings, 65, 170, 183, 192, 211, 212, 217–
    18, 220n7, 227–29
    See also capabilities; cooperation; disability;
        moral powers; primary goods
Fung, Archon, 193

Gardiner, Stephen, 287–88
Garner, Robert, 267, 271
Gaus, Gerald, 46, 59

Habermas, Jürgen, 40, 41–42
Hartley, Christie, 236, 249, 278n12
Hartley, Christie and Lori Watson, 236, 249
Hayek, Friedrich, 99–100, 101–2, 108
health / health care, 41, 62, 63, 65–66, 67, 71–72, 106,
    151, 153, 165–66, 167–68, 167n26, 176–78,
    179, 180, 186, 187, 203, 209–12, 210n11,
    211n15, 249, 257–58, 261–62, 297, 298, 332–34
    See also care; disability; equal opportunity
Hobbes, Thomas, 277–79
human rights, 40–41, 76n17, 304–10, 313,
    326, 330, 335–36, 338, 339, 342, 346–47,
    346n10, 348, 350–52, 350n30, 356, 363,
    365–66, 368–69, 377–81, 380n50
    See also decent society; duty of assistance;
        Law of Peoples; legitimacy; political
        autonomy; sovereignty; toleration
humanitarian assistance, 301, 315–16
    See also cosmopolitanism; duty of assistance;
        Law of Peoples

ideal and nonideal theory, 26, 38, 51, 219–20,
    222–23, 379
intergenerational justice. *See* just savings
    principle
intuitionism, 26, 39, 63–66, 77, 294–98
    See also original position; priority rules;
        reflective equilibrium

James, Aaron, 227–28
just savings principle, 134, 135–36, 145, 159,
    209–10, 210n11, 213–14, 279–80, 285–86,
    285n1, 285n2
    See also environment; principles of justice

Kant / Kantian, 2–3, 37, 158–59, 268–69,
    278, 283–84, 286n6, 287–88, 287n11,
    296n34, 358–59
    See also deontology; domination;
        republicanism
Kaufman, Alexander, 169
Kittay, Eva, 204, 205, 206, 219
Kymlicka, Will, 127–28, 131, 136–38, 140, 142–
    43, 150, 153, 271, 282

Laden, Anthony, 11, 236, 253n12
Larmore, Charles, 15
law / rule of law, 6–7, 16–17, 18–19, 21, 35, 79,
    96, 97, 100, 113, 119–20, 225, 237–38, 240–
    41, 243–44, 246, 247–48, 250–52, 251n7,
    252n8, 256, 257–58, 259–60, 259n38, 261,
    265, 281–84, 286–87, 296–97, 304–5, 325,
    332–35, 346–47, 348, 348n19, 350–51,
    355–56, 357n6, 359, 365–66, 368–69, 373–
    74, 377–78, 377n30, 379–80
    See also basic rights and liberties; criminal
        law; democracy; Law of Peoples;
        legitimacy; political rights and liberties;
        public reason
Law of Peoples, 301, 343
    See also cosmopolitanism; decent societies;
        human rights; public reason; sovereignty;
        toleration
legitimacy, 6–7, 15–16, 21, 23, 35, 41, 43, 45–46,
    45n26, 50, 249–50, 253, 254–55, 288, 331,
    341, 345, 346–47, 349–50, 362, 373–74,
    376–78, 377n30, 379–81
    See also decent societies; law / rule of
        law; political liberalism; public reason;
        toleration
Levy, Jacob, 59, 74–75
lexical priority. *See* principles of justice;
    priority rules
liberalism / liberal society, 5–6, 15–16, 89,
    92–93, 101, 102, 108, 112–13, 115, 119,
    167–68, 192, 203, 206, 208, 217, 219,
    239–40, 249, 254–55, 289–91, 304–5,
    324–27, 343
    See also basic rights and liberties; decent
        societies; democracy; democratic equality;
        legitimacy; political liberalism; principles
        of justice; reciprocity
libertarianism, 82, 87, 149, 150–51, 153, 241
    See also basic rights and liberties; economic
        justice; freedom; property
liberty. *See* autonomy; basic rights and liberties;
    freedom
Lippert-Rasmussen, Kasper, 131, 133

Lloyd, S. A., 236, 237–38
Locke, John, 2–3
Lowry, Christopher, 170
luck / luck egalitarianism, 67, 72, 125, 133, 148, 222, 268–69, 279, 304–5
    See also cosmopolitanism; democratic equality; distributive justice; equal opportunity; relational egalitarianism; redress, principle of

MacKinnon, Catharine, 250–52, 251n3, 252n8, 253n12
Mandle, Jon, 11, 94, 349–50, 352, 371
Mandle, Jon and David Reidy, 11
Martin, Rex and David Reidy, 11, 352
Marx, Karl / Marxism, 105, 107, 108, 112, 113–14, 118
    See also capitalism; socialism
Mayerfeld, Jamie, 368–69
Mill, John Stuart, 112–13n13, 114, 116, 120, 241
Mills, Charles, 57–59, 62, 71, 78, 84–85, 287–88
Moellendorf, Darrel, 304–5, 311, 347–48, 371–72
moral luck. See luck / luck egalitarianism
moral person. See citizen, moral powers
moral powers, 29, 95, 111–12, 152, 164–65, 166–67, 203–4, 206, 209, 215–17, 240–41, 242, 259–60, 265–66, 273–76, 289–90, 289n18, 292–93, 293n30, 297–98, 297n36
    See also animals; capabilities; citizen / citizenship; conception of the good; cooperation; dependency; sense of justice
Mounk, Yascha, 360–61

Nagel, Thomas, 127, 311
Nath, Rekha, 313
National Endowment for Democracy, 363, 368
Nelson, Eric, 184, 185, 187, 191, 195–96
Neufeld, Blain, 352–53
Nickel, James 350–52, 363
Nozick, Robert, 89–93, 91n16, 94, 98–99, 100, 108, 149, 158, 241
Nussbaum, Martha, 11, 76, 150n13, 166–67, 169, 185–86, 187–88, 189–90, 191, 192, 197–98, 205, 233–34, 236, 267, 271–72, 276, 287–88

Okin, Susan Moller, 205, 234, 236, 237–38
original position, 2–3, 5, 6, 61, 63–65, 66, 67, 70, 71, 76, 111, 125–27, 136, 148–49, 163–64, 166–67, 209, 210n11, 214, 227, 228, 267–68, 280–81, 285n1, 304–5, 324–25, 337–38, 353, 371

See also cooperation; political liberalism; primary goods; principles of justice; public reason; reciprocity; reflective equilibrium; social contract
Otsuka, Michael, 146
outlaw regimes / states, 346–47, 371–73
    See also benevolent absolutism; decent societies; human rights; Law of Peoples; toleration
overlapping consensus, 6, 15, 18–19, 209–10, 210n11, 239–40, 253–54, 253n15, 282–84, 346
    See also comprehensive doctrine; congruence; political liberalism; reasonable doctrines / persons; stability

Parfit, Derek, 157n46
Pateman, Carole, 71
patterned principles (of distributive justice), 89–91, 91n16, 130, 144, 146, 158
    See also allocative justice; distributive justice; luck / luck egalitarianism; pure procedural justice; relational equality
perfectionism, 26, 53, 105, 119, 181–82, 186, 240, 254–55
    See also comprehensive doctrine; political liberalism; teleology
Pettit, Philip, 115, 241
Piketty, Thomas, 114
Pogge, Thomas, 158, 304–10, 309n51, 311–12, 318–20, 353, 371–72, 375–76
political autonomy, 35, 46–49, 158, 314, 317–20, 331, 333, 336–38, 339–40, 351–52, 372–73, 376–78, 380–81
    See also autonomy; democracy; duty of assistance; sovereignty; toleration
political liberalism, 5–7, 21, 35, 166, 173, 181–82, 184, 227–30, 235, 238–40, 249, 271, 285, 346, 354n1, 356–58, 366–67, 371–72
    See also burdens of judgment; comprehensive doctrine; liberalism / liberal society; legitimacy; overlapping consensus; public reason; reasonable doctrine / persons; reasonable pluralism; toleration
political rights and liberties, 96, 107, 113–18, 114n22, 119–20, 170–75, 172n5, 176, 181n23, 242, 281, 380n49
    See also basic rights and liberties; democracy; freedom of speech / expression
pornography, 67–68, 242, 251–52, 251n7
    See also freedom of speech / expression

primary goods, 3, 71–72, 90–91, 135–36, 136n13, 138, 158, 163, 178, 183, 204, 215–17, 221, 223–24, 227–28, 246–47, 247n28, 289–90, 289n18
  See also capabilities; distributive justice; functionings; conception of the good; moral powers; self-respect
principles of justice, the, 3–4, 29, 30, 53–54, 64, 66, 91n16, 97, 109, 126, 133–34, 170–74, 217, 241–42
  See also basic rights and liberties; difference principle; equal opportunity; just savings principle; liberalism / liberal society; original position; primary goods; priority rules; reciprocity; reflective equilibrium
priority rules, 4, 26, 39, 40–41, 63–64, 65, 67–68, 70, 77, 82, 90–91, 95, 96–97, 100–1, 106–7, 108, 134, 254–55, 289–90, 289n18, 290n20
  See also basic rights and liberties; intuitionism; principles of justice
Pritchard, Michael and Wade Robeson, 267–68, 276
property, 89, 95, 109, 183, 246–47, 334–35, 350
  See also basic rights and liberties; difference principle; distributive justice; economic justice; libertarianism; property-owning democracy
property-owning democracy, 92, 109, 160
  See also capitalism; democracy; economic justice; property; socialism
prostitution, 251–52, 257–58
  See also feminism; women, status of
public reason, 6–7, 13, 64, 158, 239–40, 242n17, 245–46, 256, 274–75, 280–84, 288, 294–97, 298–99, 356–57, 372–75, 373–74n20
  See also comprehensive doctrine; democracy; duty of civility; legitimacy; political liberalism; reasonable pluralism; religion / religious liberty
publicity, 48–49, 253n15, 298
punishment. *See* criminal law
pure procedural justice, 91, 142, 154–55, 159
  See also allocative justice; basic structure of society; difference principle; distributive justice; patterned principles (of distributive justice)

Quong, Jonathan, 20

race / racism, 2, 57–59, 67–68, 78, 81, 150, 153–54, 171–72, 176–77, 214–15, 219–20, 222, 223–25, 228, 260, 283, 295–96, 354–55, 379–80, 379–80n48

See also affirmative action; ideal and nonideal theory; slavery
reasonable doctrines / persons, 5–7, 16, 22–23, 26, 27–28, 33, 37–38, 42–43, 44–45, 163, 181, 235, 237–38, 239, 240–41, 244–46, 253, 253n15, 261–62, 278, 279–80, 290–91, 290n24, 292, 293, 323–24, 346–47, 348, 373–74, 375
  See also comprehensive doctrines; cooperation; decent societies; overlapping consensus; political liberalism; reasonable pluralism; reciprocity; public reason
reasonable pluralism, 5, 16, 21, 39–40, 41, 42–43, 44–45, 47–48, 49, 103n29, 238–40, 245–46, 247, 248, 253–54, 280, 291, 323–24, 348, 366–67, 373–74
  See also burdens of judgment; political liberalism; overlapping consensus; reasonable doctrines / persons; public reason
reciprocity, 24–26, 33–34, 110, 149, 154–55, 159, 204, 207, 217n26, 227–28, 240–41, 254–59, 278–79, 285–86, 355, 355n3, 367–68
  See also cooperation; liberalism / liberal society; moral powers; sense of justice
redress, principle of, 127–28, 128n15, 140–43, 141n34, 143n40, 146, 147, 154, 159, 167
  See also luck / luck egalitarianism
reflective equilibrium, 2–3, 53–54, 64, 83, 125–26, 134, 143n40, 221, 239, 242, 244–45, 295–96, 374–75
  See also intuitionism; original position; principles of justice; priority rules
Regan, Tom, 269, 282
Reidy, David, 11, 20, 21, 35, 349–51, 352, 353
relational egalitarianism, 125, 143–47, 148, 337–38
  See also democratic equality; distributive justice; domination; luck / luck egalitarianism; reciprocity; republicanism
religion / religious liberty, 2, 17–19, 30, 36–37, 40–41, 53–54, 101, 102, 185, 235, 239, 242, 244–45, 289–92, 295–96, 298, 357–59
  See also basic rights and liberties; comprehensive doctrine; public reason; toleration
republicanism, 33–34, 117, 119–20, 157n48, 241, 243
  See also democracy; domination; property-owning democracy; relational egalitarianism

respect, 15–16, 18–19, 146n48, 152, 152–154,, 167–68, 189, 203, 219–20, 221–22, 223–24, 228–29, 243–44, 255, 261–62, 274, 278–81, 282, 283–84, 336–38, 340, 345, 349, 365, 369, 372–73, 375–76
  See also autonomy; citizen; cooperation; moral powers; reciprocity; self-respect
rights. See basic rights and liberties; deontology; human rights; libertarianism; political rights and liberties
Roberts-Cady, Sarah, 273
Robeson, Wade, 267–68, 276
Robeyns, Ingrid, 165–67, 168, 169, 178–79, 184–85, 190n33
Robinson, Joan, 116
Rorty, Richard, 363–64
Rosenberg, Alexander, 78–79
Rousseau, Jean Jacques, 2–3, 46–48
Rowlands, Mark, 268–69, 272

Sabel, Charles, 311
Sangiovanni, Andrea, 312
Scanlon, T.M., 64, 278, 287n10, 290n24, 304–5
Scheffler, Samuel, 130, 132, 138–39, 140, 143–47, 146n48, 150–51
Schmidtz, David, 73–74
Schwartzman, Micah, 20, 37–38, 49
Schweickart, David, 112–13n13, 120
self-determination. See decent societies; Law of Peoples; political autonomy; toleration
self-respect, 3, 91–92, 111, 163, 174, 375–76
See also conception of the good; primary goods; respect
Sen, Amartya, 56–57, 58–59, 70–71, 80–81, 83, 165–67, 169, 170, 183, 184–85, 187–88, 189–90, 197–98
sense of justice, 4–5, 47, 53–54, 96, 104–6, 212, 216n22, 225–26, 265–67, 273–74, 276, 277
  See also conception of the good; moral powers; reciprocity; stability
sexual orientation, 144–45, 225, 239
Shelby, Tommie, 59–60, 78, 176–77
Shklar, Judith, 354n1
Simmons, A. John, 55, 58, 60, 78–79
sincerity, 35–38, 44–45, 49–50
  See also public reason
Singer, Peter, 269, 282–84, 310n55
slavery, 2, 56–57, 65, 67, 71, 80, 84, 85, 142–43, 145–46, 207, 213, 229, 243, 291–92, 350, 351–52
  See also basic rights and liberties; race / racism
Smith, Patrick Taylor, 285
social contract, 2–3, 83, 267, 268, 269–70, 276

See also basic structure of society; liberalism / liberal society; original position; principles of justice; reciprocity
socialism, 97, 107, 108, 109
  See also capitalism; libertarianism; property; property-owning democracy
sovereignty, 345–46
  See also Law of Peoples; political autonomy
Sreenivasan, Gopal, 82–83
stability, 4–6, 16, 22–25, 53–54, 79, 117–18, 119, 120n37, 125–26, 210n11, 220, 223, 225–26, 253–54, 321, 361–66, 367, 368
  See also congruence; overlapping consensus; political liberalism; sense of justice
state. See basic structure of society; cosmopolitanism; law / rule of law; Law of Peoples; political autonomy; sovereignty
Stemplowska, Zofia, 55, 58, 60
Stemplowska, Zofia and Adam Swift, 55, 58
Sunstein, Cass, 65
survival guilt, 146–47
Svolba, David, 268–69
Swift, Adam, 55, 58

Tan, Kok-Chor, 316, 324n51, 347, 353, 371–72
teleology, 64, 155–158, 371
  See also deontology; utilitarianism
Thomas, Alan, 94, 109
toleration, 2, 44–45, 53–54, 76n17, 233–34, 235, 239, 323–27, 338, 339, 343
  See also decent societies; duty of civility; human rights; political autonomy; political liberalism; reasonable doctrines / persons; reciprocity; sovereignty
Tomasi, John, 94, 101–3, 102n28, 104, 105n37, 108, 109
Tomlin, Patrick, 132
two moral powers. See citizen; moral powers

utilitarianism, 1–2, 63–66, 99, 100, 186, 192, 241, 282–84, 287n9, 288, 291–92, 304–5, 310n55
  See also distributive justice; teleology

Valentini, Laura, 55, 60, 75, 77–78n19, 290n20
Vallentyne, Peter, 90n8
Vallier, Kevin, 20, 46, 118–19
van Parijs, Phillipe, 118
veil of ignorance. See original position
von Platz, Jeppe, 94, 95
von Platz, Jeppe and John Tomasi, 94

Waldron, Jeremy, 18
Watson, Lori, 236, 249
Weithman, Paul, 5n13, 11, 20

welfare state capitalism. *See* capitalism
Wenar, Leif, 11, 239n10, 321n36, 325
Wiens, David, 60
Williams, Andrew, 20
Williams, Jeremy, 20
Wittgenstein, Ludwig, 198
Wolff, Jonathan, 152–53
Wolterstorff, Nicholas, 17

women, status of, 27–28, 31–33, 67–68,
    185, 204, 206–8, 214–15, 223–27, 229,
    231, 291–92, 293n30, 295–96, 304–5,
    338, 379n47
See also dependency; equal opportunity;
    family; feminism

Zakaria, Fareed, 359